Making American Boys

BOY-STUFF IS THE ONLY STUFF IN THE WORLD
FROM WHICH MEN CAN BE MADE

BOYOLOGY

OR

BOY ANALYSIS

H. W. GIBSON

AUTHOR OF "CAMPING FOR BOYS," "SERVICES OF
WORSHIP," "QUALITIES THAT WIN," ETC.

ASSOCIATION PRESS

NEW YORK: 347 MADISON AVENUE

1922

Making American Boys

BOYOLOGY AND THE FERAL TALE

Kenneth B. Kidd

University of Minnesota Press
Minneapolis · London

A shorter version of chapter 1 previously appeared in "Farming for Boys: Boyology and the Professionalization of Boy Work," *Children's Literature Association Quarterly* 20, no. 4 (winter 1995/96): 148–54; reproduced by permission of the Children's Literature Association. Parts of chapters 2 and 6 were first published as "Boyology in the Twentieth Century," *Children's Literature* 28 (2000); reprinted with permission from *Children's Literature*; copyright 2000 by Hollins University. Parts of chapter 5 were first published as "Men Who Run with Wolves, and the Women Who Love Them," *The Lion and the Unicorn* 20, no. 1 (June 1996); reprinted with permission from The Johns Hopkins University Press.

Published by the University of Minnesota Press
111 Third Avenue South, Suite 290
Minneapolis, MN 55401-2520
http://www.upress.umn.edu

Library of Congress Cataloging-in-Publication Data

Kidd, Kenneth B.
  Making American boys : boyology and the feral tale /
Kenneth B. Kidd.
    p. cm.
Includes bibliographical references and index.
  ISBN 0-8166-4295-8 — ISBN 0-8166-4296-6 (pbk.)
1. Children's stories, American—History and criticism.
2. Boys—Books and reading—United States. 3. Feral children
in literature. 4. Boys in literature. I. Title.
PS374.C454K53 2004
810.9′92826—dc22
                    2003023381

Printed in the United States of America on acid-free paper

The University of Minnesota is an equal-opportunity educator and employer.

12 11 10 09 08 07 06 05 04   10 9 8 7 6 5 4 3 2 1

For Byron, Doris, and Kathryn, with love

Contents

Acknowledgments — ix

Boyhood for Beginners: An Introduction — 1

1. Farming for Boys — 23

2. Bad Boys and Men of Culture — 49

3. Wolf-Boys, Street Rats, and the Vanishing Sioux — 87

4. Father Flanagan's Boys Town — 111

5. From Freud's Wolf Man to Teen Wolf — 135

6. Reinventing the Boy Problem — 167

Notes — 191

Works Cited — 221

Index — 237

Acknowledgments

I have often fantasized that writing my acknowledgments would be like throwing a party. Family, friends, and colleagues could meet up, and I could thank everyone at once, champagne glass in hand and party hat askew. These words don't a party make, I know, but for now they will have to suffice.

In a sense, this project began at Friday Mountain Boys Camp, which my family ran for nearly forty years in central Texas. Thanks to the Kidd family, beginning with my grandparents, Von and R. J. "Captain" Kidd. My grandfather, too, was writing a book about boys before he died, and while this book doesn't look much like his, I owe him and Friday Mountain more than I know. I dedicate the book to my parents and sister, to whom I owe everything.

Making American Boys is also derived from a doctoral dissertation co-directed by Lora Romero and Wayne Lesser at the University of Texas–Austin. Thanks to Wayne for taking me on, and for his exemplary interest in all matters disciplinary. Committee members Ann Cvetkovich, Marjorie Curry Woods, Katherine Arens, and Shelly Fisher Fishkin were generous with their time and knowledge. I particularly appreciate Katie's warmth and advice, then and now. Thanks also to Lance Bertelsen, Jerome Bump, and Edmund Farrell for their example. Among my grad school pals, Susan Dauer, Kay Harris, Mary Lenard, and Robby Sulcer especially shared their humor and love and sustain me still. Having Susan just down the road is one of the best things about living in Florida. Ed Madden remains the one-stop source for all news academic and not.

I have been fortunate to work in two English departments in which collegiality and intellectual life go hand in hand. At Eastern Michigan University, many folks cheered me on, among them Nancy Allen, Gilbert Cross, Marcia Dalbey, Craig Dionne, Jim Dolan, Laura George, Sally McCracken, Michael McGuire, Kate Mehuron, Sheila Most, Sandy Norton, and Marty Shichtman. Ian Wojcik-Andrews has been the best children's literature colleague I could hope for, and Rhonda Kinney has taught me much about political science and friendship as we dined our way through Ann Arbor. At EMU I was granted a faculty research fellowship, thanks in large part to my chair, Marcia Dalbey.

At the University of Florida, English chairs Ira Clark and John Leavey have likewise supported me generously. Special thanks to John for enabling a semester's leave for the book's completion. A summer research grant from the University of Florida also provided key support. At Florida I've been fortunate to count among friends and colleagues Apollo Amoko, Efraín Barradas, Kathryn Baker, Roger Beebe, Patrick Brennan, Marsha Bryant, John Cech,

Patricia Craddock, Sid Dobrin, Kim Emery, Franz Epting, Jeanne Ewert, Joseba Gabilondo, Pamela Gilbert, Andrew Gordon, Terry Harpold, Tace Hedrick, Susan Hegeman, Maude Hines, Anne Jones, Brandy Kershner, Linda Lamme, David Leavitt, David Leverenz, John Murchek, Scott Nygren, Jack Perlette, Robert Ray, Mark Reid, Nancy Reisman, Leah Rosenberg, Malini Schueller, Blake Scott, John Seeleye, Rita Smith, Stephanie Smith, Bob Thomson, Maureen Turim, Gregory Ulmer, Phil Wegner, and Luise White. David Leverenz, Susan Hegeman, and Joseba Gabilondo read several chapters and offered sage advice and good cheer. The book would be languishing still were it not for the fabulous duo of Tace Hedrick and Pamela Gilbert, who talked shop but also got me out of the house. Pamela's feedback was especially crucial at several stages of revision, and I am grateful for her mentorship. Also vital has been the warm support of John and Eve Cech, who set a high standard for hospitality as well as intellectual engagement.

Some intellectual communities, of course, are more diffuse. Gratitude is due also to my friends in the Children's Literature Association, notably Gillian Adams, June Cummins, Richard Flynn, Elizabeth Goodenough, Elizabeth Keyser, Lois Kuznets, Michelle H. Martin, Anne Morey, Claudia Nelson, Marilynn Olson, Lissa Paul, Julie Pfeiffer, Jan Susina, Roberta Seelinger Trites, and Jack Zipes. They, among others, have contributed greatly to my professional growth.

I couldn't have asked for more careful or gracious manuscript readers than Carol Mavor or Michael Moon, and I thank them (and an anonymous reader) for their insights and suggestions. Special thanks to my editor, Richard Morrison, for his enthusiastic confidence in the project that became this book. Richard and his colleagues at the University of Minnesota Press made this book happen; Doug Armato, the director of the Press, even supplied the cover photograph.

My psychic twin Laura George deserves my deepest gratitude. She has read draft after draft, talked with me all night about dreams and projects, and taken me dancing in Detroit, Chicago, and New York. No one makes me laugh or think harder, and while I miss seeing her on a regular basis, I am lucky to know her. A big hug to my boyfriend, Martin Smith, who makes life sweeter day by day.

Finally, I acknowledge two friends who are no longer living, Lora Romero and Jody Norton. Lora was the codirector of my dissertation, staying on even after leaving the University of Texas for Stanford. She was funny and sharp, and I learned much from her. I received Lora's book *Home Fronts* just a few days after her death, and I have since been thinking about how books function as surrogates of the self, for better and for worse. Jody was a friend and colleague at Eastern Michigan University. Smart and astonishingly kind, he cherished his family, friends, students, and colleagues—or, as Jody would have corrected me, *hir* family, friends, students, and colleagues. Jody didn't believe in gender and wrote (among many other things) a moving essay about transgendered kids. And yet the word that comes to mind when I think of Jody is *maternal*. So, too, with Lora, despite their differences. I miss them both.

Boyhood for Beginners: An Introduction

No earthly object is so attractive as a well-built, growing boy.
—H. W. Gibson, *Boyology or Boy Analysis*

This is a book about discourses of boyhood. I argue that the ideological and practical work of boy education and supervision in America has been shaped by two main discourses: *boyology,* comprising descriptive and pre-scriptive writing on boyhood across a variety of genres, and what I call the *feral tale,* a narrative form derived from mythology and folklore that dram-atizes but also manages the "wildness" of boys. Both boyology and the feral tale are implicated in larger historical narratives about human and cultural development. Boyology is primarily an American phenomenon, while the feral tale is international and interdisciplinary in scope even as it has helped shape boyology. My focus on boyology is thus Americanist, whereas I trace the feral tale's Anglo-European lineage to better understand its American forms and effects.[1] Taken together, these discourses—especially through the shifts they undergo from the mid–nineteenth century to the late twentieth—help mark the momentous changes by which we recognize modernity. Boy-ology and the feral tale are necessarily theoretical as well as descriptive terms; they suggest patterns of representation that are otherwise difficult to tackle, especially since boyhood seems self-evident.

An allusion to biology, boyology first designated the American pseudo-science of boy analysis that flourished in the early twentieth century. I bor-row the term from Henry William Gibson, YMCA leader and author of the handbook *Boyology or Boy Analysis* (1916). Designed for readers "who are short in psychology, physiology, pedagogy, and sociology, but who are long in common sense and 'heartology'" (x), *Boyology* serves as a handbook for "boy workers" and as a literature review of the handbooks that precede it, beginning with William Byron Forbush's influential *The Boy Problem* (1901). Gibson's text provides an overview of the nature and nurture of boys, in-dulging in not a little boyologist trivia. We learn, for instance, that the "slan-guage" of the typical fifteen-year-old boy includes "Oh lu lu!", "Glory be!", "Do you feel like fruit? have an onion!", and "Rats, go to grass!" (48–49). So extensive was this advice literature by 1916 that the book concludes with an annotated "Six Foot Shelf" of 103 books and pamphlets "about boys or sub-jects analogous to boy life" (260).

Gibson was only one of the more visible boyologists, men usually affili-ated with agencies such as Scouting and the YMCA. The character-building movement, as David I. Macleod explains, was the last major type of boy work to develop in America, following 4-H programs for farm boys and mass boys' clubs for the working class. In all three traditions, boy work was a supplement to the guiding mechanisms of home, church, and school. Boyology was the narrative discourse of formal and informal middle-class character building or boy work. It entailed a philosophy, a professional orientation, and a mode of authorship. Whatever their affiliations, early boy workers rallied around "boy culture," conducting fieldwork and profiling boy types. The boy became a subject, the source of much concern and scrutiny. He was "real," self-evident but not self-explanatory. Most important, he was white and middle-class.

With apologies to Gibson and his cohorts, I use the term "boyology" to describe more broadly the American preoccupation with this boy and his authorized worker from the postbellum period through the late 1990s. Boyology is the lingua franca of boy work—both the recognized institutional forms such as Scouting and the more diffuse cultural practices that I identify. I use both "boyology" and "boy work" to refer to that larger enterprise, even if "boyology" functions as the umbrella term. I appropriate boyology not only because it designates earlier forms of literary and institutional boy work but also because it seems an appropriate label for more recent efforts, evidenced by new academic research, a growing network of "parents of boys" support groups, and best-selling handbooks that look strangely familiar. Michael Gurian seemed to speak for a whole new generation of boyologists in a 1998 edition of John Merrow's National Public Radio program *The Merrow Report*. Bemoaning feminism, Gurian insisted that American boys, not girls, are in crisis and that we need a "massive reeducation," even a "boy's movement," to redirect our attention to boys. Such a movement is apparently under way, thanks largely to Gurian and other therapists with a penchant for public outreach.

Gurian's *The Wonder of Boys: What Parents, Mentors, and Educators Can Do to Shape Boys into Exceptional Men* (1996) was followed by other best-selling titles, which make generous use of familiar literary topoi that establish "the boy" as a normative subject: Huck Finn, Tom Sawyer, the Bad Boy, the boy-savage, the "real boy," the "Lost Boy," the "boy wonder." It's no accident that *The Wonder of Boys* opens with those moving words of Geppetto: "Pinocchio! Oh Pinocchio! You're a boy! A real boy!" (xiii). This will be a book about real boys, Gurian implies, not those wooden creatures of abstraction. The irony of citing *Pinocchio* as evidence of a real boyhood seems lost on Gurian. While it's never clear if boyologists are primarily concerned with preadolescent or adolescent boys, such invocations suggest the former, with their archetypal poetics and sense of stasis. Like their predecessors, the new boyologists address a popular audience and claim expertise in the field, but they rewrite the tenets of early-twentieth-century boyology in the largely custodial terms of middle-class therapeutic culture. The generic practicality of early boyology has thus given way to a pop-psychological language of self-esteem and self-help. That shift or transformation, as aided and abetted by the feral tale, is a major concern of this study.

The term "feral tale" I've coined to suggest a resemblance between the literary fairy tale and a group of narratives that might not otherwise be intelligible as a genre. The feral tale is a literary but still folkloric narrative of animal-human or cross-cultural encounter, in which childhood figures prominently. I take my cue from Jack Zipes, who describes the literary fairy tale as part of "an institutionalized symbolic discourse on the civilizing process" (*Fairy Tales and the Art of Subversion*, 3). As a variously institutionalized symbolic discourse, the feral tale, too, has helped set standards for civilization and, unlike the fairy tale, is not restricted to the realm of popular entertainment, though now it often winds up there. It persists especially in children's literature and film (as well as exposés in the *Weekly World News*).[2] The incredulity with which we now greet such stories outside of popular entertainment belies their historical import, as well as the seriousness that used to mark their narration.

Whereas in mythology and folklore, feral children are raised by animal nurses or are the offspring of animals and gods, in subsequent genres they often just live apart from mainstream human culture.[3] There have been three overlapping types of feral subjects in oral and written narrative thus far: those fostered by wild animals, those living outside of civilization, and those living in confinement within its borders. Long the stuff of mythology and folklore, the feral tale did not figure prominently in the literature of science until the eighteenth century, when Carolus Linnaeus (Carl von Linné) devised the category of *Homo ferus,* or feral man, in the tenth edition of *Systema naturae* (1758). *Homo ferus* was a human subspecies, hirsute, four footed, and mute. Linnaeus based the classification on nine rather dubious cases, most of them children rather than adults: a Hessian wolf-boy (1344), a Lithuanian bear-boy (1661), an Irish sheep-boy (1672), Wild Peter of Hanover (1724), the Pyrenees boys (1717), the girl of Cranenburg (1717), the Songi girl from Champagne (1731), and Jean of Liège (no date). These were the cases that made it into print, if only as transcripts of eyewitness reports. The feral child thus made his (or, less often, her) scientific debut through Linnaean taxonomy and natural history.

Debate raged over the validity of particular accounts, but the feral tale found persuasion with naturalists such as Johann Tafel, Francis Galton, and later Sir James Frazer. Scientists have been attracted to these cases and myths because feral children promise insight into the mysteries of life, chief among them the origin of language. Eighteenth-century Europe was already preoccupied with the wild man figure, and the variation associated with Rousseau, the noble savage. *Valentine and Orson,* about a boy raised by bears, was still a popular work of fiction, and in other such stories the wild man usually spent his childhood suckled by animals. The wild man thus easily morphed into the wild child and the proto-romantic child of nature.

In fact, the first official wild child of the Enlightenment was a man-boy hybrid named Wild Peter or simply Peter. Discovered in 1724 near Hameln, Germany, Peter was then sent to Hanover, England, where he became the possession of the duke of Hanover. Probably around fifteen years old when discovered, Peter was represented as a man-child (even into old age), whereas subsequent wild children were younger and treated as such. Peter was examined by Dr. Arbuthnot, friend to Alexander Pope and Jonathan Swift, and the first such principal investigator of a wild child. The naturalist Joseph Friedrich Blumenbach tried to discredit the case, and with it Linnaeus's *Homo ferus* category, but already the wild child, almost always male, was a major player on the scientific stage. Traditionally the wild man was childless, and in the nineteenth century, in spite of romanticism and the noble savage legacy, he was increasingly treated as a case of arrested development, which might be why *Homo ferus* so often—and so ambivalently—took form as a boy.

The most famous case of a feral child, that of Victor, the wild boy of Aveyron (discovered in 1799)—which inspired François Truffaut's famous film *The Wild Child* (1969)—enabled new forms of child observation and training, as a test case for Enlightenment theories about language, cognition, motor skills, and socialization. First studied by the naturalist J. J. Virey, Victor was then educated by Dr. Jean-Marc-Gaspard Itard of the National Institute for Deaf-Mutes, whose pupil-centered, sensorimotor approach eventually led to advances in behavior modification, sign language, and education for the differently abled. Maria Montessori studied Itard's transcripts while developing her own pedagogical innovations in the 1930s. Victor's story has become "a tale of epic proportions in which the protagonists play highly stylized roles" (Lane, *The Wild Boy of Aveyron,* 163)—the ignorant boy and the selfless pedagogue, enacting a drama that still drives educational practice and fantasies of cultural redemption. In the 1970s, *The Wild Child* was even screened as an instructional film by the "Genie team," a group of psychologists and researchers working with a severely isolated "feral" girl in California.

That other famous feral boy, Kaspar Hauser, discovered at age sixteen near Nuremberg in 1828, learned to speak and write before his mysterious assassination in 1833. More a political than a pedagogical fable—Hauser was rumored to be the heir of the throne of Baden—the tale of Kaspar Hauser occasioned international interest from the start. Herman Melville likened his character Billy Budd, the ultimate "boy" who is doomed to die, to Hauser. Jeffrey Moussaieff Masson reports that by 1996 more than three thousand books and fourteen thousand articles had been written about Hauser (*Lost Prince*, 3–4); Masson himself appropriates Hauser as an "abused child" in a contemporary idiom, ignoring the political dimensions of this feral tale.

Around the middle of the nineteenth century, feral child narratives shifted in setting from Europe, the home of Victor and Kaspar, to colonial India and Africa. Beginning in 1843, British military and anthropological reports of children raised by wolves in India began to circulate. Rudyard Kipling drew from such reports in fashioning his *Jungle Books* (1894–1895). By the end of this period, what had previously been an Enlightenment narrative of culture's redeeming power, as in the case of Victor especially, had become an apologia for Anglo-American imperialism. Kipling's famous wolf-boy Mowgli represents a turning point, as a makeover of the feral subaltern into a heroic character, not unlike Kipling's other famous feral boy, Kim. Mowgli and Kim embody native nature alongside colonial uplift, whereas the most famous feral boys in American literature, Tarzan and Bomba the Jungle Boy, are unequivocally Anglo-Saxon and insulated against native ways (even if they too are stock characters of empire).

Like related folk genres, the feral child narrative has been understood as a transcription of both real events and psychic anxieties, though it is neither solely historical document nor psychological map. Leslie Fiedler attributes the theme's enduring popularity to its evocation of fundamental "Oedipal resonances" and our collective fantasy that "a single human being, cast away in the jungle, might recapitulate the evolutionary experience of the race" (*Freaks*, 157). I suggest instead that the motif helped dramatize and codify psychoanalysis (as well as perhaps evolutionary science before it). At least to some degree, psychoanalysis is indebted to the feral tale. And the professional study of childhood, it seems, has long revolved around the feral boy, from eighteenth-century empiricism to contemporary psychology.[4] The feral tale guarantees the legibility of childhood itself, implying a usual path of development and deviation from such.

The twentieth-century feral boy is at once normal and exceptional; he competes with the regular boy even as he morphs into that boy.[5] Although I concentrate on the collaboration of, rather than the tension between, boyology and the feral tale, that tension persists. Consider, for instance, the rumor that Elián González, the six-year-old Cuban boy rescued near the coast of Florida in 1999, was protected against sharks and drowning by dolphins. The González case, easily one of the most media-intensive events of the late twentieth century, became a touchstone for debates about the cultural and political status of Cuban Americans and the vexed history of U.S.–Cuba relations since 1959. The Cuban exile community seized upon the dolphin story as evidence of divine intervention, likening Elián to Jesus as well as Eleggúa, the Afro-Cuban deity who often appears as a child. Elián was positioned more broadly as a feral child, torn between nations and families. He seemed at once a normal "American" boy—adorably blond, wearing Tommy Hilfiger pants and waving an American flag at a backyard barbecue—and, as presidential hopeful George W. Bush kept calling him, an "alien."

The case of Elián suggests the residual power of the feral tale alongside its appropriation as a story of white, middle-class citizenship. Whereas boyology concerns itself most exclusively with white, middle-class, native-born boys, the feral tale addresses marginal and disenfranchised populations: the immigrant poor, "native" or indigenous groups, the developmentally impaired—all likened to children. Elián was already a child, which made that representational work even easier. As this book suggests, the boy subject of boyology has long served as a prototype for the representative American man, but the feral boy has historically embodied *both* the normative self and the cultural other. I examine both that dual legacy and the gradual transformation of the feral boy into a respectable citizen.

Although sightings of feral children are still reported worldwide, mostly in economically impoverished nations, the twentieth century bears witness to the Western recuperation of the feral boy as a normative subject, especially in certain genres developed for children and families. As evidence we might point to Maurice Sendak's award-winning picture book for children *Where the Wild Things Are* (1963) or, switching audiences, to the primers of the mythopoetic men's movement, notably Robert Bly's *Iron John: A Book about Men* (1990). *Iron John* narrates the transition from boyhood to manhood made possible by the wild man's recovery; so, too, does Steven Spielberg's film *Hook* (1991), considered a family film, in which an adult Peter reclaims his inner Pan to achieve full yuppiehood. Such are the translations of empire into imperialist self, in pop-psychological terms. Put another way, what was basically a grim portrait of inner life became an affirmative story of masculine selfhood. Wildness was no longer a liability but an asset, and the dissemination of ego psychology and humanistic psychology further held at bay more disturbing visions of the beast within. These feral tales, marketed variously to young people and to men, anticipated and set the stage for the return of boyology. The latest boy-rearing handbooks draw directly from the mythopoetic movement, take issue with feminism, and reassert wildness, this time in the form of testosterone and masculine brain chemistry.

The proliferating subdiscourses of boyhood have continually blurred distinctions between literary work and ostensibly scientific enterprises, such as anthropology, educational theory, and psychology. The figure of the feral boy, I argue, is central not only to boyology but indeed to residual theories about race, gender, the psyche, and culture more broadly. Whether the "wild child" originates in India, Germany, or a Native American community, the lesson this creature's career is usually taken to impart is about the white, middle-class male's perilous passage from nature to culture, from bestiality to humanity, from homosocial pack life to individual self-reliance and heterosexual prowess—that is, from boyhood to manhood.

Taming Your Inner Wolf: Scouting and Psychoanalysis

Boyology and the feral tale began to look more alike at the beginning of the twentieth century. The national differences we can see between Mowgli and Tarzan, while significant in some respects, fade entirely in the institutional scene of character building. The most striking intersection of boyology and feral iconography is Scouting, in which British and American understandings of boyhood were largely reconciled. Scouting was pioneered in 1908 by Lord Robert Baden-Powell, a British military officer who led the invasion against the Boers of North Africa. And as Hugh Brogan reports in *Mowgli's Sons: Kipling and the Boy Scouts,* Kipling was supportive of Baden-Powell's program, so much so that he gave the Chief Scout permission to adapt the Scouting idea from *Kim;* the result was Baden-Powell's *Scouting for Boys* (1908). Kipling even penned a song for the Scouts, the first line of which became the Scout's motto: "Be prepared! Zing-a-zing! Bom! Bom!" (Brogan, *Mowgli's Sons,* 30).

When Baden-Powell decided to start a junior Scouting program in 1915, he turned again to Kipling for inspiration, transforming the *Jungle Books* into *The Wolf Cub's Handbook* (1916).[6] The adaptation of a classic folkloric-literary motif hence helped launch what soon became the most successful boy work institution on both sides of the Atlantic. Animal imagoes are not limited to Cubbing but indeed permeate the whole register of Scouting. In Scouting's totemic scheme of development, animal resemblances suggest incipient or potential manhood. Scouting quickly caught on in America largely because comparable (if less successful) organizations had already paved the way for the British import. Americans embraced Scouting but were initially less enamored with Cubbing, disliking the feral imagery, in effect preferring *Kim* to the *Jungle Books.*

Scouting represents an important moment in the entangled but asymmetrical lives of boyology and the feral tale. Until the introduction of Scouting, boy work had been a more literary than institutional calling. But as Scouting began to thrive in the United States, literary boy work and even advice writing on boyhood lost cultural favor. Narrative boy work soon became the business of hacks and syndicates, in the form of series fiction. Boyology survived in the institutional form of Scouting, reinvigorated by the feral tale, which transformed the wolf-boy into a respectable citizen.

But the merging of boyology and the feral tale should be attributed not solely to Scouting but also to the narrative and cultural traditions from which it drew and to which it gave impetus. The feral boy's makeover precedes as well as follows the inauguration of Scouting, especially in popular science and popular ("mass") boys' literature. I acknowledge in chapter 5 that wolf-child reports found their way across the Atlantic and into the professional journals of American psychology and sociology without Freud's help, catching the attention of Bruno Bettelheim, among others. Even so, I want to argue that it was psychoanalysis that contributed more effectively—because more diffusely—to America's embrace of the feral boy. Psychoanalysis coincides with Scouting as a second crucial intersection of boyology and the feral tale. Freud's Rat Man and Wolf Man might at first seem unlikely cousins to Mowgli, but there is a strong family resemblance.

Sigmund Freud likely knew of the feral motif's resilience in mythology, literature, and scientific writing. He published his first feral tale, the Rat Man case history (1909), fifteen years after Kipling's first *Jungle Book* appeared, and three years before Edgar Rice Burroughs's *Tarzan of the Apes*. We know for certain that Freud had read Kipling, for when asked to recommend ten good books to the Austrian public, he listed the *Jungle Book* second.[7] Freud never analyzed stories of feral children or used them explicitly to illustrate his theories.[8] Instead, he wrote his own variants to promote his ideas about sexuality and psychic life. We might even think of psychoanalysis as a sophisticated practice of textualization of oral narrative, in that the speech of patients is transformed into case histories and other documents.

It is now a critical commonplace that psychoanalysis helped effect an interiorization or, in Hayden White's words, a "remythification" of wildness, just as colonial exploration and conquest had seemingly exhausted the world's wild spaces. As evidence, scholars usually point to Freud's theory of the id and his general understanding of the psyche as an often nasty and brutish place. We know that Freud (re)discovered the wild and even the bestial within civilized man. But Freud's crucial psychoanalytic contribution to this interiorization or remythification was in part the narrative form of the feral tale itself. That is, the feral case history is as much his legacy to twentieth-century culture as the ideas it dramatized. Freud inherited an Enlightenment story of culture and its possibilities, which he adapted as a story of civilization and its discontents through folkloric-turned-literary accounts of animal-identified men (for whom childhood loomed large). We tend to think of animals as both threatening creatures and benevolent nurturers; this polarization dates back at least to the Enlightenment, in which questions about man's place in the natural world assumed new urgency. Are we innately civil or wild? Are we improving on our savage ancestors or devolving from our gentle ones? Freud, like Darwin before him, provocatively reframed these questions. As Scouting thrived, and as the feral boy of colonialist writing became an emblem for the normative white male self through boys' literature, so too did the pervert of sexology become the dynamic male subject of psychoanalysis through Freud's feral tales.[9]

Just as his appropriation of the tale of Oedipus was vital to his theories about infantile sexuality and family life, so Freud's rewriting of the feral tale ensures as much as illustrates the adult persistence of animal identification in early childhood. Like Oedipus, the feral boy typically experiences mysterious birth and social handicaps, compensated by later success or notoriety. Not coincidentally does the feral tale resemble the Oedipus story in its emphasis on infant exposure, surrogate parenting, and family drama; the tale types are genetically related. Oedipus is classified as type 931 in Aarne and Thompson's *Types of the Folktale,* although Vladimir Propp argues in "Oedipus in the Light of Folklore" (1944) that there are four major types in the European tradition alone, in which a foundling is raised by foster parents, ranging from monks to fishermen to local monarchs.[10] Propp claims that Oedipus variants with animal foster parents were once quite common but are now all but extinct in the Western tradition, since animal nurture represents an earlier phase in the evolution of Oedipus. He cites an ancient Zulu variant about a boy raised by beasts, describing it as a kinder, gentler revision of even earlier variants that featured "a totem animal swallowing and regurgitating a youth" (96). The abandoned boy is nourished rather than devoured by the beast, setting the stage for animal bonding as a theme in more modern accounts.[11] In the next narrative phase, the beast disappears, and forest animals suckle the child. In time, the animal wet nurse yields to a woman, sometimes identified as a bitch: "the child is nursed by a woman bearing the name of an animal held sacred by the Medes" (Propp, "Oedipus," 97).[12]

Michael Carroll points out that Greek-derived Anglo-European cultures, as well as their colonized nations, show a strong preference for stories about boys and their female animal stepparents. Drawing from Freud, and (like Freud) ignoring the role and import of colonialism, Carroll interprets this pattern as evidence of the feral tale's Oedipal tendencies, arguing (bizarrely) that in earlier variants, the Oedipal motif was less disguised because ancient Greece had fewer prohibitions against mother-son incest than do modern cultures. Whereas Propp, focusing on "proper" Oedipus variants, believes that the motif evolved from animal variants into a more homogenized tale of Oedipus, Carroll suggests that modern feral tales are rewrites of the classical tale type. Either way, the feral tale is intimately connected to the story of Oedipus, as Freud seems to have intuited in his own creative refashionings, written amid the feral fantasies of Kipling and Burroughs.

And just as those fantasies give priority to the boy's relation to the father, so too does Freud in his case histories of the Rat Man and the Wolf Man. Thus the twentieth-century feral tale represents yet another evolution of the Oedipal tale type, in which mothers and stepmothers fade into the narrative background. Although Mowgli is rescued by his wolf stepmother, he is educated by his male animal companions Baloo (the bear), Bagheera (the panther), and Akela (the head wolf). He does battle with Shere Khan, the lame tiger. Tarzan's energies are likewise focused on male supporters and rivals, at least until Jane shows up. Even as Freud alerted his readers to the homosexual component of sexual and psychic life, Kipling and Burroughs underscored the homosocial foundation of selfhood. To achieve human estate, the feral boy is required to leave behind his animal mother and assume the paternal role.[13] In the psychoanalytic feral tale, the analyst or therapist assumes an Oedipal relation to the boy subject, serving as a foster father and often countering the influence of the feral or den mother. At least in its more heroic form, the twentieth-century feral tale is preoccupied with boys and men.

While psychoanalysis may seem a less obvious instance of feral-themed boyology than Scouting, that's essentially how one scholar understands Freud's project. Sarah Winter sees psychoanalysis as a refashioning of the intensive classical education and homosocial world that Freud experienced at the Sperlgymnasium. Rereading Freud's 1914 essay "Some Reflections on Schoolboy Psychology," Winter proposes that the schoolboy became the model subject of psychoanalysis: learned, ambitious, professionalized, and ambivalent about male bonds. Classical learning enabled Freud's formulations and their reception in intellectual circles. Sophocles' *Oedipus Tyrannus* helped Freud establish the Oedipal drama, and especially father-son conflict, as tragic but inevitable and potentially cathartic. "In elaborating Oedipus," writes Winter, Freud "builds a particular institutional form of subjectivity— the ambivalent, middle-class student of the all-male Gymnasium—into his general scenario of psychosexual development. Thus psychoanalysis itself is, in this specifically historical sense, 'schoolboy psychology'" (51).

In his ethnography *On My Honor: Boy Scouts and the Making of American Youth*, Jay Mechling takes a less historically attuned approach to the relays between boy work and psychoanalysis. Fairly late in the book, in a section devoted to homosociality and homophobia, Mechling suggests that

Scouting gives expression to the anal-erotic character as theorized by psychoanalysis. How else to explain, he wonders, the farting and anal-themed "folk speech" of Boy Scouts, the everyday dirty language of boys? "I puzzled over this for a long time," Mechling writes, "before my reading of Freud's *History of an Infantile Neurosis* (1918) helped me see the meanings of this anal-erotic complex in the context of feminist psychoanalytic theory about the construction and defense of fragile masculinity" (203). Mechling sees in the Wolf Man case the same defensive anal-erotic character that marks Scouting, the repression of "feminine" traits demanded by the project of masculinity. "This anal-erotic complex," theorizes Mechling, "is a 'cost' the boys pay for the repression of the feminine element in the naturally bisexual self" (204).

Mechling's remarks recall queer theorist Judith Butler's cost analysis of heterosexuality. For Butler, the achievement of heterosexual selfhood demands the foreclosure of homosexual possibility, yet the "lost" objects of same-sex desire persist in the ego-imaginary, sometimes disturbing the smooth functioning of self. Elaborating on earlier formulations of gender and/as melancholy, Butler proposes in *The Psychic Life of Power* that "the formula 'I have never loved' someone of a similar gender and 'I have never lost' any such person predicates the 'I' on the 'never-never' of that love and loss" (23). The never-never formulation may or may not be fundamental to subjectivity, as Butler argues. And the self may or may not be "naturally bisexual," as Mechling holds. In any case, the twentieth-century feral tale is fundamentally a story about maturation and is by turns heroic and melancholic.

Boyology and the feral tale make clear the mandate of heterosexual manhood, even as its "cost" finds different levels of recognition or different forms of expression. With respect to Butler's never-never formulation, J. M. Barrie's Neverland immediately comes to mind, with its hermetically sealed world of perpetual boys and menacing pirates, suggestive, perhaps, of those "lost" same-sex objects that persist in the ego-imaginary. Both Peter Pan and the Lost Boy are regular tropes of the new boyology. As I'll show later in this book, the cinematic feral tale doesn't so much say no to homosexuality as never-never, managing queer desire as a healthy form of narcissism or denying it altogether. Again and again, the feral boy is made safe, transformed into the very stuff of normal masculinity. The new boyology of the late 1990s prefers instead to manage queerness in a realistic, gay-affirmative, and individualizing idiom, refusing to consider the homo-economics of Scouting and other boy work institutions. Mechling, in contrast, returns the wolf-boy to boyology not in the form of Kipling's Mowgli—the more respectable origin story in histories of Scouting—but rather in the form of

Freud's Wolf Man, thus playing up the queerness of masculinity at issue in early psychoanalysis.

Mechling does not acknowledge the tension in his work between psychoanalytic and sociological models of masculinity, and it is not clear from whence comes the "anal-erotic complex" of Scouting. The implication is that American society is somehow to blame, but how to link the systematic suppression of "feminine" and homoerotic sensibilities to the cultural formations of masculinity in America? Butler has devoted much of her formidable energy to challenging psychoanalytic (especially Lacanian) formalism of the subject and arguing for a "sociality" unbound by "lack" and other terms of foreclosure/enclosure. It remains to be seen if this sociality can explain (or be explained by) stories of manhood in our culture, which seem at once dynamic and static.

Making American Boys: Boyology and the Feral Tale does not brave this difficult question, nor does it firmly separate psychoanalytic from historical discourse. But it does identify cultures of boy work in and through which American manhood was asserted, among them psychoanalysis itself. Because histories of Scouting are readily available, I have chosen to concentrate on other, less obvious points of intersection between boyology and the feral tale.

The Evolution of Boyhood and the "Aboriginal Self"

Boyology thrived in America long before Scouting and psychoanalysis arrived on the scene. In fact, the project of heterosexual manhood as exposed by Mechling and Butler was central to nineteenth-century boy work and to the evolutionary doctrines on which it was based. Though not so obviously institutional as the "schoolboy psychology" that Winter identifies, boyology develops its own Oedipal or proto-Oedipal narratives of man-boy relations at once familial and pedagogical—especially as the boy worker increasingly comes to supplant the father as the figure of authority and expertise. The boy belongs to his family but is also removed from it in boyologist narrative. Outside paternal agents often do the work of fatherhood, which suggests both the attenuation and maintenance of paternal power. In institutional contexts, the boy worker was allowed and even expected to intervene where the father could not. Like the institutional boy worker after him, the author of boys' books claims a special relationship to the boy. In the American Bad Boy books, for example, which I discuss in chapter 2, fathers play an insignificant role, and while that may attest to the father's remove to the workplace and loss of domestic authority, the author of boy books also stands in for the father, presiding over the boy's journey toward manhood and achievement.

Most analyses of the American boy book ignore this authorial party. In the family romance of boy work, however, the boy worker supplants the father but maintains his role. His authority comes partly at the father's expense, but rarely does he openly disabuse Dad.[14] Oedipality is achieved at the level not merely of theme but also of authorial address.[15] The boy book helped ensure Oedipality in American realism and in critical recognitions of it, which rarely address the paternal function of authorship and too often assert that boy authors were naturally rebelling against their sentimental or didactic foremothers and ushering in serious American literature. In boyology, Oedipality seems more immediately familial in tone than in the feral tale, where fantasies of exchange and displacement allow for a more allegorical/fantastical take on parent-child conflict.

At the same time, if boyology displaces the father from his traditional post, it also repaternalizes authority along extrafamilial lines, appealing variously to artisan models of male mentorship and patronage and more institutional models of male collaboration. The boy worker's claim to fame is that he is more fatherly than any single father could be, especially when he represents the social body of boy work. This is perhaps why it doesn't seem to have mattered much that some boyologists had no boys of their own. More important were their qualifications, their claims to expertise outside of (even against) the authority of parenting.

Thus not only did the feral tale probably help furnish the terms of Oedipal analysis for Freud and later psychoanalytic thinkers, but so too can boyology be understood as Oedipal or proto-Oedipal in tendency. Such a perspective in turn implies that Oedipality is, to some degree, a sociohistorical formation. Historians have in fact suggested as much, arguing that the privatization of the Anglo-European family (under the twin pressures of industrialism and imperialism) has led over time to greater emotional intimacy among family members, resulting in the sort of "hothouse" family environment that Freud takes as universal. Prohibitions based on kinship were ostensibly transformed into the incest taboo within the ever-shrinking bourgeois family or, as Foucault has it, the family cell.

Attempting to explain why psychoanalysis thrived in the United States, John Demos even proposes that the Oedipal family was "more widely and deeply normative in this country than anywhere else" ("Oedipus and America," 66). As evidence he points to an increasingly urban experience of family, a proliferation of child-rearing literature, and "a massive intensification of the parent-child bond" whose hallmarks included an internalization of discipline as conscience (71).[16] Demos points specifically to the centrality of the father-son relation, writing that "success in America meant surpassing one's father" (72). Whatever we make of the hothouse thesis, we shouldn't forget the importance of parental surrogates such as scoutmasters, who have perhaps symbolically replaced family servants. Boy work seems to support the Oedipal family while also offering relief from it.

Before the early twentieth century, American culture was already pre-occupied with the character and vitality of boys and expressed that concern through literature, advice writing, and local forms of character building. American boyology cohered around the genteel figures of the boy-savage and the so-called Bad Boy. The wild child had not yet made his dramatic debut in Scouting and psychoanalysis. The boy-savage and the feral boy belonged to different cultural traditions, even as they were on a collision course.

In American literature, a proto-professional interest in boys can be dated at least to Ralph Waldo Emerson, who in his famous essay "Self-Reliance" (1841) recruits carefree boys as American men:

> The nonchalance of boys who are sure of a dinner and would disdain as much as a lord to do or say ought to conciliate one, is the healthy attitude of human nature. A boy is in the parlor what the pit is in the playhouse; independent, irresponsible, looking out from his corner on such people and facts as pass by, he tries and sentences them on their merits, in the swift, summary way of boys. . . . He cumbers himself never about consequences, about interests: he gives an independent, genuine verdict. You must court him: he does not court you. (259)

In boyhood thrives what Emerson dubs "the aboriginal Self, on which a universal self-reliance may be grounded" (267). That Self relies not on social interaction but on "Spontaneity or Instinct" and "Intuition" (267). "What a contrast," he notes later, "between the well-clad, reading, writing, thinking American . . . and a naked New Zealander. . . . But compare the health of the two men, and you shall see that the white man has lost his aboriginal strength. If the traveler tells us truly, strike the savage with a broad axe, and in a day or two the flesh shall unite and heal as if you struck the blow into soft pitch, and the same blow shall send the white man to his grave" (277).

Striking is Emerson's faith in the regenerative powers of the primordial self, which he associates with "childlike" men (258), "Infancy" (259), and "unaffected, unbiased, unbribable, unaffrighted innocence" (259). Emerson approaches the savage obliquely, making reference neither to the indigenous Americans under erasure nor to the African American slave population that made self-reliance so easy, but instead to the naked New Zealander and his American counterpart, the boy. Emerson suggests not so much that men are softened by civilization but simply that they have lost the aboriginal strength of boyhood. "Self-Reliance" urges boyhood's recovery as the foundation for self. This recovery project links the man of letters especially with the aboriginal Self, safeguarding anxieties about authorship.[17]

I see "Self-Reliance" as a watershed of literary boy work. The essay is advice writing, after all, in which boys and savages loom large in a proto-evolutionary, even proto-psychoanalytic, scheme of masculine selfhood. Boyhood's natural virtues—spontaneity, indifference, independence—can be reclaimed in adulthood, promises Emerson, if men will emulate boys and aboriginals. Emerson's praise of boyish ways works to the distinct disadvantage of the naked New Zealander. Emerson's conflation of boy and savage serves a genocidal fantasy long familiar to the nationalistic imagination, dramatized, for instance, in James Fenimore Cooper's tales of "vanishing" Americans, notably *The Last of the Mohicans* (1831), often considered a boy's adventure story, only the most famous of a group of such texts. As Lora Romero points out, Cooper "incorporates the racial other as an earlier and now irretrievably lost version of the self . . . it is as though for him aboriginals represent a *phase* that the human race goes through but which it must inevitably *get over*" (*Home Fronts,* 41). This is also the trajectory of the racial other in Emerson's essay, and indeed in much nineteenth-century writing. The savage yields to the "aboriginal Self," which in maturing loses its barbarity but, with the boy worker's intervention, preserves its strength. From romanticism to realism, the association of the boy and the racial other requires that the latter vanish, through laissez-faire capitalism if not disease, famine, or war.

As "reading, writing, thinking" (literate) Americans, we are encouraged to appropriate the New Zealander's self-reliance and ignore those who, as Emerson puts it, "do not belong to me and to whom I do not belong" (261).[18] In "Nature" (1836), Emerson casually links child and savage, but in "Self-Reliance" he pointedly equates them.[19] Even before the official introduction of evolutionary science, boyhood was increasingly constituted through a social biology—a nascent boyology—that designated the racial other as irretrievably primitive. Later crucial to this process was the dissemination and misuse of evolutionary principles. The doctrine of recapitulation especially, as it was often reformulated, sustained the boy-savage comparison without insult to the boy, since he will outgrow and incorporate not only his savagery but also his femininity and his inclination toward homogeneity. "Self-Reliance" helps set the stage for literary boyology.

The middle-class white boy is *already* normative and must simply grow up according to his nature (if with supervision—that's where boy work slowly comes in), whereas the contemporaneous feral boy emblematizes a dangerous sort of alterity that demands management. This is the key distinction between boyology and the feral tale before the early twentieth century:

the boy-savage is normative while the feral boy must be acculturated or recuperated. The difference between these two figures derives largely from the traditions of evolutionary science with which boyology and the feral tale were associated. Long before their encounter with psychoanalysis, boyology and the feral tale were crucially shaped by the doctrines and conceits of evolutionary science.

Three doctrines were crucial to discourses of boyhood: the doctrine of recapitulation; Herbert Spencer's theory of diversification, or growth from the homogeneous to the heterogeneous; and Jean-Baptiste Lamarck's belief in the inheritance of acquired characteristics. The first, recapitulation, has received the most attention because of its extreme popularity and its overt racism and sexism. Recapitulation's chief proponent was Ernst Haeckel, whose biogenetic law held that ontogeny recapitulates the adult stages of phylogeny. Recapitulation linked three biological disciplines: embryology, which traces ontogeny, and comparative anatomy and paleontology, which attend phylogeny.[20]

Recapitulation was not the only biopolitical narrative of generally ontogenetic-phylogenetic correspondence, or correspondence between individual and group development, but it was the easiest to abuse. In America especially, popularizers converted this principle into a generic analogy, implying that Caucasian boys were temporarily equal to adult savages but would outgrow them. By the 1860s, the boy-savage association, underwritten by popular accounts of recapitulation, was axiomatic in American letters. Thus the breezy declaration of Charles Dudley Warner in his memoir *Being a Boy* (1877) that "everyone who is good for anything is a natural savage," having "the primal, vigorous instincts and impulses of an African savage" (150). The savage became boyish, and the boy comfortably savage, such that Warner, among others, could hold forth on the "race of boys" (66).[21] Such rhetoric of similitude ensured that the Caucasian boy would leave behind his natural savagery, even as his class status protected him against abuse or dispossession. Such sentiments are not incidental to boyology; they form its ideological center. Key to boyology is the boy-savage trope, and his most genteel incarnation in American literature, the Bad Boy.

Whereas recapitulation affirmed that each creature reenacted the development of its group, the second two evolutionary principles cast that development as progress. American literary and scientific narrative tended to evade the more pessimistic strains of evolutionary science, championing instead teleological principles of biosocial progress that underwrote manifest destiny. Spencer's ideas were strongly resonant with the political and social climate in the States. Borrowing from Karl Ernst von Baer, Spencer reconciled recapitulation with the principle of diversification, writing in his essay "Progress: Its Law and Cause" (1857) that "from the earliest traceable cosmical changes down to the latest results of civilization, we shall find that the transformation of the homogeneous into the heterogeneous, is that in which Progress essentially consists" (40). He specifically notes resemblances between aboriginals and schoolboys: "the authority of the strongest makes itself felt among a body of savages as in a herd of animals, or a posse of schoolboys" (42). The differentiation of labor and production likewise occurs both in primitive cultures and "among groups of schoolboys" (50). Spencer's schoolboy instances homogeneity but also promises diversification and progress; boys may now be primitive, but they will evolve.[22] In their manward march, boys recapitulate and surpass the savage, the feminine, the criminal poor, and the homogeneous in its various manifestations.

Spencer's faith in progress was also neo-Lamarckian. Lamarck's theory of the inheritance of acquired characteristics was more typically a component of the feral tale and related discourses—the literature on child saving, for instance—although it did exercise some influence on urban boy work. Lamarck observed that in some species, adaptations to environment become natural features in subsequent generations. Such an idea, of course, incorporates the threat of devolution as well as the promise of progress and was often used to condemn the immigrant poor. Even so, the Lamarckian strain of boy primitivism was potentially more ameliorative than the strictly recapitulationist account, which separated faux-savage white boys from the real thing. The feral boy rather than the boy-savage is the preferred motif of colonialists and urban reformers, since nonwhite, non-middle-class children raised in wild or dicey habitats might become productive citizens with environmental change and professional help. At the same time, feral boys are at the mercy of their surroundings, whereas white boy-savages can rest assured that they'll safely grow up.

These three evolutionary principles share an emphasis on boyhood as an indisputable reality, as a stage of life that follows the natural laws of evolution and that conjoins the macro and the micro. In boyology, influenced by evolutionary science and the newer disciplines that reworked these very principles—chiefly psychoanalysis, preoccupied with recapitation, the shift from homo to hetero, and the mediating influence of environment—boyhood was imagined first as a biological state, then as a particular culture, to which the boy worker had authoritative access. Boyhood became a synecdoche for evolution and the law of progress. The force of this tradition can still be felt in the contemporary faith in biology. The new boyologists look to testosterone, brain chemistry, and other forms of "hard wiring" as the immutable facts of life. In the feral tale, however, boyhood was less stable, in keeping with the nature of hybridity.

Generally speaking, recapitulation and Spencer's theory of progressive diversification inspired boyology, while Lamarckianism sustained the feral tale. The correspondences are not always so direct, however. For instance, recapitulation survived in Freud's theories of psychosexual life as well as in boyology; Freud's remodeling of the psyche is thus more developmental than situational in emphasis. Conversely, boyologists often emphasize the transformative power of context, which suggests that development isn't always so predetermined. The crucial point is that boyology and the feral tale inherited and revised particular evolutionary scripts. Perhaps because of the staying power of recapitulation, boyology came to absorb the more palatable aspects of the feral tale and to disavow its more unsettling ones.

Where the Boys Are

Making American Boys: Boyology and the Feral Tale sketches the evolution of boyology from its rural and small-town forms through its urban and institutional phases and finally its reincarnation in the late 1990s as a privatized self-help tradition. Boyology has not been addressed as such beyond its entanglements with machine culture and the "material unconscious" of modernity.[23] I argue that even if boyology did not go industrial until the 1890s, it emerged as a discourse much earlier and survives still. Boyology was first literary in form, then also institutional, then also psychological.

The book also traces indigenous and imported forms of the feral tale as they animated boy work, entered the psychoanalytic domain, and furthered the remythification of wildness by which (as White argues) we mark modernity. The feral tale entered boyology in its institutional heyday and made possible its transliteration. This does not mean, however, that the feral tale is reducible to boyology; they have different trajectories even as they collaborate in the production of normative subjects. The feral tale is much more adaptable than boyology and will surely mutate beyond the latter.

Early boyology was an ad hoc and private affair, such that we have only anecdotal evidence of this phase. Although the YMCA had conducted isolated, rural boy work efforts as early as the 1870s, boy workers did not organize in earnest until around the century's turn. Emergent boyology thus drew from discourses of family life and domestic ideology, with their codes of sentimentality and maternal authority. Thus the early boy worker did not assume the masculinist, outward-bound pose that we associate with Scouting or the Sons of Daniel Boone.

The institutional boy worker was much more worried about the feminization of boys than his rural predecessor. Institutional boy work in fact organized itself against the neurasthenia and enervation that ostensibly plagued urban life. Institutional boyology moved away from the sentimental mode of postbellum rural boyology to the more paranoid gender thematics of character building. Boyology thus tried to repudiate its ties with domestic ideology and child-rearing discourse aimed primarily at mothers, even as it revamped the ideals of both. Chapter 1 traces this transition, arguing that as the boy worker was legitimized by literary and then institutional boy work, his professional identity and his renunciation of the rural-domestic mode brought with it new concerns, foremost among them the character of the boy worker himself. The rise of institutional boyology dovetails with the rise of anxiety about "contrasexed" boy workers. It's never easy to distinguish normal from perverse man-boy relations, and institutional boyology has long struggled with this issue. This chapter also examines what I call "curatorial boyology," or the ethic of preservation that accompanied (perhaps hastened) the decline of both the farm and the farm boy.

Chapter 2 examines two narrative genres of boyology: first, the postbellum Bad Boy books, and then the handbooks of the first official boyologists, such as Gibson's *Boyology or Boy Analysis*. The Bad Boy genre adapted key principles of evolutionary science, transforming them into regulatory codes of literary realism. The doctrine of recapitulation and Spencer's theory of diversification were appropriated not only as themes but also as strategies of authorship, through which writers could narrate their artistic evolution. I argue in this chapter that literature has long been a significant form of boy work, even when we have not recognized it as such. The second part of the chapter examines the rise of boyology as a narrative and institutional enterprise that relied on evolutionary idiom and literary boy work but also appealed to comparative anthropology and the rhetoric of culture. Both the Bad Boy genre and the first wave of boyology primers died out by the 1920s, just as the American literary canon was being formalized. I suggest further that the hypercanonization—to borrow Jonathan Arac's provocative term— of Mark Twain's *Adventures of Huckleberry Finn* (1884) owes both to its origins in the Bad Boy genre and to a mode of boy-themed culture criticism launched by Van Wyck Brooks in the 1920s that took Twain as its central and representative figure. Debate about Twain's place in the culture and the canon, alongside a residual faith in boyology, helped establish *Huck Finn* as a masterwork.

Overseas in British India, as at home in America, the nineteenth-century feral tale was transformed from an Enlightenment narrative of culture into a politicized discourse of managed alterity, as the wild children of rational science were displaced by the feral subjects of British colonialism, American urban reform, and Native American assimilation. This is my subject in chapter 3, which also demonstrates how each of these projects then remodeled the feral tale into new forms of mass-market "juvenile" writing designed primarily for boys, just as psychoanalysis and Scouting alike were being embraced in the United States. This infantilization of the feral creature (at the level of genre) facilitated its eventual usurpation of the normative masculine self. Stories of wild men and wild children have been linked to children's literature from the field's early history, especially adventure writing, seen as literature for boys.[24] The remythification that White describes began in earnest in the eighteenth century and intensified by the twentieth, with the feral tale assuming the status and supporting role of children's literature and media.[25]

By the 1920s, literary boy work had fallen into disfavor, displaced by institutional boy work and by the mass dissemination of series books. Chapter 4 focuses on the twentieth-century career of one boy work institution that has been virtually ignored thus far (overshadowed by Scouting): Father Flanagan's Boys Town, best known through Norman Taurog's sentimental 1938 film *Boys Town*. The converted feral boy of chapter 3 has his counterpart in Whitey, the film's protagonist, at once a slum kid and a normal American boy. *Boys Town* depicts Flanagan's particular brand of fieldwork, as practiced in an ostensibly democratic boytopia like that envisioned by the Bad Boy writers and the early boyologists. On the one hand, the film reflects growing awareness of juvenile delinquency as a social problem; at the same time, it registers disenchantment with the emergent welfare state. As the film and other Boys Town productions make clear, the feral boy gets a makeover, becomes nearly indistinguishable from the normative boy of boyology. Now one of the largest child care organizations in the world, Boys Town owes much of its success to its father-founder mythology and its rhetoric of family values, to which Newt Gingrich famously appealed in 1994 when praising privatized child care.

At issue in chapter 5 is Freud's foundational use of the feral motif, and subsequent American adaptations. Freud never discussed the feral tale as such; instead, he wrote his own variants, developing his dialectic of the normal and the perverse. By invoking the rat and the wolf in particular, Freud aligns psychoanalysis with urban reform and colonialist adventure without having to explain the origins or import of these totems. The legacy of the psychoanalytic feral tale is twofold. On the one hand, the feral boy became a trope for the normal self, leaving psychoanalysis proper and taking up residence in pop-cultural forms like children's books and mainstream film. At the same time, thanks to Bruno Bettelheim and other advocates of disturbed and abused children, the feral tale has served as a clinical story of human failing(s) and even as a cautionary tale about science.[26] A case in point is the 1994 Nova episode *The Secret of the Wild Child*, which tells the story of an abused "feral" girl in 1970s California and implies that her rehabilitation by a team of doctors and scientists was not merely misguided but downright cruel.

While boys still tend to be the heroes of adventure-style feral tales, girls have now displaced boys as the primary subjects of more "realistic" variants. It's perhaps not surprising that gender makes all the difference, especially since psychoanalysis is notoriously male centered. In the mythological tradition, most feral children are boys, as are those famous wild children of the eighteenth and nineteenth centuries, Victor of Aveyron and Kaspar Hauser. Before the twentieth century, cases of feral girls or women were suppressed altogether; when discovered, notes Julia Douthwaite, feral girls were not embraced because they could not personify the Enlightenment project of *civilité*. The Wild Girl of Champagne, an eighteenth-century celebrity, has all but dropped out of the feral tale canon. Feral boys are now the hardy heroes of adventure fiction and mythopoetic tribute, and feral girls the subhuman subjects of clinical case study or journalistic exposé. Thus the famed child therapist Bruno Bettelheim draws on cases of troubled girls, reinventing the "feral" as a diagnostic term for autism in his 1959 essay "Feral Children and Autistic Children." Even so, Bettelheim and others have broken with the heroic reception and remodeling of the Freudian feral tale, addressing the challenge that Freud allegedly skirted: namely, how to account for people who cannot speak about or understand their experiences. The post-Holocaust feral tale, in fact, functions largely as a cautionary narrative about crimes of humanity, the abusive potential of science, and even the dangers of psychoanalysis.

Although this second tradition is fascinating and significant, especially with respect to gender, I concentrate on the feral tale's collaboration with boyology. As psychoanalysis gained ground in American culture, becoming at once more institutionalized and more diffuse, the emphasis in the helping professions more broadly shifted from treating mental illness to promoting mental health. Ellen Herman thus argues that the mid–twentieth century saw a normalization of psychoanalysis in terms of its client base and general function.[27] Against this backdrop, and in tandem with mass-market stories of boyhood, it's not surprising that as the century wore on, the feral tale served increasingly as a story of the middle-class white man's recoupable and even profitable inner wildness. Or, alternatively, it's not surprising that Freud's feral tales looked less and less like these upbeat American popularizations.

My final chapter serves as a conclusion to the book, attending to the new boyology of the late 1990s as facilitated by the twentieth-century refashioning of the feral boy, and in the wake of the mythopoetic men's movement.

The social conservatism of the mythopoetic movement is also characteristic of the new boyology, which remythifies wildness in biochemical, quasi-medical terms while still appealing to received literary and psychosocial wisdom about boyhood. The new boyologists are not affiliated with one another institutionally, and they have no professional ties to middle-class character building. Rather, they are therapists who write advice literature on the side. As such, they rather resemble the Bad Boy authors of the late nineteenth century, who knew each other personally and shared a sense of enterprise but were free agents. Although *Making American Boys: Boyology and the Feral Tale* tells a familiar story of professionalization and modernization across the twentieth century, it also underscores the static and recursive tendencies of these two major discourses of boyhood.

1. Farming for Boys

Why Boys Leave the Farm

Why did you leave the farm, my lad?
Why did you bolt and leave your dad?
Why did you beat it off to town
And turn your poor old father down?
Thinkers of platform, pulpit, press,
Are wallowing in deep distress;
They seek to know the hidden cause
Why farmer boys desert their pas.
Some say they long to get a taste
Of faster life and social waste;
And some will say the silly chumps
Mistake their suit cards for their trumps
In wagering fresh and germless air
Against the smoky thoroughfare.
We're all agreed the farm's the place,
So free your mind and state your case.

Well, stranger, since you've been frank,
I'll roll aside the hazy bank,
The misty cloud of theories,
And tell you where the trouble lies.
I left my dad, his farm, his plow,
Because my calf became his cow.
I left my dad—'twas wrong, of course—
Because my colt became his horse.
I left my dad to sow and reap
Because my lamb became his sheep.
I dropped my hoe and stuck my fork
Because my pig became his pork.
The garden stuff that I made grow,
'Twas his to sell, but mine to hoe.
It is not the smoke in the atmosphere,
Nor the taste for life that brought me here.
Please tell the platform, pulpit, press,
No fear of toil or love of dress
Is driving off the farmer lads,
But just the method of their dads.

Why do boys leave the farm? This question preoccupied both boy workers and agricultural historians in the early twentieth century. Industrialization, the city's allure, the usurpation of family farms by big business: these are the familiar and more global answers, the "misty cloud of theories." This anonymous poem, which graced the inside cover of the January 1920 issue of the YMCA journal *Rural Manhood,* faults instead the farmer-father for demanding the boy's labor but denying him proprietorship. The boy is responsible for the farm animals in their early stages—in fact, he is often likened to them in the residual evolutionary idiom of the day—but he cannot take their adult forms to market or call them his own. His raw resources become Dad's finished goods. *Rural Manhood* portrays the father-son relationship as exploitative and promises the self-reliant boy a farming enterprise of his own. Although boys may have read the journal, it is aimed at their fathers and warns them to give their sons some space—perhaps a few rows of corn or a small tomato garden—in order to keep the boys at home.

Rural Manhood first appeared in January 1910, as the mouthpiece of the YMCA's County Work Department, and was published ten times a year until 1920, when it folded. Title notwithstanding, it is rhetorically devoted to the preservation of rural boyhood against paternal abuse and urban encroachment. "Boys, Corn and Associations," which ran in the inaugural issue, explains that the "farm boy of to-day is immensely interested in the new agriculture," and that the YMCA is the ideal agency "for promoting better crops on the farm and larger interests in their growing by farm boys" (1:1:27). While praising farming more generally, even linking it with high culture,[1] *Rural Manhood* emphasizes farming for boys, in both senses of the phrase: teaching boys the joys and methods of agriculture, and teaching men how to cultivate healthy boy crops.

Rural Manhood illustrates the YMCA's efforts to affirm the boy worker at the expense of the farmer-father through a rhetoric of farm and farm boy preservation (never the alternative discourse of the Farmers' Movement or Populism). *Rural Manhood* claims to empower the boy and thus empowers the boy worker. Whereas programs such as 4-H and Future Farmers of America (FFA) had little incentive to undermine the father and promote the boy worker, the YMCA and the Boy Scouts of America (BSA) depended on the assumption that the family, and specifically the father, had failed the boy.[2] The FFA and 4-H promoted farming, while the BSA and the YMCA promoted "character" and Christian life. The BSA sponsored programs in rural areas but did not show much interest in farming. The YMCA, however, used farming as a platform for boy work, applauding 4-H efforts but offering a more comprehensive program.

Although boyology was not urban-industrial or institutional until the early twentieth century, it took shape as an "avuncular" and agrarian enterprise much earlier, as I show in this chapter.[3] America's dramatic transformation from a largely rural to an increasingly urban nation is, of course, a familiar historical theme. Acknowledging the significance of this larger backdrop of modernization, industrialization, and the rise of the managerial-professional class, I suggest that the evolution of boyology depended on the child study movement and what I call preservationist or curatorial boyology. As the farm boy "vanished" historically, he became an archetype of sorts, linked with the avuncular, old-fashioned (and thus suspect) boy worker who made possible the accredited work of character building.

By the time *Rural Manhood* made its debut, farming itself was in serious decline, and boys were leaving the farm en masse. While the journal was designed to affirm agrarian life, it had another function: to transform boy work itself. Nineteen ten is also the year in which Scouting began in the United States. The YMCA itself was turning toward urban projects. *Rural Manhood* also ran during the same decade that saw the proliferation of the middle-class boyology manuals and might be understood as their agricultural cousin. In fact, the first mention of "boyology" that I've come across is in E. P. Conlon's two-part "Brain Exchange on Leader Training" feature of the November and December 1914 issues of *Rural Manhood,* two years before the publication of Henry William Gibson's *Boyology or Boy Analysis.* In *Rural Manhood,* the boy worker is omnipresent in the sponsoring institution. He is not a singular character but a professional type, who reports in the first person or through conceits such as the concerned stranger in the poem quoted at the beginning of the chapter, promising boy retention in exchange for a little respect.

Whether rural or urban in emphasis (or both), character building emerged from avuncular boy work on the farm and from curatorial boyology. I thus begin not with *Rural Manhood* but with a much earlier narrative, written for children but likely read by adults, too: *Farming for Boys,* serialized in *Our Young Folks: An Illustrated Magazine for Boys and Girls* from 1865 to 1866, reissued in book form in 1868.[4] Its hero, Uncle Benny, rescues the Spangler farm and family from mismanagement in eleven exciting installments. Gentle and soft-spoken, and a "sort of distant relation" to the Spanglers, Benny is older than most boy workers and not so ruggedly masculine or professional. Benny's authority is more maternal and ministerial than traditionally paternal. Benny's intervention is so successful that Bill Spangler, teenage heir to the farm, wonders in the end "whether it was not better for a boy to have only an uncle instead of a father" (285).

In her essay "Tales of the Avunculate: Queer Tutelage in *The Importance of Being Earnest,*" Eve Kosofsky Sedgwick proposes that Wilde's play suggests an alternative imaginary to the usual Oedipal story: "Forget the Name of the Father. Think about your uncles and aunts" (59). Sedgwick traces the ways in which the avunculate—the social formation of aunt and uncle figures who may or may not be related to us—helps relieve the stifling insularity of the nuclear family, particularly for queer kids "whose first sense of the possibility of alternative life trajectories came to us from our uncles and aunts" (63). Even so, Sedgwick stresses the imperviousness of the nuclear family to the avunculate or other alternative forms of family; avuncular stories often wind up affirming traditional family values.[5] In *Farming for Boys,* Uncle Benny in fact assumes a paternal role, representing a creative solution to the entangled crises of farm and fatherhood.[6]

By the 1890s, however, the avuncular wisdom of an Uncle Benny was yielding to the more professional expertise of child study experts and agency-affiliated boy workers. In the second part of the chapter, I take psychologist and child study guru G. Stanley Hall as my representative figure and examine his investment in farm boy preservation. Although he professes great love for the farm life of his youth, Hall distinguishes himself from those "uncles" who seem more quaint than sage. The third section of the chapter returns to *Rural Manhood* and the YMCA's efforts in the early twentieth century to centralize and urbanize boy work. I also look at the institutionalization of camping, further evidence of the urban turn in boy work. But because camping is affiliated with the great outdoors, and because summer camps temporarily replace the family home, camp directors are expected to be familial and avuncular, which raises anxiety about character. The very codes of mentorship and domesticity that give impetus to rural boy work became signs of potential perversion in character building. Character builders tried to delineate types of boy workers: the amateur and the professional, the free agent and company man, the role model and the "contrasexed." The shift into urban boy work intensified—perhaps demanded—concern about proper and improper relations between men and boys. The pseudoscientific spirit of boy study in the early twentieth century was inseparable from interest in, and anxiety about, deviant sexuality.

Uncle Benny's Farm Aid

Before American writing on boyhood came to fiction, it usually took the form of advice literature. In antebellum handbooks by the likes of William Alcott and Horace Bushnell, the boy served not merely as a topic but as an authorizing subject, allowing the author to hold forth on assorted matters. As Richard S. Lowry puts it with respect to Mark Twain, "the very process of representing boys implied a certain authority, a parental authority no doubt, but also a larger expertise embodied in a rhetorical authority that reached beyond the immediate concerns of day-to-day family life" ("*Littery Man*," 96). Boy books and boy-rearing handbooks come and go, but the exercise of that larger expertise and rhetorical authority seems more constant than not, especially after the Civil War. Boyology went literary in the postbellum era, flourishing most visibly as the so-called Bad Boy genre, which I take up in the next chapter. Writing about the boy, and guiding him through life, not only helped boys become men but also helped men become boy workers or professional "boy men."[7]

Farming for Boys is a conduct manual for boys and their aspiring workers, a primer that anticipates and helps prepare for 4-H, FFA, and the rural wing of the YMCA, as well as more officially urban boy work efforts. Composed in the wake of the Homestead Act, it modernizes but also preserves Jefferson's faith in the self-sufficiency of the family farm and his vision of its administration by white male aristocrats of sound learning and morality. It is one of the earliest American texts to insist on the need for boy supervision outside of the nuclear family, updating advice books such as *The Young Man's Aid* (1839) and *The Young Man's Counselor* (1852).

The boy worker originally hailed from the farm or at least the rural community and naturally knew a great deal about agricultural methods and practices. In the Northeast, the field of boy work drew from the already established (if also only semiprofessionalized) field of agricultural science.[8] Between 1820 and 1860, Albany, New York, became a major agricultural as well as municipal center, the headquarters of important state agencies and academic institutions. It attracted renowned scientists such as Louis Agassiz and Charles Lyell and by midcentury was hosting national gatherings of the American Association for the Advancement of Science (Rossiter, *The Emergence of Agricultural Science*, 8). In 1834 Albany newspaper editor and Whig politician Jesse Buel founded the important agricultural journal the *Cultivator*, whose motto was "To Improve the Soil and the Mind." The *Cultivator* recommended the study and application of agricultural science and devoted special columns to young men interested in pursuing careers in soil chemistry; its successor was the *Country Gentleman*. The *Genesee Farmer* of Rochester was less rigorously scientific, but it too encouraged farmers to broaden their intellectual horizons and conduct their own field experiments. These journals reviewed the mushrooming literature on scientific agriculture, often dubbed "book farming."

With some revision, *Farming for Boys* might have been serialized in such journals, which are likely the kind of unspecified "agricultural papers" to which Uncle Benny subscribes, and from which he culls his lessons.

Certainly Benny is himself a country gentleman, and a cultivator of soil and mind. He is also a walking, talking book of farming. He encourages the Spangler boys and their father to read up on the literature and strategize in the field. Yet *Farming for Boys* is curiously short on detail along these lines, perhaps because it debuted in the first issue of a children's magazine, *Our Young Folks,* running from January 1865 through April 1866. An unlikely forum for agricultural science, *Our Young Folks* was the second long-running American children's periodical, preceded only by *Youth's Companion* (Darling, *Children's Book Reviewing,* 210).

Like the more prestigious *St. Nicholas,* with which it merged in 1874, *Our Young Folks* featured some of the greatest literary talents of the postwar period, including Thomas Bailey Aldrich, James Russell Lowell, Harriet Beecher Stowe, Bayard Taylor, Lydia Maria Child, Louisa May Alcott, Henry Wadsworth Longfellow, and Elizabeth Stuart Phelps. But we know nothing of the author of *Farming for Boys,* only that he or she (presumably he) also composed another agricultural serial, *Ten Acres Enough.* The subtitle of *Farming* spells out its agri-pedagogical agenda: "What They Have Done, and What Others May Do in the Cultivation of Farm and Garden—How to Begin, How to Proceed, and What to Aim At." Uncle Benny embodies the spirit of agricultural science without all the tedious details. "He rarely gave chemical reasons, or scientific terms, as the boys had no knowledge of them" (186). Benny is a yeoman gentleman-farmer, a cultivator and not a scientist. In many respects, *Farming for Boys* echoes the genteel ethos of *Our Young Folks* and indeed all the postwar children's periodicals, apparently produced and consumed not by a heterogeneous middle class but by the American gentry.

Farming for Boys appeared four years before the first official Bad Boy book, Thomas Bailey Aldrich's *The Story of a Bad Boy* (1869), also serialized in *Our Young Folks.* The narrator of *Farming for Boys,* unlike Aldrich, does not champion his carefree boys but rather deplores their laziness. Although it too invokes evolutionary metaphor, *Farming for Boys* is not a compendium of cheerful boy-savage analogies, like other Bad Boy books, such as William Dean Howells's *A Boy's Town* (1890) or William Allen White's *The Court of Boyville* (1898). It has more in common with rural examples of the genre like Charles Dudley Warner's nostalgic *Being a Boy* (1877), also set on a New England farm, and Hamlin Garland's grittier *Boy Life on the Prairie* (1899). Warner's text is perhaps the closest in spirit to the serial, describing experiences "common to the boyhood of" rural New England from 1830 to 1850—including the labor he performs, which Warner describes as never ending and vital (22).

The story is set on an old farm in New Jersey, near Trenton and perilously close to "the great railroad which runs between New York and Philadelphia" (1). The proximity of the railroad should alert us not merely to the dangers of technology but to its transformative power and perhaps its inevitability, a force less easy to manage than farm science. The farm is overseen by the industrious but ignorant Philip Spangler, a well-intentioned but woefully inept manager with little interest in technology. On rainy days he takes refuge in the local tavern, holding forth on matters political but not agricultural. He finds "farming an affair of muscle only" and hence wastes no time reading, attending farming fairs, or inspecting the latest equipment. He takes no notice of the dramatic developments in machinery inspired by the Civil War and a shortage of manpower. "The fact was," we learn, "he had been badly educated, and he could not shake off the habits of his early life. He had been taught that hard work was the chief end of man" (10).

Mr. Spangler doesn't realize that the labor of boy supervision and management is also vital. Thus during what historians describe as the heyday of farming in the East, his farm is failing, and his boys refuse to "split a single stick of wood," having been "brought up in the same neglectful way, just rubbing along from day to day, never getting ahead" (5–6). The work of boyology is to shift work from labor to management, a move that anticipates and accommodates a more urban economy. If Mr. Spangler can see himself as management, or if someone else can advocate such consciousness, then there is hope for the farm in this period of technological transformation.

Mr. Spangler has two teenage sons, Jack and Bill, and one adopted orphan, Tony King, "even a brighter boy than Joe Spangler" (11). Uncle Benny manages to rescue these boys and the farm itself from Mr. Spangler's ineptitude. Benny forms a special bond with orphan Tony, and in fact the narrative is overpopulated with uncle-orphan sets. Benny's "fatherly care" (99) for this son surrogate and the indulgence of Tony's real-life uncle, who materializes near the story's end, ultimately prevail. Armed with new information and vision, the boys enlighten their father, and all farm happily ever after.

Uncle Benny is around seventy years old when he comes to live with the Spanglers in this time of crisis. Called "Uncle" by the children out of respect for his age (an example the adults do not follow), Benny is well traveled and educated and "uncommonly handy with tools" (13). He understands both farm administration and the special needs of boys:

> The very tones of Uncle Benny's voice, his lessons of instruction
> upon every-day topics, his little kindly gifts, his confidences, his
> commendations, and sometimes his reproofs, were all important

agencies in the education of these neglected boys. He lent them
books and papers to read, taught them lessons of morality, and
was constantly directing them to look upward, to aspire, not only
as men, but as immortal beings. (51)

Benny believes that "too many boys on a farm were merely allowed
to grow up" (24–25), and he teaches his young charges that "it was impossible to earn genuine manhood except by steadily and industriously serving
out their boyhood" (99), a sentence best served under his watchful eye. Like
the domestic manager, the farm manager was expected to exercise systematic control over his domain, particularly its youth. What Nancy Armstrong
observes of domestic life (drawing from women's conduct manuals and
domestic fiction) is also true of New England farm life: it became an "autonomous text" when its administrative personnel understood their duties in
psychological and professional terms (126). Benny is not a manual laborer
but a genteel "mentalizer," who manages all operations and safeguards his
young charges from imbalances of body, psyche, and spirit.[9] Part homestead
and part frontier,[10] the farm is the ideal space for the negotiation of the
boy worker's authority. Benny's soft, ministerial tones and his affection for
his "nephews" are appropriate in the space of the farm.

Farming for Boys might instead be titled The Story of a Bad Farmer.
Farmers are apparently a hopeless lot, who "think too much of what only
themselves want, and too little of what their boys do" (71). They fathom
neither sophisticated ideas nor the basic wants of boyhood and miss the
value of certain "concessions" that are "the surest agencies for developing
the self-reliance of a boy" (71). Their sloppy attitudes and actions lead to
spiritual malaise, discontentment with farm life, and even flight to the cities.
Certainly this image of the lowly farmer provides some relief to the roman-
ticization of rural character(s) so typical of the period. Farming for Boys
offers both the pastoral and the counterpastoral in its insistence that farm
life can indeed build character, but only if a kindly character builder can do
his necessary work. This is no job for the father or other low-level father
surrogates such as the hired hand, like Jonas in Jacob Abbott's Rollo books,
who occasionally presides over Rollo's growth.

Nor is it a job for the (amateur) woman; the boy worker is by definition male. In Farming for Boys, Mrs. Spangler has virtually no presence; we
hear very little about her, or even about the girls she supervises. We know
only that she is often grumpy and is a poor cook. Farming for Boys attempts
to claim authority and prestige for the male boy worker, against both the
inept father and the increasingly housebound mother.[11] Benny must nurture
but not feminize, build character but not tyrannize. Boyology functioned as
a form of domestic ideology, even if it later disclaimed such influence.

Honey, I Shrunk the Farm

Farming for Boys uses an established Anglo-American agrarian register to dramatize its boyology. The title alludes not only to vaguely Georgic images of rural youth but to more modern pastoral texts such as *The Farmer's Boy: A Rural Poem in Four Books,* published in 1800 by England's Robert Bloomfield, which follows the blissfully ignorant, "meek, fatherless, and poor" farm boy Giles through the four seasons (Bloomfield, 5). Although *Farming for Boys* gives that pastoral theme an evolutionary twist—suggesting that the Spangler boys are on the verge of devolution or developmental arrest, like the farm itself—the project of recuperation is mapped spatially, through the farm's dramatic makeover. Fields are properly drained, manure competently spread, a brier patch transformed into a blackberry field. There's an awful lot of work going on, which we certainly don't see in the Bad Boy books, in which escape from work is a major theme.

And as we might expect from the anonymous author of *Ten Acres Enough, Farming for Boys* effects its improvements through miniaturization. Early on, the narrator urges the farmer to give his boy "the use of a half-acre of land, on which he may raise corn or cabbages or roots for himself" (25). Midway through the serial, Benny takes the boys to the farm of a neighbor, Robert Allen, only two miles away from the Spangler place (which, strangely, the boys have never visited). As a child, we're told, Robert was hired out to a farmer whose "very name had a suspicious sound,—it was John Screwme" (50). With Mr. Screwme's permission, Robert set up a bee colony, then a horseradish farm.[12] And although Mr. Screwme allowed young Robert little time for study, the boy subscribed to an agricultural paper. From "the very smallest beginnings," Benny concludes, Mr. Allen assembled a "respectable library," married Mr. Screwme's daughter Alice (no doubt happy to relinquish her maiden name), and became a model farmer.

Mr. Allen's model farm is only sixty acres, forty acres smaller than the Spanglers'. Mr. Allen even makes tiny tools for his boys to help them work more efficiently. At the serial's end, Benny and his "nephew" Tony King persuade Mr. Spangler to part with thirty acres, so that Tony and his newfound Uncle Alfred can stay local. Earlier Benny had chastised Tony for wanting too much land, saying that "one acre, under an intelligent and enlightened system of cultivation, will yield as much clear profit as five or six acres tilled in an ignorant and slovenly manner" (240).[13] As Mr. Allen puts it, "It is management altogether that makes a farmer, and mismanagement that breaks him" (142).

Inept and wasteful farmers are not the only threat to agrarian bliss; equally menacing is the city, here depicted both as a seductress hell-bent on corrupting rural boys and as a vast, uncharitable space in which such boys are easily lost and can quickly devolve. Later in the period, rapid industrialization in tandem with immigration and shifting gender roles heightened anxieties about enervation and inspired a backlash against the feminizing forces of the city. *Farming for Boys* might be understood as an early manifestation of that backlash, studded as it is with warnings of urban misery. Certainly its spirited defense of country life anticipates Teddy Roosevelt's wilderness cure, if in a more local spirit; Roosevelt in fact claimed *Our Young Folks* (which regularly extolled rural life) as a formative influence of his youth (Kelley, *Mother Was a Lady,* xiii).

Mr. Allen also manages to envelop industrial culture within his small but efficient farm, telling his young visitors that "I have learned to look upon a hen as a mere machine for manufacturing eggs. She may be likened to a sausage stuffer" (145). Thus Mr. Allen says no to the machine in the garden—to urban life as an overwhelming and inevitable reality—ironically by revisioning the farm as a small and contained site of production and management. The only praiseworthy city in *Farming* is the miniature and exemplary city of insects. Reading an extract from the Reverend Mr. (Henry Ward) Beecher urging kindness to all of God's creatures, Benny describes an upturned stone as "a city unawares . . . sit down quietly and watch the engineering and economy that are laid open to your view. Trace the canals or highways through which [insect] traffic has been carried" (153–54). The ant farm, of course, is still used to teach children efficiency and industry.

Uncle Benny's gravest concern is orphan Tony's desire to leave the farm for New York or Philadelphia. Tony, after all, has no claim on the Spangler farm. Benny's careful attentions arrest Tony's wanderlust. Final rebuttal of the urban idyll comes just after that visit to Mr. Allen's farm, in the form of an inverted Horatio Alger Jr. story, featuring Frank Smith, who (like Alger's archetypal protagonist) is "frank," "upright," and "open-hearted." Frank, also an "orphan nephew," had been raised as a future farmer by Mr. Allen but was "bent on trying his fortune in the city" (162). But his misadventures among the city's "low, swearing, drinking class of people" (165) change his mind: "You'll never catch me again leaving the farm to cry newspapers and black boots in the streets," he exclaims. "I'm made for something better than that" (168).

Predictably, the cornerstone of boy farming is Emersonian self-reliance, which later required legions of boy workers to deliver. Nearly seventy years before Laura Ingalls Wilder's *Farmer Boy* (1933), in which Mr. Wilder tells Almanzo that "You'll be free and independent, son, on a farm" (371), Uncle Benny insists that his boys test "their own resources and energies by some little farming operation of their own" (25). "You must help *yourself*," he tells Tony King, "and you will rise or sink in proportion to the energy you exert . . . there is no fence against fortune." For "fortune is an open common, with no hedge, no fence, or obstruction" (40), an image ironic in light of the triumph of enclosure and indeed Benny's own emphasis on "some little farming operation."

It may well be that miniaturization serves as a metonym for the resistance to urban life that marks traditional character building and property management. If boy and farm are both miniature and manageable, so, presumably, is America itself. In *Farming for Boys*, the United States does not assume epic proportions; we hear nothing about the wilderness or even the frontier (even though the frontier was composed largely of farms or homesteads). Uncle Benny conflates what William Dean Howells calls in *A Boy's Town* the "republic" of boyhood (65, 115) with the Jeffersonian republic, noting that Abraham Lincoln began as a poor country boy, a staple theme of presidential biographies written for boys. For Benny as for Jefferson, the farm is both emblem and building block of nation; it is also, as Benny recognizes, the American site of man making, comparable perhaps to the British public school. Uncle Benny predicts that the future president of 1900 now "lives somewhere on a farm. He is a steady, thoughtful boy, fond of reading, and has no bad habits; he never swears, or tells a lie, or disobeys his parents" (28). Presidential candidacy may no longer require a log cabin birth, but clearly a farm upbringing still offers the inside political track. With such an inauspicious background, goes the myth, the exceptional boy just might become the grandest farmer in a nation of farmers. Benny also takes his boys to watch the reenactment of the 1776 Battle of Trenton, linking it with the boys' quest for autonomy, a quest belied by his every instruction. Earlier we meet a plucky peddler boy named John Hancock.

Republican rhetoric pervades boyology of this period, whose "realism," as I argue in the next chapter, is routinely asserted against the sentimental didacticism of women writers. In many respects, the realism of the Bad Boy books has its roots in works like *Farming for Boys*, which suggests the moral and cultural authority of authorship but doesn't reflect explicitly on the vocation of writing for boys. In fact, the author of this serial is anonymous, whereas by the time we encounter the Bad Boy books, boyology is conducted in more intensely authorial terms.

In more ways than one, *Farming for Boys* is designed to shift attention from the father to the boy and his worker. It's hard to say what Benny's intervention accomplishes for Mr. Spangler, or for the father-son relationship, for while Mr. Spangler eventually gets with the program, the boys are always a step ahead of him. Once Benny is introduced, Mr. Spangler virtually disappears and never interferes with the changes. Still, for all his foolishness,

Mr. Spangler is not a bad man; the serial does not belittle him so much as treat him like another boy to be educated. Uncle Benny is likewise not simply his replacement but his improved self, better able to keep pace with a boy's needs as well as with the shifting agricultural scene.

Preserving the Boy

By the end of the nineteenth century, boyology had evolved from a rural and republican sensibility into a largely self-authorizing movement of impressive dimensions. *Farming for Boys* gave way to YMCA county work and *Rural Manhood*, to elegiac memoirs that lament the extinction of the New England farm boy and his natural habitat (such as those I cite earlier), and to the academic study of agricultural history, which had its own elegiac impulses. Like the slum child or "street rat" with which he was regularly juxtaposed, the farm boy was imagined as a simple creature best understood in/as his natural habitat, in his case the farm. Whereas Charles Loring Brace and other American social reformers hoped to convert street rats through relocation to the country, chroniclers of farm life hoped to preserve the farm boy, if not also his environment, through what we might call curatorial boyology.

This preservationist spirit also marked the child study movement led by G. Stanley Hall, which had strong ties to boyology. More particularly, we can see Hall's interest in the farm boy and his habitat in his autobiographical sketch, "Boy Life in a Massachusetts Country Town Thirty Years Ago," from the October 1890 issue of the *American Antiquarian Society*. Hall proposes that since farm life and therefore farm boys are going extinct, we can preserve both by establishing local agricultural museums and by studying in earnest the residual savagery of boyhood.

Between the ages of nine and fourteen, Hall spent his summers and weekends on a farm in Ashfield, Massachusetts. Although that "joyful period" ended in 1860, Hall remarks that "the old New England life" is still (if not for much longer) best experienced and "studied more objectively" on a farm (107). To that end, Hall collects tools and memorabilia into a local museum, modeled on the regional museums of Plymouth, Salem, and Deerfield. He interviews older farmers, records "customs, industries, [and] persons," and assembles "a map of the original farms." For Hall, the farm is not only "the ideal basis of a state of citizen voters as contemplated by the framers of our institutions" but also the "best educational environment for boys at a certain stage of their development ever realized in history" (108). Local museums like Hall's flourished in the nineteenth century; the first was organized in the 1840s, in the Patent Office in Washington, D.C., then a branch of the State Department.

Hall was known for his use of lengthy questionnaires and his obsessive compilation of pop-ethnographic data without analysis. It's no surprise that "Boy Life" catalogs farm industries that have since given way to more specialized trades that must be learned in special schools and factories away from the farm, outside of "boy-range" (125). It is also a catalog of child activities and artifacts from a dying era. In his day, he reports, children were expected to work but also enjoyed their leisure time, participating in wholesome recreations such as "snow-balling," dancing, singing, reading, nature study, and ("the rage of") trapping and hunting (115). Like the children, the wise but simple men of Ashfield congregated instinctively, especially during the "dull days of haying time," which provided "another sort of education. The men of the vicinity strolled together in a shed" and there engaged in various forms of exchange (115). Uncle Benny, it seems, is a more refined specimen of the rural avunculate: "The old uncles who came to be the heroes of current stories, and who were in a sense ideal men, were shrewd and sharp, of exceeding few words, but these oracular, of most unpromising exteriors and mode of speech, with quaint and eccentric ways which made their quintessential wisdom very surprising by the contrast." (116)

Against their vernacular wisdom, Hall offers the expertise of the modern scholar (and to some degree the modern boy worker).[14] Presumably if the farm boy is passing into oblivion, a new kind of boy expert is needed, who can speak authoritatively about boyhood past and present. Hall's anecdotes of "olden times" thus give way to a bland and rather generic brand of psychosocial analysis. He detects in farm folks the "'sense of progress,' which a recent psychologist writer calls a special, though lately evolved, sense" (122). He exhorts us to approach farm culture more academically. Why, he asks, are farm implements and agricultural rituals not typically treated "as scientific anthropological themes . . . ?" (124). Soap making, cheese making, road clearing, the "antique ceremonies and sequelae of butchering day," cider and beer making—are not these "quite as worthy of investigation, of illustration in museums, as the no more rapidly vanishing customs of savage tribes?" (124–25).

Hall's time on the farm, in tandem with his training in psychology and social science, allows him to speak authoritatively and disparagingly of farm folk. He calls them "these people" and speaks as social anthropologist: "Their commonest industries—planting, fertilizing, gathering each crop—have been revolutionized by machinery and artificial fertilization, within twenty-five years" (126). Hall is also a moralist. Farm life is fast changing, and in his view, it isn't pretty. The women are "haggard," the men "shiftless," and the children "very rare" (126). Singling out the work of Mary E. Wilkins, Mary B. Claflin, and Eugene Field, Hall describes fictional townsfolk as "types of degeneration well recognized by alienists and characterized by Morel" (126). Hall manages to preserve the farm against degeneration by describing it in the heroic past tense and by linking it to the boy's primal impulses:

> Nowhere [else besides the farm] has the great middle class been so all-controlling, furnished so large a proportion of scientific and business leaders, been so respectable, so well combined industry with wealth, bred patriotism, conservatism, and independence. The farm was a great laboratory, tending, perhaps, rather more to develop scientific than literary tastes, cultivating persistency, in which country boys excel, if at the expense of versatility. . . . during the rowdy or adolescent age the boy tendency to revert to savagery can find harmless vent in hunting, trapping, and other ways less injurious to morals than the customs of city life. (126–27)

From the dying "boy life" of thirty years ago, Hall rescues assorted boy traits and tendencies; in the last sentence of the passage just quoted, we see him move from an elegy of the farm toward an evolutionary portrait of the essential boyhood. If the farm boy is on his way out, the modern boy still enjoys his savage instincts, particularly if provided playtime in the country. Hall's curatorial enterprise is not new; he is simply encouraging everyone to cultivate local history and is promoting boyhood as a form of access to that history. What is distinctive about Hall's sketch is his blend of preservationist pastoral, evolutionist boyology, and modern social science. Hall was a founding father not only of child psychology but of American psychology more generally; he founded two important journals, *American Journal of Psychology* (1887) and the *Pedagogical Seminary* (1891).[15] Just three years after "Boy Life" appeared, Hall launched the National Association for the Study of Childhood. Hall presided over the child study movement at Clark University, where he welcomed Sigmund Freud in 1909 and trained a whole new generation of child experts. Given these investments, Hall's essay should be understood not only as a nostalgic response to the decline of farming but as a quasi-literary, quasi-psychological narrative that helped effect the transformations it laments. The farm, Hall makes clear, is fast becoming obsolete, along with the savage himself, but boy tendencies live on in each generation and can be scientifically studied.

Hall's memoir of boy life in fact participates in a larger late-nineteenth-century narrative closing of the frontier farm, culminating in Frederick Jackson Turner's "The Significance of the Frontier in American History" (1893). Delivered to the American Historical Association, Turner's paper has been credited with pioneering a new form of agricultural history that emphasized socioeconomic aspects of change (Shideler, "Agricultural History Studies," 6). The frontier hypothesis was an agricultural analysis, and in effect the frontier farm's obituary. That death, however tragic, seemed acceptable, since according to evolutionary accounts of human history, the agrarian lifestyle naturally yields to urban existence. The degree to which this evolutionary plot underwrites the history and historiography of farming has not been explored; I note only that attempts to preserve our rural heritage were not solely reactive but also constitutive of historical change.

Boy books of the period are also elegiac and preservationist in spirit. "The typical boy," writes Clifton Johnson in *The Farmer's Boy* (1894), "is a sturdy, wholesome looking little fellow, with chubby cheeks that are well tanned and freckled in summer, and that in the winter take a rosy glow from the keenness of the air" (100). (Johnson, incidentally, illustrated the 1897 edition of Warner's *Being a Boy*.) The book is organized around the seasons, and while Frank is alive, he might as well be stuffed, so little does he change from chapter to chapter. Seasons come and go, but farm and boy stay the same. Johnson insists that the farm's seclusion isolates and protects children from a confusing "multiplicity of amusements" that might trigger change, which is always for the worse (106). Charles Clark Munn's *Boyhood Days on the Farm* (1907) is much starker, written "to rescue from oblivion just a faint picture of the old-fashioned boy and his environment" (iv). Munn also takes a less sanguine view of farm life: "The farmer is the slave of his land, and the boy a slave to both" (22). Like *Rural Manhood*, the book simultaneously praises the farm and points out its shortcomings. It ends with a sad meditation on old age, death, and the passage of time, describing the farm as the "burial spot of boyish illusions" (396) and the farm boy as "fast passing into oblivion" (iii).

Johnson fashions a boy diorama, and Munn an outdoor museum of boyhood, whose visiting hours are nearly over. The melancholic note in Munn is more pronounced than in any of the Bad Boy books that I examine in the next chapter. Munn indulges in the occasional boy-savage comparison—his boy Orlo "runs naked as a savage" along the beach, letting out war whoops (195)—but in general Munn waxes more nostalgic. At one point he attributes Orlo's savage fantasies not to recapitulation but to the heady influence of James Fenimore Cooper (172). It's tempting to read such books as narratives of the "lost" boy trope so persistent in boyology. Here that trope seems less a useful fiction than a sad reality (particularly for Munn), and the only consolation is that the farm boy can be preserved in artificial forms, such as the boy book, the local museum, and the scientific paper.

In the early twentieth century, the local farm museum at first fell into disrepair and was then superseded by the larger-scale outdoor and "living" museum, styled after Colonial Williamsburg. Along with the improvement of agricultural history, the development of more sophisticated agricultural museums was one of the first stated objectives of the Agricultural History Society, founded in 1919. The AHS hoped to thus furnish historians with a sense of the nuances of American farm life.[16] Unlike indoor museums, which exhibited farm objects in traditional display formats, outdoor museums modeled communal farm and village life on a grander scale, featuring homes, shops, municipal buildings, and farmsteads, complete with period implements and furnishings. One of the more successful outdoor museums is Old Sturbridge Village in Massachusetts, and its 100-acre Pliny Freeman Farm. Old Sturbridge Village is a museum of American life from 1790 to 1840, and the farm alone includes a barn from Massachusetts, a corn barn from Rhode Island, a smokehouse from Connecticut, and a copper shop from Maine. The farm is designed to represent the "typical" New England farm; the regional differences actually work to that effect.[17]

While it might seem a stretch, I would venture that institutional boy work was likewise an enterprise that collected and constructed a range of habitats in an effort to curate the farm boy—and to authorize boy work as an urban undertaking. Boy workers still tried to build the character of farm boys, but they also tried to incorporate the farm boy ideal into their urban programs. Without the aid of the feral tale, however, boyology found it difficult to interiorize boyhood, which is why the farm boy seems a decidedly nostalgic figure. In the United States especially, the inner wolf-boy or wild child was a much more dynamic conceit, which is perhaps why the traditional boy book, devoted to the rural or small-town boy, has largely disappeared.

Boys, Corn, and Associations

Imagine, if you dare, a legion of younger, bolder, less genteel Uncle Bennys, armed with degrees and other credentials, united in purpose and print across great stretches of land through a federation of regional offices. This was the "junior" division of the County Work Department of the YMCA, whose contributions to institutional boy work are well documented by historian David Macleod. In the inaugural issue of *Rural Manhood*, editor in chief John R. Boardman explains that the "new trend in rural progress" is intervention and management; shared is "the profound conviction by rural social economists that no part of country life can be allowed to follow a merely natural or genetic order of development" (1:1:2–3).[18] Boardman calls for a "self-conscious and self-determinative" organization, to be achieved through the consolidation of rural work agencies into a central coordinating body, and through "wise educational propaganda" (3).

Boyhood proved a useful site of coordination and propaganda, and *Rural Manhood* was devoted to rural boyhood, mostly on the East Coast and in the Midwest, through regular columns like "General Association News," "Current Events," "The Country Life Bookshelf," and "Brain Exchange on Leader Training." E. P. Conlon, a county secretary in Massachusetts, describes *Rural Manhood* explicitly as an exercise in boyology, in his two-part "Brain Exchange on Leader Training" feature of the November and December 1914 issues. Conlon provides an overview of the religious dimensions of boyology without mentioning H. W. Gibson of *Boyology* fame, who himself served as YMCA state secretary in both Massachusetts and Rhode Island. Conlon and his colleagues tried to move the boy to the center of association work and agricultural reform. *Rural Manhood* regularly emphasizes the importance of the local male leader in boy's work, drawing from the positive notion of "character contagion." Its editor and essayists call for frequent leaders' training, through professional conferences and retreats, with lectures, literature digests, and "a systematic and scientific study of boy life" (3:6:195). Gone are the subtle lessons of Uncle Benny; *Rural Manhood* is a boy work manifesto.

"The Boy First," included in the journal's third issue, outlines the County Work Department's plan "to use much the larger part of its resources in work with boys between the ages of twelve and eighteen and with young men between the ages of eighteen and twenty-five, with the emphasis on the former class." This strategy is in accord "with the best scientific and practical thought" (1:3:1). The boy learns more quickly than his dad or other rural men and is a natural experimenter, endowed with "intellectual hunger" and a "native race-impulse toward sociality." Although the journal was already organized around rural boyhood, one special issue per year was devoted to the "country boy"—a tacit acknowledgment that the more generic "rural boy" was more myth than reality.

The YMCA men routinely praised "boy power": "It has been demonstrated that the most effective agency in solving the so-called Boy Problem is the boy himself—that given a worthy task and proper supervision most boys will do their work worthily and steadily" (1:3:2). Normal boys can develop their own methods for assembling and organizing, "so that the onetime boy problem now becomes a boy-power—a vital force in a community to dominate and direct every expression of boy life" (3). The central mission of the County Work Department was, to echo the May 1914 frontispiece, "Harnessing and Directing Country Boy Power." The farm boy, in short, is America's ideal citizen "by heritage and surroundings," as Edwin L. Earp (professor of Christian theology) preaches (8:6:260–62). The boy has four "great currents of human desire in his make-up": the desire to acquire property, the desire for play (which can be channeled into work), the sex desire "which, when rightly directed, leads to chivalry toward women," and the desire for God, which inspires worship (260). The boy can redeem his father and other wayward farmers, provided that first "the lost boy will be found by men who are willing to look for him" (7:1, inside cover). "We firmly disbelieve in farmers that will not improve," writes Henry Ward Beecher in his "Farm Creed," and in "farmer's boys turning into clerks" and "farmers' daughters unwilling to work" (5:1, inside cover).

Even so, boy power was clearly understood as something to be managed. *Rural Manhood* reports the establishment of summer camps and "labor camps" made up entirely of farm boys (9:1:8–12), and of farmers' boys' institutes, which were supplemental educational programs held after and sometimes during school. Designed for men and boys alike, these institutes were miniconferences devoted to topics such as corn and seed testing; sometimes they included growing and harvesting contests (4:5:178).[19] In an amusing variation on the management theme, the YMCA sponsored a number of man-building conferences for boys, in which the boys themselves delivered papers with titles such as "Education in Man Building," "Physical Power in Man Building," and "Fellowship in Man Building."

As in *Farming,* a recurrent theme of *Rural Manhood* is the boy's natural affinity with the crops and animals he raises, notably corn, chickens, pigs, and cattle. Photographs of lads with their prizewinning corn or livestock dot the journal's pages, with captions such as "A Leader in the Making" (6:6, inside cover). Valuing animals more than money, the boy of *Rural Manhood* is a future leader but not a crass commercialist. On occasion we're treated to profiles of farm boys turned successful managers and entrepreneurs, such as Errol Patrick of Ohio; his profile, "Raises Hogs and Builds Boy Character," traces his evolution from farm boy to rural philanthropist and YMCA boy worker and provides a statistical table of his early hog-rearing expenses and profit margin (9:3:100–101). Girls sometimes benefit from such enterprise (though not as regularly), as Kate Logan's "New Business for Pigs: Putting Girls thru College" attests (10:9:395). According to YMCA philosophy, the boy grows with and alongside his product, his transformation the result of both supervision and self-cultivation. His experiments prepare him for the urban managerial world, offering bigger challenges and plots, while preserving the country-genteel ethos of farming. Some contributors to the journal even encouraged farm families to let their sons try city life, since such exposure will sharpen their business sense and teach them that greater opportunity for "individual proprietorship" can be found in the country (3:4:120–22).[20]

But what about girls? Of some concern was the station of the country girl, because she ensures the perpetuity of the farm. In "The Girl on the

Farm" (1:9:22, 24), Warren Wilson notes that household science is not as progressive as agricultural science, and that kitchen "drudgery" should be a thing of the past. Eventually the country girl got her own regular issue of *Rural Manhood*, as did the working woman, but girls and women were ultimately confined to the home and to the familiar, if refurbished, kitchen. And there were limits to how technologically progressive a kitchen could be. In "Household Science: Past, Present, Future," which appears in the November 1912 number, Mrs. Frank Pattison praises women as "domestic engineers" but also chastises them for coveting unnecessary domestic machinery.[21]

The boy, however, was linked not only with urban America but indeed with American expansionism. As we might expect from Hall's praise of the Anglo-Saxon farm in "Boy Life," the farm-in-the-boy served as a mode of Americanization at home and abroad. Hall remarks that "should we ever have occasion to educate colonists, as England is now attempting, we could not do so better than by reviving conditions of life like these" (127). Apparently the more extinct the boy and the farm—the more ideologically preserved—the greater their political purchase. According to Edwin L. Earp's essay on citizenship in *Rural Manhood*, we conserve the boy because he will produce farm goods vital not only to our domestic health but to the survival of foreign nations:

> The conservation of the boy life of the countryside is the most important problem of the nation today, because as never before we need in this country a scientific agricultural population that can conserve the soil values of our rural domain, producing at the same time an increasing yield per acre of the necessary products for the feeding of the nations that depend upon our food exports. (8:6:260)

Here a missionary, expansionist agenda finds ideological cover in humanitarian talk of feeding the world through the labor of American farm boys. The YMCA, of course, became an international organization; association work was conducted in India for years, modeled on British colonialism and employing prominent diplomats, clergymen, and educators. And even *Rural Manhood* reports on overseas efforts. The April 1920 issue, for instance, is devoted to our World War I ally France, with articles such as "Products of Agricultural France," "The French Peasant," and "The Future of French Agriculture," as well as more historical articles (11:4). During the war, boy and nation converged: "The nation is at war. The boy is at war; if not physically at least mentally" (9:10:439). Even so, he is a superior product: "Our American Boys are the hope of the World and the best crop in any Country" (10:3, insider cover).[22]

Boy workers also developed strategies for the Americanization of rural immigrant as well as indigenous groups, praising farming as an antidote to the nomadic ways of foreigners. As Peter Roberts explains, the association's program for rural acculturation was divided into "intensive" and "extensive" work (11:3:102–3, 118). Intensive Americanization focused on the individual singly or in small groups and emphasized English acquisition, vocational training, and (where necessary) hospital visitation. External work hailed "men in masses," building solidarity and historical awareness through "community songs, patriotic rallies, pageants, entertainments, socials, etc." (102). Roberts speculates that farmers will be most interested in Americanization when it "bears direct relation to his interests"—that is, when it provides cheap labor (103). The Native American underwent this same process, sometimes willingly and sometimes not, and *Rural Manhood* reenacts his "disappearance" by defining the colonial white settler as the "Native American," and the recent immigrant as "the naturalized American" (11:6).

Despite efforts to keep it going, *Rural Manhood* itself disappeared in December 1920. The journal finally merged with *Association Men* when the idiom of farming could no longer sustain boy work, except in melancholic and preservationist form. But for ten years *Rural Manhood* served as an important forum for centralizing rural boy work. All current events—land speculation, elections, scientific advancements, international affairs—were judged by their impact on county work and that representative if vanishing American, the farm boy. Like *Farming* before it, *Rural Manhood* strove to preserve the farm within/as the boy, even as it admitted the inevitability of urban culture.

Character Contagion and the Camp That Failed

Like the farm, the camp was an artificial space of enclosure that required regular upkeep. Even more than the farm, it was a space of homosocial interaction, which usually dispensed with the father altogether in favor of charismatic boy workers. It offered a temporary, healing remove from the city, another way of saying that the camp was a consequence of the city (not many farm boys went camping, after all). Early advocates praised camping as an antidote to enervation, effeminacy, and sexual dysfunction, praise that put particular pressure on camp personnel. The camp director was expected to make character contagious, but safely, and after 1900, directors and counselors alike were younger, more charismatic, and more athletic in profile than their predecessors (Macleod, *Building Character*, 237). Like the colorful founders of boy work agencies—for example, Ernest Thompson Seton, Dan Beard, and Baden-Powell himself—the camp director became almost mythically masculine. Henry William Gibson's popular *Camp Management:*

A Manual of Organized Camping (1923) thus opens with "Credo of a Camp Director" (just as *Rural Manhood* had featured Beecher's "Farm Creed") and a paraphrase from Ralph Waldo Emerson: "Every institution is but the lengthened shadow of a man." Gibson asserts that the early camps "were built around contagious personalities rather than expensive equipment . . . we are impressed with the aims and ideals which characterized these men of unselfish motives, sympathetic understanding and tactful leadership, in the administration of their camps" (1).

Organized camping in the United States is usually dated to 1861, when Frederick William Gunn, headmaster of the Gunnery School in Connecticut, took his entire student body for a two-week excursion into the wilderness.[23] Many early camps were extensions of boarding schools, but boy work institutions also established camps.[24] Organized long before the BSA, the YMCA had dabbled in camping since the 1880s, when "camps" were outings, not sites (Macleod, *Building Character*, 234). Camping was originally a boy work strategy rather than an activity or location in its own right. Not until after 1900 did the YMCA substantially develop its camping program. In "Summer Camps," appearing in the April 1910 issue of *Rural Manhood,* Albert E. Roberts describes the recent evolution of camping from an unorganized, even savage, affair into a comprehensive "agency" managed by an energetic camp director with "a keen, intimate knowledge of boy life" (12).

But there were limits to that intimacy, as the period literature from Scouting and the YMCA makes clear. Character builders took pains to distinguish their interest in boys from the unprofessional interests of others. One of Baden-Powell's most trusted men in England was Dr. Robert Patterson, known affectionately by his boys as "Uncle Patterson." Patterson was in charge of the camping field at Gilwell Park, overseen by Francis Gidney. In September 1922 Gidney had bad news for Baden-Powell: at night in the medical hut, Uncle Patterson apparently conducted unofficial physical exams. The boys had complained, and the avuncular doctor was dismissed (Jeal, *The Boy-Man,* 509; Boyle, *Scout's Honor,* 5–6). Obviously this was an exceptional case; no doubt most uncles in boy work conducted themselves honorably. But it is not surprising that once such men were identified as sexual predators, they were quickly exiled. Most boy work institutions—and, it seems, the Catholic Church—remain unwilling to examine their own implication in the larger scene of male-male bonding and affection, preferring either to cover up the scandal or (if that is impossible) to demonize the offender.[25] Suffice it to say that the term "uncle" still conjures up queerness/familiarity/family in ways that are both phobic and affirmative.[26] Uncle Benny's concern for the Spangler boys, neither exactly parental nor institutional in orientation, might now raise a few eyebrows.[27]

As for the YMCA, consider W. B. Holliday's "A Camp That Failed," in the June 1919 issue of *Rural Manhood*. The star-turned-villain of this sad fable is young Henry, a family man with children and "no bad habits," a Sunday school teacher, and seemingly an ideal leader. Despite one dissenting voice, Holliday reports, the Wellsburg YMCA chapter elected Henry to head the Boys' Work Committee, and in only a short period, he worked miracles. "Boys' lives were changed and even the more conservative of the villages admitted that the County Y.M.C.A. was doing a much needed service in the community" (252). By the third year, larger quarters were procured (the former opera house, so well suited for boy work), and camps were organized. Henry, we learn, was especially skilled in bird study and photography.

Henry's fall from grace was abrupt and devastating. In that landmark third year, he decided that the boys needed a more remote campsite that could better accommodate their needs. Despite some resistance from the chapter, Henry and his boys soon "pitched their tents in a well-secluded spot about ten miles from town," where the swimming and fishing were superb. "All went serenely for a few days," writes Holliday, "then one by one the older boys packed their belongings and went home" (253). Shocking allegations followed. Having extolled Henry's virtue, Holliday now condemns his vice:

> We remembered now that Henry had some ways of dealing with boys that had not appealed to us from the beginning, but we had let seeming success close our eyes to his effeminate mannerisms. He had a peculiar way of taking boys on his lap and holding them very closely. He hugged the older boys and sometimes kissed them. He held their hands, at unwarranted times. In fact he impressed us at times as a boy-struck girl, but we overlooked the matter or mistook it for his zeal in helping boys help themselves. We knew that Henry could knit and crochet and that his especial hobby was china painting, but we had not the experience to teach us that he was one of those very dangerous types of individuals who become interested in their own sex immorally. For Henry was contrasexed. He could not withstand the temptations that a camp alone with a group of pure minded boys had presented, regardless of his good intentions. (253)

China-painting Henry is not locked up or even drummed from the community (as was poor Horatio Alger Jr. after the infamous scandal in Brewster, Massachusetts), only dismissed from his post. "The damage is done," Holliday concludes solemnly. Boy work in Wellsburg continues, but parents are less trusting. Holliday warns his readers only to choose leaders carefully, so as not to repeat the experience.[28]

In this little tale, Holliday and his YMCA cohorts are unable to read the signs of immorality, and even after they've spotted their pervert, they are less rabid in their response than we might expect, and less clear about how to prevent another such calamity. Presumably there are *warranted* times for holding boys' hands, and appropriate methods of helping boys to help themselves. Still, a finer line has been drawn, we're told. Never again will they hire a man who crochets and kisses boys; no longer will they confuse "seeming success" with reputable character contagion.

It's hard to take Holliday's naïveté seriously, especially since he revels so much in the telling of innocence lost, but perhaps a new awareness has indeed developed among boy workers, an awareness not particularly prescient or connected to any one understanding of perversion. As this and similar publications suggest, public discussions of the "contrasexed" in boy work circles lagged behind the larger cultural conversation. These organizations were intensely homosocial, and no doubt more self-conscious about their personnel and programs under this new scrutiny. I'm assuming that Holliday's comments are basically spin control. Why the sudden speaking up/about an incident such as this? And further, why did Holliday see fit to publicize the case not just locally but nationally in *Rural Manhood*? Is the episode really so instructive? Wouldn't it damage the YMCA's reputation? My guess is that Holliday's exposé is really an assertion of innocence, not of innocence lost: the camp is claimed as a place of purity against the evils of the world, not because it's a prelapsarian garden, but because it purges its demons, has procedures in place, even if no one's sure what they are.

Like the farm, then, the camp sometimes "failed," in the sense that Foucault outlines in *Discipline and Punish*, by generating its own self-perpetuating language of transgression. Camp defenders responded to crisis much in the manner of Uncle Benny, arguing that failure was not endemic to the institution but the result of mismanagement. Like Benny, farmer of boys, albeit in a different context, the camp director stressed the importance of ever more scrupulous screening of personnel, especially along lines of "gendered" masculinity. In his handbook *Camping for Boys* (1911), which predates *Boyology* by several years, Gibson offers the following tips on counselor recruitment:

> Aim to secure as assistant leaders or counselors young men of unquestioned character and moral leadership, college men if possible, men of culture and refinement, who are good athletes, and who understand boy life. They should be strong and sympathetic, companionable men. Too much care cannot be exercised in choosing assistants. Beware of effeminate men, men who are morbid in sex matters. An alert leader can spot a "crooked" man by his actions, his glances, and by his choice of favorites. Deal with a man of this type firmly, promptly, and quietly. Let him suddenly be called home by circumstances that he could not control (14).[29]

Here culture and refinement guard against immorality, but of course, precisely such qualities were elsewhere identified as proof of immorality. We do not know what Gibson means by "culture," except that it must be opposed to immorality and crooked men. The content of terms like "culture" and "immorality" shifts to accommodate the pressures of time and place and to keep boy work legitimate.

Even as he warns against "effeminate" and "morbid" men, Gibson in *Camping for Boys* instructs the aspiring camp director and counselor that "your personal life will either be a blessing or a hindrance to the boys in your tent. Study each boy in your tent" (17). Modern readers might be suspicious of men who study boys in tents, a suspicion that never occurs to Gibson despite his own distinction between healthy and morbid glances. In another section made hilarious by the passage of time through language, Gibson recommends a "'Cruiser' program," designed to help boys with their individual problems. Here's how it works: "The counselor 'cruises' around the camp throughout the day, and if he observes a camper who is not in some activity he ascertains why and tries to interest him in some phase of the program. . . . To be most effective, this type of work must be done by the counselor without the knowledge of the campers" (14).

Gibson alerts his readers to the presence of perverts even as he encourages an activity that sounds decidedly predatory in the contemporary moment of reading. However antithetical they seem, Gibson's "cruising" and the modern connotation may be linked, much like nineteenth- and twentieth-century versions of "fagging." Whether such shifts and continuities in meaning are capricious or governed by a discursive logic, it seems clear that modern usages do not adequately explain early-twentieth-century formulations, even if they derive from them.

The camp director is probably Uncle Benny's most faithful, if also most flamboyant, descendant. The camp director and counselor are more subject to protosexual specification and surveillance than Uncle Benny, the gentle boy farmer, who seems queer largely in retrospect and not necessarily in a sexual sense. This is largely due to the consolidation of the pervert along medical and sexological lines, in and around the anxious homo-culture of boy work. Even so, camping has never quite outgrown the cult of character, long since abandoned by most other forms of boy work, which emphasize the standardization of personality for boys and their workers. Camping still indulges in eccentric founder mythology and local color.

But what about the boy himself? Does his character ever veer toward a discernible, even a perverse, sexuality? Tales of homosexual escapades at camp are legion, but to my knowledge no one has studied that history. In the official literature on farming and camping, the boy is asexual at best.

Gibson seems happy to profile the morbid man but evinces discomfort with the boy's body. His detailed illustration of the boy and his diseases in *Camping for Boys*, for instance, is anatomically incomplete; the boy has a spleen, a gall bladder, and a nose, but no genitalia. Certainly the "pure-minded" boys seduced by Henry likewise lack agency. They are acted upon in some nefarious way; rumors circulate, but we never know of what exactly Henry is accused.

Keeping the boy on the farm was one way of protecting his innocence. Even if he observes animal sexual activity, the boy remains unsullied by city contacts and contrasexed boy workers. Even for G. Stanley Hall, who wrote extensively on sexuality and invited Freud to America, the farm was a place of purity to be summoned against the more invidious aspects of the modern world—and the more controversial claims of psychoanalysis. In that spirit, Hall revisited his "Boy Life in a Massachusetts Country Town Thirty Years Ago" in several later essays. The memoir of the Ashfield farm helped Hall acknowledge the power of both nostalgia and desire while still warding off the notion that the boy might be a creature of polymorphous perversity, as Freud had insisted.

In our own time, the farm boy—if not the summer camper or the Boy Scout—has finally been acknowledged as not only sexual but even sometimes homosexual, with the creation of rural gay lifestyle magazines such as *RFD*, and the publication of Will Fellow's engaging *Farm Boys: Lives of Gay Men from the Rural Midwest* (1996). A collection of "plainspoken" narratives based on interviews with twenty-six gay men who grew up on farms in the twentieth century, *Farm Boys* affirms the diversity of gay male experience and works to correct the urban bias in gay male studies. Gay boys, like farm boys, tend to migrate to the cities in search of community, but some stay behind. Fellows founded the Gay Farm Boys Project and conducted interviews across the Midwest, where he grew up. In the book's preface, he provides sample questionnaires and even a farming glossary, defining activities such as disk harrowing, dragging, rock picking, making hay, and whitewashing, as well as common crops and breeds of livestock. The narratives themselves address all aspects of rural life, including gay sexuality. In many of the accounts, the father is hostile toward, even physically abusive of, his gay son.

Farm Boys is the latest and the gayest in a series of post-1950s books about farm boys, including Archie Lieberman's *Farm Boy* (1974), a photographic record of farm family life through the perspective of an only son. Lieberman's book takes the boy from childhood through marriage, fatherhood, and the inheritance of the estate. Although Fellows did not come across *Farm Boy* until already at work on his own project, *Farm Boys* could be understood as a response to that heterosexual chronicle. It is, in any case, a moving explanation of why some boys leave the farm, and why some stay. It wouldn't be entirely wrong to describe Fellows as an avuncular boy worker, determined to recuperate and preserve the gay lives of farm boys, often against the forbidding specter of the homophobic father. While I'm not sure we've come full circle, here the boy worker and the homosexual have merged to their mutual credit, in the protective and nurturing (if not radically different) space of the contemporary queer family.

2. Bad Boys and Men of Culture

The mythic America is boyhood.
—Leslie Fiedler, "Come Back to the Raft Ag'in, Huck Honey!"

In his best-selling book *A Is for Ox: The Collapse of Literacy and the Rise of Violence in an Electronic Age* (1995), Barry Sanders warns that because of television, video games, and other mass media that allegedly compromise our growth from orality into literacy, the self is "falling away entirely from the human repertoire" (xi).[1] Orality and literacy, he argues, are both necessary for selfhood; lack or attenuation of either spells disaster. In illustration, Sanders points to the case of a feral boy, the nineteenth-century German wild child Kaspar Hauser.[2] Confined in a cell and deprived of a normal childhood, Hauser had no orality and thus no "inner life" on which to build literate character. The problem in American culture now, says Sanders, is that children have abandoned the book but "enjoy none of the advantages of pre-literates" (75). Kids no longer hear stories and pass them on. Nor do they read enough. Instead, they surf the Web and roam the malls. "These children," he ominously declares, "are America's Kaspar Hausers" (76).

Against the specter of illiterate mall rats, Sanders invokes America's heritage of spunky, self-reliant men of letters. More specifically, he praises Mark Twain as an exemplary author and representative American, bizarrely arguing that Twain's genius was so attuned to both oral narrative and literary culture that he could never have composed *Adventures of Huckleberry Finn* on a word processor, as computers prohibit creativity.[3] (Presumably Sanders drafted *A Is for Ox* on Big Chief tablets, after song and dance around the village fire.) And although Huck Finn lacks a self by Sanders's criteria, Sanders, in keeping with a particular tradition in literary criticism, treats Huck as an early version of Mark Twain. For Sanders, Huck is a much more promising figure than the German wild child, not in his own person but in his potential to become or call forth the man of letters. As I acknowledge in later chapters, the wild child is a more acceptable figure in the form of the wolf-boy and the Boy Scout, whereas Kaspar Hauser functions—for Sanders, at least—as an abject for the literate American self.

In the previous chapter, I examined the rise and decline of the avuncular boy worker, drawing from assorted narratives of rural life. This chapter addresses in sequence two narrative genres of boyology, the Bad Boy books of the postbellum period and the boyology primers of the early twentieth century, which together helped authorize boy work and extend its parameters, making possible a certain sort of culture criticism. Sanders invokes Twain not just in illustration of his argument but in an effort to appropriate

Twain's literary and cultural authority—and the authority asserted through debate about Twain and about the canonicity of his masterpiece. As Sanders recognizes, the literature of boyhood has long served as a form of, and forum for, social commentary more broadly. Thanks to the success of their boy books especially, authors such as Twain and William Dean Howells were respected as critics of culture as well as men of letters. Even as it began to lose popularity, the Bad Boy genre set the terms for another practice of writing about boys loosely allied with institutional character building, which Gibson and others referred to as boyology. The boyologists of the early twentieth century reworked Bad Boy themes and tropes to their own ends, even if they did not acknowledge literary boy work as such. But as Sanders's recent pronouncements about literacy and literature suggest, the conversation about boyhood did not stop there but rather continued in the form of cautionary tales about American society.

Just as Bad Boy writing was on the wane, boyology began to flourish, and culture criticism organized around boyhood was not far behind. We might identify as a point of origin Van Wyck Brooks's psychobiography *The Ordeal of Mark Twain,* published in 1920, just after the heyday of the first wave of boyology manuals. Brooks felt that boyhood was not a proper subject of literature but rather that which makes literature impossible. Leslie Fiedler famously pursued this line of inquiry first in his 1948 essay "Come Back to the Raft Ag'in, Huck Honey!" and later in *Love and Death in the American Novel* (1960), a landmark text in the field of American studies. Fiedler held that classic American literature is essentially a literature for boys, juvenile in comparison with the Anglo-European literary canon.

Although Fiedler points as evidence to authors besides Twain, it is Twain who has become the central figure of such culture criticism, probably since Twain was routinely praised by his friends and peers as hopelessly boyish. William Dean Howells once wrote of his longtime friend Twain that he "was a youth to the end of his days, the heart of a boy with the head of a sage; the heart of a good boy, or a bad boy, but always a willful boy, and willfullest to show himself out at every time for just the boy he was" (*My Mark Twain,* 7). Such praise quickly turned into criticism, in and through the debate about Twain's place in the emergent American canon, which was being formalized in the 1920s. In Twain scholarship and analysis of this stripe, Huck is at once proof of Twain's genius and proof of his immaturity and the immaturity of American culture from the Gilded Age onward. This is the critical tradition to which Sanders implicitly appeals in *A Is for Ox.* As I show in my final chapter, this tradition is one of several narrative inspirations for the new boyology primers of the 1990s.

This chapter, then, is about the Bad Boy genre and the first wave of boyology, and (more briefly) about the canonization of Twain and the mode of culture criticism practiced by Brooks and Fiedler. I argue that the canonization of Twain was made possible by the success as well as the failure of literary boy work and is entangled with social commentary organized around boyhood. Although I do not examine at length the various meanings of "culture" in this period, I note that the shift from the Bad Boy books to boyology and to boy-themed culture criticism is marked not only by the displacement of avuncular by institutional boy work but also by a shift in scientific or pop-scientific sensibility, from evolutionary theory to anthropology and social science more generally. While the Bad Boy authors appealed explicitly to the doctrine of recapitulation and to Spencer's theory of homo-to-hetero diversification, the boyologists, without discarding those ideas entirely, introduced the culture idea into their work, drawing from educational theory as well as anthropology.[4] Men of letters thus made way for men of culture and literary critics.

For the boyologists, culture was both a universal standard, in keeping with E. B. Tylor's classic formulation, and a term of relativity, as for Franz Boas and other advocates of cultural anthropology. Whereas Bad Boy authors were content to universalize from their own particular boyhoods, the boyologists insisted that expertise demanded fieldwork. It was not enough to have been a boy and then write about it—one must also do time as a boy worker. That ethnographic faith, in tandem with the "immaturity" critique launched by Brooks, effectively put an end to Bad Boy writing, even if the figure of the Bad Boy remains a staple of popular culture.

The Story of the Bad Boy Genre

The Bad Boy book, sometimes conflated with the generic "boy book,"[5] has been described as a subgenre of realism (Trensky), as memoir and autobiography (Jacobson), as male homosocial quest narrative (Fiedler, Boone), and as a nostalgic fantasy registering the ambivalences of a rapidly urbanized nation (Rodgers, Brown, Lowry, Hendler, Seltzer). The Bad Boy book is all of these things; it is also a form of boy work.

The Bad Boy book was indebted to evolutionary science and the disciplines it nurtured, such as criminal science, with its theories of juvenile delinquency, and professional child study, with its endless child-savage analogies. Usually it was a story of the Bad Boy author's life, if fictionalized. In Thomas Bailey Aldrich's *The Story of a Bad Boy* (1869), usually credited as the foundational text by both scholars and other Bad Boy writers (like Howells and Twain), the author-boy connection is announced in the opening paragraph: "This is the story of a bad boy. Well, not such a very bad boy, but a pretty bad boy; and I ought to know, for I am, or rather I was, that boy myself" (1). Recalling his boyhood playmates, Aldrich adds, "Ah me! some of those dear fellows are rather elderly boys by this time—lawyers, merchants, sea-captains, soldiers, authors, what not?" (2). Aldrich's sequence of vocations not only links authorship with the manly professions but indeed suggests it as among the most butch (after soldiering, no less).

Some such sense of enterprise is expressed by all of the Bad Boy authors, who were certainly among the most prominent men of American letters, far more genteel-literary in identification than, say, the humorists who sometimes inspired their work. The first generation of Bad Boy writers was particularly immersed in New England literary culture. Aldrich and Howells both edited the *Atlantic Monthly;* Warner collaborated with Twain to produce *The Gilded Age* (1873) and was a contributing editor to *Harper's.* The Bad Boy books were often serialized in periodicals such as these, and in children's magazines like *Our Young Folks,* in which *The Story of a Bad Boy* debuted just two years after *Farming for Boys* ended.

Other core books of the genre include, after Aldrich's inaugural tale, Twain's *Adventures of Tom Sawyer* (1876), Warner's *Being a Boy* (1877), Howells's *A Boy's Town* (1877), B. P. Shillaber's *Ike Partington, or The Adventures of a Human Boy and His Friends* (1878), Wilbur Peck's *Peck's Bad Boy and His Pa* (1883), William Allen White's *The Court of Boyville* (1898), Hamlin Garland's *Boy Life on the Prairie* (1899), Stephen Crane's *Whilomville Stories* (1900), Howells's *The Flight of Pony Baker* (1902), Henry A. Shute's *The Real Diary of a Real Boy* (1903), Owen Johnson's *Varmint* (1910), and Booth Tarkington's *Penrod* (1913) and *Penrod and Sam* (1916).[6] Typically excluded from the genre, despite strong resemblances, are Horatio Alger's stories of plucky street urchins and Louisa May Alcott's tales of "naughty, harum scarum little lads" (*Little Men,* 34).[7] *Huck Finn* is usually excluded on the basis of literary superiority, but as I argue later in this chapter, what Jonathan Arac has aptly called the book's "hypercanonicity" derives from its engagement with, not its transcendence of, literary boy work.

The Bad Boy genre defined itself against advice writing and domestic fiction. On the one hand, the Bad Boy author energetically insists that he is opposed to didacticism and domesticity; Uncle Benny has no place in his program. The closest we get to a boy worker within the story is the narrative voice itself, often autobiographical but rarely didactic in the traditional sense. Rather than grant men sentimental influence, the Bad Boy author declares boyhood's independence from all things feminine, including advice writing. His story of the Bad Boy is often also his own life story, the story of his own evolution from gentle boy-savagery into both manhood and literary vocation.

At the same time, the scene of literary boy work is avuncular in some respects. While I wouldn't want to characterize the Bad Boy authors as literary uncles exactly, I am struck by the continuities between avuncular boyology and Bad Boy writing. Like the boyologists after them, Bad Boy authors corresponded and collaborated, developing a professional identity around shared themes, styles, and practices. I think of these friendships and affiliations as comprising a sort of kinship system. Some of these men clearly took an avuncular interest not only in each other but also in each other's books. William Dean Howells, for instance, fondly described Thomas Bailey Aldrich's *The Story of a Bad Boy* as the first of the family and encouraged Twain to think of *Tom Sawyer* as "a book for boys, pure and simple. . . . Grown-ups will enjoy it just as much if you do" (Smith and Gibson, *Mark Twain–Howells Letters*, 110–12). To some degree, then, boy and book are siblings (if not synonyms) in this literary culture.

As the Bad Boy genre makes clear, the subjectivity of American boyhood, so significant in American letters and literary history writing, was constituted in the late nineteenth century according to a social biology that designates the Other as permanently primitive, in contradistinction to the temporarily primitive or juvenile white male self. With varying degrees of explicitness, this narrative of masculine development also separates those with literary potential from those without it. Widely read by both children and adults, the Bad Boy books celebrate the pre- or early pubescent boy as irrational, primitive, fiercely masculine, and attuned to nature. The evolutionary doctrine of recapitulation sustained the boy-savage comparison without insult to the boy, since he would eventually outgrow and incorporate his variously primitive tendencies. In some books, that more general narrative of masculine development is also explicitly thematized as a journey into letters; in others, that parallel growth is implied as self-evident.

In his march toward white male adulthood, understood as heterogeneity, the Bad Boy recapitulates and surpasses these stages, becoming, in the words of Teddy Roosevelt in his essay "The American Boy" (1899), "thoroughly manly, thoroughly straight and upright" (164). The Bad Boy book, like Roosevelt's little conversion essay, separates boy from man only to acknowledge the man in the boy.[8] As I suggested in the introduction, boyology relies on quasi-Oedipal scenarios of man-boy attachment and separation, both thematically and at the level of readerly address. In most of the boy books, fathers are absent or play a minor role, but the authorial persona is often intrusive, to the point that men seem an integral part of the allegedly autonomous world of boys. In the Bad Boy genre, the boy subject is the author's young self in thin disguise, which implies that the boy will grow (has already grown) into a special kind of man, the man of letters.[9] In our own time, that special kind of man is the psychologist, who also writes books about boys and appeals to the literature of boyhood.

The degree to which the Bad Boy book thematizes Oedipality has been for some critics a measure of its literary value, which suggests the implicit link between boy authorship and masculine success. Fiedler argues that "only in *Huckleberry Finn* is the full Oedipal significance of [adult male] deaths revealed, the terrible secret that the innocent treasure can be won only by the destruction of the Bad Father!" (*Love and Death,* 281). Addressing Howells's *The Flight of Pony Baker,* John Crowley argues that the American boy book dramatizes "a recognizably oedipal anxiety" and seeks to control that anxiety by locating the boy's savagery within the protective shield of the nuclear family ("Polymorphously Perverse," 9). These are rather traditional readings of Oedipality, however. I'm just as interested in the dad outside the text, particularly since in many respects the Bad Boy books aren't particularly Oedipal in terms of father-son conflict (plus the mother rarely seems an object of the boy's desire). At the same time, the dynamic of othering central to the genre does seem Oedipal, with the adult white male author functioning as the boy's gentle rival and his eventual form. The boy will reconstitute the "family" as an author and in homosocial, even avuncular, fashion. In the frequent textual absence of the father, and before the ascendancy of the institutional boy worker, the boy author presides over the boy's journey toward a masculinized culture of letters.

Savage Inequalities

Critics of the Bad Boy genre have long noted that the Bad Boy's delinquency is safely middle-class, and that such delinquency is both "innocent" and promises future success. Charles Dudley Warner, for example, speaks of "a bad enough boy" who later "became a general in the war, and went to Congress and got to be a real governor" (*Being a Boy,* 127). According to the evolutionary logic of the day—especially the doctrine of recapitulation and John Fiske's so-called infancy theory—the longer the period of parental dependence of a species after birth, the greater the eventual sophistication of said species. In child expert A. F. Chamberlain's words, "out of the helplessness of the child has arisen the helpfulness of men" (*The Child,* 5). Hence the nineteenth-century obsession with the family and other institutions that stress the vulnerability of youth; it is through the idea of vulnerability that helplessness and delinquency merge. Clearly both the helplessness and the delinquency of boys were thinkable only after boy labor was no longer essential to family survival. From the 1870s onward, white, middle-class families declined in size and increased in financial net worth, and more parents were able to forgo the labor of their kids, especially in the industrialized Northeast. Boys were apparently expected to be both helpless and delinquent, even helplessly delinquent.

Middle-class white boys, in short, were gentle and temporary savages. As in Emerson's paradigmatic "Self-Reliance," the boy-savage comparison in the Bad Boy books in fact separates the boy from the racial other. In *The Story of a Bad Boy*, young Tom Bailey is at once likened to slaves and distinguished from them through select images of boy-savagery and through slave dialect. Aldrich's account of his 1840s childhood begins in New Orleans, where the mischievous Tom routinely abuses "the little negro boy," the son of his beloved nurse and family slave, Aunt Chloe. Aunt Chloe is perfectly content in the South: "Dar ain't no gentl'men in the Norf noway," she asserts, once declaring: "If any of dem mean whites tries to git me away from marster, I's jes' gwine to knock 'em on de head wid a gourd!" (6). After spending his early years with such simple folk, Tom is then sent to live with more suitably New English relatives, specifically his Grandfather Nutter in "Rivermouth" (Portsmouth, New Hampshire), where he and his friends enjoy various exploits. *The Story of a Bad Boy* is the chronicle of relatively privileged children who can afford to be bad, who have the leisure time, education, and social status to abuse slaves while dancing around bonfires "like a legion of imps . . . their whole appearance suggestive of New Zealand chiefs" (76–77). We do not mistake Tom and his friends for aboriginals; they are no fonder of New Zealanders than Emerson. Nor do they have anything in common with the slaves whose labor makes possible the "Happy, magical Past" of antebellum America (4).

The often lyrical rhetoric of boy-savage equality enables a fantasy of racial recapitulation and absorption in the Bad Boy genre. Daydreaming in school, Tarkington's Penrod demonstrates his ability to do "really nothing at all," a feat "almost never accomplished except by coloured people or by a boy in school on a spring day" (*Penrod*, 59). "He [Penrod] *was* merely a state of being" (59; italics mine). In, or rather as, this state of reverie, he hears through the windows the music of a mouth organ, attributing its "excruciating sweetness" to the "wallowing, walloping yellow-pink palm of a hand whose back was Congo black and shiny" (60). The music wafts down the street,

> accompanied by the care-free shuffling of a pair of old shoes
> scuffing syncopations on the cement sidewalk. . . . Emotion stirred
> in Penrod a great and poignant desire, but (perhaps fortunately)
> no fairy godmother made her appearance. Otherwise Penrod
> would have gone down the street in a black skin, playing the
> mouth-organ, and an unprepared coloured youth would have
> found himself enjoying educational advantages for which he had
> no ambition whatever. (60)

At that particular stage, Penrod and the invisible musician could exchange places, since they share "a state of being." However, Penrod needs his education, if he is to enter the world of men. Ambition is latent in Penrod, but entirely missing in the young musician.

In case we've misunderstood the temporary nature of Penrod's savagery, Tarkington introduces "darky" brothers Verman and Herman, whose "Bangala great-grandfathers" were reportedly cannibals (240). Young Verman is "tongue-tied," his speech completely unintelligible (even more so than his older brother's dialect), and is put on neighborhood exhibit as a "savage tattooed wild boy" (153)—here Penrod himself writes a script for the brothers. Soon after Penrod meets them, they get into a scuffle with a local bully, who finds himself the victim of their wild instincts. In chapter 23, entitled "Coloured Troops in Action," Tarkington describes Herman and Verman as "beings in one of those lower stages of evolution wherein theories about 'hitting below the belt' have not yet made their appearance" (242). In his "simple, direct African way," Verman lashes out with a rake at the bully, and the "struggle increased in primitive simplicity" (243). "Primal forces operated here, and the two blanched, slightly higher products of evolution, Sam and Penrod, no more thought of interfering than they would have thought of interfering with an earthquake" (243–44). If we think that all boys are savages, Tarkington reminds us that, unlike their friends, Sam and Penrod will grow up.

In *A Boy's Town,* Howells furnishes another example of this evolutionary logic that, again through select scenarios of violence, first identifies boys with, and then distinguishes them from, the savage and the homogeneous, that is, the undiversified. Howells praises the savage virtues of boys, noting that when a boy joins a new community and is beaten up by the locals, "he became subject to the local tribe, as the Delawares were to the Iroquois in the last century," whereas "if he whippped the other boys, then they adopted him into their tribe, and he became leader among them" (68). Boys are "always stoning something . . . [usually] one another" (72). They endure "punishment with the savage pluck of so many little Sioux" (82). "If they could, the boys would rather have been Indians than anything else, but [in play] they were willing to be settlers, and fight against the Indians" (149). "The boys lived in the desire, if not the hope, of some time seeing an Indian," and when a group of "filthy savages" actually arrives in canal boats from the Wyandot Reservation en route to westward lands, the boys nearly go wild (151).

The visitors are themselves a homogeneous group, the "old men . . . not a whit more dignified than the children" (151). Free from adult responsibilities, they are an undifferentiated mass of idlers who simply haven't evolved:

> In fact they were, old and young alike, savages, and the boys who
> looked on and envied them were savages in their ideal of a world
> where people spent their lives in hunting and fishing and ranging
> the woods, and never grew up into the toils and cares that
> can alone make men of boys. They [the boys] wished to escape
> these, as many foolish persons do among civilized nations, and
> they thought if they could only escape they would be happy; they
> did not know that they would be merely savage, and that the great
> difference between a savage and a civilized man is work. (151)

The boys dream of bows and arrows long after "the red men had flitted away like red leaves" (151). Eventually, though, they "calmed down to their old desire of having a gun . . . for that was the normal desire of every boy in the Boy's Town who was not a girl-boy, and there were mighty few girl-boys there" (151–52). Industry and gun love make little savages into men, and Indians into natural debris.

Bad Boy authors present ritualized as well as impromptu conflict among boys as evidence of recapitulation beyond the individual level, as the collective reenactment of mankind's violent phases. Boys long to fight, and in fighting they demonstrate their savagery but also learn more advanced cultural styles, such as chivalry, which will prepare them for full-fledged manhood.[10] Even the more pacifist Howells sees savagery as necessary in the boyhood recapitulation—and adult authorship—of human history.

A hallmark of the Bad Boy genre is the town fight, in which contending groups of boys reenact and practice war. For example, chapter 13 of *The Story of a Bad Boy* retells the Civil War as the great winter snow fight at Slatter's Hill, a mythic confrontation between the North End and the South End boys of Rivermouth that not only "predates" but exists impossibly outside of that tragic event, so recently ended. Aldrich trivializes the Civil War by depicting it as boyish play that has gotten out of hand (and into legend). Shells become snowballs, mortal wounds minor injuries, and military enslavement a bond of love and blind devotion: "When General Harris (with his right eye bunged up) said, 'Soldiers, I am proud of you!' my heart swelled in my bosom" (147). Only in the introductory chapter does he mention the actual war. In an even more troubling mock-heroic tone, George Wilbur Peck dedicates *How Private Geo. W. Peck Put Down the Rebellion* (1887), published in between his famous Bad Boy books, to "THE 'BOYS IN BLUE' AND THE 'BOYS IN GRAY,' Who got real spunky at each other, some years ago, while playing in their adjoining door-yards, threw tomato cans and dead cats back and forth, called each other names, pulled hair, and snubbed noses until they got into real actual war" (iii).

Affirming Hall's definition of childhood play as the reenactment of ancestral patterns, such descriptions establish war as at once inevitable and trivial.

In Tarkington's *Penrod and Sam,* the Civil War and slavery degenerate into "outbreaks of cavalry" and a game called "bonded pris'ner" derivative of Tom's games with Jim at the end of *Huck Finn.* "Masters" Penrod and Sam capture Verman, who is "obliged to accompany the forces of his captors whithersoever their strategic necessities led them, which included many strange places" (1).[11] Slavery, like war, is child's play, or history harmlessly rewritten.

The Bad Boy books naturalize genocide along the same lines. In *Being A Boy,* Warner makes the usual observation that the "military instinct, which is the special mark of barbarism, is strong" in the boy (151). Having transformed his narrator John into a warrior, Warner describes John's love for history, more specifically "the Indian wars," which Warner then rewrites. In the heat of battle, the boys playing Pequots would "come swarming up the hill, with hideous war-hoops," and both sides would experience "a great many hard hits . . . always cheerfully, for it was in the cause of our early history" (91). Wannabe Indians Yan and Sam also cheerfully wage war in (former BSA Chief Scout) Ernest Thompson Seton's *Two Little Savages: Being the Adventures of Two Boys Who Lived as Indians and What They Learned* (1902), set in Canada.[12] Given their penchant for Indian craft and custom, it's no surprise that the boys prefer to "massacre" the palefaces, staging raids on their nearby families, as well as a rival tribe. Squatter and woodsman Caleb Clark, somewhat reminiscent of Uncle Benny, teaches them

> a little Indian war chant, and they danced round to it as he drummed and sang, till their savage instincts seemed to revive. But above all it worked on Yan. As he pranced around in step his whole nature seemed to respond; he felt himself a part of that dance. It was in himself; it thrilled him through and through and sent his blood exulting. He would gladly have given up all the White-man's "glorious gains" to live with the feeling called up by that Indian drum. (326)

But he cannot. Yan and Sam live in the woods only by the good graces of their guardians. Their massacres secure no corpses. Perhaps Seton is more dubious about those "glorious gains" than Teddy Roosevelt, but he too invokes the aboriginal self in the service of man making ventures, among them the boy book itself. *Two Little Savages* is not only a story about boys but also a swan song for vanishing Americans.

Whereas critics have found problematic the "boy book frame" of *Huck Finn,* debating the final section's status as "satire or evasion"—the section in which Jim is playfully imprisoned by Tom Sawyer on the Phelps plantation—I have seen little commentary on these other disturbing episodes of revisionist play, presumably because these texts are understood as boy books through and through, offering no such distinction of frame and content, or of history and fiction.

Realizing the Feminine

In Bad Boy writing and boyology more generally, the feminine suffers a fate similar to that of the savage, imagined as a stage to be suffered through and then surpassed. G. Stanley Hall avers that "adolescent boys normally pass through a generalized or even feminized stage of psychic development" (*Adolescence*, 2:625). Unlike boys, however, girls can never leave adolescence behind, and Hall links women with the "adolescent races" who "linger in the paradise of childhood" (2:649). Hall's praise for feminine virtue rests on his belief that "woman at her best never outgrows adolescence as man does, but lingers in, magnifies, and glorifies this culminating stage of life with . . . zest for all that is good, beautiful, true, and heroic." And yet she must "take her stand against all premature specialization" and "resist all these influences that make for psychological precocity," in herself as well as in her children (2:624).

Several decades earlier, the prominent American paleontologist Edward Drinker Cope had identified "impressibility" as the "'woman stage' of character" evidenced in the hero worship of male adolescents (cited in Gould, *Ontogeny and Phylogeny*, 130). And in his chapter "The Child and Woman," A. F. Chamberlain summarizes E. S. Talbot's *Degeneracy: Its Causes, Signs, and Results* (1899), which "holds that the forms of degeneracy known as infantilism, masculinism and feminism are 'practically arrests of development of the promise of the child type'" (Chamberlain, *The Child*, 399). For Talbot, "masculinism" is the survival of male characteristics in women, and "feminism" the inversion of men (399). Feminism, it seems, is unnatural in men, and while "not rare in boys," it "usually appears in a transitory form" (400). Here we can see feminism's origins as a sexological term, even as the reverse discourse was well under way.

Americans were increasingly concerned that their boys had grown degenerate. In his discussion of the discourses of neurasthenia in and around 1903, Tom Lutz points out that fears of overcivilization, overwork, and overproduction led to "cures" for nervousness that reinforced traditional gender roles and the emergent ideology of the leisure class. Boyologists tried to counter inappropriate forms of feminine influence by invoking the doctrine of recapitulation to preserve the masculine frontier as psychic (the savage wilderness of boyhood). That boys might be perceived as feminine was inevitable, insofar as femininity was linked to dependence. Recapitulation ensured a period of dependence that could easily be survived.

The Bad Boy writers thus allow their male heroes to have limited contact with girls and women, but make clear that boys do not prefer such contact and will eventually escape feminine influence, even as they grow into ostensibly heterosexual men of culture. Huck Finn is not the only Bad Boy victim of feminine plots; *Penrod* begins with the attempted sissification of the young protagonist by his mother, sister, and pageant director Mrs. Lora Rewbush. Set to play Child Sir Lancelot in Rewbush's "The Children's Pageant of the Table Round," Penrod is convinced "that he was intended by his loved ones to make a public spectacle of himself in his sister's stockings and part of an old dress of his mother's" (28). In this "unmanned condition" (30), he must "declaim the loathsome sentiments" of young Sir Lancelot (4). In a panic, the mortified boy dons the janitor's overalls and makes his grand debut, sending the crowd into hysterics. This is the first in a series of narrow escapes. As Howells explains in *A Boy's Town,* lads who participate in plays are judged "girl-boys" (76). Seton also links the feminine with the emasculating forces of society. Chastised by his mother for not leading a pious life, protagonist Yan replies, "I go out into the woods, and every bird and flower I see stirs me . . . they make me feel like praying when your Bible does not. They are my Bible" (97). He and Sam temporarily escape into the wilds, learning to hunt, make Indian clothing, and speak Tutnee, becoming "wonderfully self-reliant" (97).

Most of the Bad Boy writers foil the feminine by insisting that boys and girls inhabit separate spheres, despite their proximity. Howells reports that boys avoid each other's mothers and homes: "If he entered the house of a friend at all, it was to wait for him by the kitchen-door. . . . If he sometimes, and by some rare mischance, found himself in the living-rooms, or the parlor, he was very unhappy, and anxious to get out" (226).[13] "The boy, with boys," announces Tarkington, "is a Choctaw; and either the influence or the protection of women is shameful" (230). Like many child-rearing manuals of the period, the Bad Boy books differentiate the sexes along the lines of gentle and rough, civil and wild. Warner's John "liked best to be with boys, and their rough play suited him better than the amusements of the shrinking, fluttering, timid, and sensitive little girls" (99).

Like these writers, most educators around the turn of the century opposed coeducation and other forms of male-female socialization on the grounds that boys and girls experience different rates of growth and need different training. What seemed a potential problem for Hall and the boyologists—the earlier maturation of girls—became the chief warrant of their claims. Physically and intellectually, they argued, girls are precocious, and precocity leads to premature apogee. Invoking Fiske's infancy theory, educators and laymen alike argued that the inferior development of boys, even their susceptibility to feminine influence, attests to their future power. According to Warner, social graces come easily only to girls: "The girl takes to society as naturally as a duckling does to the placid pond, but with a semblance of sly timidity, the boy plunges in with a great splash" (102). In time, he will make waves.

The women who interact with the Bad Boys are conduits of male development and homosocial bonding. As mothers and teachers, they enable the transition from boyhood to manhood, triangulating and safeguarding male-male relations. While this traffic in women could be described as compulsory heterosexuality, relations between men and women are rarely addressed, perhaps because of the persistent fear of the feminine. When these books actually mention interaction with women, that interaction usually takes the form of the archetypal war between the sexes. In *Peck's Bad Boy with the Cowboys* (1905), for example, the struggle for women's rights is transformed into a set of "comic" encounters between temporarily liberated Indian squaws and their vengeful mates, who "will give [them] a walloping when they get back to camp" (61).

As these and other examples show, escape from the feminine and civilization is a defining theme of books written for and about boys and, as Fiedler has argued, of American literature more generally.[14] In *A Boy's Town*, Howells claims that "there was not a boy in the Boy's Town who would not gladly have turned from the town and lived in the woods if his mother had let him," and "if their ideal was the free life of the woods, no doubt it was because their near ancestors had lived it" (149). Aldrich notes that "all the male members of our family, on my father's side—as far back as the Middle Ages—have exhibited in early youth a decided talent for running away. It was an hereditary talent. It ran in the blood to run away" (258). If escape from civilization is a theme of the genre, it may also be a narrative strategy for asserting the centrality of boyhood to civilization, and for linking the subject of boyhood to the legitimate practice of authorship in the realist mode. In other words, we should not confuse the trope with its ideological effect. Like the boys for whom they spoke, the Bad Boy writers saw themselves as rebellious, as challenging the tales of pious children authored by women such as Susan Warner, Fanny Fern, Maria Cummins, and Harriet Beecher Stowe. As Aldrich explains,

> I call my story the story of a bad boy, partly to distinguish myself from those faultless young gentlemen who generally figure in narratives of this kind, and partly because I really was *not* a cherub. . . . In short, I was a real human boy, such as you may meet anywhere in New England, and no more like the impossible boy in a story-book than a sound orange is like one that has been sucked dry. (1–2)

Despite feminist reevaluations of domestic and sentimental fiction, critics have generally accepted the literary genealogy offered by the Bad Boy writers, aligning their tales with dime novels and frontier fictions as flight from, or innovative resistance to, the feminizing forces of American culture. Against didactic literature featuring "faultless young gentlemen," the Bad Boy writers ostensibly showcase "real human boys." "The real lives of boys are yet to be written," declares Henry Ward Beecher in *Eyes and Ears* (1862). "The lives of pious and good boys, which enrich the catalogues of great publishing societies, resemble a real boy's life about as much as a chicken picked and larded, upon a spit, and ready for delicious eating, resembles a free fowl in the fields" (73–74). But as Lora Romero observes, this pervasive scenario of feminine assault, against which realism is often defined, grew out of exaggerated claims about the power of domestic ideology, which was at least in part a male enterprise. Romero argues that "women's novels already contain the narratives of male rebellion against the role of women that are generally associated with male writers" (*Home Fronts,* 18). To stress the civilizing influence of women, early-nineteenth-century writers began to depict men and boys as "naturally aggressive, sensual and godless" (15). Domestic ideology relied on the archetype of boyish lawlessness and the "evasion" of heterosexual culture. The boy-savage trope is fundamental to the very literature it supposedly supplanted.

American realism in general has been understood as the genre both of democratic possibility and of custodial male bourgeois culture.[15] Responding to critics who locate the origin of realism in the attack on sentimental women writers, Elise Miller points out that writers like Howells, James, Norris, and Dreiser appropriated as their own "feminine" modes of perception and representation, to the extent that "complaints about the feminization of American literature shifted to a growing recognition of the *feminine* nature of realism" (31). In *Heroines of Fiction* (1901), to which Miller directs our attention, Howells even equates the "ever-womanly" self with the realist imagination. Like sentimental and domestic fiction, realism was preoccupied with human psychology and morality. The attack on the sentimental was also a co-optation, and realist writers imagined their assimilation of sentimentality as an early stage of their literary training. The effort to realize the feminine did not lead to the liberation of women authors or to widespread acclaim of their work. Instead the realists marshaled arguments about the developmental inferiority of women writers while appropriating the tricks of their trade. As Tom Lutz shows, James, Dreiser, Howells, and others even transformed neurasthenia, a sign of weakness in women, into a mark of superior aesthetic sensibility in men. Even if the realists learned from their female rivals, they ostensibly outgrew them.

It is easy to see the degree to which the Bad Boy genre is patterned after domestic fiction, however much it is promoted as realism. Howells's vision of realism clearly relies on the sentimental power of boyhood, as embodied in the postbellum image of the rural, savage, barefoot boy.[16] Few women writers ever produced anything as cloying as William White's nostalgic *The Court of Boyville* ("Their souls—fresher from God than are the souls of men—were a-quiver with joy, and their lips babbled to hide their ecstasies" [353]). Or consider the following passage from Aldrich: "It is with no ungentle hand [that] I summon [my memories] back, for a moment, from that Past. . . . How pleasantly they live again in my memory! Happy, magical Past, in whose fairy atmosphere even Conway, mine ancient foe, stands forth transfigured, with a sort of dreamy glory encircling his bright red hair!" (4). This passage follows closely on the heels of Aldrich's promise that he paints an unromanticized portrait of a "real human boy" (1).

In short, by identifying the feminine with sentimentality, the Bad Boy writers could authorize their claim to realistic representation, implying the natural evolution of boyhood's unthinking wildness into the man's principled choices to fight wars, captain industry, and author American literature. In this way, the effort to write "realistically" could be regarded both as a manly challenge to female sentimentalism and as a rendition of the realism of evolutionary science itself.[17]

Homo-Economics

Unlike the savage and the feminine, the homogeneous is not so obviously thematized or personified in Bad Boy writing, because homogeneity operated as a conceptual umbrella for boyhood and its developmental analogues. But the belief in homogeneity as the precondition for development is equally central to the genre. Homogeneity may be a more useful and historically sensitive concept for our analysis of boyology than other permutations of the homo that are so hotly contested these days. In Herbert Spencer's account of diversification, all forms of biological and social life instinctively evolve from the simple and uniform (the homogeneous) to the complex and diverse (the heterogeneous). Spencer's thesis, only the most familiar and influential of such formulations, suggests that the rubric homo/hetero originally applied to a spectrum of behaviors before it became largely identified with sexuality—before, as Eve Kosofsky Sedgwick theorizes in *Epistemology of the Closet*, "homo/heterosexual definition" became "a presiding master term of the past century" as pervasive and significant as "the more visible cruxes of gender, class, and race" (111).[18]

In the Bad Boy genre and boyology more generally, boys are not so much homosocial as homogeneous, the same everywhere despite their distinct characters, and even when they do not enjoy the company of other boys. Certainly they are never homosexual. The terms "homosexual" and "homoerotic" tend toward the mythic in classic Americanist criticism such as Fiedler's. The homogeneous offers another way to think about boyhood's affinities, making it more difficult to mythologize distinctions of class and race as variations on the theme of boyhood.

The homogeneous ethos of many narratives of boyhood, from the Anglo-American school story to the Bad Boy tale, assumes the safe shape of memoir, of the author's memory of an "aboriginal Self." At the same time, however, the author has grown out of that phase, and his recollective project guards against, even if it invokes, the specter of queer identity or desire. What look to us like homoerotic/feminizing moments are also toasts to the writer's inner boy-savage and his imminent diversification.

In *A Boy's Town*, Howells enacts this literary genealogy, tracing the growth of "my boy" from a scribbling "girl-boy" to a successful man of letters. Howells's use of "my boy," instead of the usual first-person "I," invites the reader to see Howells's narrative persona as an adult as well as a boy.[19] When we first meet the lad, we learn that he "had no conception of literature except the pleasure there was in making it; and he had no outlook into the world of it; which must have been pretty open to his father" (21). His father, in fact, is the source of "my boy's" growing conception of literature as a body of texts and a professional calling. For the first part of the book, though, "my boy" revels in nature and in the usual homogeneous play of boys. Only gradually does his literary ambition emerge, and natural evolution explains its force and staying power. "My boy," Howells writes toward the end of the book, developed "a desire to localize, *to realize,* what he read; and he was always contriving in fancy scenes and encounters of the greatest splendor, in which he bore a chief part" (176–77; italics mine).

Chapter 15, "My Boy," distinguishes Howells's boy self from the "other boys" chronicled in the following chapter, thus setting that self on the path toward diversification and greater individuality. Chapter 15 details Howells's early love for Greek and Roman mythology, travel and adventure fiction, and certain forms of poetry. Imitating these and other literary genres, the young Howells nonetheless "had no conception of authorship as a vocation in life, and he did not know why he wanted to make poetry" (179). After others misunderstand him, "my boy" prefers to "conceal his gift. It became 'His shame in crowds—his solitary pride,' and he learned to know that it was considered *soft* to write poetry, as indeed it mostly is" (179). This lesson in shame echoes an earlier episode, recounted in chapter 7. "My boy," explains Howells, "had his secret longing to be a dandy" and pestered his father to buy him "a little silk hat" (77). The hat brought him ridicule rather than respect from his friends, but his father made him wear it several times more, despite his "streaming tears" (77).

In "My Boy," Howells also confesses his love for theatricals, and while he defends the theater itself against Calvinist judgment, he also admits that such an obsession "was not quite a wholesome frame of mind for a boy of ten years," adding, "but I do not defend it; I only portray it" (ostensibly in the spirit of realism, here nearly compromised) (181). In any event, "my boy" is alert to the feminizing taint of all things aesthetic (prior to realism) and keeps his literary ambitions secret. This produces a split self. While "joyfully sharing the wild sports and conforming to the savage usages of the boy's world about him, he was dwelling in a wholly different world within him, whose wonders no one else knew" (171). Shepherding him through this dangerous phase is his "aboriginal Self"—he cannot be soft if he is savage. He safely leads a "kind of double life . . . the Boy's Town life and the Cloud Dweller's life" (184). Howells's book is a catalog of boy-savage analogies, with chapters entitled "Foraging," "Fantasies and Superstitions," "Traits and Characters," and "Manners and Customs"; these analogies at once protect against femininity and attest to his evolution from boyhood into manhood. (The chapter "My Boy" directly follows the chapter "Foraging.") His potentially feminizing tastes in boyhood comprised "a phase of being" necessary to his development.

In the final paragraph of the "My Boy" chapter, Howells unequivocally locates his early aesthetic tastes within a heterosocial matrix. His passion for literature and the theater is allied with his unspoken "passion for those lovely little girls" of the community (182). The theater bills were printed in his father's office, and "my boy" "always wildly hoped and feared" that the theater manager and his wife "would bring [their] little girls" with them. They never did, but the boy "contented himself with secretly adoring the father and mother, doubly divine as [the girls'] parents and as actors" (182). And of course we know that "my boy" safely evolved into William Dean Howells. All of the things that might signal a queer personality to contemporary readers—poetry, silk hats, theatricals, even literary ambition itself—suggest instead evolution from a homogeneous to a heterogeneous character.

Later in the book, Howells appeals again to the inevitability of diversification when he recalls "my boy's" attraction to a "queer companion," a poor and uneducated country boy whose "kinship with nature" was so profound that he seemed "a piece of the genial earth . . . without force or aim" (191). Their friendship is based on this shared kinship:

> My boy could not have talked to him about any of the things that
> were in his books. . . . He must rather have soothed against his

> soft, caressing ignorance the ache of his fantastic spirit, and
> reposed his intensity of purpose in that lax and easy aimlessness.
> Their friendship was not only more innocent than any other
> friendship my boy had, but it was wholly innocent; they loved each
> other, and that was all; and why people love each other there is
> never any satisfactory telling. But this friend of his must have had
> great natural good in him; and if I could find a man of the make
> of that boy I am sure I should love him. (192)

Such a man, of course, is impossible. Howells insists that the relationship was free from taint because it was so simple. "My boy's" other friends reproach him for his affection for the pastoral lad, and he grows embarrassed by their rapport. Howells admits that "the attempted reform had spoiled their simple and harmless intimacy," as education and social interaction are wont to do (193). From this point onward, their friendship declines. This anecdote surfaces in a chapter titled "Other Boys," in which Howells wistfully remarks that, unlike men, "all boys are a good deal alike" (190).

Enter the Boyologists

In her study of the Bad Boy genre, Marcia Jacobson notes that just as the genre was beginning to fail—and just as Twain was entering the canon through the culture writing of Brooks and others—Bad Boy writer Booth Tarkington became "a sort of spokesman on boyhood," writing introductions to new editions of Twain's boy books and later publishing an essay titled "What I Have Learned from Boys" (1925) in *The American Magazine* (Jacobson, *Being a Boy Again,* 150). Tarkington's *Penrod and Sam* is arguably the last of the Bad Boy books, making Tarkington a transitional figure of sorts between the avuncular Bad Boy author and the self-styled boyologist with institutional connections. As I explain in the next section, Twain was a different sort of transitional figure through whom literary boy work was transformed into the work of literary and culture criticism.

Penrod and Sam appeared the same year as Gibson's *Boyology,* and the two share more than a general concern with boyhood. Both the Bad Boy books and the boyology primers were meant to be read by men, not boys, even if some of the former found favor with younger readers. But while literary boy work was at best an informal and even avuncular affair, boyology and its primers emerged from (if also against) institutional character building. Gibson's book originated in a series of lectures to YMCA groups, mothers' meetings, parent-teacher associations, and women's clubs. A YMCA leader and authority on camping, Scouting, and church work, with twenty-six years of "actual contact" with boys, Gibson hopes that *Boyology* will foster "genuine sympathy" for "the struggles of youth" (ix).

Gibson's text is a standard example of the American primers of boy education and management published during the first two decades of the twentieth century. It serves more as an epitome of the genre than an original contribution to "boy analysis." "Boyology" was a familiar term, which Gibson and others used in their lectures and institutional work. Boyology gave boy work a philosophy, codifying a cluster of ideas about boyhood and the national character that also inspired church youth work, organized camping, and character-building agencies such as the YMCA, Boys' Brigade, Order of the Knights of King Arthur, Sons of Daniel Boone, Order of the American Boy, Woodcraft Indians, Big Brothers, and Scouting.[20] Modeled in part on urban child-saving efforts, these agencies targeted white, middle-class boys. Most were organized from 1900 to 1920, years that saw the publication of influential handbooks predating Gibson's, notably William Byron Forbush's *The Boy Problem* (1901), Granville Stanley Hall's two-volume *Adolescence: Its Psychology and Its Relations to Physiology, Anthropology, Sociology, Sex, Crime, Religion, and Education* (1904), and Baden-Powell's *Scouting for Boys* (1908), quickly embraced in the United States. *American Boy* magazine, sponsor of the Order of the American Boy, was founded in 1899 and achieved a circulation of 360,000 by 1929.[21]

By the century's turn, the boy had become an important social as well as literary subject, appearing at the expense of the "vanished" native. According to its champions, who subscribed to the doctrines of recapitulation and progressive diversification, boy culture was analogous both to earlier stages of civilization and to contemporaneous primitive societies. Typically bourgeois white men, boy workers saw themselves as ethnographers and role models. They concerned themselves chiefly with younger boys, aged eight to twelve, and adolescent boys, aged twelve to sixteen; G. Stanley Hall alone distinguished adolescence from boyhood (Hall, incidentally, was one of the few psychologists associated with early-twentieth-century boyology, whereas today psychologists run the show), and even his work suggests more continuity than difference.

The works of Forbush and Gibson provide rough bookends for classic boyology, by which I mean the post-1900 spate of organization and publication. During this period, boy work emphasized group participation as the preferred mode of character building (Macleod, *Building Character*, xvii–xviii), and the sudden deluge of boy manuals reflects that emphasis on networking and collaboration. Forbush's *The Boy Problem*, with an introduction by Hall, was the most commercially successful of the handbooks (published first in Boston, by the way). Reprinted eight times between 1901 and 1913, it established the "boy problem" as the formulaic opening of, and rationale for, the genre. By the time Gibson's *Boyology* appeared, that problem had been addressed exhaustively. *Boyology* in fact concludes with an annotated "Six Foot Shelf" of 103 books and pamphlets "about boys or subjects analogous to boy life" (260), organized in categories including general parenting, advanced child study, sex instruction, vocational guidance, church work, and recreation. Representative titles suggest the emphases of boyology: Kate Upson Clark, *Bringing Up Boys* (1899); Nathan C. Fowler Jr., *The Boy—How to Help Him Succeed* (1902); John E. Gunckel, *Boyville: A History of Fifteen Years' Work among Newsboys* (1905); E. L. Moon, *The Contents of the Boy* (1909); Lilburn Merrill, *Winning the Boy* (1908); Hanford M. Burr, *Studies in Adolescent Boyhood* (1910); Albert M. Chesley, *Social Activities for Men and Boys* (1910); George Walter Fiske, *Boy Life and Self-Government* (1910); Joseph Addams Puffer, *The Boy and His Gang* (1912); Frank Orman Beck, *Marching Manward* (1913); and William McCormick's *Fishers of Boys* (1915).

But Forbush and Gibson were the most visible spokesmen of boyology. A clergyman and physician, Forbush helped organize the Men of Tomorrow and the Order of the Knights of King Arthur in 1895 and became president of the American Child Institute (based in Philadelphia).[22] Gibson authored a number of books on camping and church work and served as YMCA state secretary in both Massachusetts and Rhode Island. Both describe the contributions of women to boyology as practical and anecdotal by nature and not by design, as pure "heartology" rather than the strategic presentation of ideas for the lay reader. Thus the boyologists could dismiss books by women with the very praise they lavished on their own volumes. Gibson calls Clark's *Bringing Up Boys,* for instance, a book of "old fashioned, therefore, good common sense," and Christine Terhume Herrick's *My Boy and I* (1913) a "chronicle of incidents occurring in the home life of normal boys" (269–70). Like Gibson, these women had actual contact with boys, but they could not claim authority in the field. They could only report from it. The commonsense and episodic chronicles of women did not expertise make, unlike Gibson's "heartology." Mothers were encouraged not to publish their own work but to join Forbush's institute, where they could attend lectures and purchase materials. Although boyology had progressive as well as reactionary impulses, Gibson's title page announces its basic agenda, featuring a photograph of a smiling adolescent boy, with the caption "Boy-stuff is the only stuff in the world from which men can be made." Boyology was not an exclusively male domain, but its authoritative figures were men.

Child Study and Character Building

Then, as now, boyology was not a discrete discourse, and its contradictions and inconsistencies make generalizations difficult. It was asserted against, even as it borrowed shamelessly from, the domestic wisdom of women and the expertise of doctors, social workers, educators, and academic psychologists. Some of the most prominent boyologists were also doctors and educators and were affiliated with the child study movement led by Hall, whose sketch "Boy Life in a Massachusetts Country Town Thirty Years Ago" I discussed in chapter 1. Child study and boyology seem to have nurtured each other more than competed for attention; it might even be a mistake to treat them as distinct in the first place. Forbush, for instance, held both a Ph.D. and a Litt.D. and authored not only *The Boy Problem* but also the *Guide Book to Childhood* (1915), a 550-page encyclopedia of child life and training. Many of the child study proponents were affiliated with universities and teaching institutes (such as the Teachers College of Columbia University), whereas the boyologists were more diverse in terms of training and affiliation. Boyology was as much a genre or mode of writing as anything else, whereas child study was conducted through a network of federal and regional chapters and through lectures and parent-training seminars. And boyology had closer ties to character-building organizations such as Scouting and the YMCA. Child study generally had a more academic provenance; the Advisory Board of the Federation of Child Study, for instance (organized in 1888), boasted John Dewey among its members.

Most accounts of the child study movement see it as anomalous in the history of child observation and nurture; I think of it as a more erudite and academic extension of boyology, with its obsessive charts and constant invocations of recapitulation and the boy book. Hall's *Adolescence*, although indebted to evolutionary science, also makes use of anthropological metaphor and is very much a study in what Gibson calls "social pedagogy." Volume 2, for instance, features a long section on oratory, literary study, classical rhetoric, and teacher education. Like the boyology books that frame it historically, *Adolescence* prolongs boyhood into early adulthood, defining adolescence as an extended period of turmoil and apprenticeship.

Hall and the boyologists made it clear that boy workers must be ex-boys, must remain boy identified, and must imitate in their own organizations the gangs of boys. Further, their recreational work with boys, like their instructional work, must build character. As Albert Chesley puts it in his compendium *Social Activities for Men and Boys,* "you cannot be social unless you are social to save . . . underneath the fun there [must be] a rock foundation of character building" (viii). The character-building activities that Chelsey recommends—among them corn roasts, clambakes, minstrel shows, Gypsy trips, Oriental research, and hustling (Bible study)—help develop "culture," or "the finer sensibilities and appreciations" of life (xiii). Culture must emanate from genuine male affection for boys, and that affection will be returned tenfold, as Lilburn Merrill explains in *Winning the Boy:*

> A friend of mine who lives with some boys said to me the other day that his boys had learned that he is human. I discovered that same fact the day before while his crowd had him down on his back at the bottom of a free-for-all heap of boy-flesh. He was encouraging the personal touch. By having a part in the spirit of boyhood you will have a chance to be chummy. After all is said that is the secret of successful work with boys. (160)

The boy worker's task was to teach, heal, and love the boy, and to restore him to his family. So still it goes. Like Gibson and his cohorts, contemporary boyologists too speak of their love for, and commitment to, boys and devote themselves to the careful cultivation of male homosocial chumminess in the name of character and family integrity. Perhaps their language will someday seem just as queer.

In their attention to character especially, the books of classic boyology resembled the late-nineteenth-century nonfiction treatises designed for young men and their families that Irvin Wyllie first identified as "success manuals." These success manuals began to appear around 1870 and flourished through around 1910; they were produced by the subscription book industry and sold door-to-door. While such advice literature dates back at least to the early part of the nineteenth century, these manuals were more uniform in style and more widely distributed; they were, in short, hot commodities in the newly established circuit of subscription bookselling. They are the focus of Judy Hilkey's study *Character Is Capital: Success Manuals and Manhood in Gilded Age America.* Hilkey revisits the earlier critical consensus that these books embodied a uniform and simple ideology of success, showing instead how such manuals helped establish such an ideology but also embodied the anxieties of this volatile era.

Like the rural narratives of boyology that I considered in chapter 1, success manuals were marketed to native-born, largely rural, and largely Protestant men of moderate education and income. And like the primers of classic boyology, success manuals were aimed as much at the parents of young men as at the men themselves, meant to guide and reassure parents as their sons sought security (if not fortune) in a rapidly changing socioeconomic order. Both the boyology books and the success manuals depend on the interplay of a rhetoric of crisis and the promise of success and renewal. Both stress the importance of vocational choice. Tracing the education and life experiences of the authors of success manuals, Hilkey emphasizes the influence of two intellectuals in particular: Ralph Waldo Emerson and Herbert Spencer. As we've already seen, Emerson and Spencer loom large in the collective unconscious of boyology (and indeed in nineteenth-century intellectual culture more generally).

According to Hilkey, character became a substitute for money, a form of cultural capital, offered as a buffer or quasi antidote to the new materialist ethic but framed in essentially materialist terms. A young man could thus be rich without money, provided he was rich in character. Such an emphasis "softened the blow of the failure of Jefferson's agrarian democracy while providing the rationale to maintain faith in self and in the efficacy of the new social order" (131). We might extend Hilkey's observations to classic boyology, which emerged in the wake of these success manuals and also sought to manage anxiety about monopoly capitalism by emphasizing what were largely agrarian and artisan values while translating boyhood into cultural capital. Clearly in the primers of classic boyology, character education is the solution to the "boy problem." A good boy has character, and a good boyologist knows how to cultivate and ensure character. Boyhood could be understood as a first form or step of character—a building block, of sorts— and as a reformulation of (adult male) character. Like character, boyhood was presumed rural and preindustrial, such that an urban boyhood seemed a contradiction of terms for quite a while, the early novels of Horatio Alger Jr. notwithstanding (though even in those, many of the street boys are from the country or embody rural character). It wouldn't surprise me if the rather flat notion of character was rooted largely in the ideology of boyhood, or at least, if the two emerged more or less together; it's not by accident that the men who involved themselves with Scouting and the YMCA self-identified as character builders.

Native-born boys were a relatively secure form or embodiment of character, more so than, say, the immigrant men who were arriving in droves. The success manuals and the boyology primers don't just ensure that this population of native-born, WASP boys can develop and claim character; they also ensure that character will belong solely to this particular group. Targeting this particular group of American subjects not only bestowed privilege but also checked the fungibility of such a generic and vague term. The primers of classic boyology emphasize the importance of character in boys especially; character is part of the native-born boy's potential, almost part of his biological makeup. Character is not a dynamic feature of personality but a stable essence. Boys are supervised by men of character not merely because such men are admirable but because those men represent the utopian future of boyhood. Eli Newberger puts it best in the title of his 1999 book *The Men They Will Become: The Nature and Nurture of Male Character.*

Like the boy books that precede them historically, the manuals of classic boyology claim universality for boyhood, representing it as a distinct world with its own features and laws. What Bill Brown calls the "chrono-topic work of the boy's book" is also the work of boyology more generally (*The Material Unconscious*, 173). Such spatialization, which tends tempo-rally toward the mythic, has long been a standard feature of the biopolitical coordination of boyhood. The German educator Friedrich Wilhelm August Froebel, for instance, notes in *The Education of Man* (1826) that the boy "forms for himself his own world; for the feeling of his *own power* implies and soon demands also the possession of his *own space* and his *own material* belonging exclusively to him" (106). Over a century and a half later and in a dramatically different culture, Michael Gurian agrees, adding in *The Wonder of Boys* that boys "tend to use up far more space than girls" (15). Girls play contentedly in small corners, while boys merit more room, and presumably more private property. "So often the boy's brain cries out to us . . . 'Give me more space!'" (16). This spatialization implies that boyhood is a universal and expansive experience, to the disadvantage not only of girls but also of boys other than those smiling Caucasians who adorn the covers of Gibson's *Boyology* as well as contemporary handbooks such as Gurian's *The Wonder of Boys*.

I have already discussed the Bad Boy genre, but in other boy book genres of the period, the boy is also an a priori positivity, a body actively engaged with the spaces of history but rarely changed by them. For example, Rupert S. Holland's *Historic Boyhoods* (1909), with chapters about figures such as Christopher Columbus, Peter the Great, Daniel Boone, and Andrew Jackson (some of which first appeared in shorter form in *St. Nicholas*), im-plies that boyhood is more constant than variable, since these heroes allegedly shared fundamental character traits. The book's illustrations include a color picture of the archetypal snow fort, where boys reenact ancestral wars. In this book, the qualities of the boy, including innate savagery, anticipate future greatness, and multiplicity serves the interest of a familiar tale. Hartwell James's *The Boys of the Bible* (1905) likewise makes boyhood a constant by recasting biblical greats such as Isaac, Jacob, David, Absalom, and Jesus himself in "The Boy Who Obeyed," "The Farmer Boy," The Shepherd Boy," "The Boy Who Would Be King," and "The Boy Jesus."[23]

More typically, boyhood is presented in the archetypal singular. Dorothy Margaret Stuart's engaging *The Boy through the Ages* (1926), first published in England, also uses the boy as a stable vantage point for historiography, tracing attitudes toward boys from cave-dwelling days to the middle of Queen Victoria's reign. "As the long pageant of boy-life through the ages passes before us," she rhapsodizes, "with its gay and sombre colours and shadows, and then narrows and recedes into the distance again, we see that the first great influence which moulded the minds of men and the lives of their sons was the love of learning" (281). Ages and attitudes pass, but the "pageant of boy-life" goes on. Most of these texts are single volumes, compilations in their own right, but some belong to a series. Francis Rolt-Wheeler's U.S. Service series sought to inspire patriotism and a sense of history by dramatizing the boy-affiliated operations of federal agencies. My personal favorite, *The Boy with the U.S. Mail* (1916), is packed with photographs and thrilling tales, told in chapters like "The Honor of the Postage Stamp" and "A Desperado Mail Carrier." "The handling and delivery of the U.S. Mail is alive with its own perils," Rolt-Wheeler warns in the preface; "Blizzards may howl and flood may rage, but 'The Mail Must Go Through.'"

In such texts, as in classic boyology and the earlier imaginative literature from which it draws, boyhood is imagined as a constant world at odds with (and imperiled by) dystopian worlds. In *The Boy Today* (1930), Mather Almon Abbott describes the boy as the victim of intellectualism, or "mental indigestion" (16), and of the "godless world," which includes the "automobile world," the "bootlegging world," and of course the "hard-boiled world." But boyhood survives these predatory forces. With guidance, the boy today is the boy of yesterday and also of tomorrow. "Boyhood is fundamentally the same as boyhood has always been," claims Abbott (113). Boyhood is at once static and dynamic, inaccessible and supervised, singular and collective.

Social Pedagogy and the Culture Idea

The anthropological idea of culture, which found canonical expression in E. B. Tylor's *Primitive Culture* (1871), offered boyhood a form of existence and intelligibility beyond the faux-biological: as a culture or subculture, analogous to, but independent of, adult society. Boy book writers had already suggested as much, and travel writers likened boy gangs to the heathen clans they encountered abroad. A less racist composite example is Bayard Taylor's travel narrative *Boys of Other Countries: Stories for American Boys* (1876), which features five short stories about boys whom Taylor met overseas, including "The Little Post-Boy" of Sweden, with whom Taylor snuggles for survival during an icy night; and Hans, a German herd boy about whom Taylor writes, in keeping with the spirit of the times: "Hans was not a bad boy: he was simply restless, impatient, and perhaps a little inclined to envy those in better circumstances" (124). Taylor emphasizes the constancy of the boy, and his enduring qualities: "I have found many instances among other races, and in other climates," he reports to his young readers, "of youthful courage, and self-reliance, and strength of character, some of which I propose to relate to you" (2). Taylor's collection is contemporaneous with Warner's *Being a Boy*, which takes the New England farm boy as its exemplary and exotic subject. The boy became both strange and familiar enough to merit his own culture, and the primers of boyology read much like domestic travel narratives.

The boyologists also made creative use of a metaphor of recapitulation congruent with the culture idea: the culture epochs concept of the German philosopher Johann Friedrich Herbart. In the 1890s, American Herbartians used this concept to revitalize curriculum theory. The culture epochs concept extended culture into the domain of ontogenetic-phylogenetic relation; the parallelism between the development of the human race and the development of the individual suggested certain "epochs" in the child's mental life that required particular kinds of instruction and activity. These epochs dictated the very materials with which educators should work, and the general emphasis of each grade level (see Kliebard, *Forging the American Curriculum*, 72–73). As with the concept of culture more generally, boy culture was not so much the sum of those stages, epochs, and materials as it was the promise and ostensible measure of their correspondence. As Christopher Herbert puts it in *Culture and Anomie*:

> What gives [culture] ethnographic significance—what enables it to generate a method of research, a set of directed assumptions, problems, and procedures—is the presumption that this array of disparate-seeming elements of social life composes a significant *whole*, each factor of which is in some sense a corollary of, consubstantial with, implied by, immanent in, all the others. (5)

The epochs concept implied precisely such wholeness and intelligibility and was inherently pedagogical and easily adapted. Froebel had already claimed that *"boyhood is the period in which instruction predominates"* (95); boy workers had only to expand the field of instruction. Forbush's *The Boy Problem* is aptly subtitled *A Study in Social Pedagogy*. "For helping this age," writes Forbush, "social pedagogy, the combination of educative forces in a social direction, is a new and most important science" (26). Despite Forbush's institutional clout, social pedagogy per se never quite caught on as a concept or practice; perhaps it sounded too radically like social activism to some. The term "boy worker," by contrast, was grounded safely in boyhood and pseudobiology, less subject to social misdirection. In any case, boyology came to eclipse rival terms and indicate the ever-expanding domain of boy work.

Forbush offers a synopsis of the "by-laws of boy-life" and the ways in which boys spontaneously organize but stops just short of the culture idea. He is too invested in what he calls "instrumentalities" (management techniques) to endorse a more holistic concept, which might engender resistance to the intervention he advocates. But the epochs concept does inform a number of boyology primers, particularly George Walter Fiske's *Boy Life and Self-Government* (1910), revised from a series of lectures and published by the YMCA's Association Press. Fiske was professor of practical theology in the Oberlin Theological Seminary, and *Boy Life* is quite practical and far less prescriptive than *The Boy Problem;* Fiske is even critical of some boy work organizations. But Fiske certainly has his own fantasy of boy culture to share, and he is just as eager to promote the proper instrumentalities. A quick detour through *Boy Life* suggests both the rhetorical appeal and the nonsense-logic of the epochs concept—a concept that, in a sense, combined recapitulation with time travel, presenting the evolutionary and racial history of boyhood as an anthropological reality.

Boy Life opens with a diagnosis of "Jimmie, James and Jim," the tripartite self of the typical boy—respectively, the "rollicking savage," the "nice little man," and the "manly boyish fellow, frank of face and sound at heart," to whom the others give birth after much labor (12–13). These personae must surface at the appropriate time. "What if Jim comes too soon?" Fiske asks. Such prematurity will result in that most distasteful condition, "precocious little manhood" (15). Jimmie, James, and Jim escort us through Fiske's text, which emphasizes the birthright of boys to found their own institutions. Fiske expresses reservations about using the term "government," recognizing that it "has the usual inaccuracy of the figure synecdoche, the use of the part for the whole" (24), but embraces the equally figurative culture epochs idea. He cites the emerging literature of "social education" but locates citizenship in a boy-driven pedagogy: "In all boy problems the boys themselves must first give us the cue; for after all, the Supreme Court of Boyville is the *heart of the boy*" (41).

This concern with the sacred hearts of boys opens the third chapter, "Boy Life and Race Life," and inaugurates Fiske's Herbartian scheme. He cites recent authorities on the boy-savage parallel—Hall, James Mark Baldwin, and A. F. Chamberlain—to establish that "recapitulation is not merely a physical fact but *psychic and social as well*," a fact "too great to be ignored by students and lovers of boys" (55). Fiske cautions his readers that the theory has its limitations and that boy lovers should not overlook "the modifying influence" of the boy's immediate environment (58). For Fiske, culture denotes that environment as well as past epochs. Fiske often speaks of "race culture," but he attributes the differences among boys to social factors, including urban distress, which hinder or accelerate recapitulation. Reviewing popular schemes of culture epochs, he provides a chart of Dr. Woods Hutchinson's five overlapping stages of "food getting," which correspond to stages of child development: Root and Grub, Hunting and Capture, Pastoral, Agricultural, and Shop and Commercial. The Hunting and Capture epoch, for instance, usually culminates in the seventh year; boys in this epoch fear strangers, practice methods of stalking, and are indifferent to pain and given to cruelty. They prefer games of stealth, including Hide and Seek, Black Man, and Prisoner's Base (64).

Fiske divides the epochs into two larger categories: stages in the evolution of government and stages of industrial evolution (66–67). He then returns to the boy's instincts, reinterpreting them as the basis for an initially laissez-faire boyology. Don't interfere with recapitulation, he warns; allow the spontaneity of urge and emotion. Encourage the development of the will, but don't disrupt the transition in boy culture from primitive democracy through tyrannical feudalism to republican social democracy. If left alone, the boy's industrial instincts will likewise cycle through acquisitive, destructive, constructive, and cooperative phases, the last of which enables commerce and the growth of cities. Boy workers, notes Fiske, can learn much from a systematic study of "boy made societies" (115), the alleged basis of modern democracy. Unfortunately, the average boy's club or gang is short-lived and does not afford the boyologist a stable object of inquiry. If only, Fiske laments,

> in our study of boy life, we could discover a modern boy colony, with a distinct social life of its own, continuing through a series of years, isolated from cities and free from adult interference, how delighted we should be! Then we should be able to study boys in a true boy's world, and watch the activities of the unfettered boy will. Then we could discover how boys, untrammeled by adult notions and customs, would develop naturally such social and economic customs of their own as their needs required. Then, too, we might see clearly whether or not the influence of race habit would work out, and the modern boy really recapitulate the progress of the race. Such a self-governing boy world, if we could discover it, would also teach us many things about our subject of self-government in boy life. (118)

A close approximation conveniently supplies itself: the McDonogh School near Baltimore. Presumably a boarding school (the description is sketchy), the McDonogh School offers boys what similar institutions do not: lots of space, in the form of eight hundred acres of farm and forest, where boys and their cramped brains may roam at will. The teachers do not regulate their recreation, and over the years certain "customs and unwritten laws" have evolved that echo the epochs of government and industry (120). As the grounds became more settled by the boys, more complex forms of land tenure and harvest emerged; unregulated use yielded to squatter rights, succeeded by private ownership and monopoly. A socialist political party even formed to protest capitalist travesties and promote land redistribution (of course, it didn't survive). The McDonogh boys, concludes Fiske, "seem clearly to have proved the truth of the culture-epochs views along social, economic, and partly governmental lines" (142).[24]

Obviously the McDonogh School was designed for boys by adults, with specific means and to specific ends, and is hardly comparable to spontaneously organized boy peer groups. Fiske's step-by-step analysis of this boy colony illustrates how seductive the epochs concept could be. Fiske lives the contradiction of boyology, declaring the autonomy of boy culture while dictating its nature and nurture. The second half of *Boy Life* provides instructions for the supervision of boy republics, including manipulation of the "boy ballot" (210). Fiske contrasts his own practice with the "benevolent despotism" of boy work uninformed by scientific study and driven solely by charisma (206). He also appeals to missionary strategy: "Foreign missions are now conducted on the principle that each nation must be Christianized by natives. . . . China is to be saved by the Chinese. . . . Boys must be won and saved *by boys*" (200–201). Or by men pretending to be boys. Even if "the adult should guide from the rear" (221), Fiske recommends the missionary position, having little use for alternative lifestyles: "How ludicrously pathetic are the little Amish boys, dressed in long pantaloons and old men's broad-rimmed hats, as soon as they get well out of the cradle" (42).

As Fiske's text demonstrates, the primers of classic boyology, whatever their worries and investments, construct a pseudoanthropological rhetoric of culture around the often contradictory axioms of boyhood. There is some consensus; boys are presumed to be primitive or savage to some degree and to spontaneously congregate, "for it is a law of nature," as Gibson explains in *Boyology*, "for bees to go in swarms, cattle in herds, birds in flocks, fishes in schools, and boys in gangs. . . . The most interesting thing to a boy is another boy" (82–83). And yet boys also mimic adult social institutions such as the city and the republic, which are anything but homogeneous. Perhaps the homo-to-hetero (or progressive diversification) paradigm I described in the book's introduction makes both forms of culture possible, but in this and other respects, boyology seems inconsistent at best, reflecting the increasing complexity of debates about culture more broadly.

Mark Twain and the Bad Boy Boom

The Bad Boy all but disappeared in early-twentieth-century boyology, only to reappear with some consistency in the advice manuals of the late 1990s, such as *The Wonder of Boys* and *Real Boys*. What happened in between, as character building organizations thrived? Among other things, the canonization of Twain within the academy, and the absorption of his characters

Huck Finn and Tom Sawyer especially into popular culture (through film adaptations, Norman Rockwell paintings, and so forth). That canonization, and perhaps that cultural absorption as well, was fostered in part by the immaturity critique launched by Brooks and the ensuing debate about Twain's accomplishments. Despite that critique, and perhaps also because of it, Twain has been recuperated as one of our most significant writers.

Twain's contemporaries clearly saw him as one of their own. Like Twain himself, Howells firmly situated *Tom Sawyer* within the conventions of Bad Boy writing.[25] Now, however, the Bad Boy genre is often invoked by scholars as merely a source for *Tom Sawyer* and especially *Huck Finn,* as in Alan Gribben's essay on "boy book elements" in these novels.[26] Many scholars try to isolate *Huck Finn* from this particular source. Anne Trensky argues that *Huck Finn* belongs "if not to a separate genre, certainly to a separate category within the genre" (510). Jim Hunter finds *Tom Sawyer* a dramatic improvement of Aldrich's *The Story of a Bad Boy* and accords *Huck Finn* "a significance beyond the literary" (431).

Twain's two boy books now have an uneasy status, attesting at once to Twain's genius and to his various alleged shortcomings, among them sentimentality, nostalgia, and immaturity. The hypercanonization of *Huck Finn* is inseparable from the lionization of Mark Twain as a literary father and representative American. Mocker of pretension at home and abroad, Twain became the rebel of American letters, a "bright disrespectful genius" who "represented a certain distinctively American attitude" (Hunter, "Mark Twain," 438). But not everyone saw it that way, and the more suspicious critical tradition of Brooks and Fiedler lives on, in Forrest C. Robinson's analysis of Twain's "bad faith," for instance, and Lawrence Howe's ideas about Twain's "double-cross" of authority.

Twain-affirmative scholars often identify Twain's use of the vernacular voice in *Huck Finn* as his chief improvement on the boy book, but that very innovation would have been unthinkable without the fetishization of the boy-savage accomplished by the Bad Boy genre. What is usually cited as the major difference between Twain's two novels, point of view, actually suggests their continuity and their custodial function. However much Twain may have troped the Bad Boy genre (and that's debatable), the story of Huck is still largely understood as a boy's story that transcends rather than dramatizes racial tension.[27]

In emphasizing the novel's affinities with boyology, I am not suggesting that the book is really about boyhood rather than race. From its publication, *Huck Finn* has served as a touchstone for debates about racial interaction and representation. More recently it has been at the center of debates about institutional racism, canon revision, and multiculturalism. The novel is indeed about race, not simply through its depiction of Jim but in its use of the boy-savage trope.

I am hardly the first to consider *Huck Finn* in relation to that genre and the rhetoric of juvenile delinquency. Steven Mailloux argues that readers of the 1880s were far more worried about the novel's alleged endorsement of juvenile delinquency than about its depiction of Jim, despite Twain's connections with George W. Cable and other opponents of racial persecution and segregation. In *Rhetorical Power,* Mailloux emphasizes that Twain's readers "were much more preoccupied by literature's effect on the 'Bad-Boy Boom' than they were on its relation to the 'Negro Problem'" (103–4). But that "Boom" was part of the "Negro Problem," as racial and juvenile delinquency were inextricably linked in the late-nineteenth-century imagination and in the practice of boy authorship.

According to Mailloux, Bad Boy writers made fun of the growing panic about delinquency, stressing the fundamental harmlessness of Bad Boys. He is surprised that Aldrich's *The Story of a Bad Boy* "exerted little pressure to change attitudes toward juvenile delinquency" (113), assuming that characters like Tom Bailey and Huck Finn convincingly illustrate G. Stanley Hall's "scientific claim that 'bad boys' weren't doomed to be adult criminals" (112). Mailloux even applauds Aldrich's "practices of realistic representation" (113), which, as we have seen, are rather strategically realistic. The otherwise astute Mailloux overlooks the fact that late-nineteenth-century American culture had a profound and distinctly literary investment in a language of delinquency that separated middle-class white kids from the criminal classes.

Taking at face value the competition of various theories of delinquency—"theories that either optimistically conceived of delinquency as a developmental stage naturally outgrown or pessimistically viewed it as a hereditary trait or irremediable degeneracy" (114)—Mailloux fails to see their shared dependence on evolutionary principles, notably recapitulation and diversification, that were interpreted and promoted along familiar ideological lines. In other words, while it's true that some theories of delinquency emphasized the incorrigibility of all juvenile offenders, most differentiated delinquency according to class and race; middle-class white boys would naturally outgrow delinquency, but for other populations, delinquency was immutable. Hence Mailloux's confusion when the Bad Boy gets recruited in the service of what looks like "pessimistic" rhetoric (in opposition, he claims, to Aldrich). Although Mailloux does not believe that evolutionary ideas are influential until the 1890s, the 1880s panic about juvenile delinquency seems very much about race and the "Negro Problem." The 1884 *Detroit Free Press* editorial that Mailloux cites, for instance, which laments "the vicious literature which is turning American boys into savages" (123), offers a counterpoint to earlier descriptions of boys as noble savages and keeps the discourse of primitivism in circulation. Literature, of course, had *already* turned boys into savages, and vice versa.

The boy-savage trope, then, is indeed related to Reconstructionist politics of race, and the success of Twain's famous novel is in part attributable to that trope's pervasive hold on the American imagination. Throughout the novel, Huck is arguably the boy-savage par excellence, and Jim the racial other marginalized through the boyologist rhetoric of homogeneity. As in the Bad Boy books, the rhetoric of racial equality disguises profound socioeconomic differences between the two characters. Their bond is often celebrated as a triumph over bigotry, but Huck's love for Jim is clearly not that of a principled abolitionist. Because he functions as an "innocent eye," Huck cannot take such a stance. The reader must supply the critique. What makes *Huck Finn* successful as an indictment of style and narrow-mindedness is Twain's refusal to editorialize. But that refusal obscures Twain's perspective on the ideology that informs the book, even as it makes clear his authorial strategies. The realism of Huck's character demands his naïveté, just as the realism of the Bad Boy books requires a gap between ignorant boy and knowing man, perhaps between innocent reader and knowing writer.

Within the novel, Twain effectively imprisons Jim in a minstrel stereotype after he and Huck pass Cairo. Twain, of course, stopped working on the book for more than two years, since to go further toward Jim's freedom meant taking the characters up the Ohio, away from the mythic drift south. Up until that point, I'd argue, *Huck Finn* is in tension with the other Bad Boy books, which are more formulaically racist. Once Twain returned to the manuscript, however, and sent his characters south, a more traditional Bad Boy narrative unfolds. Huck's reunion with Tom at the Phelps family farm and their playful reenactment of slavery seems less jarring if one does not insist on Huck's moral growth. When Huck first arrives at the farm, Aunt Sally mistakes him for Tom, and "it was like being born again, I was so glad to find out who I was" (282). Huck's rebirth as Tom, and his acquiescence in Tom's wild schemes, suggests a merger of the social outcast with the socially sanctioned Bad Boy.[28] Any marginality or special vantage Huck may have enjoyed disappears when Tom Sawyer returns. If, as some critics assert, this section dramatizes the failure of Reconstruction, it may also trivialize slavery by treating it as the innocuous pastime of boys. If Twain's masterpiece is understood not as a political fable but rather as a boy book that (at best) allegorizes national events, then the last section, and the boy book frame more generally, does not have to be an interpretive problem.

One critical line of defense is that Twain used the boy book frame to disguise subversive content. In *Was Huck Black? Mark Twain and African-American Voices,* for example, Shelly Fisher Fishkin holds that this frame is a "trickster strategy" through which Twain dramatizes the difficulty "of writing a slavery-to-freedom narrative in the 1870s and 1880s, a time when the nation was effectively reenslaving its black citizens by law and by force" (74).[29] I'm not as convinced as Fishkin that Huck's vernacular voice is so close to that of African Americans in the period, but even if Huck is somehow "black," that doesn't mean that the novel is subversive.[30] I agree with Jonathan Arac's assessment that "Huck's 'black' voice becomes more cultural capital for hypercanonization" (Arac, *Huckleberry Finn,* 183). If we champion Huck as trickster figure playing havoc with the racist texts of his day, we forget that he is still the white boy-savage. The cult of the boy-savage is another important context for the book, one that illuminates not only *Huck Finn* but also its larger life in culture. Given the evolutionary and racial fantasy endemic to boyology, we cannot assume that Huck is rebellious and that Twain's book is antiracist.[31]

This does not mean, however, that Twain and American culture can be described as immature (or irresponsible)—that Brooks and Fielder got it right after all. Like the "frame" defense, the immaturity critique takes its cue from the boy book itself, from its central themes of savagery, freedom, and imaginative play. The larger point is that criticism and defense of Twain both drew from the Bad Boy genre and together established Twain's place in the critical debate about literature and culture (and thus the canon). In the 1920s and 1930s, as Mailloux notes, *Huck Finn* was evaluated along historical and biographical lines by Van Wyck Brooks, Bernard DeVoto, and others; by midcentury, however, the conversation had become "a formalist debate about a text's unity" (91), featuring luminaries such as Lionel Trilling, T. S. Eliot, and Leo Marx. The frame or trickster defense clearly derives from both traditions of critical reading, merging formal concerns with the ongoing debate about social significance.

Lighting Out for the Territory of Culture

Brooks was arguably the first critic to pay serious attention to *Huck Finn,* and he wasn't impressed either by the book or by what he thought it embodied. "Who does not see in the extraordinary number of books about boys and boyhood written by American authors," asks Brooks in *The Ordeal of Mark Twain,* "the surest sign of the prevalence of the arrested moral development which is the result of business life . . . ?" (175). Brooks describes Twain as a divided and troubled personality and laments his failure to achieve a mature artistic vision, blaming first Twain's repressive mother and then the commercialized Gilded Age. According to Brooks, Twain capitulated to a feminized sort of commercialism by becoming a popular writer. This was Twain's "wound," at once socially and self-inflicted.[32] While others have extolled Twain's ability to fashion literature out of primitive genres like the boy book, Brooks sees Twain as hopelessly bound by boyhood's forms: "He resembled those young boys who have inherited great fortunes which they own but cannot command; the power is theirs and yet they are not in control of it; consequently, to reassure themselves, they are always 'showing off'" (22). Brooks finds Twain's failure tragic because he was destined to become a great artist; as proof, Brooks even cites Twain's Bad Boy tendencies.[33]

For Brooks, a culture critic of archetypal persuasion in search of both a national culture and that culture's representative genius, Twain is emblematic of creative America, trying in vain to escape the immature and feminizing commercialism of the period.[34] Brooks echoes at the level of literary history writing the primary assumptions of Bad Boy realism. He invokes not only psychoanalytic caveats (for which he is largely remembered) but also the evolutionary principles that underwrite them. Without naming recapitulation, he notes America's developmental compulsion to repeat: "What has been said of our civilization, that it was always beginning again, at the same level, on each new frontier, might perhaps be said of our literature also. It is always beginning again as adolescent" (70). His invocation of Spencer is direct:

> Americans were a simple, homogeneous folk before the Civil
> War, and the practical effect of pioneering and the business régime
> was to keep us so, to prevent any of that differentiation, that
> evolution of the homogeneous into the heterogeneous which, since
> Herbert Spencer stated it, has been generally conceived as the note
> of true human progress. (60)

Whereas the Bad Boy writers affirm the phenomenon of diversification, Brooks implies that Americans haven't diversified their lives or their literature.[35]

In Brooks's analysis, Twain obsessively wrote for and about boys because "he knew, or something in him knew," that "ten million business men"— "children of a larger growth" (175)—made up his masculine reading public. Twain's work allowed businessmen to "escape from the emotional stress of maturity" (213). Brooks holds the pecuniary instinct responsible for stunting our literature and the American character. He blames Twain for hawking his wares. In his view, boy authorship, instead of protecting culture from business, is a lucrative, suspect venture. Brooks's critique of Twain in the 1920s, and Bernard DeVoto's rebuttal in the next decade, set the terms for the ongoing debate about Twain's cultural status.

The Ordeal of Mark Twain has been criticized for its overreliance on psychoanalysis and its uncertain grasp of American history. In *Mark Twain's America* (1932), DeVoto calls it "lay-analysis," "a species of dinner-table annotation" (228), suggesting the struggle for cultural authority through popular scholarship. As DeVoto rightly notes, the 1920s "chose to think of Mark Twain not as a writer of books but as a man who either betrayed something sacred or was betrayed by something vile" (298). Even so, the sort of culture criticism practiced by Brooks found a sympathetic audience as well as later champions. In a later volume called *The Writer in America* (1953), Brooks anticipates Fiedler in asking, "Does not our literature reflect, just like our foreign policy, a national mind that has not yet crystallized, that . . . [is] still immature?" (69).

Although Fiedler shows more enthusiasm for Twain's particular practice of boy authorship, he too represents boyhood as a roadblock to a mature canon and a fully realized American self. Most recent accounts of the Bad Boy genre politely overlook Fiedler's uncomfortable thesis that our canonical books are our most juvenile ones in the pejorative sense, and that *Huck Finn*, that "euphoric boy's book" (*Love and Death*, 26), is merely an accomplished literary expression of our Bad Boy complex, which he identifies as both homoerotic and racist. Fiedler criticizes "the ritual praise of good-badness as the true Americanism" (*Love and Death*, 284–85). While warning against making Twain into "either a cult or a case," Fiedler, like Brooks, frequently collapses Twain and America through the very language of boyhood that he finds troubling. Noting the mythology of the Bad Boy as "America's vision of itself, crude and unruly in his beginnings, but endowed by his creator with an instinctive sense of what is right" (270), Fiedler nonetheless uses that mythology to diagnose the cult or case of Twain, remarking that while Twain understood his role as the "Good Bad Boy of Western culture," "what the mask hides is no face at all," as Sam Clemens does not survive Mark Twain (272).[36]

Feminist critics have developed Fiedler's description of American literature as immature, taking issue with his views on literature and women both, and identifying melodramas of beset manhood and other sexist stratagems. Gay-affirmative critics, by contrast, have criticized Fiedler's privileging of heteronormative masculinity as the basis for a mature canon. Robert K. Martin, searching for a queer Melville, chides Fiedler for implying "that all homosexual love is childish, or more pertinently, adolescent" (*Hero, Captain, Stranger*, 8–9). Tracing the "canonical architecture" of American race mythology, Robyn Wiegman sees Fiedler's intervention in literary studies as the first major integrationist response to the American Adam myth-symbol tradition in scholarship, a response both politically revisionary and politically suspect. Even if designed to counter certain kinds of racism, contends

Wiegman, Fiedler's reading of the canon supports the popular representation of the black liberation struggle as a masculine quest narrative of "shimmering egalitarian transcendence" (*American Anatomies,* 150), affirmed in some gay-affirmative writing and epitomized in the popular realm in black-white buddy films. She finds especially troubling Fiedler's vision of a homoerotic cultural unconscious, as it reduces the complexities of sexuality, gender, and race to a "mythic America" embodied in dark man–white man liaison and a national "literature for boys."[37] She even calls Fiedler's narrative "sentimentalized" (156).[38]

All these critics acknowledge Fiedler's role as a culture critic; they know he is writing about more than literature. What they don't acknowledge is Fiedler's debt to the very mythology of boyhood that he interrogates. Martin, for instance, seems to miss Fiedler's point that boyhood is a powerful discourse that authorizes a homoerotic and racist myth of interracial fraternity. Martin, in fact, is too invested in that myth, claiming that Herman Melville presents the interracial male couple as "an inherently democratic union of equals" capable of transcending and transforming social hierarchies (11). Fiedler makes clear his suspicion of innocence in *Love and Death:* "In our native mythology, the tie between male and male is not only considered innocent, it is taken for the very symbol of innocence itself"(350).[39] And, he holds, the homoeroticism between whites and nonwhites absolves the white man's racial guilt: "It is the Southerner's dream, the American dream of guilt remitted by the abused Negro, who . . . opens his arms crying, 'Lawsy, I's might glad to git you back ag'in, honey'" (353).

Fiedler's depiction of same-sex love as boyish is thus also a condemnation of this racist and "peculiarly American form of innocent homosexuality" (370)—even when, as here, that depiction is itself theatrically racist.[40] Fiedler's minstrelsy, and his appeal to "native mythology," work to debunk boyhood as a natural state of affairs. Imagining masculinist American literature as a homosocial literature for boys is one way of inspecting (if also upholding) the canonical architecture of boyhood.

After writing *Love and Death,* Fiedler explored other boy-savage/native relays, particularly in *The Return of the Vanishing American* (1968) and *Freaks: Myths and Images of the Secret Self* (1978), the latter of which includes a chapter on wild men and feral children. If *Love and Death* is his contribution to boyology, *Freaks* is his feral tale; it's as if Fiedler was hot on the ideological trail of boyhood even as boyhood and its analogues furnished an idiom of culture writing. The more explicit attention to boyhood is what distinguishes Fiedler's work from Sanders's *A Is for Ox* and other such tales of America's immaturity or decline. Fiedler's work shows how literary analysis draws explanatory and rhetorical power from the very material with which it "works."

In an article in the November 1992 issue of *GQ*, just before the presidential election, Gore Vidal likened Bill Clinton and Al Gore to Huck Finn and Tom Sawyer, noting the disparity between the promise of political transformation and the fact that nothing ever changes. Accompanied by caricatures of Bill and Al aboard the cherished raft, Vidal's piece reveals just how stubbornly Huck and Tom remain in our national mind. Tom, of course, never sailed that raft. Here as elsewhere, he has displaced Jim from the comic tableau of boyhood that so often stands (in) for America itself, thanks to the legacy not just of Twain but also of Bad Boy writing, boyology, and culture criticism.

3. Wolf-Boys, Street Rats, and the Vanishing Sioux

In the nineteenth century, as boyology was taking literary and institutional shape, the feral tale shifted in setting from Europe, the home of Victor of Aveyron and Kaspar Hauser, to colonial India, described by John Lockwood Kipling (Rudyard's father) in *Beast and Man in India: A Popular Sketch of Indian Animals in Their Relations with the People* (1891) as the "cradle of wolf child stories" (318).[1] In the early nineteenth century, the feral tale was typically an Enlightenment story about the redeeming power of culture. Although both Victor and Kaspar were likened to animals, their caretakers clearly saw these boys as exemplary subjects of science and as proper citizens. By the middle of that century, however, British reports of wolf-reared boys in India began to proliferate, inspiring anthropological inquiry as well as literary fantasy. However troubled, Victor and Hauser were citizens of France and Germany, respectively; the wolf-boys, by contrast, were animal-affiliated subjects of empire.

Attitudes toward alleged wolf-boys were mixed on both sides of the Atlantic. Kipling glamorized the motif in his tales of Mowgli, while men of science were more likely to dismiss such reports, or (if they believed the reports) to see wolf-boys as hopelessly subhuman. E. B. Tylor, for instance, responded to the wolf-boy reports in his 1863 essay "Wild Men and Beast Children"—published in the inaugural issue of the *Anthropological Review*—but concluded that "beast children" were the stuff of mythology rather than anthropology. As I show in chapter 5, the feral tale met with greater success in psychoanalysis, but anthropology had little disciplinary use for feral boys until early in the twentieth century.

I suggested in the book's introduction that Scouting represents the institutional intersection of boyology and the feral tale, as Kipling's tales were the inspiration for Baden-Powell's programs. This chapter examines another form of overlap, this one literary but also institutional in a different sense: the emergence of related American genres of boy's literature, from the urban conversion story to the memoir of "native" boyhood and finally the mass-market stories of a jungle boy named Bomba. These genres supplant the Bad Boy books in keeping with larger cultural shifts. As the Enlightenment effort to account for human nature through a set of liminal cases gave way to more overtly political efforts to manage the subjects of metropolis, nation, and empire, these forms of boys' literature made feral boyhood increasingly safe for mass consumption. Like Scouting, which they both anticipate and support, these genres transform the wolf-boy back into an exemplary subject.

Uniting these feral genres is a hands-on practice of paternalism, uplift, and educational zeal also characteristic of boyology. Just as the Bad Boy books adapted the evolutionary theories of recapitulation and progressive diversification in support of a particular ideology of American selfhood, so too do feral tales for boys preserve and promote the scientific and imaginative conceits of major political projects such as British colonialism, urban American "child saving," and Native American assimilation. In the mass-market scene of boy's literature, the feral boy of British inflection merges with the iconic American figures of the boy-savage, the Bad Boy, and the (juvenile) "vanishing American." Whereas the boy subject of boyology has long served as a prototype for the representative man, the feral boy has undergone a dramatic transformation, first a figure of radical alterity, then a trope for the necessity of intervention, and finally an imago for the middle-class white man's inner self.

From Wild Child to Wolf-Boy

In 1799, hunters in south central France spied and captured a boy estimated to be around twelve years old, apparently abandoned or orphaned, who had been surviving alone in the woods for much of his life. In 1800 he was taken to Paris, where scientists and laymen alike flocked to see him. As film-maker François Truffaut and others later recognized, the case approximated the "forbidden experiment"—intentionally raising a child in isolation—and became a test case for Enlightenment theories about language acquisition, cognition, motor skills, and socialization. First studied by the naturalist J. J. Virey, Victor was then supervised by Dr. Jean-Marc-Gaspard Itard, associated with the National Institute for Deaf Mutes.[2]

Itard's pioneering work with Victor was conducted to demonstrate the explanatory and compensatory power of culture. As Victor's caretaker and educator, Itard's first obligation, as he explained in the first of two formal reports, was to "produce his physical and moral development," but if this proved impossible, he could deduce "from what is wanting in him, the sum, as yet not calculated, of that knowledge and of those ideas for which man is indebted to his education" (93). Culture, then, that always "as yet not uncalculated" sum of religious mores, sexual practices, kinship systems, and so forth, may be measured both by its achievement and by its absence in Victor. Victor's ultimate failures helped Itard prove that "moral superiority which has been said to be *natural* to man, is merely the result of civilization, which raises him above other animals by a great and powerful stimulus" (140).[3] Itard published an update on his work with Victor in 1807, addressed to the minister of the interior. Itard regrets Victor's lack of progress after a promising start but hopes His Excellency will accept this "collection of facts relevant to the illumination of the history of medical philosophy, the study of uncivilized man and the organization of certain types of private education" (141).

About a century later, the scientific project of wild child study of which Victor's case is representative was remodeled into a pop-imperialist mythology. If, as Gauri Viswanathan holds, English studies helped effect imperialism in India, so possibly did the wolf-boy reports "collected" in India, circulated throughout the British Empire, and canonized as fantasy stories for boys. As Viswanathan points out, while English literature was promoted in the colony, partly as an antidote to the traditional literature of the East, Indian legends and folklore were widely known in Britain. Though not written for children, tales of Indian wolf-boys were very much about the children of empire, and it's no accident that they are still considered children's literature. These tales rewrite early missionary work in the idiom of military and scientific encounter. British troopers and explorers, not the wolf-boys, are the protagonists. Not unlike Perrault and the Brothers Grimm before them, these men slummed among the folk in the name of culture—not culture as an abstraction but British culture more specifically.

Sir William Henry Sleeman, a major general in the service for forty years, issued a widely read pamphlet in 1852 entitled *An Account of Wolves Nurturing Children in Their Dens. By an Indian Official.* Sleeman's account was reprinted in his memoir *A Journey through the Kingdom of Oude* (1858). The 1852 pamphlet seems to be rhetorical baseline for the colonialist feral tale.[4] Sleeman discusses seven cases in all, several of them recorded elsewhere in 1843 (Malson, *Wolf Children,* 44). The report is quasi-anthropological, offering both a portrait of Indian rural life and an affirmation of British superiority. Children in Sultanpoor are often carried off and devoured by wolves, Sleeman notes, and the natives are afraid to kill them, partly because of their superstitious fear, and partly because they later rob the wolf dens of the gold and silver ornaments belonging to the children. Sleeman implies that children are literally left for the wolves, dumped off to die so that they may be posthumously robbed. The seven cases Sleeman describes have a cumulative reading effect that diminishes the specificity of each. In each variant, the boy is rescued from the wolves that abducted him and taken against his will to a village by a trooper. He is filthy and hostile; he rejects clothes, cooked food, and human affection. He is indifferent to cold but often in ill health; several of the wolf-boys die soon after capture.

Despite his extensive travels, Sleeman himself neither finds nor meets any wolf-boys.[5] This does not mean, however, that he doubts the truth of such stories. Since no men are around to testify to wolf nurture, he thinks that boys stolen by wolves perish in the wild, eaten by their foster parents or other prey, or perhaps die from "living exclusively on animal food" (222). Sleeman suspects tigers as likely predators, perhaps inspiring Rudyard Kipling's tiger Shere Khan, Mowgli's archenemy. While Sleeman associates certain native habits with superstitious lore, he treats these cases realistically, as evidence of the dire conditions of Indian life that are now the responsibility of Britain. His realism is folkloric in function, offering archetype in the service of political regime. Other officers dismissed these tales as rubbish, using them as incitement to more legitimate discourse, whereas Sleeman takes them seriously; either way, they function as imperial polemic in their careful invocation of the folk.

The Kiplings later responded to this literature, and specifically to Sleeman, but so did E. B. Tylor. In a sense, Tylor takes his cue from his predecessors in wild child inquiry, since it was the first official anthropological organization, the Society of Observers of Man, that sponsored Itard's research on Victor. The society was only a month old when Victor surfaced, but by Tylor's time, British anthropology was a practice in need of some discipline. If, as is often asserted, anthropology was the handmaiden of colonialism, then no wonder Tylor appeals to the subaltern figure of the wolf-boy. In "Wild Men and Beast-Children" Tylor is rehearsing his most important contribution to anthropology, the idea of "culture," as elaborated in *Primitive Culture* (1871).

Shifting the discussion from anthropology to mythology, Tylor in his essay collapses Sleeman's cases into a master plot from which the urban child savers later borrow, noting that the cases "are so curiously consistent with one another that it is possible to make a definition of the typical wolf-child, or rather wolf-boy, as we hear nothing of wolf-girls" (26). He offers the following composite sketch: "He should be about ten years old, more or less, brutal and hideous in appearance, idiotic in mind, given to eating raw meat and garbage in preference to anything else, generally averse to wearing clothes, incapable, or almost incapable, of learning to speak, but able to understand and express himself by signs to some extent" (26). Like Sleeman, Tylor relocates wildness from the geospace of the outback to the body and psyche of the wolf-boy, whom he treats as a mythological figure.[6]

Tylor agrees that Indian boys may indeed live "in an extraordinary state of brutalization" (26), but he doubts they are raised by wolves. He decides that "the whole matter may be safely given over to the student of Comparative Mythology," because such stories are the usual stuff of Eastern folklore, and Oriental testimony more generally offers little insight into the "lowest stage of human society" (21). He concludes in the essay's last paragraph that the study of culture, like culture itself, is a top-down affair:

> The inquirer who seeks to find out the beginnings of man's
> civilization must deduce general principles by reasoning
> downwards from the civilized European to the savage, and then
> descend to still lower possible levels of human existence, with such
> assistance as he can gain from the study of the undeveloped
> human mind in children, and in the blind and deaf and dumb,
> who have been prevented by physical defects from receiving much
> of the knowledge which is current among their fellows, and who
> are therefore obliged to form their opinions from the direct
> evidence of their senses, without sharing in the treasury of
> knowledge which has been accumulating for so many ages, and
> comes almost unconsciously to ordinary children. (32)

Whereas for Itard, the wild child afforded a less tainted glimpse at the natural state of man, and simultaneously an opportunity to deduce culture, for Tylor and other social scientists some sixty years later, the feral child doesn't give us enough to go on, or is too entangled with mythology. A more systematic kind of deduction must take place; we can't simply see culture as everything that's absent or latent in the wild child. In *Primitive Culture* he defines culture as "that complex whole which includes knowledge, belief, art, morals, law, custom, and any other capabilities and habits acquired by man as a member of society" (1).[7] The wild child disrupts the process of reasoning downward or upward in pursuit of that whole. He is too singular a figure of chaos and rupture.

Why, then, does Tylor rehearse his history for ten pages? Perhaps, in part, for the same reason that Freud later made use of the motif in his own foundational enterprise: the feral boy suggests both a normative path of development and deviation from that path. As a concept, culture is generally more compelling when diffuse or ideologically vague. The trope of the feral boy was more useful than any single conception of savage or child. It links savage and child but is itself neither, implying culture through its absence—or, as for Tylor here, establishing the need for a serious form of intellectual inquiry. Tylor's assessment is not merely a dismissal; it is also a rhetorical move that became characteristic of the social sciences, devoted to the study of culture and indebted to (while anxious about) culture's folkloric and literary repertoire: the liminal figure of the wild child is invoked and then quasi-repudiated as a legitimate object of inquiry.[8]

Tylor seems also to anticipate fieldwork as anthropology's major method of cultural observation (not formalized until Malinowski's *Argonauts of the Western Pacific*, published in 1922), even as he practices armchair analysis. He devotes much attention to cultures outside of Britain and Europe but makes no mention of Victor or Kaspar Hauser. To these famous cases he prefers more rural and primitivist examples, recalling a few cases of wild children living in Germany after the Napoleonic wars, citing Henry Rowe Schoolcraft's work on Native American animism and totemism, and summarizing a Chippewa tale about an abandoned boy who becomes increasingly wolflike. As is typical of armchair anthropology, "Wild Men and Beast-Children" is comparativist in energy and attributes the feral tale to primitive cultures. Tylor emphasizes the promise of more properly scientific research abroad. Colonial anthropology, after all, had to justify not only bringing culture into the metropole, in the form of the museum, the academy, the zoo, and so forth, but also taking culture into the heart of darkness.

Taking his cue from Sleeman rather than Tylor, Valentine Ball also gives an account of wolf-reared children in the province of Oude, in his *Jungle Life in India* (1880). In 1872 Ball had learned of a boy smoked out of a wolf den and taken to the Sekandra Orphanage. Ball corresponded with the superintendent and in 1873 presented a paper about the case to the Asiatic Society of Bengal (455). Determined to prove the plausibility of the case, Ball visited the orphanage in 1874 while conducting a geological survey. There he met not one but two ostensible wolf-boys. Ball tells us very little about the behavior of these boys, referring only to their "arrested growth" and their inability to "maintain an erect position" (461). Their defects seem congenital rather than the result of hardship, and Ball's quasi-medical realism is perhaps calculated to ward off the likely incredulity of his peers. Ball asks his readers to suspend judgment until a new wolf-boy surfaces, who can be inspected "by a joint committee of judicial and medical officers" (466). While Ball appeals occasionally to evolutionary science, his observations are couched largely in the language of exploration and proto-ethnography.[9]

Given this rich mix of folkloric and scientific feral speculation, it's not surprising that Rudyard Kipling introduced his own wolf-boy in a quasi-anthropological, colonialist sketch called "In the Rukh." Published just a year before the first *Jungle Book*, "In the Rukh" narrates Mowgli's life after the jungle, and his entry into adulthood and the Raj. In search of his identity, Mowgli meets Gisborne, a forest officer in Northern India, who adopts the wolf-boy. Mowgli becomes a ranger himself and marries the daughter of Gisborne's servant. In an introduction to the *Jungle Books*, Daniel Karlin sees the story as "a half-baked anticipation" (13) of the real Mowgli and thus omits this story in the Sussex/Penguin edition. (No one has yet treated "In the Rukh" as children's literature.) We could argue, of course, that the *Jungle Books* are just as colonialist and proto-ethnographic as "In the Rukh." In any case, Kipling's revision from wolf-boy report to jungle fantasy is telling. Mowgli is a far nobler creature than the pitiable wolf-boys of colonialist reportage; he is superheroic, strong, intelligent, easily in charge of the animals that so lovingly raise him. Kipling thus sets a precedent for the transformation of the native feral boy into the idealized masculine self, through the medium of popular adventure literature—a transformation so dramatic as to veer quickly into cliché, as Tarzan degenerates into Bomba the Jungle Boy.

Charles Loring Brace and the Urban Conversion Story

The British colonialist feral tale had its counterpart in feral tales of street boys in urban America, narratives affiliated with the "child-saving" movement and forensic writing on the immigrant poor. In "Wolf-Reared Children" (1882), which appeared in *St. Nicholas: An Illustrated Magazine for Young Folks,* Charles Loring Brace, urban reformer and founder of the Children's Aid Society, draws an unflattering portrait of the Indian wolf-boy, then asks his readers, "Did the children who read *St. Nicholas* in comfortable homes ever think that there are wolf-reared children in such a city as New York?" (543). After detailing the Indian wolf-boy's bestial ways, Brace describes how a particular New York wolf-boy turns his life around with the help of the Children's Aid Society. For Brace, the wolf-boy is redeemable as long as his environment can be changed, and as long as the boy is not too markedly ethnic or foreign. Brace's account, like those of British colonialists, revises the feral tale frame: the colonialist or child saver goes native in the metropolis in an effort to redeem and rehabilitate.

Brace's work emerged from several decades of concern (even panic) about immigrant street children in urban America. In New York City, juvenile vagrancy and crime had been a matter of serious public interest since midcentury at least. In 1849, Captain George Matsell, the chief of police in New York City, called his citizens to task, noting the "constantly increasing number of vagrants, idle and vicious children of both sexes, who infest our public thoroughfares, hotels, docks, &c." (58). Clergymen rather than businessmen were the first to respond to this "infestation," perhaps because nineteenth-century sentimental Protestantism supplied a conversion metanarrative easily reworked for street children. Under the pressure of millennialism and evangelical revivals, conversion on a grand scale became the mandate of Sunday schools and various social agencies. Joseph Kett notes that most people insisted on "the need for a 'tangible and manifest' conversion experience as a capstone of childhood nurture" (*Rites of Passage,* 118). Eventually such schools shifted their attention toward the children of their church members, but not before conversion became nearly synonymous with childhood (119).

A minister himself, Brace came from an old New England family; his mother was related to the famous Beecher family, and his father had ties with the Hartford Female Seminary. His travels in Hungary and Germany convinced him to turn to charitable work and to model child saving on the German plan of education for vagrant children, as embodied in the *Rauhe Haus,* or "rough house." In New York, Brace and fellow clergymen such as A. D. F. Randolph, William C. Russell, and others first tried to organize special Sunday meetings for vagrant boys. Not surprisingly, the boys did not respond favorably to these meetings. In a series of articles in the *New York Daily Times,* Brace pronounced the meetings a failure and called for the creation of a larger umbrella organization. Early in 1853, Brace and his colleagues established the Mission, which soon became the New York Children's Aid Society, a state-chartered but privately controlled philanthropic organization. Most of Brace's programs were administered through the CAS, including the establishment of industrial schools, reading rooms, and lodging houses, and the controversial practice of relocation or "placing out." The CAS was funded primarily by private donations (the Astors were generous patrons) and various fund-raising projects.[10]

In sociological accounts, the child-saving movement is alternately described as a humanitarian "triumph of progressive liberalism" and as a systematic assault on the lower classes (Platt, *The Child Savers,* xiv). Brace's career has likewise been imagined as both heroic and reprehensible. My own sense is that the child-saving movement, like most such social phenomena, was simultaneously progressive and custodial, drawing from a wide range of overlapping but also contradictory images and ideologies. Certainly it seemed an odd mix of Protestant theology and evolutionary rhetoric. Brace himself was fascinated by the work of Darwin and consistently argued that the evolutionary process always led toward "higher forms of life" (cited in Emma Brace, *The Life of Charles Loring Brace,* 302). Against more deterministic theories of degeneration, Brace even insisted in *The Dangerous Classes of New York* (1872) that "the natural drift among the poor is towards virtue" (45).

Child savers generally shared Brace's rhetoric of progress when it came to children but were less optimistic about adults, particularly when it came to Eastern Europeans. But even child saving was bound up with racist typologies of the exotic and the feral and, like other discourses of social hygiene and sanitation, tracked the criminal poor in the name of pest control. Although they do not consider child saving specifically, Peter Stallybrass and Allon White demonstrate how thoroughly the period's literature of urban reform drew comparisons between specific animals (pigs and rats especially) and specific populations of the body politic (the Irish, the "native" poor, and so forth). Alarms about street children had been sounded in early-nineteenth-century England and Europe; street children were routinely described as "street Arabs" and "street rats."[11] Through a web of legal, medical, literary, and social science writings, the laboring classes of America were similarly depicted as subhuman.[12] Animal analogies were especially popular in America.[13] In his exposé of New York slum life, *How the Other Half Lives* (1890), Jacob Riis details the habits of the young street Arab and likens him to the weasel ("which, among all the predatory beasts, he most resembles"), to rabbits, even to "the fleet-flooted mountain goat" and other "herding" forms of wildlife (148–50). Not coincidentally did Riis support Brace's projects.

Like Riis, Brace describes slum children as feral in *The Dangerous Classes of New York.* "Sometimes they seem to me," he writes, "like what the police call them, 'street rats,' who gnawed at the foundations of society, and scampered away when light was brought near them" (97). The rat, of course, has its own troubled history of representation, as much tainted by its association with the urban poor as vice versa. Brace brackets "street rats" with quotation marks, as if to signal his doubt about such a phrase, but he repeats it nonetheless, rarely holding back in this sensationalistic book. He attributes the condition of slum kids to nurture as well as nature but still thinks them biologically inferior. Even as he expresses faith in their ability to grow a character, he likens them to "a swarm of cockroaches" (176).

In response to urban crisis, Brace, Riis, and other social reformers in America advocated not the redistribution of wealth but a change in individual circumstance, achieved by relocating the street rat from his natural habitat (the slum) to boy work institutions and to the great outdoors. "From the lodging-houses and the schools," reports Riis, speaking of the work of the CAS and other agencies, "are drawn the battalions of young emigrants that go every year to homes in the Far West, to grow up self-supporting men and women safe from the temptations and the vice of the city" (156). This strategy, officially known as "placing out," was an ambitious undertaking.[14]

To argue for the efficacy of placing out and the conversion of the slum child more generally, Brace wrote a number of essays and sketches, among them "Wolf-Reared Children" (1882). In this sketch, Brace abandons the street rat language of *The Dangerous Classes* in favor of a more flexible rhetoric of wolf-boys. He begins by outlining the history of the wolf-boy in British India, appealing to Ball's *Jungle Life in India.* Although his language is more tentative than Ball's when he summarizes the wolf-boy literature, Brace uses the motif to advance his own agenda and assert proto-anthropological authority. He casts New York as an urban jungle and acknowledges that New York's "wolf-boys" were not actually raised by wolves but rather resemble the wolf-boys of India in their inhumanity and savage desperation. These children are "born to hunger, and cruel treatment," live "in miserable dens and holes," and "are as ignorant of love and hope, and of the missions, and churches, and schools of this city as are the infants found in the wolves' dens of the mountains of Oude" (543–44). They have been "taught only in the schools of poverty, vice, and crime," and their "ways are not our ways." They have "wolfish habits," and their feral brains make them "more cunning, more dangerous, than the animal" (544).

Fortunately, "they can be saved and made into reasonable human beings. Would you like to hear how this is done? Well, here comes one of the wolf-reared children to the office of the Children's Aid Society, in Fourth street, New York." This is Pickety, the urban wolf-boy, with eyes "bright and cunning" and a face "so dirty and brown that you hardly know what the true color is" (544–45). Pickety's savior is the benevolent Mr. Macy, who has much experience with street boys.[15] Mr. Macy sends young Pickety down to one of Brace's lodging houses, at 287 East Broadway, administered by a superintendent, Mr. Calder, and of course a matron, Mrs. Calder. The Calders in fact did work for Brace; Mr. Calder was superintendent at the lodging house in Rivington Street in the early 1870s and may well have been in charge of the East Broadway center. There Pickety is bathed and clothed; he is given a new shirt, but not new trousers, and thus "his hastily formed plan of slipping away with a whole suit of new clothes is nipped in the bud" (547). The lodging house is both home and schoolhouse, featuring a dormitory, a library, and a conservatory. In the accompanying sketches, plants and flowers adorn its halls and staircases; as Brace explains in chapter 27 of *The Dangerous Classes,* the "ministry of flowers" works wonders. Brace consistently likens the house to a ship, recalling the perilous passage of immigrant families across the Atlantic. This ship, however, is securely anchored and in tip-top shape. The dormitory is "clean as a ship's deck" (549), and careful "watch" is kept. At night, the superintendent lectures Pickety and the other little wolf-boys on honesty and obedience to God and guides their secular lessons. Such sessions were conducted at night because most of these children worked from eight to ten hours during the day, despite the efforts of many reformers, Brace among them, to modify such practices.

Under Mr. Calder's care, Pickety quickly learns to read and write, and most important, to do his sums. Apparently the lodging house is not only a (nautical) home for wayward boys; it is a financial and career support center and includes a "savings bank" and a fund for starting boys in business. Not wishing to be a "pauper," Pickety gets into the newspaper business, selling the *Telegram* and the *Daily News.* Gradually our lad embraces a "straightforward and manly life" and transfers his savings to a real bank (551–52). He loses "much of his wolfish, savage nature" and does "not wish to go back to his jungle and den." He even begins "to have a desire to earn and own something, and to get on in the world" (552). Pleased with his handiwork,

Mr. Calder explains that "the best possible employment for a young working-boy in this country was farming," and that he should venture out West (552). In *The Dangerous Classes*, Brace similarly insists that "the best of all Asylums for the outcast child, is the *farmer's home*" (225).

So Pickety heads to Kansas, where eventually he becomes a successful farmer and even "a very good scholar" (554), much like Uncle Benny from *Farming for Boys*. Pickety's subsequent letter to Mr. Macy is articulate and cheerful; he thrives in the great outdoors. The final two illustrations make up a before-and-after sketch: the first depicts the original wolf-boy, dirty and ragged, smoking a cigarette; the second features a stout, well-dressed, bespectacled gentleman surveying an idyllic countryside (the caption reads "A Thriving Farmer on His Own Land"). This transformation has been accomplished, sums up Brace, "through the civilizing, Christian influences that had been thrown around him" (554). In The *Dangerous Classes,* Brace speaks fondly of the "lambs" of Cottage Place; Pickety has simply been a lamb in wolf's clothing.

The case of Pickety dramatizes the realities of poverty, but too close an association of Pickety with the Indian wolf-boys of Oude (who, unlike Mowgli, remain wolfish) may remind readers of the hopeless "street rats" of *The Dangerous Classes of New York*. Brace is thus quick to imply that Pickety is poor and badly trained but decidedly human and even vaguely Caucasian. Most of the street children placed out by the society were native-born Americans and so-called old immigrants, children of German, Irish, and English descent. We know from his ethnological work that Brace had less faith in the recuperative powers of other groups, notably people of Mediterranean and East European descent, and here, perhaps, he draws a distinction between the permanent street rat and the redeemable wolf-boy, as well as between the wolf-boy of India and his counterpart in urban America. "Wolf-Reared Children" hints at no particular race or ethnicity; we know only that Pickety later takes a Christian name.

For Brace, the American wolf-boy is redeemable as long as his urban environment can be changed, and as long as that boy is not too distinctly or stubbornly alien. While New York might drive anyone wild, the damage may not be permanent. Pickety seems finally indistinguishable from the middle-class subject of boyology, because he seeks professional help, and because he takes an interest in money. In his writings, at least, Brace struggles to reconcile an older, more dismissive tradition of feral figuration (the street rat) with a newer feral sensibility that seems to acknowledge, if in very select terms, the importance of immigrants to the national mix.

Were he actually middle-class, of course, Pickety could enjoy a life of relative leisure, for while the street child who steals or simply works to survive is judged to be degenerate, the Bad Boy I discussed in chapter 2 is expected to be greedy and lazy: "it exactly suits the temperament of a real boy to be very busy about nothing" (Warner, *Being a Boy*, 113). As a "criminal" and "outlaw" worthy of "punishment" (*Penrod*, 76), he is an entrepreneur on the make. The boy's selfishness enables him to survive in the ruthless business world for which he is inevitably bound. These traits are apparently not outgrown but rather conserved, and even lower-class boys have their pecuniary impulses. Thorstein Veblen's *The Theory of the Leisure Class* (1899) describes the "tendency of the pecuniary life . . . to conserve the barbaric temperament, but with the substitution of fraud and prudence . . . [for] that predilection for physical damage" typical of early man (125). Veblen describes this continuity as the "hereditary present," and his challenge to economic applications of Darwinism ironically depends on his faith in recapitulation. Unlike Emerson and the Bad Boy writers, Veblen criticizes entrepreneurial self-interest, but like them believes it boyish. Veblen in fact organizes his tenth chapter around a discussion of the "predaceous features of boy life" that drive grown men to hunt and play sports (196).

In much social science writing of the day, capitalism is imagined as both cause and effect of the Caucasian boy's recapitulatory development. Drawing from Malthus, Darwin, and Spencer, William Graham Sumner insists in his laissez-faire manifesto *What Social Classes Owe to Each Other* (1883) that "from the first step that man made above the brute, the thing which made his civilization possible was capital. Every step of capital won made the next step possible, up to the present hour" (61–62). Biologically reenacting history, boys—even underclass boys—naturally love to accumulate, even if they have to be instructed in the proper methods of banking. "Do we believe that the child recapitulates the history of the race?" ask Kline and France as late as 1928. "If so we may not be surprised to find the passion for property-getting a natural one" (Thayer, *The Passing of Recitation*, 64). Forbush puts it succinctly: "A boy is capitalized hope" (20). Riis agrees; if the boy is treated as "an independent trader," granted both "trust" and trade, then "habits of thrift and ambitious industry are seen to grow up" (153).

But if the white boy became almost a synonym for capital (and "character" a form of cultural capital), laissez-faire capitalism made it clear that for every hopeful Pickety, there's a lifelong pauper. Street rats will never evolve, and it's okay to abuse them. As Sumner patiently explains, "a man who can command another man's labor and self-denial for the support of his own existence is a privileged person of the highest species conceivable on earth" (15). While child savers recognized that circumstance influenced one's station in life, they also deferred to a naturalistic narrative of competition and survival that shored up as well as disrupted ethno-evolutionary perspectives on race and class. Brace's rat-wolf distinctions qualify his cheerful story of conversion.

Revising the usual critical scenario of middle-class disdain toward and control of the working poor, Keith Gandal argues that during this period, the slum became a sort of frontier space for the middle class. He suggests that the middle class emulated the poor, aspiring to their industry and adopting their fondness for popular entertainments. While it's clear from the placing-out movement that not all middle-class urban reformers embraced the slum, Gandal's work helps explain why the feral has been appropriated as a middle-class discourse. Brace's own work pulls in both directions— against such a refashioning (as in the "street rat" rhetoric) and in favor of it (as in Pickety's makeover).

"Wolf-Reared Children" reads much like the typical Horatio Alger Jr. novel, with its white-bread protagonist succeeding against all odds, with a little help from male mentors. Brace's success story is coterminous with Alger's fiction and helped standardize stories of lower-class boys trying to make good. We might argue that Alger, unlike Brace, gave up on the farm and accepted city life, but the continuities are still clear. Alger's Ragged Dick, for instance, is feral by his own admission; "I can't read much more'n a pig," he tells his friend Fosdick, "and my writin' looks like hens' tracks" (105); soon enough, however, Ragged Dick becomes Richard Hunter, Esq. Like many of Alger's titles, *Ragged Dick* (1868) strikes me as an amalgam of the Bad Boy novel (which it predates, actually) and Brace's conversion story. Missing from *Ragged Dick,* however, are the pervasive animal comparisons typical of forensic writing and the feral tale. Nor is Ragged Dick portrayed as a boy-savage, perhaps because boy-savagery is so thoroughly linked with white male identity, or because Alger recognized that such language would not help him redeem the street boy. In any case, Alger's work represents one strain of popular boy's literature, which by the early twentieth century was produced largely by syndicates.

Incidentally, the feral tale survives as a forensic genre of urban displacement and despair, as evidenced by the contemporary literature on the "mole people" of New York City—people living in subway tunnels, hidden vaults, and other forgotten underground spaces. Jennifer Toth brought the phenomenon to national attention with her account *The Mole People: Life in the Tunnels beneath New York City* (1993), and while not everyone found her account persuasive, others produced similar such studies. Titles focusing on homeless children and teenagers include Jim Goldberg's moving photo-essay *Raised by Wolves* (1993).[16] These accounts are more sympathetic to the plight of the homeless, but as exposés, they are indebted to the classic quasi-forensic photojournalism of Riis and Lewis Hine, among others.

Animal Spirits

There seemed to be a very considerable class of lads in New York who bore to the busy, wealthy world about them something of the same relation which Indians bear to the civilized Western settlers. They had no settled home, and lived on the outskirts of society, their hand against every man's pocket, and every man looking on them as natural enemies; their wits sharpened like those of a savage, and their principles often no better. Christianity reared its temples over them, and Civilization was carrying on its great work, while they—a happy race of little heathens and barbarians—plundered, or frolicked, or led their roving life, far beneath.

—Charles Loring Brace, *The Dangerous Classes of New York*

Ours was a life that called for strength, quick wit, and skill. But we were as much at home as the little fellow who sells newspapers on a busy street dodging here and there between swift-moving traffic. I believe, though, that outdoor training is very valuable and that every boy should have the advantage of living a clean outdoor life.

—Luther Standing Bear, *My Indian Boyhood*

Taken from texts published nearly sixty years apart, these two excerpts suggest the persistence, if also the flexibility, of a set of feral equivalencies. For both Brace and Luther Standing Bear, the street boy and the Indian are similar, if not quite synonymous. Brace, trying to identify street boys, takes Native Americans as a standard reference point, as nomadic, uncultured, and boyish. The children of these diverse groups resemble the equally homogenized "Indians" in Brace's mind. For Standing Bear, a Dakota Sioux who left his tribe to attend the Carlisle Indian School in Pennsylvania and became a successful writer, it's the street boy who is a familiar if now positive figure, industrious and cheerfully at home in his wild environment. Through that boy, he seems to think, we can access the Indian. Standing Bear was writing in the 1930s, when attitudes toward Native Americans had shifted toward the romantic. While he implies that mainstream culture could learn from the Sioux, there are no Others to speak of in his memoir; his plucky "little fellow" looks more like Alger's Ragged Dick than Brace's street rats.[17]

Aside from scattered references such as this, Brace does not concern himself with the Native American. Even so, his analogy makes clear that for him at least, the drama of the feral boy is the everyday life of indigenous people. For Brace, Native Americans are not merely nomadic; they exist without and outside of civilization, even if they form a culture of sorts. In a sense, Standing Bear agrees, if for different historical reasons; *My Indian Boyhood* is not only autobiography but also elegy, a tribute to a dying, if noble, culture, much like the farm boy elegies that I discussed in chapter 1.

He ends the book with a description of his first and last buffalo hunt, writing that "it lives only in my memory, for the days of the buffalo are over" (190). Standing Bear has a difficult task, to re-create the tribal life that had largely disappeared by the 1930s. *My Indian Boyhood* appeared just five years after Zane Grey's *The Vanishing American* (1925) became a motion picture in 1926, and although the 1930s witnessed a resurgence of interest in the conservation of Native people, the force of the vanishing American trope in literary and popular culture, as documented by Brian Dippie, remained strong. In fact, the publication of memoirs such as Standing Bear's might be understood as a literary form of conservation, consonant with the Indian Reorganization Act of 1934, an effort to restore tribal lands. As the twentieth century began, more and more memoirs of Indian childhood appeared, suggesting that an ideology of boyhood especially helped "preserve" Native life.

From very early on in our national history, Native Americans were associated with an indigenous, masculine Americanism, even as a competing ideology of an uninhabited landscape justified their extermination. Their likenesses were put on our money and our state seals, and many whites, Thomas Jefferson among them, imagined that white-Native intermarriage was good national policy. This nativist vision of American selfhood later underwrote boy work efforts, as Philip J. Deloria's fine study *Playing Indian* makes clear. Deloria suggests that boy workers like Ernest Thompson Seton developed a two-part strategy for appropriating the Native American. First, the Native American was imagined as "exterior" to, and insulated from, modern culture, uncompromised in his authenticity and masculinity. Second, a correspondence was asserted between that "exterior Indian" and the inner native of the white man—or in Emerson's phrase, the "aboriginal Self." This correspondence represented a solution to the dilemma of modernity, which "centered on finding ways to preserve the integrity of the boundaries that marked exterior and authentic Indians, while gaining access to organic Indian purity in order to make it one's own" (Deloria, *Playing Indian*, 115). That dilemma has origins in various schemes of self making, among them the remythification of the feral.

Although recent scholarship has shown that as early as the 1830s, Native Americans themselves debated their place in the union, it's also true that by midcentury, Native Americans were understood as an internal problem rather than an independent population. In 1849 the Bureau of Indian Affairs was transferred from the War Department to the Department of the Interior. American ethnology was increasingly a governmental tool in the resettling of Native Americans on reservations as well as farms, suggesting a further interiorization in terms of physical space.[18] Assimilation was generally the goal of schools for Native Americans, such as the famous Carlisle Indian School. Assimilation, of course, looks pretty progressive in the context of genocide and slavery, but assimilation had its own custodial impulses, among them the interiorization of the native. Thus an often melancholic language of encapsulation and incorporation pervades proto-modernist Native American writings around the turn of the century, especially those offered in the name of boyhood. As I imply throughout the book, children's literature sometimes functions as racial elegy, or conversely, such elegy has sometimes been declared children's literature. The texts of boyhood at the turn of the century in effect memorialize lost American boyhoods.

As an example, I turn to another Dakota Sioux, Charles Alexander Eastman, who devoted his life to Native American affairs. I concentrate on Eastman rather than Luther Standing Bear because Eastman's work appeared earlier and, like Brace's "Wolf-Reared Children," was serialized in *St. Nicholas.* Still described as the finest literary magazine ever produced for children, that magazine was very much a New York operation, named, in fact, for the city's patron saint. From 1873 to 1905, when it was edited by Mary Mapes Dodge, *St. Nicholas* focused on urban issues, including philanthropic outreach to the poor. The magazine championed such philanthropy alongside the preservation of indigenous cultures—a dual emphasis far from coincidental. Brace was invited to write for *St. Nicholas* and used it to promote his vision. While Eastman likens his boyhood self to neither an energetic newsboy nor a feral boy per se, his own conversion story is not so different from the one that Brace tells. In *Indian Boyhood* (1902), Eastman conserves "Indianness" (as he prefers it) in the eternal present of the boy book.

In 1873, a year after Brace published *The Dangerous Classes,* a fifteen-year-old Dakota Sioux boy named Ohiyesa was suddenly reclaimed by his long-lost father and whisked away from his Manitoba home to the United States. His father, who now called himself Jacob, had converted to Christianity and was farming in South Dakota. "I felt as if I were dead and traveling to the Spirit Land," Eastman later wrote, "for now all my old ideas were to give place to new ones, and my life was to be entirely different from that of the past" (*Indian Boyhood,* 288). In time, Ohiyesa, already part Caucasian through his mother, became Charles Alexander Eastman, a writer, lecturer, physician, and Boy Scout and YMCA leader. Eastman spent his adult life mediating between Native American and white culture(s), through his lectures, his agency work, and his eleven books.

As attending physician at several reservations, Eastman came into conflict with government-appointed agents. He witnessed and documented the infamous confrontation at Wounded Knee, in which a nonviolent Sioux protest was misinterpreted and met with massacre. To the dismay of many, he criticized his employer, the Bureau of Indian Affairs, even calling for its abolition. He supported Native American citizenship and in 1911 helped found the Society of American Indians, a pan-Indian organization devoted to health care and education. Despite his conviction in the integrity of indigenous life, and his determination to preserve that life in his writings, Eastman advocated assimilation. His acculturation was widely praised, and he toured the lecture circuit as had ex-slaves and other "ex-Indians" before him, testifying to the transformative power of Anglo-American culture. Eastman was an ideal spokesman, a distinguished graduate of Dartmouth College and Boston Medical School, fluent in English and familiar with Greek, Latin, French, and German. The only way that Eastman could overcome his cultural effacement was to recast his indigenous heritage as a past life.

Eastman's first autobiographical book, *Indian Boyhood,* describes his early life among the Sioux, from 1858 to 1873 (until age fifteen). By 1858, the year of Eastman's birth, most of the Dakota Sioux land had been transferred to white settlers through various treaties, in exchange for rations of food and money, often delivered late or not at all. The increasing presence of missionaries, traders, and military personnel pressured the Dakota Sioux to abandon their heritage. Eastman's two memoirs attempt to celebrate that heritage, emphasizing to white readers the complexity of Sioux religion, government, schooling, and family life. Eastman acknowledged that he wrote *Indian Boyhood* to entertain his own children and to document a culture already lost. *Indian Boyhood* is similar to other Native American memoirs, such as Zitkala-Sa's *American Indian Stories.* But Zitkala-Ša's sketches appeared in the *Atlantic Monthly,* not in a children's magazine like *St. Nicholas.* Moreover, *Indian Boyhood* was promoted and received as a boy book.

Like those books, *Indian Boyhood* mediates childhood through not merely the nostalgic voice of the adult but also the voice of the literary boy worker. Eastman opens with the query "What boy would not be an Indian for a while when he thinks of the freest life in the world?" (2). Such fantasy is a key feature of the Bad Boy genre especially. In *A Boy's Town* Howells tells us that "if they could, the boys would rather have been Indians than anything else" (149). Eastman's emphasis in *Indian Boyhood* on Native stoicism reassures readers that cultural effacement is painful but endurable. He often refers to himself in the third person and describes his fellow Sioux as "primitive housekeeper[s]" (238), "aboriginal maids" (240), and "savage philosophers" (279). He documents rites of courtship and mourning, and calls the Sioux bear dance "an entertainment, a religious rite, a method of treating disease—all in one" (172).

Both *Indian Boyhood* and *The Soul of an Indian* (1911) emphasize the Native American's affinity with animals, even if they stop short of invoking the feral tale per se. In *Indian Boyhood* we discover that Ohiyesa is being raised by his tough and savvy grandmother, Uncheedah. "As a motherless child, I always regarded my good grandmother as the wisest of guides and the best of protectors," writes Eastman (21). As it happens, young Ohiyesa (then known as Hakadah) is adopted by nature at large. He has "extended conversations in an unknown dialect with birds and red squirrels" (8). Birds would often "alight on my cradle in the woods" (8). He has a pet grizzly bear. Uncheedah routinely frightens him with tales of child-abducting owls.

Eastman emphasizes that in Sioux culture, humans are not the only creatures to shape the behavior of native children; certain kinds of animals are also important, even conferring gifts on the unborn or "impressing" them with unfortunate traits. In preparation for hunting, "the leading animals are introduced," presented as friends who kindly offer their bodies for sustenance (50–51). Boys are encouraged not just to respect but to *become* the animals they hunt, to "be as cool as the animal himself" (54). These and other examples of animal proximity give way to the story of a boy and his dog. For his first offering, Hakadah must sacrifice his beloved pet. In this section of the book, we see the eight year old tearfully relinquishing the dog to the Great Mystery.

In *The Soul of an Indian,* Eastman retells for his largely non-Native audience a Sioux creation myth, the story of Ish-ná-e-cha-ge, or the First-Born, made in the image of man yet superior to him. The First-Born walks and talks peacefully among the animal people. He soon grows weary, however, and forms for himself a companion—not a woman fashioned from his rib but "the Little Boy Man," "an innocent child, trusting and helpless," created from a splinter in the First-Born's toe (124). The First-Born's duty is to guide the Little Boy Man through life. The animals love Little Boy Man; his only rival is the trickster Unk-to-mee, the Spider, who prophesies that one day the playful boy will rule over all of them. Eventually the Spider sows dissent among the animal people, and they make plans to kill Little Boy Man; this is the creation myth's fall, a fall not between our first parents and God but between the boy-man and the animals.

The forensic-anthropological impulse is even more pronounced in Eastman's second memoir, *From the Deep Woods to Civilization* (1916), and in his intervening volumes on Native folklore.[19] *From the Deep Woods to Civilization* chronicles his transformation from savage nomad into white citizen, made possible by his mastery of English and his conversion to Christianity. Affectionately Eastman calls his boyhood self a "wild cub" (23) and recalls its "savage gentleness" (67). Because that self was also his Sioux self, the disappearance of the Native likely seemed to be the inevitable result of growing up. Pursuing ever higher levels of education, Eastman met illustrious men of culture such as Matthew Arnold, Longfellow, Francis Parkman, and appropriately, Emerson; later he also encountered Twain, Howells, and G. Stanley Hall. Eastman praised Emersonian notions of "industry," "economy," "thrift," and self-reliance.

Given the historical pressures, it is not surprising that while Eastman devoted his early career to reservation medicine and political activism, he spent his final decades working for the Young Men's Christian Association and the Boy Scouts of America. Eastman organized forty-three Native American chapters of the YMCA, converting Sioux people to Christianity. He helped establish the Boy Scouts of America, which emerged not only out of Baden-Powell's program but also from American boy work programs such as Daniel Beard's Sons of Daniel Boone and Ernest Thompson Seton's Woodcraft Indians. Seton, whose *Two Little Savages: Being the Adventures of Two Boys Who Lived as Indians and What They Learned* appeared the same year as *Indian Boyhood*, is generally credited with incorporating Native American practices into Scouting, but Eastman also deserves mention. He also founded a summer camp in New Hampshire, where his presence lent legitimacy to Nativist activities. Eastman has vanished from the scene of institutional boy work, remembered now as a boy book author and folklorist; as Frances Karttunen puts it, "he has his real monument in edition after edition of the Boy Scout handbook" (*Between Worlds*, 169).

Whiteness in the Steaming Grotto

In Brace's "Wolf-Reared Children," the figurative wolf-boy, once taken from his hostile environment, is transformed first into a farm boy and then into a successful farmer. In Eastman's two-part autobiography, the adult man of culture recollects his Native boyhood, embodying the principles of evolution that for so long underwrote the developmental story of boyhood. Both narratives are nostalgic in their desire for the simplicity of boyhood. That nostalgia, however, looks forward as much as backward, in the same sense that modernism depends on primitivism for its sense of the future.

By the early twentieth century, the feral boy had come to represent the ideal American male self, very much in the tradition of Emerson's "aboriginal Self" and the literary boy-savage, but also thanks to the American appropriation of the feral tale that I have been tracing. Tarzan, of course, is our most representative jungle man—even if he's English, not American—and much has been written about Tarzan in relation to modernist primitivism and political conservatism. Eric Cheyfitz, for example, reads the series as a fiercely Anglo-Saxonist response to the second wave of immigration in America, and Tarzan as a reconfiguration of James Fenimore Cooper's

Natty Bumppo and other faux-native figures.[20] But another jungle character, Bomba the Jungle Boy, is a better example of the British-derived tradition of the feral tale, or of the wolf-boy's transatlantic makeover and association with American popular literature of boyhood.

Unlike Tarzan, Bomba is a boy, and he remains a boy, in keeping with the static character demands of series fiction. Moreover, Bomba is not actually a feral boy, only a jungle boy; he's neither raised by animals nor isolated from other humans. Like Tarzan, Bomba lives in a largely male and homosocial world, but his relationships with adult male figures are not as wrenchingly Oedipal as are Tarzan's. The series is not only a (more) "juvenile" variant on the jungle theme but also an instance of feral-tale boyology consolidation, in which the story of a normal if unusual boyhood displaces any real engagement with difference or singularity (the usual hallmark of the feral tale). Moreover, the production history of the Bomba series makes clear the transition from single authorship to syndicate collaboration, as the first ten volumes were apparently written by Edward Stratemeyer himself before his death halfway through the series.

In the late 1920s, the Stratemeyer Syndicate introduced several boy superheroes that led out their lives in exotic locales. The most successful of the bunch was Bomba, a white boy stranded in the upper Amazon. Written in fact by Stratemeyer, the series was promoted as the work of "Roy Rockwood," who had brought young readers Dave Dashaway, the Great Marvel series, and the Speedway Boys (Prager, *Rascals at Large*, 310). The first book, *Bomba the Jungle Boy*, appeared in 1926; the last, *Bomba the Jungle Boy in the Steaming Grotto*, in 1938. The series also inspired twelve films starring Johnny Sheffield (and Otis the monkey).[21] The Bomba series was part of the early-twentieth-century boy book industry; many such series were produced by the Stratemeyer Syndicate and other outfits. Thus we have left behind the genteel world of literary boy work or boy authorship for a more institutional model.

Given the preoccupations of the period, it's not surprising that the Bomba series is set in Latin America; especially in the later volumes, we see reflections of both "good neighbor" trade policy and various imperialist ventures. Although the United States had withdrawn its military from all Latin American nations by 1936, it had not relinquished the goal of political and economic dominance in the hemisphere. Like the stories of Mowgli and Tarzan, the Bomba books have little to say about imperialism directly, but Bomba's frequent struggles with real natives and his emergent white pride suggest a familiar consciousness.

Like Mowgli and Tarzan, Bomba is a striking physical specimen. Although he looks older, he is only a boy; in the series he ages from fourteen to eighteen. His fine features and athletic physique offer a sharp contrast to the sorry wolf-boy of British India. Like Tarzan, Bomba manages to be more native than the natives without being mistaken as such. Armed with his wits and some primitive weapons, Bomba battles a daunting array of jungle beasts, including anacondas, alligators, boas, cooanaradis, jaguars, piranha, and vampire bats. He defies poisonous and mood-altering flora, including the marijuana plant. Excepting the occasional Spaniard and generic half-breed, Bomba's human enemies are savage headhunters and cannibals; every volume introduces a more terrible tribe. Mountains move, volcanoes erupt, and rivers flood, but Bomba perseveres, always speaking modestly of himself in the third person. In the words of one of his white admirers, Bomba has the "body of a boy and the heart of a hero!" (*Swamp of Death*, 69).

Unlike Mowgli and Tarzan, Bomba grew up under the care of a white man, Cody Casson, a reclusive naturalist who has since grown feeble and feebleminded. We learn in the first volume that Casson gave Bomba the rudiments of an education and promised to tell the boy about his mother and father later, but sadly for the lad, Casson suffered an accident and never recovered his memory. Bomba searches for information about his past as Casson fades in and out of consciousness. Bomba becomes his caretaker and is forever clasping Casson to his breast as he whisks him out of one burning hut after another. Our hero has no foster mother and few female pals, only the squaw Pipina and Sobrinini, a crazed ex-European opera diva turned snake-woman.

Bomba longs for his unknown parents and the company of white men who, in his dreamy words, "slap each other on the back." Although he speaks various animal dialects and is fond of his animal friends—among them the parrots Kiki and Woowoo, the monkey Doto, and Polulu the puma—he clearly feels superior to them:

> "Bomba loves you all. He does not want to leave you, but he must go. He will always think of you, and some day he may come back to you. But Bomba must go. He must find the men who have souls, the souls that are awake. For Bomba has a soul. And he must find the white men. For Bomba is white."
> He tore the puma skin aside and displayed his chest.
> "Look, Woowoo! Look Kiki! Look, Doto!" he cried in an ecstasy of joy and pride. "Look all of you. I will tell Polulu too. I am white! Bomba is white!" (*Bomba the Jungle Boy*, 204)

The Bomba books appeal to a distinctly American form of homosocial quest narrative. They combine this narrative with a family plot. Just as Huck has his faithful Jim and Ishmael his Polynesian pal Queequeg, Bomba relies on his devoted native companions. When, for instance, he tears himself away from bosom buddy Gibo in *Bomba the Jungle Boy among the Slaves* (1924), they "parted with a long look into each other's eyes that told of the strong affection that united them" (86–87).

In the Bomba books, the family plot is equally homosocial, even homoerotic. Unlike the Bad Boy books, the series emphasizes the importance of the father. Although Bomba lovingly carries around a portrait of his mother, it is the father who dominates Bomba's consciousness. As is typical of boyology, other male authority figures stand in for the father. Casson, of course, is Bomba's most important father figure and boy worker, and in the first ten books, Bomba encounters other white men who eventually lead him to his lost father, and who contrast sharply with half-breeds who claim paternity but are false fathers. In the first volume, for instance, in a chapter called "Beaten Off," Bomba saves the lives of Gillis and Dorn, two English rubber hunters. Bomba adores these men of culture and commerce. Only his dedication to Casson prevents him from going with Gillis and Dorn, who give Bomba their affection, and better yet, two dangerous white male weapons: a pistol and a harmonica.

These and subsequent white men, however, are not just father figures; they are also learned explorers and scientists, who regard Bomba as a fascinating case study. Even the amnesia-plagued Casson is a famous scholar and naturalist, who originally went to the Amazon to do research. To the degree that they preside over and supervise Bomba, they recall boyology and the child study movement led by G. Stanley Hall. Although he seems extraordinarily capable on his own, in his various encounters with white men, Bomba is pronounced "an untutored child of nature" (*Bomba the Jungle Boy*, 20), a "creature of the wild, inarticulate" (83), and "wholly devoid of knowledge" (*Swamp of Death*, 28–29). For these men, Bomba is simultaneously noble savage, ascendant white man, and ignorant boy.

Bomba is finally reunited with his real father in the tenth volume, *Bomba the Jungle Boy and the Lost Explorers* (1930). In that volume, a turning point in the series, Bomba rescues several white male explorers from a jaguar, a giant tarantula, and other menaces. Their party includes a wounded—and unconscious—man who turns out to be Andrew Bartow, Bomba's father, who has been searching for his boy all these years. Bomba somehow knows this man is special; he is "thrilled by the touch of those lean, bronzed fingers on his face" (*Lost Explorers*, 106). The other explorers are in turn mesmerized by the handsome Bomba, even "temporarily hypnotized . . . into forgetting the dangers that pressed upon them from every side" (110). In the end, Bomba is reunited with his parents and spirited off to that urban jungle, New York City (the setting of so many contemporary cinematic feral tales).[22]

The volume in which Bomba and his father are reunited was apparently the last written personally by Stratemeyer before his death. At that point, other writers from the syndicate took over, suggesting a shift from a more traditionally authorial relationship to the boy book to a more institutional one. But even in the beginning, the Bomba books were not vehicles for authorial pride or prestige; mass-produced series books are rarely "about" an author's vision or style—and certainly not about his own boyhood. The Bomba books, then, do not constitute a traditionally literary culture of boy work, as do the Bad Boy books; by the 1920s, boy authorship was no longer so respected a practice, and boy books were finding a wider audience that actually included children, much like the dime novels of yesteryear.

The final volume, *Bomba the Jungle Boy in the Steaming Grotto* (1938), is a rambling, surreal narrative of shipwreck and survival, starring our hardy hero, now eighteen years old, and introducing Norwegian sailors, an American castaway and his foulmouthed baby hyena, and fire-breathing serpents reminiscent of Komodo dragons.[23] By this point, Bomba is decidedly adult and nonnative. Although we are assured in the last line of the book that he loves the jungle "above civilization" (209), Bomba thinks like a man of science and industry. He discovers the medicinal qualities of plants and nuts. He determines to capture one of the strange serpents: "If these creatures were of value on the island, why should they not prove so in coal mines, or in places where gas was a menace to human life?" (165). If not that, he figures, the creature belongs in a zoo (166). Or scientists might want to kill and dissect it (208).

Bomba has no troubled depths or dark desires, only a longing for family. His wildness is entirely contained. Bomba's character is the static sort of boys' series fiction. Whereas the wolf-boy retains some animal affinity and cultural otherness in the name of complexity—in literature as in Freudian psychoanalysis—the jungle boy of popular fiction represents an alternative sort of remythification, nearly a denial of otherness altogether aside from the most cartoonish of contrasts. At this point, the feral tale looks nearly identical to boyology, which likewise denies complexity or ambivalence even as it insists on an essential boyhood that only authorized workers can access.

4. Father Flanagan's Boys Town

> But Billy came; and it was like a Catholic priest striking peace in an
> Irish shindy. Not that he preached to them or said or did anything in
> particular; but a virtue went out of him, sugaring the sour ones.
> —Herman Melville, *Billy Budd, Sailor*

So far I've described boyology as a literary and institutional form of boy work and shown how boyology and the feral tale became virtually indistinguishable in and through particular genres of boys' popular literature as well as character-building organizations. At issue in my next chapter is the harmony of boyology and the feral tale within and beyond psychoanalysis. But first I want to address another important venue of American boy work, one overlooked in histories of character building: Boys Town, now known as Boys and Girls Town. Founded in 1917 by Father Edward Joseph Flanagan, an Irish immigrant priest, to provide safe haven for abandoned and abused boys, Boys Town quickly captured the American imagination, thanks to Flanagan's inventive outreach and especially the success of the 1938 film *Boys Town*, directed by Norman Taurog.[1]

Boys Town is ideologically more affiliated with ministerial child-saving efforts than with middle-class character building. Whereas Brace's Children's Aid Society and other such organizations were administered by Protestants and ministered primarily to Protestant children, Boys Town represents a Catholic tradition of boy work. Even so, Boys Town has always enjoyed a certain remove from the Catholic Church, and many of its programs are comparable to those sponsored by Protestant child care institutions. In fact, Flanagan, supported by the church but operating largely on his own, helped ease the tension between Protestant and Catholic child welfare work. As a result, Boys Town is one of the best-known child care institutions in the nation, and Father Flanagan is perhaps our most famous boy worker. By the 1940s, Flanagan was "internationally recognized as the world's foremost expert on boys' training and youth care" (*Boys Town: Memories and Dreams*, 11). He remains familiar long after the character builders are forgotten; even the flamboyant Baden-Powell is obscure by comparison.

That a priest should serve as a boy worker isn't surprising, since the priest is already institutionally presented as a "father." Presumably the priest does not need an affiliation with boy work institutions (which are generally middle-class and Protestant in orientation). At the same time, as the recent sex abuse scandals in the Catholic Church have made painfully clear, the priest's authority as a boy worker is shaky at best, since his relationship to children is more paternal or avuncular than professional in the secular, institutional sense of the term. I am not implicating either Father Flanagan or Boys Town in the abuse cases that have proliferated in the last several years. As far as I know, there are no cases pending against the men of Boys Town, and Father Valentine J. Peter, the current director of Boys Town, has written a response to the sex abuse crisis entitled "We Stand with the Children," which emphasizes his commitment to protecting child victims and the truth. I suggest, rather, that the boy work of Boys Town depends on a cult of priestly character that is neither middle-class nor institutional (nor, obviously, Protestant) in form and is thus subject to greater suspicion, or at least a different kind of suspicion, in the current moment of paranoia about child abuse. At the same time, as I show in this chapter, Boys Town is understood as an exemplary child care institution, one from which our ostensibly dissolute society can learn.

Because the priest is already seen as an exceptional figure, expected to be celibate and perhaps less stereotypically masculine, any accusation of improper sexuality (perhaps any sexuality at all) threatens to bring the house down. A scoutmaster accused of improper relations, by contrast, is less likely to be seen as representative of Scouting itself, or as an embodiment of Scouting's virtue or vice. Scouting is a notoriously homophobic institution, precisely because anxieties about, as well as confidence in, the adult-child relationship are central to the enterprise. To that degree, the comparison between Scouting and Catholicism holds, and certainly we've lately seen open criticism of Scouting from gay Scouts and scoutmasters alike. The presence of gays in Scouting is a different issue from accusations of sexual abuse, but I suspect that much of the latter is fueled by a general paranoia about same-sex desire. In any case, Scouting is not the church, and even if it collapsed as a social institution, the middle-class project of boy work would likely continue in other guises. More to the immediate point, the scoutmaster's normative masculine character is ensured both by his institutional affiliation and by his status as a family man, whereas the priest's authority derives from the church and from his symbolic remove from ordinary family life.

Most priests, of course, are not boy workers in any official sense. Father Flanagan is exceptional among priests as a boy worker, even if he capitalized on his priestly authority to found Boys Town. And to be a successful boy worker, Flanagan had to demonstrate his resemblance to character builders as well as child savers. In both the 1938 film and the only biography of Flanagan, Fulton and Will Oursler's *Father Flanagan of Boys Town* (1949), Flanagan is thus portrayed as gentle but rugged, in touch with his feminine side but ready to defend Boys Town with his fists as well as his faith. These and other pro-Flanagan vehicles produce a suitably masculine form of sentimentality to legitimate the Boys Town enterprise, akin perhaps to Gibson's muscular "heartology" in *Boyology*, but less immediately dismissive of feminine interest.

That such representation of Flanagan's character is tricky territory becomes clear in the Oursler biography. Published just after Flanagan's sudden death in 1948, *Father Flanagan of Boys Town* is at once an authorized biography of Flanagan, a history of Boys Town through 1948, and a meta–conversion narrative of the boys who encountered Flanagan personally.[2] The Ourslers champion Flanagan as a modern-day saint, using a heroic mode of language that seems, in the contemporary moment, campy and even accusatory. Chapter titles in book 1 alone, for instance, include "A Shepherd Boy with Bleeding Hands," "Banished from Rome," "One with the Apostles," and my favorite sequence, "A Priest among the Dregs," "A Priest and a Little Boy," and finally "A Priest in Court" (chaps. 12–15). Such a sequence might seem ominous to readers today, but the Ourslers are more concerned with assuring us of Flanagan's manliness (charity being so feminizing) than with warding off accusations of sexual vice.[3]

More specifically, they insist that Flanagan embodied the best of both sexes and that his masculinity was never compromised by his more feminine traits. In their eyes, Flanagan is both gentle nurturer and fierce Christian soldier. Although Flanagan routinely called his boys "dears," the Ourslers insist "there was nothing namby-pamby or weakly insipid in this attitude; he was a man of hard common sense" (10). "A tall figure he made, looming and erect even when seated" (21). Here they describe the first encounter of "Stubby," a prototypical lost boy, with the famous priest:

> And Stubby could see and appreciate the power in the pale and rugged face. There was a granite look to him, as if the great brow and long jaw and straight nose had been carved from rock of great strength. And yet, with that visible and unmistakable masculine force and power, there was an almost womanly luster in the soft blue eyes. When necessary, this man could be father and mother both. (21)

The Ourslers also describe the priest's wisdom as intuitive, not grasped by the secular intellectuals or child experts of his day, more akin to the "native wit" of boys (5)—suggesting even an indigenous form of masculine sentimentality, as if Flanagan's work with the "natives" ensures and reflects his own experiences and ideals. Central to the success of Flanagan's boy work is this code of maternal-paternal authority and rugged sentimentality. The 1938 film offers a similar picture of Flanagan, emphasizing his willingness to engage in violent combat on behalf of his cherished boys.

By showing Flanagan's fierce devotion to boys, *Boys Town* affirms what historians have described as a return to paternalism in the diagnosis and treatment of juvenile delinquency in the first two decades of the century. Reform schools had been under serious attack since the late nineteenth century, and in the next several decades the juvenile court took over the parental function of the state (legally sanctioned as *parens patriae*). Although the juvenile court could still send children to reform schools, its primary function was to educate and rehabilitate delinquents through probation and other paternalistic forms of monitoring. Flanagan started Boys Town literally by going to court and offering to take delinquent boys home with him. *Boys Town* emphasizes Flanagan's emotional connection with such boys, and the success of his particular program of privatized, paternalistic child care. Whereas Scouting and YMCA programs were seen as supplemental to the home, Boys Town was home itself, at once alternative and traditional (thanks in part to the ambiguity of the "father").

In Flanagan's work we can see the historical tension between the state and the private sphere in child care and social welfare policy. Boys Town has long been praised as an exemplary child care institution precisely to the degree that it is financially independent and self-sustaining. To this day, Boys Town receives no funds from the Catholic Church, nor does it contribute any monies to the church. According to its Web site, public support now accounts for 30 to 40 percent of the operating funds, with 25 to 35 percent coming from various program revenues (including state agency reimbursements, grants, and medical insurance), and the other 30 to 40 percent from Father Flanagan's Trust Fund. No wonder former Speaker of the House Newt Gingrich appealed in 1994 to Boys Town as a model example of privatized child care, advising Hillary Clinton and her fellow Democrats to watch *Boys Town* as evidence. For Gingrich at least, Boys Town represents a patriarchal solution to social malaise that doesn't require the redistribution of wealth or even federal aid—and reinstitutes Father as the central figure of the family. While Gingrich appropriates the film to his own ends, he's not entirely wrong about the cultural and political tendencies of the film and of the institution itself.

Flanagan and the Personal Touch

As a founding father, Flanagan was a complicated character, hardly consistent in his ideas and efforts. To give just a few examples, he was well versed in the period literature on juvenile delinquency (domestic and European) and rejected most of it as too pessimistic. At the same time, he subscribed to a deterministic view of slum life and felt that adult criminals were beyond his reach. He argued against trying children as adults but also had little faith in juvenile courts and reform schools. Well-educated and smart, he was also stubbornly anti-intellectual. He was committed to social justice, and to racial tolerance, declaring Boys Town open to all boys "regardless of creed, color or race." Yet he worked closely with FBI director J. Edgar Hoover, an advocate of "Christian vision" in law enforcement (Oursler, 118); Hoover hired many former residents of Boys Town. Flanagan denounced the corrupting influence of media but was quick to use it to his own ends. If he famously held that "there is no such thing as a bad boy," he decried "bad environment, bad training, bad example and bad thinking" (*Boys Town: Memories and Dreams*, 1). Flanagan was a progressive reformer, and also a priest. Boys could not be saved, he thought, without God, and Boys Town was at once an alternative to, and a reincarnation of, the religious nuclear family.

Flanagan took his cue from the repaternalization of child care as promoted through the juvenile court system. The first juvenile court was established in Illinois in 1909, in an effort to transfer parental power to the entire legal system. Timothy Hurley, president of the (Catholic) Chicago Visitation and Aid Society, explained its function thus:

> The fundamental idea of the Juvenile Court is so simple it seems anyone ought to understand it. It is, to be perfectly plain, a return to paternalism. It is the acknowledgement by the State of its relationship as the parent to every child within its borders. Civilization for years lost sight of this relationship, and as a consequence the utter demoralization of society was threatened. (Mennel, *Thorns and Thistles*, 132)

In his account of the juvenile court, Robert M. Mennel adds in a footnote that Hurley had good reason to be happy with this system, as it allowed Catholic charities to serve as guardians for Catholic children whom the court placed on probation (132). Thanks to the juvenile court, young offenders were treated as delinquents rather than criminals, a transformation hailed as progressive at the time.

Central to the juvenile court system were the judge and his support staff of probation officers, usually male. The judge typically emphasized his paternal powers—and the simplicity of his reason and ethics—in dealing with troubled children, particularly boys. Mennel cites the philosophy of Judge Tuthill, the first juvenile court judge: "I talk with the boy, give him a good talk, just as I would my own boy, and find myself as much interested in some of these boys as I would if they were my own" (135). Or as another such judge put it, "It is the personal touch that does it" (135). These judges recommend that the arrangement of the courtroom be altered so that the judge is seated closer to the boy, for easier access: "If I could get close enough to him to put my hand on his head or shoulder, or my arm around him, in nearly every such case I could get his confidence" (135).

The most outspoken advocate of the juvenile court system, and of the personal touch, was Benjamin Barr Lindsey (1870–1943), a circuit court judge in Colorado, whose career Mennel discusses at length. Lindsey challenged the more deterministic perspectives of criminologists and child experts (among them G. Stanley Hall) and, in a letter to Flanagan himself, highlighted the importance of compassionate men in the juvenile court system, writing "So much depends upon *personnel*" (Mennel, 137)—or, perhaps, upon the personnel touch. Like the character building agencies, the juvenile court system preferred such personnel to the biological father, whom Lindsey characterized as "careless," "unworthy," and even "dangerous" (Mennel, 145). Such distrust of the father also resulted in the parental delinquency laws passed during the first decade of the twentieth century. The laws designed to protect children often stripped away the rights of parents in favor of the allegedly more capable state.

In Taurog's *Boys Town*, the state is the villain, along with the residual "reform schools" (which presumably include the industrial and vocational schools designed as alternatives to more punitive lockups). Disenchantment with the juvenile court system was widespread by the 1930s; it was attacked as both too conservative and too liberal. Progressive reformers were more interested in combating problems such as poverty and crime than in treating this thing called juvenile delinquency. In any case, there were few social or judicial alternatives to the court system during this period. Social work, for instance, was just being professionalized at this time. Rather than interrogate the concept of delinquency, or the class aspects of unrest, *Boys Town* reformulates it as a problem misunderstood by the public and best treated by a paternalistic and "simple" Christian program, not by the ineffectual, bureaucratic state. At the same time, the civic structure of Boys Town safeguards it as a properly democratic and American enterprise. In this respect, the film does not misrepresent Flanagan's practices. By emphasizing the goodness of his boys, Flanagan not only appropriated the state's right to father but extended it beyond delinquency. Flanagan began his home with ostensibly delinquent boys and then took in neglected and abused boys.

The transfer of authority from judicial boy worker to priest was relatively painless, even if some judges and probation officers resented Flanagan's interference. Flanagan began his boy work career by pleading on behalf of boy offenders in juvenile court. At the request of Omaha judges, he began serving as an unofficial probation officer, meeting with his boys once a week under a street lamp in front of the Northwestern Bell Telephone Company (away from the hobo-saturated atmosphere of the Workingmen's Hotel). More and more boys were paroled into his care. A turning point came when he was entrusted with seven lads ("gang leaders") arrested for a crime spree in Omaha. The boys were perceived by the public as seriously criminal, and Flanagan's advocacy for them was widely criticized at the time.[4]

According to his biographers, Flanagan promptly took these seven boys out to play baseball. The film misses this opportunity to link baseball, boyhood, and reform and instead collapses the "crime wave" seven with the first five residents of Father Flanagan's Home for Boys, depicting them as docile and misunderstood. The real Flanagan brought his five boys home on December 12, 1917, and though he continued to visit juvenile court, more often than not boys were sent to him, as the Home for Boys became better known and supported. Whatever the film's inaccuracies, the cinematic Flanagan is generous with the personal touch. In scene after scene, the actor caresses the shoulder of a troubled lad, in a quasi-secularized laying on of hands.

The personal touch is precisely what's at issue in the current sex abuse scandal. As is also true for teachers and other child care workers, priests now touch children at their own peril, as virtually any contact might be understood as sexual. To my knowledge, no one has ever questioned Father Flanagan's motives for, or practices of, boy work, thanks to the "historicity" of Flanagan and the sentimental work of the film.

Whitey Comes Home: Taurog's Boys Town

Even those who haven't seen the 1938 film may know of Boys Town, thanks to various publicity schemes over the years that emphasize the pathos of the neglected or abused boy. For instance, there's the quintessential Boys Town image of a sturdy lad carrying a lame boy on his back, exclaiming, "He ain't heavy, Father. He's my brother!" Both the phrase and the image have been legal trademarks of Boys Town since the 1940s; the image is properly titled *Two Brothers* and was probably inspired by a photograph taken in the 1920s of Howard Loomis, who wore a leg brace, piggybacking another Boys Town resident, Reuben Granger, "He ain't heavy, Father. He's my brother!" was eventually put to music and featured on the album *Boys Town Sings America* (prepared for the Bicentennial) and covered by assorted performers, including the Hollies and the Osmond Five. The *Two Brothers* statue replaced the *Homeless Boy* statue located for years near the Boys Town entrance and featured in the film. The *Two Brothers* image also adorns the Boys Town Christmas seals on fund-raising letters, a strategy adopted in 1949. The famous image even found its way onto a Faberge limited-edition egg in 1991; Mickey Rooney returned to Boys Town that year to unveil the egg, a gift from Borsheim's Fine Jewelry and Gifts (Lonnborg, *A Photographic History*, 140). There have been other enabling sentimental symbols with less currency today, among them Carlo, the first dog and mascot of Boys Town (who was later stuffed, so reluctant was Flanagan to retire him). Flanagan protected his boys from the outside world, but he also sent them back into that world as fund-raising performers in the traveling Father Flanagan's Boys' Shows. Winsome lads would perform song and dance numbers designed to melt hearts and empty pocketbooks.

But it is through the strategically sentimental film that most people know about Flanagan and Boys Town. Adapted from a story by Dore Schary and Eleanore Griffin, *Boys Town* stars Spencer Tracy as Father Flanagan, and Mickey Rooney as Whitey Marsh, a delinquent turned good citizen. Tracy won his second Academy Award for his performance, and the film further boosted the career of Rooney, who was quickly becoming the most successful actor in Hollywood.[5] *Boys Town* romanticizes Catholic charity and paternal love and criticizes Depression-era America for its disavowal of needy kids. It is critical not only of an apathetic public but also of state reform schools and the juvenile court system. At the same time, *Boys Town* suppresses the real-life Flanagan's more progressive programs and concentrates on the spiritual project of boy saving as embodied in the priest.

As such, *Boys Town* is allied with both melodrama and what Mary Lenard calls "sentimentalist discourse," in which religious authority and pathos are invoked in the name of social reform (*Preaching Pity*, 4). Lenard points specifically to Victorian novelists, but Taurog's film similarly appeals to the religious authority of the priest and the pathos of the needy boy to advance the cause of Boys Town. Although the film doesn't liken Flanagan explicitly to the anthropologist, preferring instead the residual idiom of the moral crusader, *Boys Town* does suggest Flanagan's similarity to the boy worker by showing him in the field with the boy-natives (who are in fact recent transplants). In *Mestizo Modernism,* Tace Hedrick demonstrates how a sentimental masculinity invoking an indigenous and ostensibly timeless form of culture underwrote Latin American modernist projects in the early twentieth century. She also shows the influence of evolutionary theory on these projects, and on the project of nation building more broadly. While in this chapter I leave such larger questions about sentimentality and culture unaddressed, we might think of *Boys Town* as an exercise in masculine and indigenous sentimentality designed to sustain the nation-state in the miniature form of Boys Town—a form that has now apparently gone global or exceeded the boundaries of the nation-state.

In any case, Taurog's film emphasizes Flanagan's utopian vision of a democratic, self-governing boy sanctuary and condenses the experiences of Boys Town's diverse residents into the conversion story of an archetypal boy tellingly named Whitey. Whitey's struggles with, and eventual love for,

Flanagan suggest an Oedipal drama of father and son, which affirms (and helps effect) the remythification of child care as a paternal concern in the wake of disenchantment with reform schools and even the juvenile court system that supplanted them. Historically this remythification came at the expense of the boy's actual father, who was typically blamed for his son's dysfunction. Just as the film remakes Father Flanagan from priest into the ideal parent, so it also transforms the immigrant wolf-boy of American child saving into a more acceptable protagonist, along the lines of Pickety's make-over in Brace's "Wolf-Reared Children."

But even when we first meet him, Whitey is hardly a threat to Tracy's Flanagan or to viewer sensibilities. At first Whitey is tough, then he shapes up, but he's still the same blond Caucasian kid. Not once is he described even as a friendly boy-savage, like his cousins in the Bad Boy books; by 1938, such a description would have had more menacing connotations. Although the film is dedicated to Flanagan "and his splendid work for homeless aban-doned boys, regardless of race, creed or color," it features not a single African American child, not even in the shots of boys en masse in the dining hall and dormitory. Nearly all the boys are white. The town barber, Mo, is Jew-ish, as we discover at lunchtime on Whitey's first day in town. We watch the boys saying prayers in English, while Mo prays in Hebrew, and a dark-haired boy in silence, his eyes wide open, presumably practicing his own indige-nous form of worship. The victim of Whitey's ridicule, Mo later puts Whitey in blackface, smearing shoe polish all over him. You "look like a mammy," laughs Mo.[6] But in the end, all the boys rally around Whitey, who renounces his rebellious ways and is elected mayor of Boys Town.

Boys Town poses Flanagan's recuperative work against the sordid life of the streets, and against the men who lead boys astray (bad or false fathers). The film begins and ends with adult criminals who terrorize city streets in the dead of night, from whom Flanagan must rescue his boys. Unlike the scenes set in Boys Town, which show boys frolicking in the sun as Father Flanagan works in his airy study, the frame sequences are brooding, shad-owy, and claustrophobic, as in gangster or crime films. Flanagan himself assumes a tougher, streetwise persona when he ventures out into the larger world. *Boys Town* is one in a line of crime films in which hardy priests save the day. Such films are preoccupied with immigration and urban transfor-mation, so it's not surprising that priest characters, like the criminals they encounter, are often marked as immigrant. Les and Barbara Keyser observe that gangster films were largely made out of difficult (if not irreconcilable) cultural and religious tensions, with "protagonists positioned on the cutting edge between cultures, countries, and creeds" (*Hollywood and the Catholic Church*, 47–48). Pressure from the Legion of Decency and the Catholic

Church helped transform priests in crime films from shady characters to major heroic figures, even if some (particularly the Irish priests) remain feisty and fond of violence. "Super-padre would be born around the time Superman came crashing down from Krypton," continue the Keysers, "and for years a few Latin mumblings and a breviary could quiet the most savage beast and transform the most hardened heart" (62).[7]

Father Flanagan doesn't just stick up for his boys; in the beginning of the film, he also serves as confidant and counselor to a man condemned to die (another convention of the gangster-priest film). In the opening scene, set before Flanagan has established Boys Town, we encounter a prisoner named Dan about to be executed for murder. Newspapermen have come to take his statement, and Father Flanagan to console him. Dan asks the priest about what happens when we die. "Dan," Flanagan responds, "life and death should be left to the creator of life and death." We might be tempted to read this as a critique of the state's arrogant biopower, its sentence of death, but in fact it's the state's hypocrisy that's really being criticized. A few moments later, Dan makes clear that the death penalty for adults is not the problem, but rather the state's refusal to shelter the needy young, to take responsibility for potential as well as actual criminals. He screams at the ensemble of journalists and jailers, "Where was the state when a lonely, starving kid cried himself to sleep in a flophouse, with a bunch of drunks, tramps, and hobos?" One friend, he says, would have made all the difference. Viewers are asked to sympathize not so much with the dying man as with the innocent boy he once was. Father Flanagan listens in silence, head bowed, brow furrowed.

The doomed man's words echo in Flanagan's head as he heads back to town. In the next scene, Flanagan watches helplessly as street kids rumble and damage private property. He then goes to the Workingmen's Hotel and announces to its residents that he has realized it's "too late" for men such as themselves, who are hopeless drunks, tramps, and hobos; from now on, he is turning his attention to boys. Although the film distorts the actual events, it is true that Flanagan gave up what his biographers describe as "the hotel for lost men," which he established for itinerant laborers hard hit by the 1913 drought. As the Ourslers report in their chapter "A Priest among the Dregs," Flanagan had sometimes sheltered boys in his hotel, assigning them to the attic, away from the most degenerate men inhabiting the basement, known as the "Lower Regions."

Rather than argue for the state's responsibility for finding an alternative to reform schools, Father Flanagan established a private, nonprofit home for boys, not financially supported by the church but sanctioned by Flanagan's bishop and eventually embraced by the church. Flanagan was released from his duties at the hotel so that he could concentrate on boy work. Boys Town was thus founded upon the difficulty of saving men, particularly working-class men, and upon the state's renunciation of everything but punishment. The film's main plot repeats and develops this theme through the story of the orphaned Whitey and his convict brother, Joe. Joe, also in prison, asks Flanagan to take Whitey to Boys Town so that he will not grow up like himself.

Flanagan finds Whitey in a dilapidated apartment, playing cards with his pals, and tries to reason with the boy, describing the various vocational programs of Boys Town, and telling him, "You know, I think you might like farming; it's good for you, it keeps you out in the open, it'll put hair on your chest." When Whitey refuses to go, Flanagan drags him to the compound. Whitey's youth has clearly been misspent. He gambles and smokes. He is arrogant, hostile, and theatrically queer, dressing and acting like a cross between a dandy, a hood, and P. T. Barnum. When he runs for mayor, Whitey forms a marching band and mounts campaign slogans on cattle and horses.

Rooney's performance borders on campy, but of course such theatricals soon give way to the tearful piousness of a grateful orphan-turned-son. Near the end of the film, Whitey leaves Boys Town and wanders through downtown Omaha, where he accidentally gets shot by his brother Joe, escaped from prison, who has just robbed a bank with his gang. Whitey at first refuses to squeal on his brother and is blamed for the crime, but (with his brother's permission) Whitey finally comes clean when he learns that the bad publicity will lead to the closing of Boys Town. Accompanied by Father Flanagan, the entire population of Boys Town forms a vigilante posse and descends upon the criminals' hideout (shades of the prison house here). They overpower the thugs (for whom we have no sympathy) and clear Whitey's name. Six months later, a kinder, gentler Whitey is elected mayor and can't utter a single sentence, instead sobbing against Father Flanagan's chest as the priest caresses him and intones, "There is no bad boy"—all to the stirring tune of "My Country Tis of Thee."[8]

In the film, the epic and rather whitewashed project of boy rescue ignores the socioeconomic roots of abuse. Ostensibly opposed to the idea that boys are naturally bad, and thus that cultural conditions produce what closed-minded people see as innate criminality, Tracy's Father Flanagan nonetheless explains the project of boy saving in distinctly custodial terms: "Every boy who becomes a good American citizen is worth $10,000 to the state," he explains to a potential benefactor. Or as he says when arguing for a move to the country: "I have fifty boys I've taken from the slums and the streets. Right now they're on their way to becoming competent human beings." Apparently you can take the boy out of the slum, and even the slum out of the boy, by relocating him to this boytopia. *Boys Town* appeals not so much to social Darwinism as to an accelerated sort of Lamarckianism. Given a healthy environment and a strong father figure, Whitey manages to save himself.

Whitey's conversion is also aided by another dramatic episode, which sets into motion the events I've just described and helps establish the *Two Brothers* mythology and the film's revisionist Oedipality. Soon after his arrival, Whitey is befriended by a young boy named Pee Wee, the darling of Boys Town, who gets a piece of candy from Father Flanagan each day that he has been good. Although not lame, Pee Wee likes to ride piggyback, but Whitey at first sneers and calls Mo a "sucker" when he indulges Pee Wee. Gradually Whitey comes to enjoy Pee Wee's dogged devotion. One day, after being humiliated in the boxing ring, Whitey decides he's had enough and starts to leave Boys Town. Pee Wee pursues him and is hit by a car. Whitey breaks down emotionally, bawling, cradling Pee Wee in his arms, and swearing to God he'll do anything if only Pee Wee lives. Pee Wee lives. The film makes use of that sentimental staple, the sick or dying child, to play on audience sympathies and speed along Whitey's transformation. Whitey must be humbled before God and his surrogate but must also accept his role as an example for the Pee Wees of the world. Father knows best, and Whitey must grow up to take his earthly place, in effort and spirit, if not in legend. The only women we see are the nuns who work in the infirmary. Otherwise it's boys, men, and more of both, acting out a melodrama of beset boyhood.

There are other sentimental scenarios in the film: the worthless child's toy put down as security for loans, the last-minute redemption of Christmas by a kindhearted merchant, and so forth. And there are endless scenes of boys crying. *Boys Town* makes the most of its own sentimental power, particularly against the purported realism of journalism. In the film, Flanagan's most powerful adversary is Mr. Hargraves, a powerful newspaper mogul who believes in juvenile delinquency, commissions articles that reflect that faith, and dismisses Flanagan's efforts as "sentimental nonsense that flies in the face of public opinion." The film itself is a volley in the public relations battle that Flanagan waged all his life with a cynical public. The success of the film established Flanagan as a boy worker and legitimated the ongoing work of Boys Town, work that was at once highly sentimental and highly paternalistic.

Central to the Ourslers' biography, as to the 1938 film, is the connection drawn between Flanagan's plucky self-reliance and the eventual success of his operation. The Ourslers begin by tracing Flanagan's rise in the world, from his humble beginnings in Ireland through his stop-and-start education and finally his ordination in 1912. Flanagan was plagued by health problems all his life, having been a sick and weakly child, and the Ourslers emphasize his frailty both to accentuate his selflessness and to suggest a parallel between the transformations in his own life and the transformations he effected in others. They offer anecdotes from his boyhood that anticipated his future calling. For example, as a boy, Eddie tended to cows on the family farm; one day, when the cows were less than cooperative, he became angry, screaming, "Bad cows! Wicked, bad cows." To which his father replied: "Eddie, there is no such thing as a bad cow. They only don't know any better!" (27). Later, Flanagan's work as an accountant for a meatpacking company offered another useful apprenticeship, teaching him crucial financial skills: "If they could do it for beef, we can do it for boys!" decides Flanagan (74).

The Father Chain

It's impressive that an Irish immigrant priest presiding over a diverse group of boys became such an exemplary figure of American boyology. Irish immigrants faced great discrimination at the hands of Anglo-American Catholics as well as Protestants. Flanagan emigrated from Ireland to America in 1904 at the age of eighteen, to study for the priesthood. By the time Flanagan was working in Omaha, the tide of bias had turned somewhat, thanks largely to Catholic participation in World War I. Immigrant Catholic laymen were eager to prove their loyalty to America, especially as anti-American sentiment grew in their countries of origin; as a result, Catholics signed up in droves for military service at the beginning of the war. In 1917, the year in which Flanagan founded Boys Town, the Knights of Columbus, an organization for Catholic men, was recognized by the federal government as a service organization for Catholic soldiers (until then an exclusive role of the YMCA). After the war, in the wake of the Pastoral Letter of 1919, American bishops formed the National Catholic Welfare Conference as the successor to the National Catholic War Council. This new organization coordinated Catholic work on a national level and helped counter anti-Catholic sentiment.[9]

"The 1930s," writes David O'Brien in *Public Catholicism*, "were the golden age of Catholic social action" (167) and, as a consequence, of greater Catholic visibility in America. Prior to this period, non-Catholics rarely registered any substantial knowledge of the church, aside from the occasional attack on the controversial but hugely influential "radio priest," Father Charles Coughlin. With massive unemployment, farmers in revolt, and the banks closing, many Catholics supported FDR and his New Deal policies, even drawing comparisons between those policies and papal teaching. In the late 1930s, Catholics became increasingly committed to labor and social justice efforts, and known for that commitment. Particularly important was the Catholic Worker Movement, founded by Dorothy Day, which (contrary to Day's intentions) helped to mainstream the church's image. It became ever easier to accept a priest as a social worker or reformer and to see him as pro-American. For a while, "militant Catholicism, complete with the monarchical papacy, coexisted with an at times almost chauvinistic Americanism" (O'Brien, 196).[10] But gradually that Americanism or nativism prevailed. The post–World War II period witnessed a further consolidation of what many historians call "American Catholicism" or simply "Americanism," a Catholicism more consonant with American values. Typically the election of JFK is seen as an end point in this process of integration. While this progressive historical model of the church has been challenged by James Terence Fisher, most historians agree that as the century wore on, the church was no longer seen as a church of immigrants, as more and more Catholics joined the American middle class even as they supported labor and progressive causes.[11]

Flanagan is conspicuously absent from the histories of American Catholicism that I surveyed, even though many are organized around bishops and important priests. Flanagan was not a political player in the church; he never rose to prominence in the ecclesiastical hierarchy. Still, at the time of his death in 1948, Flanagan was one of the best-known religious leaders in America, whose opinions and advice were highly regarded by political leaders at home and overseas. It seems clear that Flanagan, though a Catholic priest and always affiliated with the church, achieved the kind of cultural status enjoyed today by the Dalai Lama or the late Mother Theresa, even as he was regarded as thoroughly American. In most accounts of his life and work, the fact that he is a Catholic priest seems almost beside the point, and certainly no one questions his patriotism. The 1938 film is generically Christian, designed to appeal to a broad audience. The Ourslers, who call Flanagan "the most beloved clergyman in the United States," claim that "Jews and Protestants actually contributed to his work as much as his own people" (3). They emphasize his "complete catholicity," preferring the lowercase to the upper, citing Flanagan's commitment to the American Christian Palestine Committee and to the new Zion (7). The command to love one another, they write, "was his catholicon, his universal panacea, not only for wayward boys but for the world; the only leaven in a heathen age that could cause a general change" (10).

Flanagan's "complete catholicity" depended on his remove from the church rather than his connection with it. When Flanagan set out to establish his home, he did so with the blessings of Archbishop Jeremiah Harty. Persuaded that the work was important, Harty relieved Flanagan of his pastoral duties so that he could devote all his energies to Boys Town. The archbishop also "loaned" Flanagan two nuns and a novice from the School Sisters of Notre Dame (*Memories and Dreams,* 2). But Harty could not offer any financial support; Flanagan was on his own. Boys Town has always been a nonsectarian affair in terms of funding, administered by a board of trustees with various religious backgrounds.

But Boys Town is hardly your average nonsectarian child care facility (if there is such a thing). Responding in 1985 to the question "Is religion still a part of life at Boys Town?" the outgoing Boys Town executive director Father Robert P. Hupp answered in the affirmative, pointing out that Catholic and Protestant religion classes have equal time in the curriculum, and that a full-time priest and Protestant minister address the spiritual needs of Boys Town residents (while a neighboring rabbi attends to the Jewish children) (Hupp, *The New Boys Town,* 20). The Boys Town administration has always respected boys with non-Catholic religious backgrounds and does not try to convert them. But Boys Town has always been directed by a Catholic priest, "to symbolize Father Flanagan," according to the Web site. Flanagan was succeeded by Monsignor Nicholas H. Wegner, who ran Boys Town from 1948 to 1973. Father Hupp served until 1985, when the fourth and current executive director, Father Peter, was appointed. Simply put, Boys Town would not be Boys Town without a father figure, without reincarnations of Flanagan. Thus while Boys Town is not traditionally Catholic, this father chain is integral to its mission and to its public life. The singularity of the priest-director ensures the familial feel of Boys Town, no matter how vast its domain.

Father Peter, the latest in the chain, confidently asserts his own expertise. In a two-volume set of success stories from Boys Town, Peter chastises abusive parents and stresses the need for "compassion and competence" on the part of child care professionals (*"I Think,"* 7).[12] In the first of these stories, "Dad, Do You Love Me?" Father Peter helps a young man acknowledge the sad truth—"I told Joe that he and I both knew the answer to that question" (10)—but that he, Father Peter, does love Joe, for and through the Heavenly Father. Father Peter discusses sound and humane strategies for building self-esteem, gaining a child's trust, and so forth, providing checklists and defining key terms for the lay reader. He addresses some tough issues head-on, including incest and other forms of sexual abuse. These stories make clear that Boys Town residents are not the good bad boys of American fiction, nor are their fathers the good bad fathers of *Farming for Boys* or the Bad Boy genre (unless we mean Pap Finn). I've argued in this book that the boy worker discredited the father in order to justify his own calling, and while I suspect this practice is residual in priestly boy work, it's also obvious that some parents are profoundly unfit, and that the staff of Boys Town care deeply about their work and write honestly about its complexities. In any case, Father Peter preserves the spirit of Father Flanagan even as he rises to new challenges.[13]

Boys Town, furthermore, has always been imagined as a mini-America, as refuge, home, and melting pot for the teeming juvenile masses. Boys Town stages a reenactment of the arrival and Americanization of immigrants in the United States. From all over the nation, and sometimes from other countries, boys emigrate to Boys Town, leave their pasts behind and start over, adapt to its culture and (hopefully) thrive. They are free to come and go; there are no walls or gates, only opportunities for work and personal transformation. Under the father's watchful eye, residents learn democracy, electing their own mayor, responding to civic and social problems, maintaining law and order. They leave with a high school diploma, vocational training, and a strong pride of place. It's not surprising that Father Peter described the 1980s expansion of Boys Town beyond Omaha as a "new manifest destiny"; it was only a matter of time before Boys Town claimed new territory.

And why not? Consider some of its latest triumphs. In 1997, Boys Town developed a partnership with the Chicago Public Schools to help train staff working with at-risk students. In Philadelphia, Boys Town renovated an inner-city building and converted it into a shelter for runaway girls. What's wrong with this picture? My concern is that Boys Town's remarkable success will help justify the privatization of child care programs nationwide; and in fact, the Boys Town National Resource and Training Center is now helping several states begin that transition. Whatever its day-to-day realities, the popular mythology of Boys Town reinforces, at least in the rhetoric of Gingrich and other opponents of public assistance, a traditionally masculinist and patriarchal (if weirdly homosocial and sentimental) image of the family while sanctioning the federal abandonment of actual families.

Boys Town against Boys Town

The evolution of Boys Town over the years reflects the rough trajectory of boyology more generally, from its rural and small-town forms to its more urban incarnations. Flanagan started his sanctuary in 1917 in Omaha, Nebraska, renting a two-story red brick house that was the German-American Home before it became Father Flanagan's Home for Boys. In 1921, he purchased the ninety-four-acre Overlook Farm on the outskirts of Omaha, later acquiring surrounding property. Now spread out over 1,300 acres, Boys Town is roughly the size of a land-grant state university campus. Boys Town now designates not just the Omaha campus but a complex network of residential programs located in metropolitan areas such as Chicago,

Los Angeles, Las Vegas, San Antonio, New Orleans, Orlando, Philadelphia, and Washington, D.C. "We're taking our healing out from the heartland to the whole nation," explained Father Peter in 1986. "It's a new manifest destiny" (Lonnborg, *A Photographic History*, 46). From Home to Farm to Town and beyond, Boys Town has gone national, even global, in the very late capitalist moment of the corporation's eclipse of the nation-state. In some sense, Boys Town has never been limited by the traditional boundaries of space and place, only by money and other resources; its move overseas and into cyberspace seems to have been effortless.

The programs of Boys Town are diverse; some are even progressive by contemporary standards. Newt Gingrich, however, seems to imagine Boys Town as it is depicted in the classic film, as a cheery, rural, rather traditional place presided over by a wise priest. One of the stranger political episodes of 1994 occurred when Gingrich, then Speaker of the House, advised Hillary Clinton and her fellow Democrats to watch Norman Taurog's film *Boys Town* (1938). His rationale: they might then appreciate the wisdom of a GOP proposal to relocate the children of unwed teenage mothers to orphanages.[14] Gingrich was concerned not with saving kids but rather with saving society itself from the depredations of welfare moms and their troubled offspring. Gingrich's recommendation provoked outrage, if also some scary praise. Even many opponents of assistance programs were horrified by Gingrich's eagerness to break up families and to institutionalize at-risk children. Former Boys Town residents were themselves quick to protest. "His mean-spiritedness is hardly the tone Boys Town—the movie and my home—means to impart to children," wrote former resident J. B. Tiernan-Lang in a *USA Today* opinion page. Tiernan-Lang speaks of the lessons he learned at Boys Town, adding that Gingrich might "benefit from the family, religious, and social values and skills Boys Town teaches those he and his colleagues consider the flotsam of society."

Gingrich refused to back down and not long afterward hosted a screening of the colorized version of *Boys Town* on Turner Network Television (TNT). His commitment to popular forms shouldn't surprise us; Gingrich has been a staunch advocate of the simple wisdom of such entertainments, such as *Field of Dreams* (1989), which he urged everyone to see during the baseball strike (Quart, "A Second Look," 55). Thus, with the American flag in the background, Gingrich introduces Taurog's film and offers commentary during commercial breaks. He confesses that he is a fan of sentimental and "idealistic movies" about America, such as *Boys Town* and *Forrest Gump* (1994). He muses that should the film be remade, Harrison Ford would make an ideal Father Flanagan (suggesting the need for a butcher or less maternal Flanagan). Gingrich also draws political lessons from the film, representing

Flanagan as a tough disciplinarian who shows his boys that "life is hard and you have to work at it," and that economy pays off. The film itself, however, makes clear Flanagan's tender, liberal sympathies and his disdain of the financial cost of child rescue. As Leonard Quart notes in "A Second Look," "Gingrich takes a film whose sentiments are much more humane and compassionate than his own, and turns it into a justification for Republican welfare policies" (57).

Even so, Gingrich's politics are not so far removed from the politics of the film. As Quart points out, the film does not offer any kind of socio-economic critique of society, but rather "palliatives—a gym, a boy's home—havens, but not social solutions" (55). Given that New Deal programs were virtually dead by 1938, we might view the film as marking the start of disenchantment with public assistance that has resulted in the devastating attacks on relief programs in the Reagan-Bush years. Even if *Boys Town* hardly authorizes Gingrich's sense of Boys Town as a repository for welfare kids, the film stages the crisis of juvenile delinquency such that removal of troublemakers from the public sphere and into the care of a devoted priest seems a good way to go. As Gingrich recognized, the film recommends privatized care of a vaguely Catholic persuasion in lieu of federal intervention. It's not surprising that Gingrich uses *Boys Town* to endorse an institutional structure that looks like the patriarchal nuclear family writ large and kept spiritual. Writing in *Policy Review*, on the heels of the Gingrich commentary of 1994, Brian Jendryka offers a similar assessment: "As illegitimacy mounts and more and more American families fall apart, Boys Town is a model for foster care system in crisis, and an attractive alternative to a welfare system that undermines parental responsibility" (44).

Thinking that Gingrich had too easily confused the film with the real place, and already curious about this peculiar institution, I visited Boys Town in 1997 with my friends Lois Kuznets and Elizabeth Goodenough while in Omaha for the Children's Literature Association's annual meeting. I hoped that a visit to the home campus might make clearer the ideological shape of Boys Town. We went first to the visitors center and signed up for a tour. After we browsed for half an hour or so in the gift shop—which shouldn't be missed—our guide showed up. It turns out that residents conduct the tours. Chris was a sharp and funny high school sophomore who lived on-site and also worked at a steak house in Omaha. His first question was "So, do you guys have a car?" We were a little surprised that he was allowed to ride around with strangers, but we discovered that Flanagan's famed trust in people lives on at Boys Town, where visitors can also take self-conducted tours at their leisure, and where the Dowd Memorial Chapel/Father Flanagan Shrine is open to the public year-round. Chris climbed into our rental van and began directing us through the campus. He explained that the residents of Boys Town compete for the position of guide and are paid for their work.

Incorporated as a village in 1936, Boys Town today boasts more than one hundred buildings, among them seventy-five individual family homes. There are also two chapels on site, the (Catholic) Dowd Memorial Chapel, and the Chambers Protestant Chapel. More than eight hundred youths live on-site each year, coming from every state in the union, as well as U.S. territories and several foreign countries. Residents attend the Monsignor Wegner Middle School and the Boys Town High School (complete with a great hall) and may also attend classes in the Vocational Career Center. The Program Planning, Research, and Evaluation Department, organized in 1989, sponsors the Boys Town Reading Center, which conducts research on literacy issues and aids curricular planning (Lonnborg, *A Photographic History,* 48). Boys Town has its own post office, town hall, credit union, and fire department. Prominent stops on the official tour include the beautifully preserved Father Flanagan Historic House, and the Hall of History, opened in 1986, on the 100th anniversary of Flanagan's birth. For some reason, we did not go into the Leon Myers Stamp Center; among its many attractions is a 600-pound ball of stamps made by residents in the 1950s.

As we learned, Boys Town is now a vast organization, administering not only residential programs but also emergency and family shelters, family counseling and other "preservation" programs, foster care services, and Common Sense Parenting, a parent-training program. The year 1975 saw the establishment of the Boys Town National Research Hospital, a premier diagnostic and research facility for children with language, speech, and hearing disorders. There is also the Father Flanagan High School for inner-city youth in Omaha. The Boys Town Press offers an extensive selection of "resources for youth-serving professionals, educators, and parents" (I quote from the front cover of the 1997 catalog). The national hotline was established in 1989, now plugged on television by boy stars such as Jonathan Taylor Thomas. And naturally there's a Web site. Even so, the Village of Boys Town remains the symbolic center of the enterprise, such that the urban colonies seem firmly rooted in America's heartland. It is a popular Midwest tourist attraction and a National Historic Landmark site, a living museum of Flanagan's boy work in its original and contemporary forms.[15]

There have been significant changes over the years in the policies as well as the physical arrangement of the site. The dormitory system was abandoned in the early 1970s. Most of the residents now live in groups of five to eight, under the care of family-teachers, specially trained married couples who teach the trials and tribulations of family life.[16] As we drove from the visitor's center past the first cluster of family homes, Chris explained that of the

550 current residents of Boys Town proper, 330 were boys; the first girls were admitted in 1979, and the transition was quite successful. Some of the girls live in apartments, but most live in the homes. In 2001 (several years after our visit), Boys Town officially became known as Girls and Boys Town, after a vote by the residential body. The name change applies only to national programs and centers; the Village of Boys Town, Boys Town High School, and other structures will apparently keep the original Boys Town name.

Our tour was limited to the historical buildings of Boys Town; we did not go inside the residential buildings, or the schools, or any place where we might encounter other residents. In keeping with what I have called curatorial boyology, the tour is designed to showcase the history and evolution of Boys Town, not provide access to its citizens or explain its daily operations. We spent the most time at the Hall of History, which features a range of materials and display formats and is both a museum and a research center, with a Boys Town historian and archivist on hand to answer questions. The hall is arranged chronologically, so that you move through the decades exhibit by exhibit. There are audio and video clips augmenting photographs and paper documents; one audio box had this instruction: "Please push the button to hear the story of my neglected boyhood."

That sad story is told ad nauseam in various ways, with appeals to various sensibilities (although Liz pushed every button in the place). Spencer Tracy's Oscar award is on display in the hall. Even Captain Marvel joins forces with Flanagan in one comic strip featured in the hall, dated March 24, 1941, in which the superhero rounds up some delinquent boys and says, "If you fellows were in Boys Town you'd learn that it's wrong to rob" ("Captain Marvel and the Omaha Adventure"). Other exhibits document the strange career of Father Flanagan's Boys' Shows, featuring the "World's Greatest Juvenile Entertainers," launched in the summer of 1922. Traveling in old circus wagons, the troupe toured first Nebraskan towns and then larger swaths of the Midwest and even the South, performing what the display describes as a minstrel show. Nonetheless they often met opposition from the KKK, since African American boys were part of the cast. The Boys' Shows later gave way to the Boys Town Choir, now internationally known. The hall includes one of the original Boys' Show wagons, as well as a Boys Town bus, inside of which visitors watch a video narrated by Father Peter.

Chris was proud to be at Boys Town. The admission process, he told us as we finished our visit, is very selective. "You have to apply," he explained, "and it's not easy to get in. You have to really want to come here." It became clear to us that for Chris and many other residents, Boys Town is a prestigious institution, akin to a prep school, with a distinct and enabling tradition. On occasion, Chris would allude to a less successful past, but always as a backdrop for his current accomplishments and his plans for the future. Simply by taking us around, he was asserting ownership of the place and participation in its history, its rituals, and its promise of a better life. For Chris and many others, being a graduate of Boys Town is similar to being an Eagle Scout: it signals exceptional character. Jendryka begins his article "Flanagan's Island" by recounting one of many reported acts of Boys Town–style heroism. When an Amtrak train jumped its tracks and plunged into Alabama's Bayou Canot in September 1993, Boys Town graduate Michael Dopheide repeatedly risked his own life and saved the lives of thirty passengers. He credited his years at Boys Town: "No matter what, no matter how difficult the situation is, you're still going to help, you're still going to carry this person to safety" (44).

We didn't talk with any other residents and in fact saw very few of them on the grounds, so I don't know how representative Chris's attitude toward Boys Town might have been. But as we finished the tour, I kept thinking of the contrast between Chris's proud sense of investment and even ownership and Gingrich's understanding of Boys Town as a holding pen or rehab facility. Not every former resident of Boys Town saves thirty people from drowning, but nonetheless the graduates of Boys Town compare favorably to kids raised in the traditional families touted by conservatives. Measured against the national norm, in fact, Boys Town alumni are more likely than their nonresidential peers to attend college, hold down high-paying jobs, and attend church, and less likely to use illegal drugs (Jendryka, 45). Given this success, maybe all American kids should be raised in Boys Town, even the children of Congressfolk.

Or maybe not. Flanagan seemed more interested in saving the souls of his young charges than in producing good citizens, which seems to be the current agenda. Education at Boys Town emphasizes skills—job skills, vocational skills, and social skills. Residents must master more than thirty distinct skills (including accepting criticism and accepting no for an answer). Each resident begins his or her stay with an "empowerment card," a record of positive and negative points keyed to appropriate and inappropriate behavior. Residents carry their cards everywhere they go. They must accumulate 10,000 points every day to keep basic privileges (such as watching TV, using the phone, or listening to music). Eventually, as the kids internalize their good behavior and master the skills, they quit carrying the cards. Boys Town administrators insist that this system works because it teaches accountability and cause and effect (Jendryka, 46). It's hard to imagine Flanagan endorsing such an instrumentalist, normalizing program of "empowerment."

And as it turns out, the typical Boys Town family is decidedly more nuclear than the average American family. The family teachers are not chosen for their ability to model creative lifestyles; their job is to demonstrate "how a healthy, traditional family should work" (Jendryka, 47). Administrators cite the single-parent family as a significant factor in the decay of the American family—surely music to Newt's ears. There is little room for individuality or eccentricity at Boys Town. The day is highly structured, activities closely monitored.

It's hard to assess this system without actually living on-site. Clearly a quick and limited visit doesn't tell one much, and even now, after further research and reflection, I'm not sure what to make of Boys Town. On the one hand, it's hard to quarrel with what looks like success. Boys Town kids learn to participate fully in the life of a family, to share in its work and play, to attend and participate in family councils, to respect their caregivers and "siblings." If we believe testimonials, each child's voice is heard and respected, a novel experience for many. Residents apparently learn to live with diversity; families may be made up of kids with different ethnic, class, and regional affiliations. The family-teachers stay in constant contact with the schoolteachers, which accounts for a very high graduation rate at Boys Town High School. (Teachers, incidentally, enjoy very small classes and often work in pairs, too.) Corporal punishment is not allowed, and striking a child just once results in automatic termination.

At the same time, as Gingrich has intuited, a traditional understanding of family prevails (despite the fact that these are not biological families): two-parent, heterosexual, and rather top-down. And religious. Although Boys Town is nonsectarian, residents cannot refuse religion. According to Father Peter, religion "is the single most important characteristic of a Boys Town education" (Jendryka, 51), and family-teachers set special times for prayer and the study of scripture. Non-Jewish kids are allowed only to decide between the Protestant and Catholic faiths. Atheism is not an option; presumably neither is Buddhism, Islam, or any non-Judeo-Christian faith. In e-mail correspondence, I asked the public relations director whether residents were allowed to identify as atheist or agnostic; I received no answer. I also asked if there were any support services in place for lesbian/gay youth, and if Boys Town affirms the Catholic Church's condemnation of same-sex relationships. Silence again.

Not for a moment do I doubt that Boys Town works wonders for most of its residents, many of whom take pride in their institution and distinguish themselves in the outside world. Still, I can't help but wonder about the lives of kids for whom a "healthy, traditional family" is oppressive. I don't personally believe that religion should be the basis of scholastic or family education. And while I applaud the idea of a diverse group of children learning to live with each other under the loving, nonviolent supervision of trained adult caregivers, I don't like the dismissive attitude toward family constellations that the Boys Town philosophy ironically construes as unnatural.

It's worth remembering that, as Sedgwick points out in "Tales of the Avunculate," the Name of the Father so often takes the Name of Family these days (72). If, in the symbolic field of Boys Town, Father Flanagan resembled and supplanted the wise men of the juvenile court in the early part of the century, Father Peter and his system of parent-teachers may represent not so much a bold new trend in institutional child care as a reconfiguration of the traditional family in the name and spirit of the Father. In his advocacy of Boys Town, Gingrich isn't recommending that we entrust our children to just any old institution, but to the institution of the nuclear family. The presiding father of Boys Town is both administrator and patriarch, whose presence lends authority to, and finds support from, heterosexual, two-parent family configurations. (The family units, furthermore, protect the priest from suspicions of abuse in our current moment of panic.)

To make matters more complicated, Boys Town may not represent insulation against modern society so much as one of modern society's most successful ventures, if we imagine Boys Town as a miniature nation-state quickly being transformed into a nonprofit corporation in the wake of globalization. By praising Boys Town, Gingrich endorses the privatization of social services without actually having to acknowledge such, since Boys Town is not typically considered a corporation.

All of which makes me strangely nostalgic for Father Flanagan's overtly paternalistic but still avuncular brand of local boy work. With original sin creeping in the back door of contemporary pop psychology and cultural exposé, it's certainly hard now to imagine a priest persuading juvenile court to release wayward boys into his care. Perhaps Flanagan appealed to a doctrine of original innocence in childhood that seems to be eroding, along with our faith in father figures. I'm nearly inclined to agree with Gingrich that *Boys Town* should be mandatory viewing, not for its homogenized tale of Whitey, or its alleged endorsement of privatized institutional care, but rather for its sentimental faith that there's no such thing as a bad boy, and that priests make ideal (if singular) boy workers.

5. From Freud's Wolf Man to *Teen Wolf*

You take a guy like Morrow that's always snapping their towel at
people's asses—really trying to *hurt* somebody with it—they don't just
stay a rat while they're a kid. They stay a rat their whole life.

—J. D. Salinger, *The Catcher in the Rye*

In the early sections of *Book I: Freud's Papers on Technique, 1953–1954,*
Jacques Lacan makes use of two reports that suggest the significance of the
feral tale in psychoanalysis. The first is a pioneering case study published
by Melanie Klein in 1930 about her work with a four-year-old boy dubbed
"little Dick." Drawing from Klein's own remarks about the boy's lack of
interest in communication or social interaction, Lacan concludes that the
boy exists "completely in reality, in the pure state" of presymbolic life.
Lacan's faith in that "pure state" calls to mind the 1801 report of Jean-Marc-
Gaspard Itard on his work with Victor of Aveyron—an earlier write-up
of an experiment with a child isolated from humanity. But whereas Itard
had hoped to uncover "the features of man in the pure state of nature" in
order to assess the nature of culture (91), Lacan's interest is language; he is
explaining the Real. Lacan emphasizes that little Dick's state is perfectly normal and only seems strange to us because we have fallen into language.[1]

The second report in *Book I,* the case of Robert, is given by one of Lacan's
seminar students, Rosine Lefort, and recounted at length in chapter 8, titled
"The Wolf! The Wolf!" Neglected, abused, and (unlike Dick) violently disturbed, Robert is "acutely confused as to his own self, the contents of his
body, objects, children, and the adults who surrounded him" (94). He is also
wolf identified from early childhood. He names his own panicked image in
the mirror as "wolf!" and his only words are "Miss!" and "wolf!" (92). Here
Lacan emphasizes the fundamental misrecognition of the mirror stage, and
the disjunction between imago and bodily chaos that gives rise to fears of
fragmentation and otherness.[2] The case of Robert serves as a bridge between
Lacan's discussion of the dynamic between the superego and the imaginary—
specifically, of the superego's tendency to become a "ferocious figure" (102).

But why should that ferocious figure be a wolf? When pressed by Lacan,
Lefort speculates that nurses terrorize children into proper behavior with
fairy tales of devouring wolves, and that the fear takes hold because the
wolf naturally represents the devouring mother (101). As evidence she cites
unspecified "children's stories" in which oral sadism abounds. Lacan himself
remarks that the wolf "raises all the problems of symbolism: it isn't a function with a limit, since we are forced to search out its origin in a general
symbolisation" (101). That general symbolization includes the life of secret

societies, rituals of initiation and totemism, even "identification with a character" (101). Not surprisingly, neither Lacan nor his students acknowledge the possibility that fairy tales or children's stories about wolves and werewolves have found their way into the psychoanalytic repertoire, or what we might call, after Michèle Le Doeuff's tropological study of philosophy, the "psychoanalytic imaginary."[3]

The case histories of little Dick and Robert the wolf-boy clearly derive from different traditions of the feral tale. Like Victor, little Dick is feral without being animal identified, and as is typical with the Enlightenment variant, his condition is less dramatic and promises insight into the human condition. Neither Klein nor Lacan identifies Dick as a feral child, but their descriptions at once echo Itard's report and anticipate Bruno Bettelheim's 1959 diagnostic appropriation of the feral as a term for the autistic child—who likewise exists in a "pure state," silent and often quite indifferent to the outside world.[4] The case of Robert is resonant with other wolf-boy stories, from the myth of Remus and Romulus to the reports in British India that inspired the Mowgli tales. But of course Robert has a more immediate ancestor in Freud's Wolf Man, in *From the History of an Infantile Neurosis* (1918). Like Lefort, Freud attributes his patient's wolfishness to both cultural experience—reading wolf-themed fairy tales in early childhood—and the ostensibly natural fears of infantile life.

My concern in this chapter is twofold. First, I examine Freud's imaginative remaking of the feral tale from folkloric and literary material as well as sexology. Freud did not imagine the feral tale as such, although he might easily have done so. He did not liken stories of animal identification or cohabitation to screen memories, or to the Oedipus myth, to which such stories are structurally related. That's because Freud needed such stories to affirm man's uneasy affinities with the animal kingdom, and his psychosexual evolution from ostensibly primitive, autoerotic sexuality to genital heteronormativity—an evolution tricky at best, as Freud was quick to insist.[5] The feral boy is a perfect vehicle for Freud, for that boy can embody otherness selectively, remaining a figure of ambivalence while becoming nearly identical with the properly civilized adult.[6] Feral children are biologically human but lack some of the cultural markers of humanity; Freud thus appropriates the familiar figures of rat and wolf as psychoanalytic totems. Although his patients are adults, he concentrates on their early lives, in effect treating them as hapless boys. Freud's feral boys don't lack culture entirely but rather have established an uneasy relation to it, functioning adequately in public while suffering in private. Like the neurotic, the feral boy lacks the capacity to understand and account for himself, which is what psychoanalysis claims to foster. To that degree, we are all feral subjects. Stressing the power of instincts, Freud writes in the Wolf Man case that the typical child "knows nothing" of "remote cultural aims" (165), implying that everyone is feral in that sense.

As Janet Malcolm notes, as psychoanalysis developed as a discipline, Freud "grew less and less interested in the special plight of the people to whom unspeakable things happen" (*In the Freud Archives*, 77). These "psychoanalytic foundlings" have since occupied child psychotherapists, particularly those trained in object relations theory and ego psychology (77).[7] Neither the Rat Man nor the Wolf Man would qualify as a "psychoanalytic foundling," having survived into adulthood (in however an infantile state). Thus while Freud set the feral standard, using animal analogies to paint an ominous picture of the psyche, later theorists and case writers invoked the animal metaphor also to represent the unspeakable things that cripple and even destroy the child, such as bad parenting, sexual abuse, and even the terrors of the Holocaust. In the clinical literature, the term "feral" designates moderate to severe psychological trouble.

At the same time, as the psychological industry has largely shifted its focus away from treating mental illness and toward promoting mental health, the very idea of inner beastliness that Freud helped disseminate has been appropriated as the stuff of normal masculinity, as a productive, rather than a potentially destructive, force. Thus the psychoanalytic feral tale has a dual history, at once a narrative vehicle for the cultural normalization of the feral boy and still a story of profound psychosocial difference. I am fascinated by this second tradition, which spans the work of Klein through Bettelheim through Julia Kristeva through Jeffrey Moussaieff Masson's recasting of Kaspar Hauser as a poster boy of child abuse and "soul murder."[8] The split between these two strains unfolds along predictable lines of gender as well as genre. Since the early twentieth century at least, the feral girl is almost always more marked by her feral condition, and the most highly publicized recent cases of feral children involve abused and neglected girls. But because my larger topic is the entangled history of boyology and the feral tale, I concentrate on the more heroic feral boy inaugurated by Freud's case studies.

My second concern is thus the popularization of the feral boy along literary and residually psychological (if not always strictly psychoanalytic) lines. While it may seem counterintuitive to associate Freud with American popular culture, the psychoanalytic feral tale made possible not only the interiorization or "remythification" of wildness of which Hayden White and other scholars have spoken but also the juvenilization of the feral tale. Thanks in large part to the success of psychoanalysis in the United States— and its diffusion as ego psychology and object relations came to modify and displace Freudian discourse—Maurice Sendak's wolf-boy Max in *Where the Wild Things Are* (1963), one of our most famous picture books, is now the prototype of a normal boy. Nor is it surprising that werewolf movies were popular in the midcentury heyday of adolescent mass culture; monster movies (often very parodic) remain a staple of teen mass media. As evidence I turn to Michael Jackson's breakthrough music video *Thriller* (1983), Rod Daniel's film *Teen Wolf* (1985), and several other contemporary cinematic feral tales marketed to youth. In these and similar productions, the sub-versiveness of Freud's insights yields to a defensive celebration of normative identity and family values. Heterosexual manhood is identified with, and made possible by, the masculinized inner wild child. Although such films are designed for children and teenagers, they often feature an adult male character who must recuperate or manage his inner wild boy. In this sense, at least, productions for children and productions for (and about) white, middle-class American men seem indistinguishable. Again and again, the conceit of the inner wolf-boy displaces wildness, refuses the feral tale's queer potential.

Sex and the Singular Feral Boy

As I noted in chapter 3, Dr. Itard had argued vis-à-vis Victor of Aveyron that the study of wild children could make culture intelligible, whereas E. B. Tylor, writing in 1863, preferred a more ethnological model of culture that had no analytical place for *Homo ferus,* only normal children. Freud merges these two attitudes in his depictions of feral children as both neurotic and normal, animal identified yet human. In the Rat Man and the Wolf Man case histories, Freud rewrites the sexological pervert as feral, claiming for psychoanalysis a diagnostic authority similar to that of sexology, but also offering greater hope for self-understanding and even self-improvement.

But the Rat Man and Wolf Man were hardly the first feral boys whose sexual problems engaged the curiosity of scientists and clinicians. Victor and Kaspar Hauser were also sexual misfits by most standards, and the feral tale was preoccupied with sexuality long before its encounter with psycho-analysis. In Itard's 1801 report to Napoleon's imperial government on his work with Victor, which rather resembles the case histories of Freud, Itard notes that in his attempt to "awaken the nervous sensibility by the most powerful stimulants" (105), he administered warm baths and

> prescribed the application of dry frictions to the spinal vertebrae, and even the tickling of the lumbar regions. This last means seemed to have the most stimulating tendency: I found myself under the necessity of forbidding the use of it, when its effects

> were no longer confined to the production of pleasurable
> emotions; but appeared to extend themselves to the organs of
> generation, and to indicate some danger of awakening the
> sensations of premature puberty. (107)

He adds that Victor has been suffering through puberty, "the appearances of which cast considerable suspicion on the origin of certain affections of the heart, which we regard as very *natural*" (140). Itard admits that Victor's excitations are not heterosexual in nature but thinks it impolitic to undermine social prejudices "in themselves perhaps respectable, and which, beyond all doubt, constitute the most amiable, as well as the most consoling illusions of social life" (140).

In the 1807 update, Itard, a lifelong bachelor, makes clearer his discomfort with Victor's sexual unorthodoxy. Itard isn't surprised that the boy remains selfish in nature, but he finds "astonishing" the boy's consistent "indifference to women, in spite of all the signs and symptoms of a well-developed puberty" (175). This simply "defies all explanation" (175). "Every day, I waited for a breath of that universal emotion which stirs and stimulates all creatures, expecting it to move Victor in his turn and enlarge his moral existence" (175). No doubt Itard's rhetoric of innocent expectation and puzzlement is largely for the benefit of His Excellency, the Minister of the Interior, but it is true that Itard's inability to direct Victor's libido in the proper direction was one reason he quit working with the boy. Feuerbach likewise found disconcerting Kaspar Hauser's indifference to women and his preference for women's clothing. In his fascinating reading of the Hauser case, Michael Newton proposes that Kaspar might have been the love object of Lord Stanhope (likely Hauser's murderer). In any case, neither Victor nor Kaspar achieved what Freud called genital heterosexuality, the final stage of sexual development.[9] Not surprisingly, Freud shared Itard's ambivalence about the naturalness of heterosexual desire when he profiled his feral boys; he too judged it one of our "most consoling illusions," even if he didn't entirely debunk it.[10]

Although Itard worked before the advent of sexology, the kind of interest he shows in Victor's sexual development, particularly as a barometer of the boy's success in culture, is characteristic of that discipline, which took shape after the dissemination of evolutionary science. Until around 1890, sexology was primarily a German and French enterprise, with sexual psychopathology dominating the scene, especially in psychiatric circles. Several prominent German sexologists, however, were advocates of the decriminalization of homosexuality, chiefly Karl Ulrichs and Magnus Hirschfeld, but also Richard von Krafft-Ebing.[11] While the sexologists reveled in the proliferation of sexual types—among them the zooerasts, exhibitionists, fetishists, and even heterosexuals—they did not uniformly endorse essentialist categories or social discrimination.[12] Freud thus inherited a German-led sexological tradition imbued with the same contradictory impulses that characterize his own writings.

Freud understood the power of this tradition. He specifically courted medical practitioners who specialized in sexual pathology, hoping to interest them in psychoanalysis. In 1908 and 1909, Freud had published essays on hysteria while bringing his theories of infantile sexuality in line with sexology. As Stephen Kern and Frank Sulloway confirm, Freud's attention to child sexuality was anything but novel; many sexologists had already done impressive work in this area, including Sanford Bell in America (a former student at Clark University) and Albert Moll in Germany. In fact, Freud was beaten into English print by Moll's *The Sexual Life of the Child,* translated into English in 1913, which offered the first overview of child sexual life and the extant literature. Introduced by child expert and Columbia professor Edward L. Thorndike, the book affirms the more custodial typologies of Krafft-Ebing and Havelock Ellis against Freud's innovations. Bell's theories were more biogenetic in spirit; he likened childhood sexuality to amorous activity in puppies, seals, grouse, and goldfinches (Hale, *Freud and the Americans,* 107). Upstaging these researchers, Freud transformed a subfield of sexology into a major aspect of psychoanalysis. Children, he felt, are sexually liminal, neither entirely human nor animal, as Moll and Bell respectively presumed.[13]

Before writing his feral tales, Freud provided a systematic outline of sexuality that might be understood as a primer for a new kind of child study, distinct both from European sexology and from the American child study movement: *Three Essays on the Theory of Sexuality* (1905). Darwinian in form and theme, this text offers an account not only of perversion but also of neurosis (which Freud calls the "negative" of perversion). I think of *Three Essays* as the first phase of Freud's portrait of sexual malaise, while the feral tales, closer in tone and spirit to *The Interpretation of Dreams* (1900), form the second phase. *Three Essays* opens with an essay on the sexual aberrations, perhaps because sexology as a field of study had organized itself around deviance, but also because sexual aberration was still a safer subject than child sexuality. The next two essays are devoted to infantile sexuality and to puberty, respectively. In *Three Essays,* childhood and adolescence are nearly synonymous with perversion, and perversion with everyday life. Freud scoffs at the notion that the masturbating child is a social menace. He pays virtually no attention to the sexual types of the sexologists and even blithely observes that intercourse with animals "is by no means rare, especially among country people," for whom "sexual attraction seems to override the barriers of species" (14).

At this stage in his career, Freud had no direct clinical experience with either children or alleged perverts. No matter: perversion and childhood are for Freud aggregates of memory, overlapping psychic states, a relation of ontogeny (the development of the individual) and phylogeny (the development of the larger group or species). Freud insists that the child persists within the adult, just as the inner invert survives heterosexuality. Humans, he writes in a much-quoted passage added in 1915 to *Three Essays*, "are capable of making a homosexual object-choice and have in fact made one in their unconscious" during childhood, which means that "the exclusive sexual interest felt by men for women is also a problem that needs elucidation and is not a self-evident fact" (12).[14] The child is likewise redefined in that work as both a dynamic, physical person and a static psychic reality. Adulthood, like heterosexuality, is neither self-evident nor inevitable, even if linked with culture.

Freud pursues the identical ideas in his feral tales, emphasizing that the psychic traffic in animals reflects a state of lesser development, but not necessarily pathology in the sexological sense. Freud never personally encountered a feral child or foundling. As usual, he converts a lack of clinical experience into theoretical bravado, describing adults as children, and neurotics as essentially feral, or developmentally deficient. Thus while the Rat Man and the Wolf Man were adult patients, Freud emphasizes their infantile fears and fantasies. But although he associates them with animals to make them compelling as sexually vexed subjects, Freud isn't interested in proliferating species of perversion in these tales or in *Three Essays*. Instead, he represents his patients as human beings with animal associations, capable of achieving culture with guidance.

Freud's work was thus a substantial departure from sexological primers such as Krafft-Ebing's *Psychopathia Sexualis* (1886), a compendium of psychosexual disorders, among them erotic delirium, necrophilia, coprophilia, bestiality, coprolagnia, lesbianism, viraginity, dementia, frottism, and of course (male) homosexuality.[15] Krafft-Ebing's brand of sexology is characterological and taxonomic, emphasizing inherited dispositions and more static types of perversion. No subject is diagnosed as more than one kind of pervert, although the lines of definition seem arbitrary; masochists are sometimes masochists, and sometimes homosexuals, but rarely both. *Psychopathia Sexualis* was groundbreaking in its multiplication of singularities, but it told no stories of cultural modification or liminality.[16]

Freud's theoretical innovation, his rhetorical skills, and his interest in his patients' imaginative lives resulted in a dramatic transformation of the sexological profile. In effect, Freud interiorized sexology, recasting sexual types as stages of affinity and cathexis. Itard's report on Victor, with its less certain commitment to organicism and inheritance, seems closer to Freud's work in interpretive spirit than texts such as *Psychopathia Sexualis*. Freudian psychoanalysis did more than de- or repathologize the pervert along sexological lines; it rewrote the pervert as feral, suspending him somewhere between nature and culture.[17] Even so, psychologists and social scientists alike continued to worry about the nonnormative sexuality of feral boys; summarizing the eighteenth-century case of Wild Peter, anthropologist R. M. Zingg writes (in 1939) that "what proves, above all, the more than brutish and invincible stupidity of Peter, [is] just as complete an indifference for the other sex" (Singh and Zingg, *Wolf-Children and Feral Man*, 186–87).

Freud's literary relays between animal and boy help naturalize the bourgeois project of psychoanalysis against, if also alongside, sexology. The class and racial dimensions of Freud's theories go underground, even as repressed sexual dynamics (homo and hetero alike) rise to the surface.[18] In the Rat Man case, it is an Ibsen play, a properly literary text, which enables this mode of analysis, whereas in the Wolf Man case, literary fairy tales constitute the interpretive scene.

The Rat Currency

On June 3, 1909, while preparing for his first and only visit to the United States, Freud wrote to Carl Jung that "I suddenly feel like writing up the Salzburg Rat Man, and if you like I can give you the piece for the second number [of the journal *Jahrbuch für psychoanalytische und psychopathologishe Forschungen*]" (*Freud/Jung Letters*, 227). Later that month he reported that the case "just pours out of me, and even so it's inadequate, incomplete, and therefore untrue. A wretched business. I am determined to finish it before leaving and to do nothing more before setting sail for our America" (238). Freud finished the piece in early July. In September he delivered his five lectures at Clark University in Worcester, Massachusetts, accompanied by Jung and their Hungarian colleague Sándor Ferenczi. Clark's president, the psychologist Granville Stanley Hall, had invited Freud and twenty-eight other specialists in the sciences and the humanities to participate in the school's vigentennial celebration. Freud's topic was childhood sexual neurosis, central to the Rat Man case, officially titled *Notes upon a Case of Obsessional Neurosis* (1909). "Neither psychoanalysis nor the United States," writes Philip Cushman, "has been the same since" (140). Just as the narratives of Anna O. and Dora had earlier helped Freud transform hysteria studies into psychoanalysis proper, the Rat Man case allowed Freud to share his faith in infantile sexuality and Oedipal dynamics with a highly sympathetic American audience.[19]

The Rat Man came to Freud in October 1907. He was Ernst Lanzer, a twenty-nine-year-old lawyer, whose initial complaints included suicidal impulses and fears that injury would befall his female lover and his father. His concerns about death, and his uncanny ability to predict the death of relatives, earned him a reputation as a "carrion crow." Stranger still, he worried that he or his loved ones would be subjected to a cruel, allegedly Eastern war punishment described by his sadistic army captain: a pot is filled with rats and then tied upside-down on the victim's buttocks, and the rats gnaw their way out through the anus. From the beginning, Freud worries about his patient's transference. "He repeatedly addressed me as 'Captain,'" remarks Freud, "probably because at the beginning of the hour I had told him that I myself was not fond of cruelty like Captain M., and that I had no intention of tormenting him unnecessarily" (15).[20]

In keeping with *Three Essays*, Freud emphasizes the Rat Man's early sexual life, declaring that early events "were not merely, as he supposed, the beginning of his illness, but were already the illness itself. It was a complete obsessional neurosis" (9). Section G, "The Father Complex and the Solution of the Rat Idea," is the centerpiece of the case. Freud explains that unresolved father-son conflict has been reanimated (literally) by the rat story, in tandem with the Rat Man's dilemma regarding whom to marry, his impoverished true love or the daughter of a wealthy cousin. Several years after his father's death, the patient had sexual intercourse for the first time, and according to Freud, "an idea sprang into his mind: 'This is glorious! One might murder one's father for this!'" (43). This proto-Oedipus complex is exacerbated by the story of rat torture, especially since the patient's father was also a military officer. That story "had jarred upon certain hyperaesthetic spots in his unconscious"; it was "a question of 'complex sensitiveness'" and overdetermination (49).

Fortunately, Freud is up to the interpretive task. Over the years, "rats had acquired a series of symbolical meanings, to which, during the period which followed, fresh ones were continually being added. I must confess that I can only give a very incomplete account of the whole business" (52). Next he declares unequivocally that "what the rat punishment stirred up more than anything else was his *anal eroticism*, which had played an important part in his childhood and had been kept in activity for many years by a constant irritation due to worms" (52). Worms, however, are not as symbolically laden in this case as rats. Apparently rats came to be associated with money, as *Ratten* (rats) is nearly *Raten* (installments). "In his obsessional deliria," notes Freud, "he had coined himself a regular rat currency":

> Little by little he translated into this language the whole complex
> of money interests which centered around his father's legacy to

> him; that is to say, all his ideas connected with that subject were, by way of the verbal bridge "Raten-Ratten," carried over into his obsessional life and became subjected to his unconscious. (*Three Case Histories*, 52)

The patient also associated rats with syphilis and thus the penis, evocative of anus-invading worms. The association *heiraten* (to marry) further complicates the scene.

Apparently, however, none of these associations revealed the nature of this specific neurosis. The breakthrough came one day when the Rat-Wife in Ibsen's play *Little Eyolf* (1894) mysteriously came up during analysis and supplied the most crucial association of all: "that of *children*" (53). Freud explains neither the play nor its place in the analysis, but in brief, Ibsen's title character is a child injured while his parents make love. The parents fault each other, and then Little Eyolf, under the spell of the Rat-Wife, drowns himself. Afterward the parents accept responsibility for their neglect. Freud observes (in a footnote) that the Rat-Wife is probably adapted from the legend of the Pied Piper of Hamelin, who enticed both rats and children to a watery grave. In legends, the rat appears not as repulsive but as "something uncanny—as a chthonic animal . . . used to represent the souls of the dead" (53).

This literary association of rat and child secures other Oedipal recollections. Earlier in this section, Freud shares that the patient recalls being punished as a young child not for sexual activity but for having bitten someone (46). Freud explains (again in a footnote) that the recollection was a screen memory for a more embarrassing sexual misdeed. Having established the rat-child link via Ibsen—literature confirming the Rat Man's oral report—Freud now reveals that the patient understands his childhood self as a rat: "But he himself had been just such a nasty, dirty little wretch, who was apt to bite people when he was in a rage. . . . He could truly be said to find 'a living likeness of himself' in the rat" (54; here Freud quotes from *Faust*).[21] "According, then, to his earliest and most momentous experiences, rats were children," concludes Freud (54).

Ibsen's play, however, suggests another possibility that Freud doesn't develop, namely, that parents are rats, an interpretation later pursued by Bettelheim. Little Eyolf is clearly the victim of neglect. He is feral (seduced by the Rat-Wife) because his parents do not care for him. He is injured while they have intercourse, which seems a rather literal enactment of the psychic injury of the primal scene. For the Rat Man, however, no such scene of adult sex and infant terror is to blame, despite Freud's invocation of the play. Instead, the primal scene is presumably a solo act of masturbation interrupted and punished by Dad, and distorted as the memory of having been a "nasty, dirty little wretch." If the Rat Man is not to blame for his neurosis, neither are his parents, in Freud's view, nor their surrogates. The captain may be cruel, but he (like Freud) is not responsible for reanimating prehistoric fears.[22]

Freud's gloss on *Little Eyolf*, then, de-emphasizes the impact of parental neglect and accentuates infantile sexuality and its repression and representation via the rat imago. The problem is not abuse but self-abuse. Had Bettelheim introduced Ibsen's play into the analysis, he would surely have found fault with the Rat Man's parents. For Freud, the important detail is the child's self-identification as a rat, the result of the usual psychodramas and not otherwise disabling. In Freud's eyes, the patient's multiple rat associations underscore his a priori anal eroticism and his rivalry with his father. These basic drives and dynamics form the bestial core of an ostensibly civilized man. Fortunately, the neurosis dissolves once the rat currency is decoded.

Little Eyolf is not the only literary key to the case. American psychotherapist Leonard Shengold speculates that the Rat Man's captain might have read about the rat punishment in an 1899 novel by Octave Mirbeau called *The Torture Garden*, widely known in Europe. The garden is in China, and the book's climax revolves around the story of a rat torture, told to a young woman but not enacted in the text. The tale hinges on a fantasy of abuse, not an actual episode of violence. Freud and his patient reconstruct this already Orientalist fantasy as a horror story, one that emphasizes the dominance of fantasy while implying the cruelty of the Rat Man's captain.[23]

We might conclude that Freud is too committed to infantile sexuality to consider alternative explanations for the Rat Man's condition. Freud, after all, was frantically working on this case history during his preparations for his 1909 visit to America, where he announced the importance of infantile sexuality.[24] Perhaps Freud really did overlook parental responsibility in the Rat Man case. But what's distressing about the current debate about Freud's position on abuse is the twofold insistence that abuse is a self-evident event, and that Freud's position amounts either to affirmation or to denial.[25]

Peter Middleton suggests another way to think about culpability in the Rat Man case. In "Are Men Rats?" Middleton argues that the Rat Man's difficulties are best understood in the context of World War I and the mass habituation to male violence that enabled and accompanied it. If Freud is guilty of anything, suggests Middleton, it is complicity with the structures and strictures of masculinity. In his view, psychoanalysis adopts the cultural logic of masculinity, a logic that forbids the expression of emotions and the development of empathy among and for men. As Middleton emphasizes, Freud ignores the Rat Man's violent tendencies toward women and assumes that his military interests are normal. Middleton also speculates that the Rat Man's mythic stature as half-man, half-animal functions to emphasize the process of man making. The Rat Man is not only still an animal; he is also still a boy. Working from an academic men's studies perspective, Middleton shows how Freud initiates the Rat Man into the world of men.

For Middleton, such hazing merits no celebration, as it does for the boyologists. Rather, it is cause for alarm. "The rattiness of the patient," he writes, is "masculine violence," and "psychoanalysis is a successful rat catcher because it knows how to speak to such animals" (84–85). Examining the Freudian and post-Freudian writing on ego consolidation, infantile aggression, and the death drive, Middleton holds that male violence shapes the psychoanalytic rules of engagement. Residual in the Rat Man case "is something about masculinity that is unspeakable within the existing framework" (101). If male violence is unspeakable in Freud's tale, implies Middleton, then perhaps critical discourse can attest to that horror.

Who's Afraid of the Big Bad Wolf?

The specificity of the animals with which Freud's two patients identify should give us pause. Freud implies that the animal affinities of Rat Man and the Wolf Man are idiosyncratic and even incidental, operating much like the ethnographer describing his subjects in a manner allegedly mimetic rather than interpretive. But the rat and the wolf were the most popular animal figures in the racially and class-inflected Anglo-European literature of colonialism and urban reform. Freud wasn't simply paying homage to his patients' eccentricities; these identifications have a history, one that informs but also exceeds psychoanalysis.

The rat, Freud tells us, is a natural symbol of self-loathing—even if Freud must introduce an Ibsen play in order to decode the "rat currency" behind his patient's symptoms. As Peter Stallybrass and Allon White point out, while Freud examines the rat as a signifier in the Rat Man's tortured psyche, he "nonetheless treats the concept of 'rat' as unproblematically given, the 'natural' symbol of his patient's repression" (144). The rat, ostensibly a creature of the slum, is a symbol of bourgeois anxiety about health and hygiene, mediated through folklore and literature.[26] Freud's feral currency works as a lingua franca for the psychic slum, where the primitive and the evolved variously meet and dodge one another. With the debut of psychoanalysis, urban reform gives way to sexual exposé and healing. Or in the residual idiom of colonialism, in which the wolf-boy figures, Freud maps and conquers the psychic jungle, devotes himself to native uplift. Given such refashionings, it seems a mistake to pluralize Freud's feral monikers as archetypes, as does one otherwise astute psychotherapist, Leonard Shengold, who holds forth on the traits of "rat people."[27]

The wolf-boy enters Freud's work through the literary fairy tales of the Brothers Grimm, who transformed oral folktales into stylized literary fairy tales that largely reflected and legitimized the values and shifting political affiliations of Germany's educated middle class (Zipes, *Fairy Tales and the Art of Subversion,* 47).[28] In appealing to wolf-themed fairy tales, Freud sets the stage for later psychoanalytic case studies of folklore such as Erich Fromm's *The Forgotten Language: An Introduction to the Understanding of Dreams, Fairy Tales, and Myths* (1951) and Bettelheim's *The Uses of Enchantment* (1976).[29] Like Little Hans, the Wolf Man as a young boy was preoccupied with the "widdlers" of horses and other beasts. But unlike Hans, he turned to the fairy tales of his culture, to animal avatars, for sexual information. He became preoccupied with a story from William Caxton's *Reynard the Fox,* about a wolf who went fishing with his tail during winter and lost it when it froze and fell off. Also formative was his reading of "Little Red Riding Hood" and "The Seven Little Goats," in which "kids" are gobbled up by a wolf and then rescued from his belly. Freud doesn't specify, but his summaries suggest that he's referring to the versions of the Brothers Grimm. These stories inspired the Wolf Man's dream of the wolves, from which Freud assembles the primal scene, proposing that images of wolves remind the boy of the parental *coitus a tergo more ferarum* he witnessed but repressed. The upright wolf represents his father, who penetrates his mother from behind. Freud notes that the Wolf Man has never been afraid of wolves going on all fours or even lying in bed; his fear depends "upon the creature being in an upright attitude" (*Three Case Histories,* 198).

As in the Rat Man case, Freud portrays his patient as a man suffering not so much from sexual dysfunction per se as from an inability to distinguish between bestiality and humanity at the level of the unconscious. A wealthy young Russian, Serge Pankejeff first consulted Freud in 1910, a year after Freud's trip to America and the publication of the Rat Man tale. Freud concentrates on Pankejeff's early anxiety-hysteria, which developed just before the boy's fourth birthday and later changed into an obsessive religious piety. This focus allows Freud to isolate infantile neurosis and construct the case around an animal-identified childhood. Through a fairy-tale register, Freud reconstructs the act of *coitus a tergo more ferarum* that so terrified the boy, aged one and one-half, causing him to scream and pass a stool.

Recently, scholars working in two usually distinct fields, rhetoric and queer studies, have read that primal scene, and the case more generally, as the story of Freud's homoerotic or anal-sadistic use and abuse of Pankejeff.[30]

I find such analyses compelling, and I share Dianne Sadoff's belief that this case evidences the homosexual's displacement of the hysteric as Freud's favorite disciplinary figure. Even so, I think critics overstate the case. Freud is often chastised for withholding the "missing" portion of the primal scene—the stool that interrupts coitus—until near the end of the analysis. Stanley Fish understands this strategy as yet another indication of Freud's sadistic tendencies; in his view, Freud withholds the missing portion in order to take a whopping dump on his patient. But it's equally plausible that Freud delays the information to avoid the kind of punishing logic to which Fish subscribes. Freud sees the boy's stool as a gift, not a counteroffensive. He describes the boy's defecation not as frightened protest but as erotic generosity. "Faeces are the child's first gift, the first sacrifice of his affection, a portion of his own body which he is ready to part with, but only for the sake of someone he loves" (239). And as with the Rat Man, Freud links faeces and money with the child; the (male) child is again the privileged term in the feral currency. "At a later stage of sexual development faeces take on the meaning of a *child*" (240); "in a roundabout way, then, through their common relation to the 'gift' meaning of faeces, money can come to have the meaning 'child,' and can thus become the means of expressing feminine (homosexual) satisfaction" (241).[31]

Moreover, scholars who presume Freud's strategies to be abusive overlook the fact that the Wolf Man's sexuality is coded not only as anal but also as animal. Most accounts of the Wolf Man case emphasize Freud's use of *a tergo* to specify the style of coitus seen by the boy. But Freud further modifies *coitus a tergo* with *more ferarum*, meaning wilder, more beastly. In one instance, that second Latinate stands alone, when Freud explains that such a preference is an "archaic trait" of the anal-erotic disposition: "Indeed, copulation from behind—*more ferarum*—may, after all, be regarded as phylogenetically the older form" (199). Freud may not identify *Homo ferus* as such, but he acknowledges feral intercourse with this sequence of taxonomic terms.

Not only does Freud present the Wolf Man as feral in terms of his sexual traits; after describing the primal scene, he even proposes that the Wolf Man might not have witnessed his parents thus engaged but rather have seen an act of animal copulation, which he displaced onto his parents. Typically this theory is presumed to be a weak link or concession in Freud's otherwise aggressive campaign for the reality of primal scene number one (the witnessing of parental sex). But in my view, critics overestimate Freud's loyalty to the parent primal scene. The animal hypothesis could just as easily serve as the primal scene, particularly since the case is saturated with animal symbolism. The Wolf Man is so animal identified, in fact, that Freud's sudden revelation of the parent primal scene seems more an abrupt reversal than a smooth revisitation of the case thus far. This is why I understand the case as a feral tale, as the story of a boy imprinted on animal rather than civil intercourse, no matter what forms were engaged in that ostensibly bestial behavior. As in the Rat Man case, what's significant about the Wolf Man is his animal persona. But while the Rat Man mistakes his childhood self for a rat, the Wolf confuses wolves with the parents who raise him, not identifying those parents as abusive just yet, but nonetheless paving the way for Bettelheim, who shifts attention away from the child's fantasy life and toward those wolfish parents.

Freud develops a narrative legend for the patient's psychic map, turning first to fairy tales, and then to the dream of the wolves. These imaginative renderings don't prove anything in terms of sequence or causation, but they do affirm the man-animal relay. The dream of the wolves had already been published in a 1913 sketch, "The Occurrence in Dreams of Material from Fairy-Tales," although Freud's interpretation was several years in the making. The dream, which occurs just before the boy's fourth birthday, is simple: he suddenly awakes at night in his bed and sees six or seven white wolves perched in a walnut tree outside his window. Terrified, "evidently of being eaten up by the wolves," he screams and wakes up for real (*Three Case Histories*, 186). Accompanying this description is the patient's sketch of five (not six or seven) wolves in the tree, which Freud reproduces. The Wolf Man himself associates this dream with the wolf illustration that so terrified him, which he attributes to a picture-book version of "Little Red Riding-Hood." Freud decides that the wolf is a father surrogate, and that the fairy tale behind the dream was in fact "The Wolf and the Seven Little Goats"; "Little Red Riding-Hood" was its screen.[32] The dream of the wolves functions much like the folkloric tradition itself, distorting not only the *coitus a tergo more ferarum* but the interceding picture-book illustration and the wolf tales. Mother and father metamorphose into the six or seven wolves of the second folktale, with the immobility of those wolves suggesting the "strained attention" with which the boy witnessed the scene (192). An animal scenario is linked with the primal scene, if not as the original event, then as imaginative reformulation of it.

Freud implies that the wolf association is quite natural, in that *coitus a tergo more ferarum* is beastly behavior and would instinctively be perceived as such, even by a young child. Although he acknowledges that the boy's literary encounters with wolves are idiosyncratic, he also appeals to the wolf's status as man's most familiar surrogate in folklore, preceding the experiences of any single child. Through the mediation of the fairy tale, the wolf phobia seems natural.

While the rat is perhaps more familiar in real life, the wolf is known through folklore as a creature who flourishes outside of human society. Such images of the bestial outside are recruited as signifiers of the psyche's secret life, to the degree that they become almost trite. In folklore, of course, the wolf is a sexual predator; "Little Red Riding-Hood" is often a cautionary tale for innocent girls. But as in Angela Carter's short story "The Company of Wolves," in which the wolf merges with the hunter into a more dynamic personality, the Wolf Man in Freud's narrative is a figure at once menacing and pathetic. The Wolf Man is, in short, a human being, if a neurotic. The symbolic language is so familiar that "Wolf" even migrates from patient to teacher and therapist. Freud reveals that the Wolf Man's Latin master was called Wolf, which further animated the father-wolf complex. With his diagnosis of *coitus a tergo more ferarum* and his use of the feral, Freud too is Latin master, father figure, and Wolf.

The Wolf Man is for Freud primarily a boy with a problematic but not horrific psychosexual complex. That, at least, is the story he tells. Unlike the Rat Man, who was killed in World War I, Pankejeff lived to a ripe old age and never completely recovered from his symptoms, despite the help of Freud and later analysts Ruth Mae Brunswick and Muriel Gardner. If the Rat Man case helped launch Freud's career, the Wolf Man case became emblematic of a more mature psychoanalysis and its postwar discontents, which helps explain the persistence of the abuse hypothesis.

Freud also romanced the feral boy more briefly in *Totem and Taboo* (1913). In that book, it is again the feral boy through whom Freud elaborates his central theme, this time the psychic resemblances of savages and neurotics. Compared with the Rat Man and the Wolf Man, Arpád the chicken-boy is a minor character, but he plays a pivotal role in illustrating what Freud describes as the "positive" or unharmful infantile recurrence of savage totemism. Freud likens psychoanalysis to folklore, in a sense anticipating my take on the feral tale. What folklore has taught us about racial psychology, he suggests in *Totem and Taboo*, psychoanalysis will teach us about neurotic psychology (4). Freud poses as anthropologist, and his synopsis of aboriginal life is the classic portrait of the wolf-boy writ plural: aboriginals are "poor naked cannibals" who build no homes, raise no crops, and eat no refined food (4). It is to those wretches that the life of Arpád the chicken-boy—aka the "Little Chanticleer"—returns us.

Freud first heard of Arpád through his Hungarian colleague Sándor Ferenczi. In a letter to Freud dated January 18, 1912, Ferenczi describes his young patient as "a sensational case, significant enough to be a brother of 'Little Hans.' A boy who is now five, *Bandi*, was bitten on his penis by a rooster when, at age 2½, he urinated into a poultry cage (bleeding, pain, bandages). *Since that moment,*" Ferenczi continues, "the boy's entire psychic life revolves around chickens and roosters" (Freud and Ferenczi, *Correspondence,* 330). As with Little Hans, Freud makes it clear that he does not find the boy's behavior pathological. Instead he uses it to confirm his theory that the Oedipus complex is the vestige not merely of savage totemism but of an actual episode of jealousy, incest, and parricide in the Darwinian horde of our remote past. With the help of Arpád, Freud inaugurated a modern narrative of psychic activity predicated on ontogenetic avowals and revisions of the phylogenetic script.[33]

Where the Wild Things Are

Born unhousebroken and half wild, dabbling in their own feces and popping into their mouths whatever unlikely objects they can grab, [children] remain for a long time unsure—as the Alice books imply and Book IV of *Gulliver* explicitly states—whether they are beasts or men: little animals more like their pets than their parents.

—Leslie Fiedler, *Freaks*

For Freud, all children are feral early in life, and this perspective survives in both Freudian interpretive schemes and pop-cultural feral tales. Leslie Fiedler, for instance, makes essentially the same point in the epigraph from his book *Freaks,* subtitled *Myths and Images of the Secret Self.* Freud and Fiedler alike underscore the fundamental weirdness of all children alongside the exceptionality of those who seem irredeemably different. Most children figure out they're human, unless they are never embraced by culture. Even in Freud's work, there's a difference between children who snap out of their confusion and those who don't. Little Hans, for instance, resolves his horse-father complex in a properly Oedipal fashion; he does not become the Horse Man.[34] Fiedler appeals not only to Freud but to the twentieth-century practice of child analysis, which holds that children are not (yet) civilized, even when they seem perfectly normal.

Child analysis in the United States was a hybrid discipline, born of Hall's child study movement as well as other social science ventures. In this chapter, I argue that Freud's feral tales helped make space for the American wild boy, but there's another, perhaps more direct, line of feral tale influence in the United States as well. The same wolf-boy reports that so preoccupied Kipling also drew the attention of psychologists and sociologists in England and the United States. The esteemed psychologist Arnold Gesell, for instance, who founded the Yale Clinic of Child Behavior in 1911, was fascinated by the well-known but also well-disputed case of the wolf-girls of Midnapore, India. The girls, christened Amala and Kamala, were allegedly found in a wolf den in 1927 and were raised by the Reverend J. A. L. Singh in an orphanage. Anthropologist Robert Zingg generated interest in the story, corresponded with Singh, and wrote a bibliographic essay to accompany Singh's diary account in their collective effort, *Wolf-Children and Feral Man* (1939). Gesell himself wrote a book on the subject called *Wolf Child and Human Child* (1940), in which he cites scientific studies but also Kipling's *Jungle Books.*

Gesell was roundly criticized for his acceptance of Singh's testimony and Kipling's fiction, or for succumbing to myth. Zingg's and Gesell's collective faith in the feral child was not, however, an isolated episode of professional lunacy. *Wolf-Children and Feral Man* features forewords from four distinguished experts in the fields of human heredity, sociology, and psychology, including Gesell. Gesell would never have published *Wolf Child and Human Child* had he not already established himself as an expert on the human child. For Gesell, as for Freud, all children are clinical, if not pathological subjects; the existence of developmentally challenged children suggests a continuum of childhood experience, and the need for accredited specialists. Bruno Bettelheim's interest in feral children was also spiked by the Midnapore case; before long, Bettelheim was pointing to feral children as undiagnosed cases of autism.

While I see no direct connections between psychoanalysis and Scouting, the eventual success of Cub Scouting in America seems also to echo the normalization and juvenilization of the feral tale as expedited by psychoanalysis and social science. Scouting thrived in the United States after being introduced in 1910, but Cubbing itself was slower to catch on.[35] Early on, Scout leaders disliked the feral imaginary. But by 1956, Cub Scout membership had surpassed the combined membership of the Boy Scouts and Explorers. Moreover, the feral thematics of den mother and Cub seem to have bolstered both the 1950s cult of domesticity and the attendant "Momism" diatribes. It's easy to see the Oedipal logic of the Scouting program. Den mothers cultivate in Cubs an appreciation of home, and scoutmasters take over when boys come of age and embark on more outward-bound adventures. The wolf-boy of folkloric derivation and psychoanalytic and social science inflection thus became a standard American conceit by midcentury, if the success of Cub Scouting is any indication.

Like Scouting, psychoanalysis quickly became popular in the United States, especially after Freud's famous lectures at Clark University in 1909. Within a decade, psychoanalysis was a hot topic in the popular press. Best-selling books and countless magazine articles made Freud's theories available to the lay public, often giving psychoanalysis a rather optimistic spin. Popularizers played up the potential of psychoanalysis for personal and political transformation, against Freud's own warnings about the difficulty of such. Even as Freud's celebrity was spreading, the white primitive was in pop-psychological vogue, yet another version of the pragmatic American self. As evidence Joel Pfister points to titles such as William J. Fielding's *The Caveman within Us: His Peculiarities and Powers; How We Can Enlist His Aid for Health and Efficiency* (1922) (Pfister, "Glamorizing the Psychological," 183).

Scholars have furnished different explanations for the extraordinary success of psychoanalysis in the United States. While John Demos proposes that the American family was uniquely Oedipal and thus uniquely receptive to Freud's theories, Nathan G. Hale emphasizes instead the appeal of psychoanalysis as an alternative to the somatic style that dominated psychiatry. But the most intriguing (if also the most speculative) hypothesis comes from Philip Cushman, who holds that Freud's notion of the unconscious energized the American capitalist machine.[36] Freud's real successor in the movement, Cushman declares, was not a person but a nation, the United States. There the unconscious "became a vehicle for the single most important cultural dynamic of the twentieth century: the consumerization of American life" (143). The unconscious served as the new American frontier—Cushman calls it "the enchanted interior"—and the American self was refashioned as inherently needful and acquisitive. Psychoanalysis helped justify consumerist individualism naturalizing socioeconomic stresses as the necessary conditions of a "deep" psyche, shifting attention away from the material realities of work and play. Mass advertising and marketing, contends Cushman, sought to identify, or rather generate, the needs of the collective unconscious, and the federal government invested much energy in the creation of psychological expertise, such that psychotherapeutic practice was soon big business.[37]

Whereas most historians of psychoanalysis understand object relations theory and ego psychology as progressive, in that they challenge the allegedly more pessimistic Freudian vision of psychic life, Cushman sees in these movements the cultural triumph of American consumer society. In his view, the idea of the enchanted interior, or the new frontier of the unconscious, is what made possible mass culture from the 1950s onward. Beginning in this period, white, middle-class Americans "were characterized by a sense of unconditional entitlement; they felt entitled to money, commodities, experiences, food, special treatment, respect (sometimes deference), speaking the mind, expressing their feelings, getting their way" (221). Ellen Herman, too, takes issue with the consensus progressivist portrait of psychoanalysis and psychology at midcentury, emphasizing instead the degree to which ego psychology underwrote Cold War hostilities, with its emphasis on self-fortification and defense. The normalization of psychology as a professional practice—the general shift away from treating mental illness and toward promoting mental health—has since enabled and accompanied the perception that psychological treatment is an appropriate response to distress.

While speculation along these lines is tricky at best, it's likely that Freud's narrative forms were just as influential in America as his theories, even as those theories were reworked in a more generic psychological idiom. It is the folkloric nature of Freud's work, I think, that helps account for the success of his feral tales (whereas Gesell's *Wolf Child and Human Child* is largely forgotten). Even if he did not provide the key that unlocked the American commodity machine, as Cushman believes, Freud made possible—and made exemplary—variants of the feral tale that emphasized the "enchanted interior" both singular and collective. And as psychology reoriented itself to everyday life, we can see in children's popular culture a corresponding surge of psychological interest in fairy tales. The forms of boys' literature at issue in chapter 3 were instrumental in the feral tale's mass dissemination, as were mass media adaptations of classic fairy tales (especially those by Disney), but psychoanalysis also helped set the cultural stage.

Psychoanalysis, reports Alan Dundes, has long been preoccupied with folklore and the literary fairy tale. In fact, "almost every single major psychoanalyst wrote at least one paper applying psychoanalytic theory to folklore" ("The Psychoanalytic Study of Folklore," 21), among them Freud's contemporaries Karl Abraham, Ernest Jones, Carl Jung, and Otto Rank. Such "application" seems to have been a foundational practice of the discipline, and psychoanalysis is folkloric in other ways as well (case histories, as I've already pointed out, are transcripts of oral narrative). At the same time, the European fairy tale canon, especially the work of Charles Perrault, the Brothers Grimm, and Hans Christian Andersen, is generally understood as the foundation stone of children's literature. Most survey classes and introductory texts of children's literature begin with folklore, then move on to picture books and finally more sophisticated written genres.

The evolution of scholarly writing on children's literature follows this path as well. Although criticism of children's literature dates back at least to the beginning of the twentieth century, the field only became legitimate in English studies with the introduction of Marxist, psychoanalytic, and poststructuralist analysis. In *Fairy Tales and the Art of Subversion,* for example, Jack Zipes describes the literary fairy tale as the "classical genre for children" (from the book's subtitle) and sets the stage for a Marxist-materialist understanding of children's literature. His perspective is also residually psychoanalytic—in his words, "an historical psychological point of view"

(33)—in suggesting a correspondence between "psychogenetic" and "sociogenetic" factors in the socialization of children through fairy tales. It's hard to imagine children's literature without folklore, and children's literature criticism without Zipes, Marina Warner, Maria Tatar, and other scholars who examine the fairy tale (if not the feral tale).

It was, of course, Bruno Bettelheim's best-seller *The Uses of Enchantment* that made psychoanalytic interpretations of children's literature available to the greater reading public. Like Melanie Klein before him, Bettelheim thought that fairy tales were useful in gauging and ensuring mental health. Thanks to Richard Pollak's devastating biography *The Creation of Dr. B* (1997), as well as some detective work from Dundes, we know now that large chunks of *The Uses of Enchantment* were plagiarized. In more ways than one, then, Bettelheim's book responds to an already pervasive sense that fairy tales have much to say about childhood's trials and tribulations.

That conviction extends to more official forms of children's literature as well, even if no psychoanalytic study of, say, picture books has resonated in quite the same way with the larger reading public. Instead, the successful picture book speaks its own psychological truth about childhood. Nowhere is this imperative more evident than in Sendak's picture book *Where the Wild Things Are,* a Caldecott Medal winner and one of the best-selling children's books of all time. Donning a wolf suit, Max makes mischief "of one kind and another" and gets sent to his room by his mother, who calls him "Wild Thing!" Falling asleep, he travels to the land of the wild things, where he rules supreme until finally coming home to find his supper waiting—still hot.

Recently Jennifer Shaddock has interpreted *Where the Wild Things Are* as an imperialist fiction, with "its reliance on a frame of feminine domesticity and masculine voyage through which the hero finds authority and control over the natives of the land he discovers" (155). The sea voyage, the tropical landscape, the odd familiarity of the natives: these are the tropes that Sendak adapts. Shaddock also acknowledges the standard bibliotherapeutic interpretation, namely, that the story allows children to express anger without repercussion. In other words, it's a journey not merely into the heart of darkness but into the darkness of the heart. Shaddock then argues for a parallel between imperialist narrative and psychological fantasy. Insisting on the significance of Sendak's own cultural influences, and particularly the radical movements of the 1960s, she proposes that Sendak deconstructs the classic opposition of civil and wild by recognizing that rebellion is "a natural and healthy impulse" (158–59).

Shaddock valorizes at the generic psychological level what she criticizes in more political terms. But shouldn't Sendak's 1960s psychological refashioning of the wild and the civil concern us precisely as such, especially if we're charting the persistence of imperialist poetics in the psychological field? It might be more productive to see in Sendak's book the cultural ascendance of ego psychology, for instance, or at least faith in psychology more generally. The humanist psychology of Abraham Maslow and Carl Rogers, which emerged out of 1960s progressivism, likewise contributed to the gentle (even genteel) understanding of inner wildness at play in Sendak's inventive book. Earlier in the century, proponents of ego psychology had already argued that fantasy was vital to the mastery of psychological reality, that imaginative escape shores up the self.

Where the Wild Things Are is also notable for its gentle domesticity. In Manhood in America: A Cultural History, Michael Kimmel links the popularization of psychoanalysis and psychology from the 1920s onward to the cult of domesticity in which men as well as women participated. Kimmel argues that because the workplace was no longer an adequate zone for demonstrating masculinity, men turned their attention homeward, paid more attention to child-rearing advice, and participated in family activities more than ever before (or ever since). Where the Wild Things Are links outward-bound activity to the safe space of home, and although Max's father is nowhere to be seen, the book surely appealed to the father's as well as the child's sense of imagination and adventure, even as the bedtime reading of stories was very much a domestic ritual. As far as I know, no one has studied the appeal of picture books to adults. In our own time, picture books remain popular coffee table books and conversation pieces, thanks to their artistic appeal and their evocation of family togetherness.

In any case, Where the Wild Things Are makes inner wildness utterly safe. Sendak's classic book is a story of managed wildness, and as John Cech notes, there are traces of the Bad Boy (even Huck Finn) in Max as well as the more generic wild boy (Angels and Wild Things, 130–36).[38] Thus psychologist Michael Thompson, one of the new boyologists whose work I address in chapter 6, calls Where the Wild Things Are "the best book on boy anger" (165) in his Q&A primer Speaking of Boys. "Sendak beautifully illustrates my point about little-boy anger" he muses; "[boys] are dependent and furious at the same time" (166). Give your little boy some time out, Thompson advises, and he will repudiate truly wild things. Readers return to Where the Wild Things Are not because it has stood the test of time, as Shaddock implies, but because it has helped to set standards for that test. Thanks to psychological culture, and in keeping with it, Max knows how to wear his wildness.[39] Gone are the fears that crippled Freud's Wolf Man, and even the more generic angst of Kipling's hero, who sang, "I am two Mowglis . . . Ahae! My heart is heavy with the things I do not understand" (The Jungle Books, 6).

Teen Wolves

Where the Wild Things Are is just one example of the remythification that I've been describing, and in some ways it is an exceptional one, as most picture books don't so explicitly adapt the wolf-boy motif. Although the feral tale remains a popular form in children's literature, the cinematic feral tale even more consistently treats psychic wildness as enabling rather than disruptive. Moreover, cinematic feral tales tend to affirm heteronormativity through a carefully managed homo-narcissistic feral theme.

Consider, for instance, werewolf movies, which have been popular in America since the 1940s, when the Nazis were likened to wolf-men (Skal, *The Monster Show*, 211–27). In films such as *The Wolf Man* (1941), *Frankenstein Meets the Wolf Man* (1943), and *The Werewolf* (1956), lycanthropy signaled human depravity. In the 1950s, however, with the rise of teen culture, a different genre emerged that linked werewolf-dom or lycanthropy with male adolescence. American International Pictures assembled a cycle of films "whose appreciation," according to S. S. Prawer, "was almost entirely tongue-in-cheek—a perfect example of 'camp' manufacture and reception of the iconography of terror" (*Caligari's Children*, 15). These cinematic terrors included *Teenage Zombies* (1957), *I Was a Teenage Frankenstein* (1958), *Teenager Monster* (1958), and *Werewolf in a Girls' Dormitory* (1961). On-screen, the monstrous teen body afforded anxiety and amusement, horror alongside camp.

As a teenager I was obsessed with monsters and misfits; I read countless books about Bigfoot and the yeti. Even so, I don't remember seeing any werewolf films before 1983, when I attended a Boy Scout jamboree held in Austin, Texas. The most popular booth by far featured an entire troop performing, in costume, a rendition of Michael Jackson's just-released video *Thriller* (1983). I had seen the video on MTV; still, I was astonished to see several dozen boys perform it at a Scouting event. In retrospect, the spectacle doesn't seem that odd; teen culture has always dallied with the monstrous.

Thriller spawned a revolution in the music video industry, which has always relied heavily on teen audiences.[40] In the video, Jackson's character walks his girlfriend (played by *Playboy* playmate Ola Ray) along a wooded lane and asks her to "be my girl." She agrees; he gives her a ring. Then he makes a strange confession: "I have somethin' I wanna tell ya . . . I'm not like the other guys." Michael then transforms himself into a gruesome werewolf and dances with a pack of zombies and ghouls risen from their tombs. Ola flees her boyfriend, and just as he tries to grab her, she wakes up in the theater with the "real" Michael. They go home safely, but at the video's end, Michael grins demonically at the camera.

Directly inspired by John Landis's dark horror-fantasy film *An American Werewolf in London* (1979) the fourteen-minute *Thriller* was a huge commercial success. It revived interest in Jackson's LP of the same name, which quickly became the biggest-selling album in history. The video also provoked a storm of controversy; religious organizations denounced it as occult propaganda before it had even been released, which later prompted Jackson to omit the song from his concert performances. The video can easily (perhaps too easily) be interpreted as a coded statement of Jackson's liminal identity or, as Kobena Mercer argues, as a complex parody of heterosexual presumption. Mercer's essay appeared before the 1995 allegations of child abuse leveled against Jackson, which make *Thriller*'s confession of feral difference particularly ominous: just how exactly *is* Jackson different? Incidentally, *Thriller* was the inspiration for a feature film that Michael was planning with Steven Spielberg, a new version of *Peter Pan,* in which Michael would play Peter. Spielberg was unable to secure the script rights until much later, when he made the dreadful *Hook* (1991), starring Robin Williams. Said a Hollywood studio chief of Jackson: "I think he would have been a very good Peter Pan. Other than that, I don't know what you do with him" (Kennedy, "Time to Face the Music," 30).

Thriller suggests both the potential subversiveness of the werewolf motif and its narrative containment. Such containment may be endemic to the horror film, which tends to parody its own codes. Such parody does not necessarily subvert the genre but may reaffirm its nature as self-mocking. Many horror films indulge in a comic version of homosexual panic, associating, often through parody, the monstrous with the sexually liminal.[41] These films register anxieties about male-male relations—specifically, the anxiety that friendship will be misread as desire. Horror and teen films alike obsessively invoke and repudiate the specter of perversion.

Rod Daniel's *Teen Wolf* (1985), loosely inspired by *I Was a Teenage Werewolf,* likewise conflates the iconography of the feral child with lycanthropy in a parable of adolescent angst. Our hero's lupine impulses separate him from his peers but secure him to his father; werewolf culture, it seems, is all in the family. *Teen Wolf* is set in mythical Beacontown, a small community in which high school basketball games are epic social events. Our hero is Scotty Howard, an all-American boy with only two problems: he's small and easily bullied (and thus played by the elfin Michael J. Fox), and he's bored. There's nothing to do in Beacontown except work in Dad's hardware store and hang out at the local hot spots. Scotty pals around with his fellow basketball players and his tomboyish friend Booth, who has a crush on Scotty. Scotty has eyes only for the voluptuous Pamela, girlfriend of his basketball enemy, Nick.

The film opens in slow motion with the classic adolescent scene of the basketball game. Scotty and Nick square off in a struggle for possession of the ball, and suddenly Scotty growls menacingly, and the surprised Nick backs off. In the locker room after the game, Scott discovers a long strand of hair adorning his boyish chest. Puzzled, he consults his coach. The sports coach, of course, is a boy worker par excellence, a mentor figure for adolescent boys—but not this coach, who is totally inept and unprofessional. Scott tells him, "I'm going through some changes," and his coach, refusing to hear the details, waves him away with the banal reassurance that change is normal. Later, in the hardware store, Scotty's ears register the shrill frequency of a dog whistle. From the beginning, his wolfish tendencies suggest but also parody adolescent turmoil. Like many boys, he seeks assurance that he's normal.

Scotty's existential crisis intensifies at a college party he crashes. Everyone is drinking heavily and playing adult party games. Scotty and Booth are locked together in a closet; once inside, aroused presumably by raging hormones, Scott turns into a werewolf and ravishes his friend. When they emerge from the closet, Scotty has ripped through the back of her dress; the beast in the closet is violently heterosexual. Horrified by his savagery, Scotty rushes home and locks himself in the bathroom. In the mirror he watches his own transformation into a werewolf. His father demands to be let in, in a standard scene of surveillance. "Whatever it is," he tells his son, "you can tell me. I'll understand." "Not *this* time," replies Scotty. Finally forced to open the door, Scotty finds himself face-to-face with his father, also now a werewolf. "An explanation is probably long overdue," admits Mr. Howard.

The consequent father-to-son chat parodies awkward scenes of parent-child sex education and even more awkward scenes of coming out for lesbian and gay youth. Scotty's potential difference is quickly recuperated as family tradition and male homosocial bond. "Being what we are is not without its problems," admits his father, "but it's not all bad. Your mother went head-to-head with this thing, and so can you." It is not clear if Mom was also a werewolf, or if she learned to play Beauty to the Beast. Regardless, she is missing from this moment, in which the father, in male guru fashion, warns Scotty that he will enjoy "great power" but also "greater responsibility." No doubt Robert Bly would be pleased with Scotty's ability to manifest the Wild Man, and with Mr. Howard's spiritual guidance.

The film seems to parody progressive attitudes toward difference. "Werewolves are people just like anyone else," asserts Mr. Howard. "The werewolf is a part of you, but that doesn't change what you have inside." Even so, Scotty is terrified that his peers, particularly the guys, will reject him. In school the next day, he is obsessed with his newfound identity and finds himself bombarded with allusions to wolves, from Thomas Wolfe to the legend of Remus and Romulus. After school, he confronts his best friend, the cool and charismatic Stiles. "I've got to talk to you about something," says Scotty, eyes averted, and hands pocketed. "Are you going to tell me that you're a fag?" asks Stiles, threateningly. "If you're going to tell me you're a fag, I don't think I can handle it." At this Scotty looks outraged. "I'm not a fag," he spits, and backs away. "I'm a werewolf." As proof he promptly transforms himself, and the amazed Stiles embraces him, declares, "You're beautiful," and christens Scotty Teen Wolf, or simply T. W. Stiles's acceptance of T. W. marks Scotty's transition from beast to local celebrity; with Stiles's clever marketing strategies, T. W. becomes homosocially hip and heterosexually desirable, despite his insistence that "I'm no different than anyone else."

In *Teen Wolf*, the werewolf functions much like a related liminal creature of great notoriety: the vampire. Critics have commented on the historical association of vampirism and deviant sexuality, crucial to several teen films about vampires, notably Joel Schumacher's *The Lost Boys* (1987). Schumacher's film associates vampirism with a form of male bonding that refuses adulthood, commitment, and marriage. One of the film's protagonists, the teenager Michael, is seduced by the stylish vampires and is soon drinking blood and sleeping all day. Even so, he is horrified by his latent vampire tendencies. Another teen film that toys with vampirism as metaphor for sexual degeneracy is Jimmy Huston's *My Best Friend Is a Vampire* (1986). In this film, the parents of a troubled teen watch him acquire strange habits and companions and conclude that he's homosexual (they study the gay-affirmative primer *Now That You Know*), only to discover that he's just a vampire. Both films return the teen protagonist to the safe enclave of the heterosexual family after mimicking the codes of gay disclosure.

So, too, does *Teen Wolf*. Scotty's wolfishness affirms not his potential transgressiveness but his heterosexual appetite and reckless male instincts. The sexual mythology of the werewolf seems more staunchly heterosexual than that of the vampire, or at least less ambiguous, which may explain its greater popularity in children's literature. Unlike the vampire, the werewolf is an interior or latent creature, an occasional, violent manifestation of the primitive male self. The figure of the werewolf is thus easily appropriated by the storm-and-stress model of male adolescence. As T. W., Scotty indulges all of his wild desires; in one of the film's many irresponsible scenes, T. W. goes "surfing" atop a moving van driven by Stiles. As Stiles so eloquently puts it, "We got some fine new wheels, we got some good tunes, and a total disregard for public safety." Unlike the wimpy Scotty, T. W. is a surfer-stud who realizes his full sexual potential. Pamela, who scorns Scotty, is drawn to "the Wolf," and as she goes down on our hero, she declares, "You're an animal!" In time, Scotty learns to police his inner wolf, but only after he's been accorded the proper social and sexual respect.

The film's homosexual parody/panic underscores the importance of Scotty's male friendships and antipathies. Reassured of Scotty's heterosexuality, Stiles is his fast friend. T. W.'s prowess on the basketball court inspires both peer admiration and jealousy. T. W. even "comes out" as a werewolf on court in the middle of a game, and soon the entire town endorses his alternative lifestyle, since he's winning the games. As Scotty puts it, "Everybody likes the Wolf." The only character who calls Scotty a "freak" is his nemesis Nick. Even though Scotty rejects Pamela, his rivalry with Nick parallels the earlier conflict between Mr. Howard and the man who is now principal of Beacontown High, also organized around a woman, the late Mrs. Howard (r.i.p.).

Teen Wolf relocates the werewolf from the forest to high school; *Teen Wolf Too* (1987) takes him (Scotty's cousin) to college on a sports scholarship. Whatever his career plans, he is hardly a figure of transgression. Rather, he is Bly's Wild Man, horny and hairy but upwardly mobile. In the 1957 *I Was a Teenage Werewolf*, the troubled teen Tony (played by the late Michael Landon) is treated by a psychiatrist, who turns the teen into a werewolf through drugs and hypnotism; Tony is at once victim and social rebel. Scotty, however, couldn't be more conventional, even in his wildest form. His comfortable wildness suggests the popular acceptance and management of psychoanalytic metaphors, as opposed to the suspicion and even paranoia about psychiatry that drives *I Was a Teenage Werewolf*.

This chipper identification of the werewolf with the adolescent continues in popular horror fiction for young adults, notably R. L. Stine's Fear Street series, the adolescent equivalent to the wildly popular Goosebumps books. In the Fear Street series, there is much to be afraid of, including werewolves, vampires, and assorted human villains, but the scariest thing of all is adolescence itself. A typical example is *Bad Moonlight* (1995), which tells the story of a high school girl, Danielle, and her tumultuous coming-of-age. When the narrative begins, Danielle has not yet entered puberty; "I look twelve instead of eighteen," she complains (2). Her friends form a rock band and one by one turn into werewolves. Danielle worries that she, too, will go the way of the wolf. Stine plays with the now-standard tropes of wolfish adolescence, titling one chapter "First Blood." The heteronormative teen werewolf has become so standard in series fiction that Stine even parodies it in his Goosebumps book *My Hairiest Adventure* (1995). The protagonist fears he is turning into a werewolf, only to discover that he is really a dog, transformed during infancy through medical experimentation and now reverting back to his true form.

Familiar from folklore, the wolf-boy or werewolf is the most hetero-sexual of our feral heroes. The only openly gay appropriation of the motif that I know about is the film *The Wolves of Kromer* (1998), billed as a love story and a satirical fairy tale, but not as a children's film. The residents of the English town of Kromer plot against the "wolves" who live in the woods, beautiful young men who have been ostracized for their homosexuality (played by real male models). Directed by Will Gould, the film revolves around Seth, who has been thrown out of his home after coming out as a wolf. Seth falls in love with Gabriel, and they struggle to survive. Whatever its merits, however, this independent art film will probably never been seen by most children or teenagers.

Films besides *Teen Wolf* that do target children and teenagers play down the sexual as well as social alterity of the feral child. While Walt Disney's 1994 live-action *The Jungle Book* manages to avoid the overt racism of its 1967 animated predecessor (also by Disney)—which assigns black dialect to an Indian monkey named "King Louie" in the wake of the civil rights movement—the film stars the Asian American actor Jason Scott Lee as the Indian wolf-boy Mowgli and pairs him up with the fetching daughter of a British colonialist. The family/romance plot so central to Disney films frames Mowgli's socialization and even colonialism itself as heterosexual exploits. Mowgli's quick mastery of letters and manners is astounding when juxta-posed with the slow progress and frequent relapses of most famous feral children. Using giant flash cards and a slide projector, Mowgli's lady friend Kitty and a character named Dr. Plumford (played by John Cleese) teach Mowgli the alphabet, then complete words, and then bits of British culture. Soon our wolf-boy is taking tea, falling in love, and dancing to the "Blue Danube Waltz." This heteronormative socialization story continues with *George of the Jungle* (1997) and Disney's animated *Tarzan* (1999).

Probably the best recent cinematic example of the feral boy's makeover is *Hook*, which transforms J. M. Barrie's melancholic story about a boy who won't grow up into a yuppie fable of fatherhood. Barrie introduces Peter in *The Little White Bird* (1902) as a "Betwixt-and-Between," part bird, part boy, a "little half and half" (166–67). Barrie didn't imagine *Peter Pan* as children's literature, but the story soon became understood as such, particularly since children loved productions of the play (which was a Christmas pantomime). Certainly Disney capitalized on the story's appeal to children, and every film version since has softened Peter's strangeness, allied him with the generic stuff of magic dust and escapist fantasy. In *Hook*, directed by Steven Spielberg, Peter Pan—played by Robin Williams (who else, if not Michael Jackson?)—has left Neverland, married Wendy's granddaughter Moira, and become Peter Pan, a corporate lawyer. In short, a pirate. Returning to Neverland in search of his children, whom Hook has abducted, Peter eventually gets in touch with not only his inner Pan but his inner Pa; the "happy thought" that enables him to fly again is "I'm a daddy!"

Hook is a "family film" as much as a film for children; it's difficult to separate the two genres. *Hook* belongs to a string of films in which a man retrieves his lost boy-self through role reversal or some magical return to childhood, among them *Like Father, Like Son* (1987), *Big* (1988), and *Vice Versa* (1988). *Jungle 2 Jungle* (1997) belongs in this category too, since Tim Allen's urban character eventually comes to appreciate and even imitate the "native" ways of his son, who has been living somewhere in the Amazon. These films have much in common with feral/jungle films like *Crocodile Dundee* (1986), *Walk like a Man* (1987), *Encino Man* (1992), and *Jumanji* (1995), all of which feature a childlike or primitive man who charms and puts to shame polite society.

Although I've concentrated on the wolf man/boy's makeover from the serious subject of psychoanalysis to the comic stuff of mass media and culture, I should acknowledge that rodents are also now the lovable heroes of children's books and films. Witness the *Stuart Little* productions, for instance, and *Mrs. Frisby and the Rats of NIMH*. Even the anal anxieties of Freud's Rat Man find comic revival in Eddie Murphy's *Dr. Dolittle* (1998), in a scene featuring a giant, oversexed gerbil (don't ask, don't tell); earlier in the film, Murphy's character administers mouth-to-mouth to a rat.

Caleb and the Merboy

Ironically, feral tales in the form of contemporary children's books offer greater ideological flexibility or variance than do cinematic feral tales. Presumably the creators and producers of film hope for the largest possible market, whereas children's book authors and publishers target particular groups of readers vis-à-vis familiar genres (even if a certain homogenization of the field seems to be the trend, as the Harry Potter craze indicates). For whatever reasons, writers of children's books take more chances with their material (contrary to the assumptions of some). The feral child is a fascinating creature, and the feral tale thus remains a staple of children's literature. Titles include Allan W. Eckert's *Incident at Hawk's Hill* (1971), Jane Yolen's *Children of the Wolf* (1984), William Mayne's *Antar and the Eagles* (1989), Sylvia Peck's *Seal Child* (1989), Dennis Covington's *Lizard* (1991), Caroline Stevermer's *River Rats* (1992), Eric Jon Nones's *Caleb's Friend* (1993), Karen Hesse's *The Music of the Dolphins* (1996), Elaine Landau's *Wild Children: Growing Up without Human Contact* (1998), Harry Mazer's *The Wild Kid* (1998), and Mordicai Gerstein's two retellings of the Victor of

Aveyron case, *The Wild Boy* (a picture book), and *Victor* (a young adult novel), both published in 1999. These texts reflect the forms and emphases of the feral tale at large. Some are purely fictional, others are fictionalized accounts of historical cases; several are cautionary tales about scientific exploitation.

As with the cinematic feral tale, so with these books: the more mainstream the production, the more custodial its vision. For instance, the most canonical of these texts, Eckert's *Incident at Hawk's Hill* (1971), a Newbery Honor Book, tells the story of six-year-old Ben, who lives temporarily with a female badger. Ben is afraid of his father, and Eckert relocates the boy from his human home to the badger's den, where he can work through his Oedipal drama. In this book, as in many feral tales, the feral boy must finally leave behind his animal stepmother to reconcile with the father and achieve human estate. In the novel, the animal mother is first honored and imitated by the boy but soon turns abject as Ben renounces her and accepts his father, his own masculinity, and, as Lacan would have it, the symbolic order (previously he was struggling with school; now he quickly learns his letters). Other texts, however, are more inventive and less fraught about gender roles, notably *Seal Child* and *The Music of the Dolphins*.

I began this chapter with Freud's case histories of the Rat Man and the Wolf Man. I conclude with a melancholic feral tale for children that preserves the creative spirit and generous vision, if not the narrative complexity, of Freud's work. In his picture book *Caleb's Friend* (1993), Eric Jon Nones celebrates the unusual beauty of a merboy and his strong bond with a young boy named Caleb. Caleb, too, is handsome, with thick brown hair and full lips, probably around twelve years old. After his father dies, Caleb works on boats belonging to other men in his fishing village. To soothe himself at night, he plays the harmonica given to him by his father. One night, after "the catch was especially good," Caleb begins to play the harmonica and accidentally drops it over the rails of the boat. A boy with ivory skin and long hair appears at the rails, deposits the harmonica on deck, and disappears. The next day, while mending nets, Caleb sees the boy again. The fourth illustration reveals Caleb's mysterious friend to be a graceful, androgynous merboy. The next day, the merboy reappears. "I thought I might not see you again," Caleb says. "I wanted to thank you." The merboy doesn't understand human speech, so Caleb clasps the harmonica close to his heart, then gives the merboy a wild summer rose, saying, "I brought this for you." The merboy smells the rose, clutches "the flower gently to his heart," and slips into the sea.

The plot thickens when the merboy gets caught in the village fishing nets. The fishermen can't believe their good luck. Caleb pleads with them to release the creature, but the fishermen decide that they will sell the merboy to a merchant, who in turn explains, "Normally I don't buy freaks, but maybe some circus sideshow will want it." A two-page spread shows the merboy on display in a warehouse, where everyone comes to gawk. Caleb is moved to action; at night, he breaks into the warehouse, puts his friend into a wheelbarrow, and wheels him across the dock to freedom.

After another subplot, in which the merboy saves the village ships from destruction during a storm, Caleb and the merboy meet one final time. Caleb plays his harmonica, and the merboy dances across the water. Caleb dangles his legs in the water as the merboy pops his upper torso just above it, flesh matching flesh, almost coalescing into a single boy. But soon it's time to part for good:

> The boy in the water reached toward Caleb, pretending to take a rose and smell its fragrance.
>
> Caleb's heart missed a beat. How could he explain that roses bloomed only for a short time and already they were gone? He thought a moment, then took his harmonica and placed it in the palm of one white hand, folding his friend's fingers closed around it. As he had so many weeks ago, the boy from the sea pressed the gift to his heart and quietly sank down into the water.
>
> From then on, until he was a very old man, Caleb returned to the village every year. He would walk along the shore, listening, remembering. Then he would throw an armful of roses across the water and watch as they drifted out to sea.

With these final lines, first love keeps on giving, into sadness perhaps, but also into the pleasure of memory. The merboy's liminality eroticizes the friendship but also ensures its innocence. Their distance keeps the bond mythical and chaste; the merboy could not survive in Caleb's world, or Caleb in his, suggesting a painful separation of self and other. To Caleb and readers of the book, the merboy is distant and beautiful; so often, it seems, queer love takes estranging form(s), for better and for worse. We cannot see the merboy as a freak, and we are outraged that anyone might, but all the same he seems a singular creature, even as he is fundamental to Caleb.

The merboy's vanishing act makes possible this melancholic love. Certainly the book's management of same-sex love tells us much about the heteronormativity of the picture book genre. Even now, with the development of a substantial body of gay-themed literature for young adults, books for younger readers do not often depict gay love openly. But at least *Caleb's Friend,* unlike the cinematic feral tale, offers a point of departure from the usual straight story of psychosocial development that has emerged out of psychoanalysis, if against Freud's own sensibilities.

6. Reinventing the Boy Problem

"Is your son physical, aggressive, difficult to manage at home and at school?" asks John Merrow in a 1998 edition of his NPR program *The Merrow Report,* available on audiocassette as *Will Boys Be Boys?* If so, join the club. Merrow's guest, therapist and best-selling author Michael Gurian, explains: "Males tend to be testosterone driven. You and I when we were fifteen years old got seven surges of testosterone per day," and "testosterone is not a nurturing hormone; testosterone is a hormone that wants sex." Those seven surges, in tandem with "hard wiring" in the brain, clearly distinguish boys from girls, claims Gurian in the interview. He calls for a "boy's movement" to shift attention away from the trials of girls and toward the misunderstood nature of boys.

The feature article of the May 11, 1998, issue of *Newsweek,* written by Barbara Kantrowitz and Claudia Kalb and entitled "Boys Will Be Boys," was perhaps the first major journalistic chronicle of this emergent "movement" (others have since followed). The major texts of the movement are boy-rearing manuals aimed primarily at parents, beginning with Gurian's *The Wonder of Boys: What Parents, Mentors, and Educators Can Do to Shape Boys into Exceptional Men* (1996), and soon followed by another popular title, William Pollack's *Real Boys: Rescuing Our Sons from the Myths of Boyhood* (1998). These remain the most influential of the genre, which also includes Bill Beausay's *Teenage Boys! Surviving and Enjoying These Extraordinary Years* (1998), James Garbarino's *Lost Boys: Why Our Sons Turn Violent and How We Can Save Them* (1999), Dan Kindlon and Michael Thompson's *Raising Cain: Protecting the Emotional Life of Boys* (1999), and Eli H. Newberger's *The Men They Will Become: The Nature and Nurture of Male Character* (1999). All of these authors are therapists, and some, notably Gurian and Pollack, have been active on the talk show circuit, as news of the boys' movement—and of its centerpiece, the "boy crisis"—has gone national, especially in the wake of school shootings at Columbine High and elsewhere.

In some respects, little of this boys' movement is new. What Kantrowitz and Kalb call "a hot new field of inquiry: the study of boys" (55) seems instead a revisitation of early-twentieth-century boyology. Certainly *The Wonder of Boys* and *Real Boys* look a great deal like *The Boy Problem* and *Boyology, or Boy Analysis.* As with the first boyologists, the new experts on boyhood claim expertise in the field through their writing and speaking engagements. The differences, however, are just as instructive as the similarities. Whereas the first boyologists were closely affiliated with character-building agencies such as Scouting and the YMCA, the new boyologists are largely psychologists in private practice or with university affiliations. The new boyologists are authorized not by institutional boyology but by their professional license to make literary-psychological references, even diagnoses.

To support their theories and observations, the new boyologists appeal to familiar boy types or archetypes as manifest in literature and popular culture: the real boy, the Bad Boy, the Lost Boy, the boy wonder, and specific characters such as Pinocchio, Peter Pan, and (as always) Huck Finn. Such is the legacy of literary boy work. In the new boyology, *Pinocchio* and *Hamlet* share the illustrative or anecdotal limelight with classic boy books and boy-centered folktales, as well as films like *Stand by Me* and *The Lion King*. The new boyologists invoke classic boy characters as standards for evaluating the realism and efficacy of our own culture. "If Huck Finn or Tom Sawyer were alive today," Gurian remarks in the *Newsweek* piece, "we'd say they had ADD or a conduct disorder" (56), implying that we no longer understand or tolerate the boy's natural energy. Here Gurian doesn't so much refuse medical typology as reject particular (pejorative) diagnoses; elsewhere he's quite happy to privilege medical or quasi-medical explanations of human functioning. Such recycling of particular boy characters and boy types points to the persistence of narrative boyology.

The new boyology was made possible not only by a consistent American interest in boys but also by the transmigration of the feral tale and the normalization of wildness that I've traced in this book. In many ways the new boyology epitomizes the last two decades of pop-psychological and self-help writing about men and masculinity. In chapter 5, I suggested that Freud adapted the feral tale to dramatize psychological wildness and to establish psychoanalysis as, in effect, a civilizing project. But by the end of the twentieth century, Freud's vision of a complex inner beastliness had largely yielded (in both the helping professions and in popular culture more broadly) to an upbeat, quintessentially American understanding of the boy as unproblematically wild. As evidence I looked primarily at children's books and family films. In this chapter, I argue that the new boyology takes its cue not only from early-twentieth-century boyology but also from more contemporary self-help and pop-psychological genres that presume the male subject to be innately and positively wild. The space of inner wildness carved out by psychoanalysis has not only been made safer but been resignified in vaguely biological terms. Unlike Freud, who articulated psychoanalysis against psychiatry and a conventionally medical view of human behavior, the new boyologists conflate psychology with biology, often appealing, like Freud, to archetype and myth, but without Freud's nuanced understanding of such.

The new boyology is indebted to two contemporary self-help genres: the primers of the mythopoetic men's movement, and (to a lesser extent) parenting manuals published from the 1980s forward. The mythopoetic men's movement in fact concentrated on boyhood and found inspiration in folkloric, even feral, discourse. The poet Robert Bly was its best-known spokesman; certainly his best-selling book *Iron John* (1990) remains the ur-text for weekend warriors. Central to Bly's fantasy of male revival is his rewriting of the *Der Eisenhans* or "Iron Hans" fable, as told by the Brothers Grimm in 1850. From this fable Bly concludes that "every modern male has, lying at the bottom of his psyche, a large primitive being covered with hair down to his feet. Making contact with this Wild Man is the step the Eighties male or the Nineties male has yet to make" (6).

Even as the new boyologists of the late 1990s invoke, like Bly, mythic-psychological (even totemic) characters, they also represent wildness as a biochemical or neurophysiological reality. Although the early boyologists such as Gibson pay some attention to the boy's physiology and health, they concentrate on his moral and intellectual character. If we believe Gurian, however, boys will be boys largely because of those seven daily shots of testosterone, because the boy brain is wired for action. All the while, the mythic-psychological model of boyhood is residual in the new boyology, sometimes in unacknowledged tension with the biological model. Whatever their claims about the boy's fundamental nature, the new boyologists simultaneously assume that the boy's behavior can be altered to some degree. Character can apparently be shaped, even as the wildness of boys is immutable.

Further linking the mythopoetic men's movement and the new boys' movement is a profound animosity to girls, to "feminization," and to feminism, since feminism is linked to politics and social change—and is presumably opposed to the hard facts of biology. This, too, is reminiscent of the first wave of boyology. In *Winning the Boy* (1908), for example, Lilburn Merrill lambastes a woman lecturer whose physiognomy and dress reveal "the mistake that had been made in creating her a woman," whose real mistake was to challenge Merrill's expertise (35). He joins a long line of authorities who decry the monstrous issue of women, prefiguring the misogynistic Momism of the 1940s as well as intervening and more contemporary alarms about feminization.[1] More recently, the mythopoetic men's movement has developed its own nutty narratives of feminization. Bly's revision of *Der Eisenhans* pits the boy against his domineering mother.[2] We must free our inner wild man, he holds, by stealing the key of autonomy from under our mother's pillow. "A mother's job is, after all, to civilize the boy, and so it is natural for her to keep the key" (11).

The new boyology likewise takes issue with feminism and feminization by appealing to a mythic understanding of masculinity's wild essence (against the feminine project of domestication). The new boyology asserts itself against the recent attention to girlhood as inspired by feminism, as exemplified in the AAUW report *How Schools Shortchange Girls* (1992) and other "girl crisis" writing, notably Mary Pipher's *Reviving Ophelia* (1994). Boys are allegedly just as at risk as girls, the boy advocates counter, but we've ignored the warning signs. We've misunderstood biology, and in our haste to redress sexism, we've ignored the needs of boys and thus the looming boy crisis.[3] In *The Wonder of Boys,* the first "gender myth" that Gurian attacks is that girls "have life much worse than boys" (xvii). For Gurian, "gender" is a dirty word used in the plot against boys; he prefers "biology" and "nature" as proof of irreconcilable differences between the sexes.[4] Our culture's faith in a child's social conditioning indicates "our arrogant belief that it's possible for human beings to create society that is not driven primarily by nature" (28).

The boys' movement is imagined variously as a pioneering defense of boyhood, as a rejoinder to an exaggerated girl crisis, and as a parallel crisis that also demands attention. The rhetoric of boy crisis is at once sexist and indebted to feminism; it also echoes the language of civil rights while ignoring the racial and class biases of our culture. That the new boyology should function as a referendum on feminism and indeed all of the social reforms of the last thirty-plus years isn't surprising, as boyology is at heart a conservative American ideology of masculine self-making.

To be sure, the statistics offered in these new books on boyhood and the boy crisis are alarming, and these books at least call attention to some pressing social problems. Boys, for instance, are more likely than girls to drop out of high school and college, to commit petty and violent acts of crime, to attempt suicide, and to be diagnosed with ADD and learning disabilities. Pollack is right to emphasize in *Real Boys* the dangers of the "Boy Code," through which boys learn to deny their emotions in the name of honor and self-reliance. Books like *The Wonder of Boys* and *Real Boys* usefully interrogate attitudes that naturalize such problems as the inevitable stuff of boyhood. There is cause for concern, however, not only about these phenomena but also about the assumptions and consequences of boy crisis writing. Most of the new boyologists refuse the idea of gender in favor of a biological separation of the sexes. They tend to ignore axes of definition and displacement such as gender, race, and class, arguing that social imprinting is "soft wiring," negligible in comparison to the hard wiring of biology. The consensus seems to be that attention to class and race, as well as denial about sexual difference, has caused the crisis. At the same time, these texts posit something called "boy culture" that seems part hard wiring, part soft wiring, at once inviolate and a site of intervention.

The new boyology is the distinctive product of boyology and the feral tale alike, shaped by a discourse of interior wildness originally sponsored by psychoanalysis that now presumes biological, rather than psychological, essence/difference. Thanks to a shared media culture (and at least the illusion of community), the new boyologists do not need institutional fraternity in the form of boy-themed organizations. They need only psychotherapeutic credentials, university affiliations, and a certain appreciation of literature. The very publicity of their work serves to further legitimate that work. Only such qualified men can make the mysterious world of boyhood available to the lay public, translate its vernacular into contemporary parlance.

Boyhood and the Deep Masculine

The mythopoetic men's movement of the 1980s and 1990s, like the new boyology after it, emerged out of contradictory cultural responses to feminism and civil rights discourse. Bly and his cohorts responded to feminism by developing an explicitly mythic or folkloric understanding of masculinity that incorporated both static and dynamic models of character. As social historian Michael Kimmel reports in *Manhood in America,* the "men's liberation" movement of the mid-1970s was "a curious mixture of a social movement and psychological self-help manual," at once reactionary and forward-looking in its strategies and conceits (280). Kimmel identifies as this movement's founding text Jack Sawyer's essay "On Male Liberation" (1970), which quickly spawned book-length manifestos such as Warren Farrell's *The Liberated Man* (1974), Marc Feigen Fasteau's *The Male Machine* (1975), Herb Goldberg's *The Hazard of Being Male* (1975), and Jack Nichols's *Men's Liberation* (1975), among others. Taking their cue from feminism, and (if less explicitly) from the civil rights struggle and the gay rights movement, men began to question stereotypical assumptions about masculinity. "At its core," writes Kimmel, "men's liberation provided a coherent critique of the Self-Made Man; in its eyes *he* was the failure" (281). The self-made man is for Kimmel the reigning archetype of American masculinity; hence the significance of any ideology challenging rugged male individualism.

The men's liberation movement faltered, however, by the 1980s, moving away from a culturalist or constructionist understanding of gender. The bullying style of Presidents Reagan and Bush helped affirm the self-made man and recast men's libbers as whiners and wimps. Several key players in men's liberation abandoned feminism, notably Warren Farrell, who now urged men to "embrace traditional masculinity" (Kimmel, 303). As Kimmel emphasizes, this backlash set the stage for the mythopoets and for a self-help psychological literature aimed at men. By the mid-1980s, a virulent anti-feminism marked popular writing on masculinity. In *The Rape of the Male*

(1986), for instance, Richard Doyle—of the Men's Rights Association—holds that men, rather than women, are the real victims of rape, abuse, and violence more generally. Fathers' rights groups emerged to fight the ostensibly unjust practice of awarding custody to mothers. Like Susan Jeffords, Kimmel sees the 1980s as a period of frenzied reassertion of a separatist understanding of masculinity that appealed to the rugged physical body as baseline and metaphor. The hyper-macho aesthetic of Hollywood was linked to the reincarnation of the wild man by Bly and other mythopoets, notably Sam Keen, author of *Fire in the Belly: On Being a Man* (1991).[5]

Attitudes toward boyhood among mythopoetic men were twofold. On the one hand, boyhood was vital to the achievement of rugged masculinity. Echoing nineteenth-century recapitulationists, Bly argues in *Iron John* that "the boy is mythologically living through the past history of man," and that the "ancient practice of initiation [is] still very much alive in our genetic structure" (36). Thus, as Kimmel notes, Bly's "search for the deep masculine" is "developmentally atavistic, a search for lost boyhood, an effort to turn back the clock to the moment before work and family responsibilities yanked men away from their buddies" (320). Bly's scheme, in other words, was actually a social explanation of masculinity's "crisis": we've lost our connection to our fathers and forefathers, he argued, and so we need corrective rituals and a new sense of solidarity. Thus the emphasis on boyhood. At the same time, the mythopoets chastised men for remaining boys, emphasizing the importance of adult responsibilities. Thus in *King, Warrior, Magician, Lover: Rediscovering the Archetypes of the Mature Masculine* (1990), Robert L. Moore and Douglass Gillette distinguish boy psychology from man psychology, holding that the successful Oedipal child's "shadow self" is the auto/homoerotic mama's boy, who compulsively masturbates, reads pornography, and avoids heterosexual sex and marriage.

Anticipating this mythopoetic distinction between the normative boy and the mama's boy—and invoking one of the most canonical feral tales in children's literature—was Dr. Dan Kiley's best-selling self-help book *The Peter Pan Syndrome: Men Who Have Never Grown Up* (1983). To his credit, Kiley uses passages of *Peter Pan* to question our society's giddy adoration of childhood. But in the process he valorizes heterosexuality as adult, predictably depicting the modern "man-child" Peter Pan as determined to avoid women and responsibility. Peter, in Kiley's account, is a potential homosexual, a "soft, effeminate boy," a narcissist, "a very sad young man whose life is filled with contradictions, conflicts, and confusion" (22–23), in short, "sex-role conflict" (103). Homosexuals, theorizes Dr. Dan, "have actualized the feminine side of their personality, but are left with grave doubts about their masculine identity" (114). Boys who try to express their emotions must either suppress them or "drop out of the heterosexual derby and actualize [this] feminine side" (31). This is the Peter Pan Syndrome, or PPS. While he claims not "to imply that all gay men are gay because of PPS," he finds it "ironic and sad that there is considerable political support for the feminist and gay rights movements, but nothing to boost the morale of the man who wants permission to cry in the arms of a woman he loves" (31).

The Peter Pan Syndrome resonated with and revived in a related idiom the critique of masculine immaturity that I discussed in chapter 2, launched by Van Wyck Brooks and sustained by Leslie Fiedler's influential analysis of the American literary canon as an escapist literature for boys. This immaturity critique, however, yielded by the early 1990s to the mythopoetic faith in a regressive yet still properly masculine appeal to boyhood, as codified in Iron John. Thus the new boyologists worry little about narcissism or nostalgia when they reconsider and romanticize boyhood. The popular fascination with boyhood does not suggest to them, as it did to Brooks in the 1920s, an unhealthy obsession indicative of national immaturity. Rather, they take boyhood as the most noble and serious of subjects, at once appealing to the mythopoetic interest in boyhood and shifting that interest to "real" boys. Boyology thus becomes the key to the deep masculine, not its roadblock.

Historians of masculinity point to the resistance of men to understanding masculinity as a cultural force, to their faith in the deep masculine. In Stiffed: The Betrayal of the American Man, her controversial but often persuasive examination of masculinity in post–World War II America, Susan Faludi emphasizes the effects of a sense of social powerlessness on men from the postwar period onward, among them a denial of the very socioeconomic forces that shape their lives, as well as the "backlash" against women that was the subject of Faludi's previous book. Whereas women have responded to social isolation and victimization by developing new forms of community, she holds, men have instead isolated themselves further, in effect capitulating to the very logic of self-reliance and immutable character that oppresses them. Unlike Kimmel, who argues that the interiorization of self-made ideology has lately given way to a more outward-bound preoccupation with the physical body, Faludi believes that men still look inward in addressing their problems.

A sociologist, Kimmel prefers to diagnose social types and even archetypes even as he historicizes American masculinity. As a result, he himself appeals to, if not the "deep masculine" exactly, a distinctly American ethic of self-reliance that "lie[s] deep in our nation's past" (2). Kimmel writes that a "deep, underlying structure" of masculinity undergirds the contemporary crisis of manhood (ix). He holds that men's fear of humiliation represents "something deeper" than homophobia, which he redefines—unfortunately,

I think—"as more than the irrational fear of homosexuals," as the bedrock "fear of other men" (8). Although he criticizes the mythopoetic gurus, Kimmel also represents men as the victims of Oedipal tyranny. Consider the following passage, in which he reconstructs the "psychodynamic element in the historical construction of American manhood," as revealed in Andrew Jackson's impetuous, violent "flight from feminizing forces":

> Having killed the tyrannical father [monarchical England], American men feared being swallowed whole by an infantilizing and insatiable mother [the Bank]—voluptuous, voracious, and terrifyingly alluring. Jackson projected those emotions onto "others" so that by annihilating or controlling them, his own temptation to suckle helplessly at the breast of indolence and luxury could be purged. Jackson's gendered rage at weakness, feminizing luxury, and sensuous pleasure resonated for a generation of symbolically fatherless sons, the first generation of American men born after the Revolution. (36)

Here Freudian drama explains the historical scene. But might not the othering dynamic that Kimmel identifies also be explained as proto-psychoanalytic? Surely the historical shift from patrician and artisan models of manhood to the self-made man that he traces—and then that man's *unmaking* at the century's restless turn—helped foster, as much as evidence, Oedipality? And surely the image of Jackson longing to "suckle helplessly at the breast of indolence and luxury" owes something to the feral tale, both in its more traditional folkloric form and as retouched by psychoanalysis?[6]

Faludi's book is less mythic in assumption, even as she practices depth history writing in a different sense. Faludi is a journalist, but unlike other journalists writing about masculinity, Faludi does not invoke the feral in her analysis, perhaps because she is trying to redeem boys and men from such animal and abject associations. She does not make use of types, aside from the controlling metaphor of the "stiff(ed)" man. The rhetorical power of *Stiffed* derives from its accumulation of data and its interweaving of exemplary stories and anecdotes. Faludi even fashions herself as a boy worker of sorts. What makes the experience of powerlessness particularly devastating for men, she contends, was the 1950s faith in the mass potential of boys. Rather than castigating 1950s society for elevating the boy over the girl, Faludi explains that *Stiffed* represents her own struggle "to understand the perilous voyage to manhood undertaken by the men I once knew as boys— boys who [knew] that the world would soon be theirs" (47).

All stories of masculinity, of course, depend upon as much as examine certain tropes, rhetorical conventions, and analytical practices. We can see in the new boyology and in new scholarship on masculinity a lively mix of archetypal poetics and pseudo-ethnographic language, and my own book likewise combines typology with selective sampling, relying on key metaphors to tell an ostensibly coherent but perhaps still mythic story about boy work.

Parenting Manuals and the New Boyology

Child-rearing manuals written for parents, as well as the primers of the mythopoets, helped pave the way for the new boyology and anticipate its dual emphasis on nature and nurture. In 1862 Henry Ward Beecher wrote in *Eyes and Ears* that the "real lives of boys are yet to be written" and that tales of impossibly good boys "resemble a real boy's life about as much as a chicken picked and larded, upon a spit, and ready for delicious eating, resembles a free fowl in the fields" (73–74). While eschewing such colorful comparisons, *The Little Boy Book: A Guide to the First Eight Years* (1986), a forerunner of the new boyology primers, is likewise offered in the spirit of realism and utility: "If you are the parent of a little boy, you may have discovered that the children described in many books for parents are not like your son at all. . . . [This is] the kind of book we wished we'd had" (xv–xvi). Cowritten by Sheila Moore and Roon Frost, *The Little Boy Book* emphasizes sexual difference against the liberal propaganda of the unisex child. Cartoon strips such as *Dennis the Menace* and *Family Circle* repeat the book's theme, reflecting "the enduring qualities and hilarious antics of boys every parent will recognize" (xvi). In one, a filthy Dennis plays gleefully in the mud with an equally filthy girl, with the caption "Gee, you're lots of fun! Are you *sure* you're a girl?" (41). Dennis mistakes activity rather than anatomy as the stuff of gender. If she plays like a boy, he reasons, she might be a boy; readers laugh, knowing better.

Chapter 1, entitled "What Little Boys Are Made Of," provides additional proof of the gender gap as confirmed by biology and bodily performance, equally comic but more literary: the story of Huck Finn's failed attempt to pass as "Sarah Williams" from Hookerville. Clad in a sunbonnet and a makeshift dress, Huck visits Judith Loftus in a reconnaissance mission to find out what rumors are circulating about himself and Jim. The disguise, as Moore and Frost emphasize, fails miserably; Huck throws like a boy and sews like a boy. Huck's behavior betrays him; he cannot repress his masculinity. "Why, I spotted you for a boy when you was threading the needle!" declares Judith in Twain's text (75). Claim Moore and Frost: "Whether the tasks be threading a needle, throwing a ball, climbing a tree, or learning to write the alphabet, we often notice that boys and girls do them differently" (2). Until this century, few questioned such an obvious reality. The little boy of Roon and Frost isn't exactly the free fowl of Beecher or the hardy Huck, but he is decidedly Dennis: dirty and irrepressibly real, less a true menace than a stubbornly masculine challenge.

Parenting manuals such as *The Little Boy Book* made cultural room for the new boyology books, which are so far written exclusively by men. They, too, are parenting manuals, but they simultaneously celebrate the world of boyhood in a residually if not explicitly mythopoetic vein, declaring, for example, the "wonder" of boys. Bringing parenting manuals one step closer to the new boyology are books written only for fathers, such as Bernard Weiner's *Boy into Man: A Father's Guide to Initiation of Teenage Sons* (1992). This handbook recounts the rebirth experiences of six adolescents forced by their fathers to spend a weekend in the wilderness of northern California. Ensconced in giant papier-mâché hands, the fathers "summoned" their sons from school to the campsite, where they spent their days baking bread, drumming, having their feet washed, and listening to the shaman's stories of "the King, the Prince, the Wildman and Coyote/Trickster" (40). On the front cover is a photograph of the men costumed as these characters. Before leaving home, the boys had to steal the key of autonomy from underneath their mothers' pillows, in direct accordance with Bly's instructions in *Iron John*. Despite their support, the mothers were barred from participating, though each wrote her son a special letter, and the ceremony included a brief speech from the masked "figure of Woman" (34). The handbooks of the new boyologists likewise assert that boys have been deprived of meaningful male rituals and intimacy.

Although the boy book has largely disappeared as a boy work venue, one contemporary author, Bruce Books, revived the tradition just as the new boyology was getting under way. Published by Hyperion as a children's book, Bruce Brooks's *Boys Will Be* (1993) is a collection of essays cross-written for boys and their fathers. It is a parenting manual of sorts, in that Brooks appeals to his own experience as a father and also positions himself as an authorial father figure. *Boys Will Be* opines on a wide array of topics, including headgear, bullies, body odor, books, "risky pals," Arthur Ashe, and hockey. Recalling Gibson's assertion in *Boyology* that "boy stuff is the only stuff in the world from which men can be made," Brooks explains that *Boys Will Be* is "a book about boy stuff, written for boys to read, by a former boy who is now raising two boys of his own" (5). He then adds that "it is very likely that a federal judge can force me to write a precisely-equal-length book for girls," with articles about "the pros and cons of sparkle in lip gloss, or the twelve best ways of sucking up to teachers and making them think you are just the most devoted little helpful student in the whole wide world" (5). He implies that boys are blamed for society's woes and that girls should just stop bitching about their sorry lot.

Boys Will Be, with its hostility to progressive politics and social change, is a must-read for aspiring weekend warriors. Brooks's little truisms about boy stuff echo those of the character builders, whom he specifically mentions in the last chapter. Boys will one day discover the joys of sex and marriage, but "during a certain age boys enjoy the company of only boys. . . . This is the nature of life" (10). In that homogeneous "boy society" (14), language is a means not of communicating but of signifying; boys are apparently trickster figures, as Shelley Fisher Fishkin has argued of Huck Finn. Echoing Leslie Fiedler, Brooks playfully uses archetypes such as the Good Boy (GB) and the Not-Quite-Bad Boy (NQBB) to distinguish his own son (a GB, of course) from "Risky Pals" or the neighborhood riffraff. He insists on the universality of fights and takes pride in his young son's scent: "Spencer's aroma was definitely an animal scent too, but one made by a more refined gland. It was musky but smart. It contained a mild wildness" that barely distinguishes the boy from the family dog (57). Brooks's wife wrinkles her nose, preferring the effeminate smell of baby products. After all, "girls never seem to give off a pungent natural aroma" (59).

Boys Will Be is a nasty attack on girls, mothers, "clever social work theorists" (42), and misguided librarians (63). Brooks devotes an entire chapter to "ten things you cannot expect your mom to come close to understanding." Ironically, he criticizes the character builders for ignoring the needs of the boy. These men were wrong to assume the "innate savagery and deceitfulness of boys" (127). "The disrespect here is more than a matter of suspicion or distrust. It is a matter of ignoring what the boys themselves might want, because someone else always knows what's best for them" (128). Brooks's claim to authority is different from that of classic boyology only in his revision of the boy-savage trope; he too asserts a sexist boy culture whose realism he can access as both an author and a father. The book betrays his caveat that "becoming a man means more than endlessly living out a fantasy of boyhood" (119). *Boys Will Be* appeared three years before Gurian's *The Wonder of Boys.* Unlike Gurian, Brooks is ostensibly speaking to boys as well as their fathers (since it is a children's book). Brooks's sentiments are neither natural nor benevolent; they depend on hateful cliché.

Engendering the Boy Crisis

Given the narrative traditions from which it emerged, it's not surprising that the new boyology is quite sexist. Gurian represents the troubling end of the spectrum, since he is convinced that feminism has distorted "the simple information our ancestors have always known—that boys and girls have been wired differently for millions of years and need special, gender-specific attention" (*The Wonder of Boys*, xiv). He doesn't see his reactionary under-standing of boys as problematic for girls. "We ended up with two daughters," he chuckles on *The Merrow Report*. "What's nice about having two daughters is that nobody can accuse me in their right mind of being antifemale; certainly a father of two daughters is hopefully not going to do anything that's antifemale."

In *Real Boys*, William Pollack responds to Pipher's *Reviving Ophelia* by reminding us that "Hamlet fared little better than Ophelia" (6). Pollack is the codirector of the Center for Men at McLean Hospital–Harvard Medical School, where he also holds a professorship. One of his colleagues is Carol Gilligan, whose recent research on separation anxiety in preschool boys has energized the boys' movement.[7] Pollack thanks Gilligan in his acknowledg-ments, noting—unlike Gurian—that boys have much in common with girls and that work on masculinity owes much to women's studies. But while Pol-lack's book represents a kinder, smarter brand of boy study than Gurian's, it too pits boy against girl. Discussing Nancy Chodorow's research on mother-child identification, Pollack contends that since boys have trouble establish-ing a masculine self against that maternal bond, it follows that "being a boy or being masculine is not so much based on the positive identification with father but on the negation of the male child's tie to mother." In other words, *"Being a boy becomes defined in the negative: not being a girl"* (28). Here Pollack acknowledges that gender identity is binary but also reverses in psychological terms the social fact asserted by feminists: being a girl is typically defined in the negative, as not being a boy. Pollack's formulation has a reality claim, if not effect: he implies that boys are now invisible, the victims of a stable and positive girlhood. Real boys, he explains, hide "behind a mask," while girls live in plain sight.

Christina Hoff Sommers, author of the controversial *Who Stole Femi-nism?* has recently joined the fray with *The War against Boys: How Misguided Feminism Is Harming Our Young Men* (2000), not a boy-rearing book but rather a critique of the movement. Sommers, who used to teach at Clark University (where G. Stanley Hall built his child study empire), inveighs against both the feminist "myth of the fragile girl" and the reactive rhetoric of boy crisis. She too believes that boys are in trouble, particularly academic trouble, but is incensed that boy crisis writers portray boys as pathological, as naturally dumb and violent. "American boys face genuine problems that cannot be addressed by constructing new versions of manhood," she writes. "They do not need to be 'rescued' from their masculinity" (15). She singles out Gilligan and Pollack for some bruising criticism and is persuasive in her critique of their research methods. But Sommers hawks her own brand of crisis, one that shouldn't surprise us, given her political leanings and her affection for literary critic E. D. Hirsch. In her final chapter, "War and Peace," Sommers attributes the troubles of boys to "an extraordinary period of moral deregulation" (212) and to the legacy of Rousseauian-style pedagogy; she prefers Aristotle and hopes for a "Great Relearning" in which moral education will take center stage. Also telling are her appeals to long-entrenched American fears of feminization and her near-fanatical adoration of all things male.

Whereas Kimmel and Sommers both underscore—if from quite different perspectives—the gender politics of crisis writing, some scholars of masculinity, like the new boyologists themselves, naturalize rather than question the role of gender in social history and thus authorize the contemporary language of crisis. I've already questioned Kimmel's metaphors of the "deep." In his chapter on "boy culture" in *American Manhood* (1993), to give another example, E. Anthony Rotundo claims that nineteenth-century boys were "embedded in a feminine world," confined to home and forced to wear girly clothes. Such practices, he holds, ran counter to boy-savage instincts. In response, boys formed sadomasochistic gangs: "One of the bonds that held boy culture together was the pain that youngsters inflicted on each other" (35). "Boys loved to compare themselves to animals," he notes, "and two animal similes seem apt here. If at times boys acted like a hostile pack of wolves that preyed on its own kind as well as other species, they behaved at other times like a litter of playful pups who enjoy romping" (45).

Rotundo's boy culture is too derivative of Kipling and Baden-Powell, too consonant with the sexist sentiments of boyology and the feral tale. A more persuasive explanation is that adults loved to compare boys to animals in the nineteenth century, as now. *American Manhood* is not only an analysis of boy culture but one of its more studied expressions. Howard P. Chudacoff employs similar language in identifying the boyhood roots of bachelor subculture: "Reckless, boisterous, aggressive, and running in packs, boys used outdoor spaces to pursue their independence away from adult supervision. In the process they engaged in a self-apprenticeship for bachelorhood" (221). Here again, animal bonding and a pack mentality among boys herald adult male independence. Both Rotundo and Chudacoff, like Kimmel, are otherwise careful historians of masculinity, which makes the persistence of these conceits all the more striking.

The new boyology likewise insists that boys need to express their wildness against the stifling, feminizing constraints of contemporary society. Across the twentieth century, the boy-rearing handbook demands the labor of women but obscures that labor with both explicit dismissals of feminine caretaking and with "realistic"/wondrous portraits of boys just being boys (preferably outdoors). To some extent, the feminization argument allows the new boyologists to align themselves with the classic project of boy work. They assert their own expertise against women caretakers especially, even as they also insist that boyhood has a nature that is innately wild and prior to all things maternal.

Drawing from the engaging scholarship on girl culture that has recently appeared, we could venture that boyology has shaped the lives of boys much as domestic ideology has influenced the lives of girls. Boyology and domestic ideology may be not only analogous but also discursively interdependent. Boyology seems also a form of gender role socialization and surveillance. The differences between boyology and domestic ideology, of course, are as instructive as the continuities. While there may be a "girl crisis" movement (against which Sommers summons her strength), the best-sellers of Mary Pipher, Peggy Orenstein, and others have not been interpreted in the national press as constituting a *girls' movement* or a "hot new field of study." Probably such a movement would look too much like feminism, made abject in/by boyology. As a modern subject, the girl has been less self-evident than the boy, more surreal or abstract even in crisis—represented more as a "question" than a "problem."[8] In response, some critics have overemphasized the girl's sentimental power.[9] It seems as if boys have a more substantial presence in American life and letters thanks to the ideology of realism, such that, even endangered, they seem more self-evident, their problems more concrete and pressing. Sommers, for instance, downplays evidence of serious problems among girls (such as eating disorders), suggesting that they pale next to the academic woes of boys. In any event, the master narrative of the new boyology is simple: boys are misunderstood and thus in crisis. They are physically and mentally different from—more endangered, more important than—girls.

In classic and contemporary writing alike, boyhood is imagined as a biological and social state in need of proper attention (not feminist analysis). Thus in the 1916 *Boyology,* Gibson devotes chapter 1 to physical characteristics, explaining that the boy is "like a little beast, and many things that make the difference between a man and a beast make no difference with him. He is, though, a man in the making" (3). Gibson dwells on the boy's beastly nature before describing his civic and spiritual tendencies, which make manhood possible. The average boy, we learn, has around 1,700 square inches of skin, each of which contains "about 3,500 sweating tubes, or respirating pores" (10).[10] In the new boyology, this emphasis on biology takes center stage. Chapter 1 of Gurian's *The Wonder of Boys* is titled "Where It All Begins: The Biology of Boyhood" and is followed by chapter 2, "The Culture Boys Create." Gurian doesn't describe the boy as beastly—such a description would undermine his attempt to ennoble the boy—and Gibson's vision of boy culture as a friendly gang would worry most contemporary readers. Gurian even acknowledges that boys form a culture, but he treats that culture as dictated by nature.

Gibson and Gurian alike promise to transform biological facts into cultural capital, celebrating the mystery of boyhood to their own interpretive credit. The boy, writes Gibson in his foreword, "is the original sulphite, keeping everybody awake and interested when he appears upon the scene. He will ever be a new subject for discussion and analysis, and in need of friendly interpreters" (ix). Gurian hopes to topple myths with the antifeminist facts of life, so that everyone can experience the wonder of boys. Boyhood is at once self-evident and in need of interpretation, a familiar but always novel subject.

Mothers have failed their sons, but so have fathers; hence the need for experts and their intervention programs (which are notoriously vague). In *Raising Boys: Why Boys Are Different—and How to Help Them Become Happy and Well-Balanced Men* (1998)—a title that reflects the dual faith of boyology in essence and malleability—Steve Biddulph even proposes that most cases of Attention Deficit Disorder (ADD) are really cases of DDD: Dad Deficit Disorder (21).[11] Sommers likewise points to deadbeat dads in her version of the boy crisis. If, as Sommers avers, fatherlessness leads to violence and delinquency, then boyology as a recuperative, masculinizing force isn't only admirable—it's imperative.

Culture Talk and the Lost Boys

If, as I acknowledged in chapter 2, early boyologists such as Forbush and Gibson made creative use of Herbartian epochs theory to identify the developmental stages of boyhood, the new boyologists draw from the residual language of cultural anthropology and ethnography to valorize their fieldwork and establish their credibility. Much like the mythopoetic men before them, these new experts borrow from and imitate classic field studies, so that titles like *Real Boys* speak transparently of the subjects under scrutiny, like ethnographies named after their subjects. Generally, however, the new boyologists do not conduct fieldwork. Some scholars have conducted fieldwork among boys—notably Jay Mechling in research on Scouting, and Gary Alan Fine in his study of Little League idiocultures—but the new boyology prefers the rhetoric of fieldwork to the real thing.

In *The Wonder of Boys,* for example, Gurian is quick to emphasize his worldliness; born in the 1950s in Honolulu, he has lived in India, Wisconsin, Wyoming, Colorado, Israel, Turkey, and now Spokane, Washington; his father worked on the Southern Ute reservation in northern New Mexico. Many chapters of *The Wonder of Boys* begin with an invocation of experiences abroad: "In eastern Brazil, among the Shavantee"; "There is an old Italian saying"; "It is a clear day. An old woman and a young woman wander to an already chosen place at the outskirts of their aboriginal village." The third chapter, "Boys Need a Tribe," advances Gurian's thesis that boys need a three-family tribe comprising the nuclear family, the extended family, and the family of man. The boy's second birth into manhood is to be guided by fathers and male mentors who can revise the initiation rites of aboriginals; Gurian advocates everything but ritual fellatio and converts the classic folk-tale "Jack and the Beanstalk" into a story of quasi-sexualized initiation. The old man gives Jack the "magic seeds" he needs for his "initiatory Journey" (135). "When boys around us climb their beanstalks, they spend more time in the masculine realm" (137) and thus learn "a sacred male role for the new millennium" (250).

That sacred male role, as we might expect, is business as usual in terms of class and race. Consider Gurian's warning in the *Will Boys Be Boys?* segment of NPR's *The Merrow Report* about the danger of pop culture icons as third-family members: "If Dennis Rodman is in my family, he's going to be a black sheep, I would think . . . If I'm trying to raise kids . . . and Dennis Rodman's in my family at the Thanksgiving dinner," that influence will be hard to combat. He then clarifies: "I'm picking Dennis Rodman out, you know; it could be anyone who's just kind of a crazy man setting the wildest, weird example." Is this the judgment of a worldly man who respects cultural diversity?

Real Boys is more politically progressive, but just as indebted to a rather selective form of ethnography and to the universalizing mythos of boy-hood. Pollack draws from his clinical practice and his ongoing research project "Listening to Boys' Voices," conducted at Harvard Medical School. This project, which has since produced its own book, involves "studying hundreds of young and adolescent boys, observing them in various situations, conducting empirical testing, and talking with their parents" (xxi). That's about all the information we get about the project. In the introduction, Pollack returns us to the boy problem, writing that "boys today are in serious trouble, including many who seem 'normal' and to be doing just fine" (xix). They hide behind the repressive Boy Code. His rhetoric of crisis isn't consistent; in the beginning he stresses the severity of the boy problem, but later he praises the ingenious coping strategies of boys. Pollack adapts as much as questions the frontier myth: "I believe one of the reasons boys find the frontier so appealing is that they feel they are inhabiting a kind of emotional and physical frontier of their own" (348–49).

Pollack's real boys seem to exist outside of adult culture, and even culture more generally; occasionally we hear about particular boys, but for the most part, listening to boys' voices means listening to Pollack tell us, selectively, about boys' voices, much in the vein of early ethnography, in which the field-worker rarely acknowledges the influence of his or her own assumptions on the research. These real boys seem almost phantasmic; Pollack must export and interpret their realism for us. *Real Boys* depends on a culture of boyhood familiar from the portraits of Tom, Huck, and other real boys—impossibly removed from the elements that make up and threaten that culture.

Perhaps because cultural or comparative anthropology has largely supplanted a more evolutionary (and more singular) understanding of culture, the boy-savage trope so popular with the Bad Boy writers and the first boyologists has disappeared in the new boyology, except in its most hyperbolic forms. In Forbush's *The Boy Problem* and Gibson's *Boyology*, savagery is invoked not only because there was a clear distinction between racial others and the middle-class white boy but also because savagery was often a less pejorative concept than we might assume, associated with self-reliance and entrepreneurial spirit. Although attitudes toward racial others ranged greatly, the boy-savage represented the positive virtues of savagery, safely contained in the middle-class home. In the works of Forbush and Gibson, boy work is a simple process of channeling boy-savagery into useful pursuits. In the more recent *The Wonder of Boys* and *Real Boys*, however, savagery is linked with dangerous external forces that threaten the family. Savagery is thus evacuated from middle-class boyhood and attributed to both society at large (the urban jungle) and specific populations (inner-city gangs). Gurian invokes "culture" precisely to ignore cultural differences.

If the new boyologists imitate the codes of cultural anthropology in their "fieldwork" with boys, their understanding of culture is astonishingly narrow. Not only do they fail to consider cultures outside of U.S. parameters; they fail even to recognize that white middle-class society *is* one culture among many. All this culture talk functions (as with the mythopoetic men's movement) to shore up white middle-class masculinity. Forbush and Gibson found it easy at the beginning of the century to praise the boy-savage and to suppress issues of class and race, and the new boyologists show the same disinclination to adopt a truly multicultural vision in the late 1990s. The only example of such an approach that I've seen is Franklin Abbott's *Boyhood, Growing Up Male: A Multicultural Anthology* (1993), which also resorts to the "real boys" trope.

Rhetoric of worldliness to the contrary, the new boyologists address themselves almost exclusively to white, middle-class audiences. The hostile tone toward feminism and social activism isn't incidental; to acknowledge the complexities of gender, race, class, and region in the lives of children and their families—indeed, to acknowledge any social complexity at all—would threaten the whole movement. It's painfully obvious that the young subject of boyology is the middle-class white boy. There's no information in these books about how to live below the poverty line, or how to survive racism or homophobia or job de-skilling. Are dropouts real boys? What "wonder" might a boy experience or embody in the crumbling and disavowed inner city? Put simply, most of the new boyologists deny these real problems in favor of the generic boy crisis, a crisis of self-esteem and gender oppression.

What of boys who fall outside the pale of boyology? A survey of the literature reveals that if such boys cannot be denied outright, they are vilified with a vengeance. Boyology as a rule doesn't have much to say about boy failures, since presumably there's no such thing as a bad boy, even if the specter of the *truly* bad boy looms in every ominous boyologist caution (are *you* raising Cain?). Such dirty work is left to those who relish it, such as Jonathan Kellerman, whose *Savage Spawn: Reflections on Violent Children* (1999) criticizes progressive thinking about violence and mental illness. The book is part of Random House's Library of Contemporary Thought, a series in which popular authors assess cultural affairs. Like the new boyologists, Kellerman is a child clinical psychologist, the founding director of the Psychosocial Program of Children's Hospital at Los Angeles, and currently a professor of psychology and pediatrics at the University of Southern California. He is also the author of more than fourteen murder mysteries, and it is as fiction that *Savage Spawn* makes the most sense.

Horrified but not surprised by the shooting sprees in Jonesboro, Arkansas, and elsewhere, Kellerman insists that psychopathy is different from other childhood disorders, and he takes issue with the liberal revision of psychiatric terminology. Psychopathy, he says, "has a nice, novelistic ring to it. It's a juicy term, connotative of evil, and this is a juicy, evil creature we're dealing with" (46). Kellerman urges a more Calvinist apperception of the bad seed and speaks the language of paranoid science fiction; here he describes Tim, the first psychopathic boy he encountered in private practice: "It was as if I were sitting across from a member of another species" (15). The following chapter, entitled "A Species Apart," reviews "the natural history of habitual evil" (19) and concludes, "The sad truth is that there *are* bad people" (34). Throughout, he refers to psychopathy as "the beast." He reminds us of the "stubborn and rebellious son" in the Book of Deuteronomy, stoned to death by his community. To Kellerman's credit, he is critical of our society's tendency to scapegoat media violence, but that's largely because he believes that psychopaths are born, not made.

Kellerman's engaging analysis of the clinical literature on psychopathy is compromised by all the hyperbolic rhetoric of otherness. He does not recognize that his own savage rhetoric might reaffirm racist thinking especially. Further, the book's secondary function is to present the social reforms of the last several decades as an exercise in foolishness, in keeping with the ethos of boyology. Kellerman is particularly dismissive of Marxist-inflected social science that redefined criminality as the product of class oppression. In his view, America went soft on crime, and so Kellerman looks elsewhere for effective examples of crime fighting (to Saudi Arabia, for example, where homosexuals are beheaded). This sort of analysis seems contrary to his otherwise minoritizing discourse of juvenile violence. If psychopaths are not influenced much by environment, we might wonder, then why these concerns about softness and other dire consequences of the leftist agenda? Kellerman's lost boys are radically other: they are savage spawn.

Among the new boyologists, only James Garbarino attributes violence to racism rather than implying that minority kids are savage spawn. He begins *Lost Boys: Why Our Sons Turn Violent and How We Can Save Them* (1999) by treating the recent shootings as evidencing not a recent crisis but rather "the terrible phenomenon of youth violence [that] has been commonplace for the past twenty years" (5). This crisis is the legacy of our country's sorry history of "institutional and interpersonal racism" (4). While he too appeals to the Bad Boy imaginary (playing on the Lost Boy trope and likening Kip Kinkel to Huck Finn), Garbarino actually examines social institutions such as the school and the prison system. The result is one of the better books of boyology, even if Garbarino has his own troubling idiosyncrasies and middle-class biases. To his credit, he opposes the boot camp solution to teenage delinquency, as profiled on talk shows these days, but rails against popular entertainment more generally, espousing classical music over "Marilyn Mansfield" (he means Marilyn Manson) and gangsta rap.

Having worked for years in inner-city Chicago, Garbarino nonetheless refuses to demonize his subjects as cold-blooded killers; from the opening pages, he makes clear his commitment to the perpetrator's essential humanity. Garbarino takes the trouble of reconstructing the pre-shooting days of Kip Kinkel and others, not to offer some vague and namby-pamby excuse (as Kellerman would have it) but to emphasize opportunities for identification and intervention. "Recognizing the humanity of troubled boys does not mean ignoring or rationalizing their lethal behavior" (94). Garbarino refreshingly takes to task those who decry youth violence but support the death penalty.

Whereas for Kellerman, the Lost Boy is the abject figure of normal selfhood, Garbarino insists on a common humanity beneath different life experiences. Kellerman claims that the psychopath could belong to any social class, but his descriptions resonate powerfully with racist tropes of boyhood and refuse the influence(s) of social life. Garbarino, by contrast, is genuinely worried about racism and youth violence and argues that these constitute the real boy problem. His efforts point toward a more responsible practice of boyology, and it's no coincidence that he makes fewer allusions to the classic literary tropes and figures of boyhood, despite his *Lost Boys* title.

Now That We Know

While the new boyology primers are sexist and tend to ignore issues of class and race, they are usually gay affirmative. Not one echoes the phobic sentiments of Kiley in *The Peter Pan Syndrome*. Both Gurian and Pollack argue for greater tolerance of gayness in boys. Pollack even devotes an entire chapter of *Real Boys* to homosexuality and homophobia. Both men, however, insist on the physical naturalness of homosexuality, on a minoritizing discourse of biology. Gay boys are thus acceptable to the degree that their sexuality can be explained in terms of biology, rather than (as for Kiley) cultural feminization. Gurian appeals to Simon LeVay's controversial thesis that the hypothalamus of the typical gay man is half the size of that of his heterosexual peer (232)—LeVay's research was based on gay men who died of AIDS, which Gurian never mentions. In a more generous (if still ludicrous) essentializing spirit, Pollack speculates that "homosexuals may be the genetic carriers of some of mankind's rare altruistic impulses" (216).

Gurian and Pollack pay more attention to sexuality than to the effects of racism or violence or class struggle, not only because of the success of the gay rights movement but also because gayness is unavoidable in even the most selective sample of white middle-class boys. But for the new boyologists, homosexuality is a variation on the normal theme of sexuality and biological development. This line of thinking isn't necessarily progressive or enabling. In fact, in some ways, it's quite consistent with homophobic tradition. Gay boys are no longer de facto Lost Boys, it's true, and yet the Peter Pan Syndrome isn't yet obsolete. In boyology, as in the larger cultural field, gay boys, as nonnormative subjects, are alternately lost and found.

A less deterministic line of inquiry into boys, gayness, and American culture is offered by Jay Mechling in *On My Honor: Boy Scouts and the Making of American Youth*. Drawing from scholarship in women's studies, men's studies, and queer studies, Mechling shows how Scouting participates in the larger social project of adult masculinity. That tenuous, vulnerable project seems to depend on homosocial bonding alongside homophobic articulations of normalcy. Casual nudity among men and boys, Mechling suggests, helps establish "a frame of heterosexual intimacy; the frame sends the metamessage

'I can be naked in front of you because we are both heterosexual and not potential sex partners'" (198). Mechling downplays the homoeroticism central to (if also disruptive of) that heterosexual frame, but he is right to emphasize that the most aggressively homosocial forms of masculine community, Scouting among them, are also among the most homophobic and heteronormative. Mechling acknowledges the presence of gay boys and men in Scouting, calling attention to the gay-positive movement Scouting for All, and discussing the consequences of the 2000 ruling by the Supreme Court to uphold the Boy Scouts' ban on gays. Mechling is gay affirmative while also emphasizing that the production of adult masculinity is ambivalently and anxiously organized around permutations of the "homo."

If the new boyology is any indication, gay-affirmative discourse can be counterproductive if it concentrates too much on the individual body as such and doesn't also attempt to analyze—using whatever language might be fruitful—the production of heteronormative masculinity. In her powerful essay on the social annihilation of queerness among children, titled "How to Bring Your Kids Up Gay: The War on Effeminate Boys," Eve Kosofsky Sedgwick points specifically to the culpability of the "helping professions" such as psychology and psychiatry. Through close readings of monographs on "sissy boys," Sedgwick shows not merely that psychologists and psychiatrists expect their patients to be heterosexual but that such professionals routinely see "the prevention of gay people as an ethical use of their skills" (163). Sedgwick does not endorse the sort of gay-affirmative language we see in the new boyology manuals; rather, she identifies that discourse as implicitly if not explicitly homophobic. The sissy boy, she remarks, serves as the "haunting abject" (157), not only of heteronormative masculinity but also of some gay-affirmative, gender-separatist discourse (in which the gay man is a "man's man"). "Advice on how to help your kids turn out gay," she writes, "not to mention your students, your parishioners, your therapy clients, or your military subordinates, is less ubiquitous than you might think. On the other hand, the scope of institutions whose programmatic undertaking is to prevent the development of gay people is unimaginably large" (161).

It's possible that the success of lesbian/gay advocacy has come at the expense of feminism, at least to the degree that antihomophobic rhetoric is organized against the so-called myth of gay effeminacy. Sedgwick notes that the depathologization of homosexuality by the American Psychiatric Association was attended by the repathologization of gender nonconformity in the form of a new diagnostic category in the *Diagnostic and Statistical Manual (DSM):* "Gender Identity Disorder of Childhood." That is, it's okay to be gay—at least, more so than it used to be—as long as you're not a girly boy or perpetual tomboy. The antifeminism of Gurian and the others is what in fact authorizes the (re)incorporation of gayness into the masculine world of the new boyology. Hence the pressing need for a feminist as well as gay-affirmative analysis.

Can This Boyology Be Saved?

As Sedgwick says in another provocative essay, "Tales of the Avunculate," "redeeming the family isn't, finally, an option but a compulsion; the question would be how to *stop* redeeming the family" (72). So too, perhaps, with boyology and perhaps masculinity more broadly. Historians of masculinity seem to feel compelled to offer hope for the future in the form of kinder, gentler masculinities. Faludi, for instance, urges men toward a feminist-affiliated "rebellion" against their stiffed condition. She hopes men will end their isolation and pursue "a brotherhood that includes us all" (608). Kimmel likewise calls for a "democratic manhood" against the self-made man. "Democratic manhood," he explains, "means a gender politics of inclusion, of standing up against injustice based on difference" (333). "This is not," he clarifies, "a call for androgyny" (334). But Mechling recommends just that, saying that "there are very good reasons for the Boy Scout to seek Scoutmasters and other volunteer male leaders who demonstrate an androgynous masculinity much broader in its range than stereotypical male performances" (231). More androgyny in our culture, Mechling thinks, "would end the need for misogyny and homophobia in the construction and maintenance of masculinity" (232).

It's hard to strike a productive balance between critique of, and optimism about, gender, between the hermeneutics of suspicion and utopian faith. I like the idea of encouraging androgyny, for instance, even as I worry that the very idea of androgyny tends to affirm male-female distinction. And both democracy and "democratic manhood" have been rather oppressive institutions. Although it has clearly functioned as an ideological cover for some unfortunate attitudes and ideas, I do not want to vilify boyhood any more than I hope to recover its innocence. And yet the racist, sexist, and class-specific impulses of boyology make it tempting to identify boyhood itself as a form of white male privilege. The new boyology especially seems a formidable obstacle to responsible work with children of all ages, races, nationalities, genders, and sexualities.

Maybe a democratic or androgynous boyhood as envisioned by these scholars would be just the ticket. But I suspect after Sedgwick that the proliferation of model masculinities would be symptomatic of the so-called (and seemingly perpetual) boy problem as much as a viable response to it. How, then, to stop redeeming boyology? One strategy, embraced by literary critics especially and inspired by feminist practices of reading, is to identify literature for and about boys that challenges what R. W. Connell calls "hegemonic masculinity," by which he means "relations of alliance, dominance and subordination" rather than any particular mode of masculinity (*Masculinities*, 37). Taking their cue, in fact, from Connell, contributors to a recent volume entitled *Ways of Being Male: Representing Masculinities in Children's Literature and Film* identify texts that "regender" boyhood. Editor John Stephens argues in the introduction that literature is uniquely qualified to serve as a counterhegemonic discourse on gender, to the degree that subjectivity and "intersubjectivity" are at issue, especially in metafictional texts. While I do not agree with all of its assumptions, *Ways of Being Male* is instructive both as a model of progressive scholarship on masculinity and as a guide to progressive contemporary children's fiction.

Another option is to identify the ways in which discourses of masculinity "work" in the disciplinary sense—that is, how they establish the rhetorical and procedural ground rules for their own legitimacy. Here Connell is even more helpful, as he identifies three major discourses for the twentieth-century project of masculinity: "One was based in the clinical knowledge acquired by therapists, and its leading ideas came from Freudian theory. The second was based in social psychology and centered on the enormously popular idea of 'sex role.'" The third "involves recent developments in anthropology, history, and sociology" (7). Connell addresses each of these discourses alongside but also against knowledge about gender derived from political activity and the experience of everyday life. While Faludi and Kimmel offer astonishingly thick descriptions of American masculinity, Connell is better able to identify what we might call the "disciplinary imaginary" of masculinity and men's studies. With this model in mind, I have tried as much as possible to identify the disciplinary dimensions of boyology and the feral tale.

Narrative and institutional cultures of boy work are deeply embedded and perversely resilient, so that even the most progressive of the new boyology manuals look like business as usual. I find myself wishing that most of the forms of boy work I've identified would simply go away. As a gay man who hated Scouting as a kid, I hope that legal challenges to Scouting's phobic conservatism prevail in the long term. If I have any residual affection for boy work, it's more familial than institutional, as my family ran summer camps in Texas for many years, one for boys and one for girls. Attending camp and working as a counselor was formative for me and prepared me to be a teacher. Yet today I have mixed feelings about camping as a boy work venue, especially to the degree that it accommodates the wealthy. I've written *Making American Boys: Boyology and the Feral Tale* as a way of working through my growing ambivalence about boyology in all its forms, chief among them literature. To the degree that it's possible, I'd like now to leave boyology behind.

Notes

Introduction

1. In *Kipling's Imperial Boy: Adolescence and Cultural Hybridity,* Don Randall persuasively argues that in Anglo-European culture, the adolescent boy has long been understood as a hybrid creature, and thus as an exemplary subject of imperialism. Caught between stages of life, that boy embodies and thematizes conflict between the primitive and the modern, the savage and the civilized. The boy variously represents both colonizer and colonized. He "serves as an organizing figure in discourses that address questions of cross-cultural encounter" (25). Put another way, boyhood is a contact zone. Randall makes a compelling case for the cultural significance of the imperial boy—indeed, for the very legibility of the boy as implicitly if not explicitly imperialist. His hybrid imperial boy, of course, is of British extract, the product of several centuries of trade, expansion, and military presence in India. It's worth asking what corresponding and divergent traditions mark American culture.

2. Mowgli, Tarzan, and Peter Pan probably come to mind, but we might also mention Edward Scissorhands, Batman, the Little Mermaid, and the Animorphs, among other changelings, cyborgs, and so-called freaks, caught between cultures or modes of life.

3. Most people know the myth of Remus and Romulus, twin sons of Mars, suckled by the she-wolf Lupa with additional care from a woodpecker. Such stories abound in Greco-Roman and Native American mythology especially, though the motif also surfaces in the folklore of Brazil, Canada, China, India, Indonesia, Ireland, and Zanzibar, featuring such unlikely foster parents as goats, monkeys, pigs, ostriches, cows, dogs, deer, bears, and eagles. In Greco-Roman lore, the children, usually boys, are supernaturally strong and wise, thanks to an unorthodox upbringing. Even the mighty Zeus was nourished by a goat-nymph.

4. In his fascinating study *Feral Children and Clever Animals,* Douglas Candland reviews four famous cases of feral children (three post-Linnaeus) to emphasize the self-fulfilling prophecy of clinical psychologies. Each of these cases, Candland contends, exposes the medical and scientific discourse of its day, not any truth about "the silent mind" of feral children (70). Candland uses these cases to defamiliarize the major psychologies of the twentieth century: psychoanalysis, behaviorism, and phenomenology. Candland does not address the sociohistorical emergence of childhood or child study, but he acknowledges that those who studied the feral child were often child psychologists.

5. This normalizing trend is disappointing, given the feral tale's tendencies toward an appreciation of queerness or singularity. Poets especially have capitalized on the wild child's fundamental strangeness; consider, for instance, James Dickey's infamous "Sheep Child" (1966), Thom Gunn's "The Allegory of the Wolf Boy" (1957), and Seamus Heaney's "Bye Child" (1972).

6. Baden-Powell rewrites the Mowgli tales to suit his own ends. He teaches the Wolf Cubs how to howl: "The call of the pack all over the world is 'We'll do our

best'; so when your Cubmaster comes into the circle you chuck up your chin and, all together, you howl out—making each word a long yowl: 'A-Ka-la!—We-e-e-ell do-o-o-o ou-u-u-r BEST.' Yell the word 'best' sharp and loud and short and all together" (cited in Brogan, Mowgli's Sons, 43). To which a bemused Kipling replied that "you must remember that among wolves, the Head-wolf's name is always one that can be howled easily," correcting Baden-Powell's pronunciation of Akela, lupine leader in the Jungle Books.

7. See Peter Gay, Reading Freud, 100–105; also on the list was Mark Twain's Sketches.

8. In The Interpretation of Dreams, Freud recounts the only nightmare from childhood that he remembers, in which he saw his mother carried into a room by bird-headed people and then laid upon the bed. Freud recognizes these figures as gods from an Egyptian funerary relief, as pictured in the Philippson Bible that his family owned, and interprets his nightmare as a fulfillment of his wish that he might possess his mother (622–23).

9. Freud, of course, says nothing about the effects of imperialism on psychic life or of any influence beyond that of the immediate family; he wasn't inclined to understand his new discipline in terms of the remythification of wildness.

10. Propp's essay, the first major exploration of the Oedipus story in "folkloristics," never mentions Freud but emphasizes psychodynamics as much as tale morphology.

11. Vassilka Nikolova similarly points out that exposure is a major component of the Attic myth of Oedipus used by Sophocles ("The Oedipus Myth," 97).

12. Given Propp's faith in progressive tale evolution, the implication is that the woman will become a less natural or permanent caregiver, which might explain why Mowgli and Tarzan must relinquish their animal stepmoms. What Freud claims for the evolution of the psyche itself, Propp claims for the evolution of folklore, and it is tempting in turn to characterize Freud's feral tales as the totemic phase of psychoanalysis.

13. In pop-diagnostic accounts of disturbed boys, such as Eleanor Craig's One, Two, Three: The Story of Matt, a Feral Child (1978), a female caseworker acts as a surrogate mother and restores the boy to some assurance of masculinity. Like the Freudian family romance as reinterpreted by Margot Backus in her book on Anglo-Irish gothicism, the feral tale wears two family faces, the idealized and the demonic—even if the demonic now tends away from the traditional gothic in favor of the diagnostic abject.

14. While Bill Brown argues in The Material Unconscious that the "chronotopic work" (173) of the generic boy book insulates boyhood against the dangerously modern world of working men, Richard S. Lowry and Glenn Hendler focus on the ways in which the genre interpellates men by addressing boys. These critics do not examine the practice of writing for and about boys, but their understanding of man-boy dynamics more generally helps us think about that vocation. Through a reading of Tom Sawyer, Lowry proposes that the "seemingly divergent topoi of boy and man" in postbellum boy books represent boyhood as an insular space while also

designating it as the "space in which . . . masculinity could best be formed" ("Domestic Interiors," 111).

15. I do not address the autobiographical dimension of the Bad Boy genre except as it pertains to the genre's cultural work. Marcia Jacobson has already given us a useful study along these lines, arguing in *Being a Boy Again* that the genre's "special appeal lies in its autobiographical aspect" (3). Her chief focus is that aspect, although she does provide occasional explanations for its cultural appeal and tenacity. In her introduction, she acknowledges that the boy book had a complex genealogy and served a variety of interests. "In presenting an entertaining and sometimes sentimentalized picture of a bygone era," she writes, "the boy book distracted from the difficulties of the present and paradoxically allowed for unreflecting accommodation to it" (16). All of the "boy books" that she discusses have been identified as Bad Boy books.

16. Mother, thinks Demos, was increasingly the sole custodian and supervisor of the child, the source of fierce love and resentment (as for Sendak's wolf-boy Max). The father was away at work, and sons were expected not only to live up to, but also to surpass, his success. Hence the distinctively American hothouse family, and the insidious growth of that hothouse flower, psychoanalysis. Demos makes clear his sense that Oedipality, however much the consequence or inflection of sociohistorical forces, is prior to them, existing as "developmental potential in all persons, no matter what their location in time and space." Thus "Oedipal issues" in his view can "become highly charged for many people" at particular historical junctures (74). Apparently as humans we already have (or are had by) Oedipal issues. The essay titled "Oedipus and America" appeared in 1978 but was reprinted in *Inventing the Psychological: Toward a Cultural History of Emotional Life in America*, edited by Joel Pfister and Nancy Schmog. In an afterword, Demos stands by his argument and particularly his sense that Oedipality is an innate building block of the psyche.

17. In *Monumental Anxieties*, his study of nineteenth-century American authorship, Scott S. Derrick observes that a writer's determination to become an author may supersede and even dictate a book's content, the narrative subject itself serving "as the narrativization of this desire" for authorship (23). Given the anxieties attending composition in the literary world, the boy seemed an ideal subject around which to assert semiprofessional status. Certainly for aspiring authors, located uneasily between the home and the workplace, the boy safeguards "monumental anxieties": masculine identity, vocational calling, financial stability, the promise of "coherent, autonomous subjectivity," and the ability to resist those scribbling women (22–23).

18. "Nature," adds Emerson in "Self-Reliance," "suffers nothing to remain in her kingdoms which cannot help itself" (270). "Society everywhere is in conspiracy against the manhood of every one of its members," he warns; "never varnish your hard, uncharitable ambition with this incredible tenderness for black folk a thousand miles off. Thy love afar is spite at home" (260–61). Such sentiments led John Fiske and Herbert Spencer to mistake Emerson for a herald of evolutionary philosophy. Spencer even visited Emerson in Concord, apparently the only tribute he ever paid a fellow intellectual.

19. In "Nature," Emerson links the linguistic patterns of children and savages, who "use only nouns or names of things, which they convert into verbs, and apply to analogous mental acts" (197).

20. For an intriguing account of this principle and its life in social science and popular culture, see Stephen Jay Gould's *Ontogeny and Phylogeny*.

21. The association of boy and savage was hardly so standard, positive, or proto-authorial in earlier periods of American history. Seventeenth-century colonists such as William Bradford and John Winthrop routinely described native Americans as savage and infantile, and the image was so commonplace that Washington Irving satirized it in *A History of New York* (1809). During the Market Revolution, the racist motif of the black child/savage gained momentum, underwritten by the Great Chain of Being metaphor, which held sway into the early nineteenth century. But in literature at least, we see a less pejorative association of boy and savage in the early nineteenth century as well, or rather a more strategically racist association through which the boy was assigned all the noble traits of the savage but none of his ostensibly ignoble ones. Eventually the boy-savage became a trope for the lettered self, a century or so before the feral boy was similarly reclaimed.

22. In the first volume of *The History of Sexuality*, Michel Foucault identifies the masturbating schoolboy as one of four modern subjects of sexual surveillance and regulation. The biopolitical "right to life," argues Foucault, shapes our understanding of the bourgeois schoolboy and the forces that imperil him. By masturbating, that boy "was in danger of compromising not so much his physical strength as his intellectual capacity, his moral fiber, and the obligation to preserve a healthy line of descent for his family and his social class" (121). Whereas Spencer looks to the schoolboy as evidence for his theory of diversification, Foucault and Winter both see the schoolboy as a subject around whom modern discourses of sexuality unfolded. Put another way, Foucault and Winter recognize the schoolboy as a thoroughly modern subject. Schoolboy psychology, I suspect, had origins in evolutionary science.

23. Charting what he calls the "anthropology of boys" in *Bodies and Machines*, Mark Seltzer suggests that boyology appeared at the end of the nineteenth century as part of the body-machine complex, a coordination of the individual and national body in response to anxieties about the depletion of virility and agency. For Seltzer, boyology represents both a reassertion of the "natural" in the machine and an acknowledgment that working men are *made* from boys. Mining the "material unconscious" of the 1890s, Bill Brown similarly proposes that this preoccupation with boyhood was an attempt to spatialize boyhood as "a site where a residual America can be preserved . . . where nationhood can be embodied outside history" (176), thereby protecting culture from modernity.

24. Early on, Wild Peter of Hanover attracted the attention of Anglo-European literati, among them Jonathan Swift and Daniel Defoe. Swift visited Peter while in London preparing for the publication of *Gulliver's Travels* (1726), and Defoe devoted a book-length satire to the case, which echoed the issues germane to *Robinson Crusoe* (1719). Lively was the interplay of scientific and literary interest in primitivism

in and around Peter's case. I note only that *Gulliver's Travels* and *Robinson Crusoe* are understood by historians of children's literature as the first nondidactic books appropriated and widely read by children. They were, of course, quite didactic in a different sense and set the tone for protocolonialist classics like *A Swiss Family Robinson* (1812), *The Coral Island* (1858), *Treasure Island* (1883), *Swallows and Amazons* (1930), and newer stories of disaster and survival.

25. And as I've already observed, that literature is often, if not always, colonialist. Fiedler repeatedly invokes the wisdom of colonialist children's literature as proof of "the sort of primordial fears which I have been examining, about scale, sexuality, our status as more than beasts, and our tenuous individuality" (34). "Reading any of L. Frank Baum's Oz books, for instance," he writes in *Freaks*, "or James Barrie's *Peter Pan*, or *Alice in Wonderland*, or *Gulliver's Travels*, we cross in our imaginations a borderline which in childhood we could never be sure was there, entering a realm where precisely what qualifies us as normal on one side identifies us as Freaks on the other" (28). Fiedler argues that children's books provide a form of optimistic closure or resolution, a way of warding off strangeness missing from the freak show itself. But the feral tale's relationship to psychoanalysis, colonialism, and children's literature, telegraphic in Fiedler's discourse, obviously has a complex and productive history.

26. Here we hear echoes of a classic assumption of the feral tale: man is abusive, whereas nature is benevolent, even recuperative. "Nature's mercy," writes Michael Newton in his recent book on feral children, "admonishes humanity's unnatural cruelty: only a miracle of *kindness* can restore the imbalance created by human iniquity" (5).

27. In his second volume on the history of pyschoanalysis in the United States, Nathan G. Hale also describes the postwar period as the "golden age of [psychoanalytic] popularization," citing as evidence the publication of Ernest Jones's three-part biography of Freud (1953–1957) and the phenomenal success of Dr. Benjamin Spock's *Common Sense Book of Baby and Child Care* (1946). See Hale's *The Rise and Crisis of Psychoanalysis in the United States: Freud and the Americans, 1917–1985*.

•   1. Farming for Boys

1. Its longtime editor Henry Israel, for instance, praises the Belgian sculptor Constantin Meunier for his devotion to the "rustic force and beauty of the toiler" (103) and suggests that Meunier's sculptures show the possibility and utility of art in rural America. See "Meunier's Toilers of the Field in Stature," in the March 1914 issue (5:3:103–5).

2. Although YMCA boy work dates back to the 1870s, it accelerated after 1900, when it finally began to pay attention to the farm boy, in response to the success of the 4-H club movement. Farm boys had no institutional room of their own until 4-H clubs were founded in the early 1900s to boost farm production and morale. Unlike the YMCA and the BSA, 4-H was originally a grassroots movement, beginning with scattered after-school meetings and local corn contests in the Midwest

(Wessel and Wessel, *4-H: An American Idea*, 5–6). "Corn club work" for boys spread quickly to other states and attracted the attention and support of the USDA. Girls participated instead in tomato canning, learning how to preserve foods safely and efficiently. By the time *Rural Manhood* began production, 4-H work had garnered county, state, and federal support, culminating in the creation of the Cooperative Extension Service in 1914, which coordinated the clubs and linked them with land-grant colleges. The official histories of 4-H and of Future Farmers of America (not established until 1928) have little to say about the abusive father. These organizations were extensions of public schools, sanctioned by the federal government, and had no investment in promoting boy work per se. For an overview of the strategies and programs of 4-H, written for club directors, see T. T. Martin's *The 4-H Club Leader's Handbook: Principles and Procedures.*

3. In *Bodies and Machines*, Mark Seltzer suggests that the rise of boyology occurred at the century's turn, "as part of the reasserting of the natural in machine culture, and, correlatively, with a modeling of the nation on the male natural body" (152).

4. For easier reference, all citations are from the book.

5. A contemporary example of the uncle-rescue formula is John Hughes's comedy *Uncle Buck* (1989), which stars the late John Candy. Buck is an affable, slobbish bachelor uncle who redeems an uptight (and upper-middle-class) family from suburban dysfunction when the parents are called away by an emergency and ask Buck to babysit. By the film's end, he has bonded with the family's three children (one of whom is played by the young Macauley Culkin, before *Home Alone*) and has decided to start his own family with his long-term girlfriend.

6. No doubt Benny is designated an uncle because that makes him more appealingly familial; it may also locate him in the literary tradition of African American uncles of vernacular wisdom and great family loyalty (Stowe's Uncle Tom being the prototype, and later examples including Joel Chandler Harris's Uncle Remus).

7. Tim Jeal titles his biography of Baden-Powell *The Boy-Man.*

8. By the 1830s, New York farmers were worried about their worn-out soil, depleted of vital minerals by land-skinning practices. These farmers adapted European methods of farming, including crop rotation, draining, deep plowing, and fertilizing. Also by the 1830s, books on agricultural chemistry were readily available to the American public. Particularly influential were the texts of the German chemist Justus Liebig, who inspired and presided over (if from a distance) the "soil analysis craze" of the 1840s and early 1850s. Most American agricultural chemists of note toured the German laboratories, including Samuel W. Johnson, who later established the nation's first agricultural experiment station in Connecticut in 1875.

9. As Lora Romero explains in her chapter on Harriet Beecher Stowe, the terms "manualizer" and "mentalizer" come from the pro-slavery apologist Henry Hughes, to describe the respective work of the slaves and their white owners; see *Home Fronts*, 77–79.

10. In *Hard Facts*, Philip Fisher identifies the family farm as one of three "privileged settings" for the consolidation of American culture in the nineteenth century.

Although he concentrates on the ways in which the Jeffersonian vision of the farm grappled with the "hard fact" of slavery, I share his conviction that the farm served as an important "vanishing point" "toward which lines of sight and projects of every kind converge" (9).

11. Farm women were increasingly displaced from traditional farmwork by technological innovation and a masculinization of agricultural business. With the developments of farm technology, farm women turned from routine farm chores like milking and livestock care to domestic work; scholars refer to this as the "defeminization of agriculture," which I find problematic, and about which there is little consensus.

12. Originally young Allen was ridiculed for cultivating horseradish, but it is that very luxury-turned-staple—evidence of the increasing agricultural specialization in the East—that secures his income (566).

13. Like Benny, Mr. Allen is a farmer-scholar who provides practical advice and intellectual nourishment. He too understands how to manage boys. Give the boy some tools and his own work space, Allen advises, and the boy will shun mischief and the "rude crowd in the street" (138).

14. Hall continues with amusing anecdotes about other farm types, including old pals and neighbors (notably a horse jockey, a rebel Baptist deacon, and a suspected witch). Nearly every aspect of farm life he declares "of perennial interest to boys" (122).

15. Hall began his research on childhood while a student at Johns Hopkins; his first publication was entitled "The Contents of Children's Minds" (1883). Though an American and a student of William James at Harvard, Hall had also been schooled on the continent in psychology and physiology, working as a postdoctoral student with Wilhem Wundt, just as Wundt's famous laboratory of experimental psychology was being assembled. Hall had a dual interest in empirical psychology and in evolutionary psychology and, like Freud, accorded sexuality a primary role in human development. Having trained at the University of Jena in the 1870s, when Haeckel's biogenetic law was being debated throughout Germany, Hall often invoked recapitulation to account for developmental stages in children. He was also heavily influenced by Herbert Spencer, particularly his *Principles of Psychology* (1872). In 1893 Hall helped organize the National Association for the Study of Childhood and for the next ten years devoted himself to the cause. In 1909 he invited Freud and Jung (among others) to lecture at Clark University, where he served as president.

16. Some historians prefer to describe the museums as "living farms" or "curatorial agriculture," to emphasize that these are not always traditional museums.

17. Darwin Kelsey, who served as the director of historical agriculture at Old Sturbridge Village, notes that the Skansen Museum of Stockholm, founded in 1891, is generally credited as the first successful outdoor museum (which today includes more than 120 buildings). See Kelsey's "Outdoor Museums and Historical Agriculture" for an overview of the movement, and John Schlebecker's essay in the same volume for an assessment of the methods and challenges of "curatorial agriculture." Although Schlebecker's essay is a bit too meandering, he expresses the difficulty of

finding "the proper biological elements" rather succinctly, asking "Where does one find the sort of pig which ran around in the Ohio woods in 1820?" (101).

18. *Rural Manhood* was published monthly except for July and August; for ease of reference, I usually refer to issues by volume and number rather than month and year, unless I want to emphasize the latter.

19. The journal even acknowledged the success of Scouting and promoted its American program, providing reviews of BSA material and tips on organizing troops (see, for instance, 1:7:32).

20. The city is not always imagined as the source of evil and corruption, but an antiurban sentiment does pervade the journal. The May 1914 issue, for instance, includes Charlotte Perkins Gilman's apocalyptic poem "A City of Death," originally published in the *Forerunner*, which likens the city to hell on earth. Here's the last stanza:

> A city whose own thick mephitic air
> Insidiously destroys its citizens;
> Whose buildings rob us of the blessed sun,
> The cleansing wind, the very breath of life;
> Whose weltering rush of swarming human forms,
> Forced hurtling through foul subterranean tubes
> Kills more than bodies, coarsens mind and soul,
> Destroys all grace and kindly courtesy,
> And steadily degrades our humanness
> To slavish acquiescence in its shame. (5:4:214)

21. For a contemporaneous book-length account of the country girl, see Martha Foote Crow's *The American Country Girl*, originally published in 1915. Crow dedicates her book to "the seven million country life girls of America, with the hope that they may see their great privilege and do their honorable part in the new Country Life Era." Chapters are thus entitled "The Daughter's Share of the Work," "The Household Laboratory," "Efficient Administration," and "Pageantry as a Community Resource," to list just a few.

22. Not surprisingly, *Rural Manhood* eulogizes Teddy Roosevelt as the "ideal American": "He gave all that he was. He gave it to country folk as to all other folk, and he saw country life with a whole mind; we still sorely need him" (10:2, inside cover).

23. For more information on the camping movement, see Macleod, *Building Character*, chap. 13, and Eleanor Eells's *History of Organized Camping: The First One Hundred Years*.

24. Earlier, of course, there were military camps; Alger's first novel, *Frank's Campaign* (1864), a Civil War story, is subtitled "Or, The Farm and the Camp."

25. The need to profile the sexual pervert and to define man-boy sex as abuse characterizes even the most nuanced accounts of these sexual scandals. Patrick Boyle, for instance, acknowledges that since its founding in 1908, Scouting has been a "magnet" for boy lovers, and that Scout leaders (beginning with Baden-Powell himself) have worked hard to suppress that unpleasant fact. Boyle suggests that the intensely homosocial atmosphere of Scouting may be conducive to abuse, rather

than arguing that sexual play was just one form of boy access that Scouting provides for men. Why, I would ask, is it the only such form deemed abusive or sinister? In their account of sexual abuse in the Catholic Church, Elinor Burkett and Frank Buni argue that the priesthood creates an unhealthy atmosphere of social isolation and sexual repression, but they stop short of indicting the church itself, or exploring sexuality in and around Catholicism. Charles M. Sennott's exposé of Covenant House in New York is better along such lines, for while Sennott focuses on its fallen founder and icon, Father Bruce Ritter, he faults the Catholic Church for suppressing early accusations of sexual misconduct and traces the "Faustian pact" Ritter made with the corporate Far Right to keep the charity affluent.

26. "Uncle" serves as a euphemism for a homosexual man in several 1990s gay-affirmative picture books, notably Mary Kate Jordan's *Losing Uncle Tim* and Illana Katz's *Uncle Jimmy*. In these books, the men are actually uncles of the young protagonists and are also homosexual men dying from AIDS. The uncles remain outside of the immediate family and are figures of pathos as well as love.

27. In a different vein, Munn's *Boyhood Days on the Farm* traces the boys' affection for the quasi hermit, quasi uncle "Old Renus" who lives alone in the woods. "Of course such an eccentric old fellow would naturally attract boys," writes Munn, particularly against the warnings of "well-meaning and pious mothers" (43).

28. Holliday is also the author of another *Rural Manhood* cautionary tale of woe titled "Jim Jenkin's Dad," which Israel summarizes thus: "A story of the third generation of a family which has splendid latent leadership qualities. It has gone to seed and 'Jim Jenkins' is the boy problem of Ourtown" (10:7:293).

29. Here Gibson is apparently quoting from a source for which he provides no citation.

2. Bad Boys and Men of Culture

1. Professing respect for the complexity of oral culture and children's culture, Sanders likens children's listening powers to those of "a clairvoyant, or a Guatemalan 'echoman'" (34), even as he insists, "I do not mean to equate oral peoples with children. Far from it" (33). He has nothing to say about the benefits of visual literacy.

2. Sanders calls Hauser an "obscure, nineteenth century example," but that's hardly the case. Jeffrey Moussaieff Masson notes that more than three thousand books and fourteen thousand articles have been written about him (*Lost Prince*, 4).

3. Sanders also wants to return mothers to the home, to bolster the nuclear family. "That's the first step—a mother and a father" (242). So much for tribal child rearing. Sanders shows little interest in what oral cultures actually entail, particularly those differing from whatever oral culture made possible the golden age of American selfhood.

4. Glenn Hendler notes that while *Tom Sawyer* and other Bad Boy books detail the homogeneous nature of boyhood, they finally affirm the more heterogeneous world of men. Hendler argues that homogeneity and other "destabilizing characteristics of boyhood" are rejected and projected upon Others, while boys become more

singular and "self-possessed," in keeping with adult male mandates ("Tom Sawyer's Masculinity," 47). I understand these two traits of the genre that Hendler identifies—the trend toward heterogeneity, and the projection of boyhood's "destabilizing characteristics" onto Others—as literary correlates of Herbert Spencer's theory of diversification, and the doctrine of recapitulation, usually attributed to Ernst Haeckel. In the Bad Boy genre, which largely keeps the evolutionary faith, the boy is first allied with, and then separated from, the savage, the feminine, and various incarnations of the homogeneous.

5. By "boy book" I often also mean the generic series book, which in America began with Jacob Abbott's Rollo books, and with the postbellum stories of William T. Adams ("Oliver Optic") and Horatio Alger Jr., and the later series of Gilbert Patten and, of course, Edward Stratemeyer. Like other popular genres, the boy book varies little from text to text. Nearly interchangeable are Tom Swift, Tom Slade, Frank Merriwell, the Rover Boys, and (later still) the Hardy Boys, not to mention boy heroes of technical or Scouting persuasions. In this chapter I use the term "boy book" to designate this more generic form, which includes the Bad Boy texts.

6. Edward Eggleston's *The Hoosier School-Master* (1871) and Edward Everett Hale's *A New England Boyhood* (1893) occasionally get mention, but neither is particularly concerned with the Bad Boy, and both are arguably more evocative of antebellum place and time (Indiana and Boston, respectively) than of boyhood per se.

7. Alger's novels are usually described as series fiction or as another genre, the "rags-to-riches" story (something of a misnomer), while Alcott's novels are generally understood as domestic or family stories, despite their Bad Boy impulses. The boys of Alger and Alcott are often orphans or of less secure social class (Laurie in *Little Women* notwithstanding); they also live and work more overtly in the world of adults than do their Bad Boy cousins. Still, Alger's streetwise boys and Alcott's little boy-savages seem quite at home in Bad Boy company. In *Little Women*, Alcott even names her major scapegrace Tommy, five years before Tom Sawyer shows up, and speaks of Jo March's many experienced "years of boy culture."

Given such resemblances, it seems surprising that the little men of Alger and Alcott weren't also seen as Bad Boys, but Alcott and Alger were outsiders in the East Coast literary culture that created the genteel but masculine Bad Boy. Alger was perceived as too commercial and crude, and Alcott too sentimental; neither had the right stuff to be a Bad Boy author. Hendler points out that Alger's novels were often linked with the sentimental and emasculating novels of women, since they required their plucky boy heroes to "lose themselves in a sympathetic identification with an even less fortunate boy" (36). Ironically, Alcott and Alger now receive more critical attention than most of the Bad Boy writers combined; the first book-length study of the genre, Marcia Jacobson's *Being a Boy Again*, didn't appear until 1994, long after similar treatments of Alcott and Alger. Of course, the Bad Boy genre was never understood as great literature—just as better writing than series fiction and sappy domestic stories. For an interesting comparison of Alger and Alcott, with brief reference to the generic boy book, see Thomas H. Pauly's "*Ragged Dick* and *Little Women*." On Twain and Alcott, see Crowley, "*Little Women* and the Boy-Book."

8. In his suggestive study *The Material Unconscious,* Bill Brown notes the tendency of classic boy books to resist developmental narratives in two ways: by preventing character growth, and by spatializing boyhood, transforming it into a hermetically sealed site "where a residual America can be preserved . . . where nationhood can be embodied outside history" (176). Boyhood is imagined as an independent and timeless world, with its own features and laws, inaccessible to adults. Brown also points out that the Bad Boy writers resorted to both a language of typology (the Bad Boy) and to particular examples of type (individual variations on the theme), shoring up the reality effect of the genre.

9. Drawing from various theorists of autobiography, Marcia Jacobson recasts the boy book as "an autobiographical form essentially defined by a separation of narrator and protagonist" (21), and examines the various degrees of such separation in classic texts of the genre. *Being a Boy Again* provides both detailed analysis of individual texts and a wealth of juicy biographical anecdote. She argues that the boy book was typically inspired by loss or trauma, such as the death of family members or even, in Charles Dudley Warner's case, despair over childlessness. She traces patterns of male humiliation and triumph in Twain's novels, seeing Tom's and Huck's adventures as expressions of Twain's theatricality and vulnerability, which "were his father's legacy" (69). Her analysis is engaging and largely persuasive.

10. As the 1914 *Handbook for Scout Masters* explains, "The period of Boyhood or the Gang period corresponds racially to the tribal period, and is characterized by the development and dominance of gang influences over the boy's whole allegiance. The early Adolescent or Chivalry period is racially parallel to the Feudal or Absolute Monarchial period with its chivalric virtues, vices, and actions" (Cited in Macleod, *Building Character,* 97). Presumably chivalry makes possible further advancements in culture. This chivalrous narrative of history is endemic to boyologist tracts like Forbush's *The Boy Problem,* which teach boy workers how to manipulate the gang and feudal impulses of male youth, and how to narrate their success.

11. Tarkington was an avowed recapitulationist, writing that "just as in his embryo man reproduces the history of his development upward from the mire into man, so does he in his childhood and his boyhood and his youth reproduce the onward history of his race, from the most ancient man to the most modern" (cited in Woodress, *Booth Tarkington,* 177).

12. Seton was born in England, spent his boyhood in Canada, and came to America in the 1880s, where he became a famous naturalist and founder of the Woodcraft movement. He considered himself the true founder of Scouting, but as Michael Rosenthal points out, Scouting is more than Woodcraft in military garb, and credit really goes to Baden-Powell. See Rosenthal, *The Character Factory,* 65–81, for an account of the collaboration and rivalry of these two men.

13. "My boy's" mother is the quintessential angel in the house, who tends the home while her husband runs the town newspaper. Howells calls her "the family sovereignty" (75).

14. It is central to Howells's novel *The Flight of Pony Baker* (1902), which Crowley has analyzed in Freudian terms in his essay "Polymorphously Perverse?

Childhood Sexuality in the American Boy Book." Crowley locates the Bad Boy genre in relation to the doctrine of recapitulation and Freud's theories of sexuality. He points out that Freud insists (via evolutionary theory) that since the child "recapitulates the archaic sexual pleasures of his evolutionary ancestors," his sexual life will naturally be "perverse" (7–8). *The Flight of Pony Baker* is thus both an enactment and a repression of sexual awareness, as boyhood escape from the polymorphous sexuality of childhood.

15. Nancy Glazener aligns realism directly with "such sinister intellectual enterprises as racial anthropology, sexology, and phrenology" (*Reading for Realism*, 23). Like these (other?) sinister disciplines, realism shows a strong "penchant for classification" (23).

16. See Sarah Burns on barefoot country children in nineteenth-century American art and culture.

17. Glazener later notes that in the 1870s and 1880s, realism was also asserted through a medical model, against the "addictive" discourse of sentimentality. Realist books were likened to medicine and healthy food.

18. Sedgwick traces in various texts the enactment of this "definition" through binarisms such as secrecy/disclosure, domestic/foreign, public/private, in/out, masculine/feminine, innocence/initiation, and knowledge/innocence—all of which permeate Bad Boy writing and the more generic boy book. She shows that homophobia is fueled by the anxiety that masculine sentiment will degenerate into feminine sentimentality, that identification (homosocial bonding) will be (mis)read as desire. Noting the prevalence in late-nineteenth-century culture of "images of agonistic male self-constitution," she links homophobia with the fear of feminization.

19. For an analysis of this strategy, see Jacobson, *Being a Boy Again*, 73–75.

20. For more on character building in its assorted forms, see Macleod, Jeal, MacDonald, Rosenthal, and Seltzer.

21. *American Boy* was published in Detroit by William C. Sprague. In its inaugural issue (November 1899), Sprague offered the following rationale for his new project: "This paper is for boys—American boys, the brightest and best boys on the face of the earth. It is not a family paper, tho' men and women with boys' hearts will read it. It is not a child's paper, of which we all know there are enough already" (Reck, viii). *American Boy* was designed instead for "the wide-awake, aspiring American boy who is just turning the corner into manhood" (viii). In 1929 it purchased the ailing *Youth's Companion*, which boosted its circulation. It began to fail during the Depression and finally folded in 1941.

22. Forbush was a disciple of both Hall and of the YMCA's dynamic leader, Luther Gulick, who was cofounder with his wife Charlotte of the Camp Fire Girls.

23. The 1916 edition features a lovely engraving of David and Goliath on the front cover and a list of popular boys' series published by Altemus Books, including the Grammar School Boys, the High School Boys Vacation series, the Young Engineers, and the Submarine Boys series.

24. In *The Education of Man*, Froebel had already offered a similar sketch of the evolving boy colony, before the epochs concept was officially launched: "Again, what

busy tumult among those older boys at the brook down yonder! They have built canals and sluices, bridges and seaports, dams and mills, each one intent only on his own work. Now the water is to be used to carry vessels from the higher to the lower level; but at each step of progress one trespasses on the limits of another realm, and each one equally claims his right as lord and maker, while he recognizes the claims of the others. What can serve here to mediate? Only *treaties,* and, like states, they bind themselves by strict treaties" (111).

25. Of Tom, Howells writes that "his courage is the Indian sort, full of prudence and mindful of retreat as one of the conditions of prolonged hostilities. In a word, he is a boy, and merely and exactly an ordinary boy on the moral side. What makes him delightful to the reader is that on the imaginative side he is very much more, and though every boy has wild and fantastic dreams, this boy cannot rest till he has somehow realized them. The story is a wonderful study of the boy-mind, which inhabits a world quite distinct from that in which he is bodily present with his elders, and in this lies its great charm and its universality, for boy nature, however human nature varies, is the same everywhere" (*My Mark Twain,* 106–7).

Tom Sawyer had its origin in an 1868 story based on Twain's Hannibal childhood, which biographer Albert Bigelow Paine, and not Twain himself, titled the "Boys Manuscript." It was also Paine who, after his authorized 1912 biography *Mark Twain,* produced *The Boys' Life of Mark Twain: The Story of a Man Who Made the World Laugh and Love Him* (1915). *Tom Sawyer*'s many affinities with Bad Boy writing have been discussed at length elsewhere; to the list I add only Twain's disdain for sappy woman authors. In his 1865 sketch "The Story of a Bad Little Boy," Twain had already parodied "Sunday School" fiction. In *Tom Sawyer*'s longest authorial aside, he laments that "there is no school in all our land where the young ladies do not feel obliged to close their compositions with a sermon; and you will find that the sermon of the most frivolous and the least religious girl in the school is always the longest and the most relentlessly pious" (137). His disparagement of the "schoolgirl pattern" (141) runs several pages, anticipating his satire of the late Emmeline Grangerford in *Huck Finn.* Later he speaks of "a committee of sappy women" (203) who petition for a pardon for Injun Joe, linking the savage and the feminine at the level of plot, and in the service of male authorial hubris.

26. Gribben avers that critics have underestimated the influence of Aldrich's *The Story of a Bad Boy* on Twain's two boy books and offers a detailed reading of the continuities.

27. We see this pattern again and again; one recent example is Disney's painfully upbeat 1993 film adaptation, *The Adventures of Huck Finn.* The movie poster featured a photograph of Huck and Jim floating down the Mississippi, with the caption "Haven't you ever dreamed of running away from it all?"

28. Tellingly, in the 1993 Disney film version *The Adventures of Huck Finn,* Tom does not appear at all; his role is assumed by Huck. The "boy book frame" disappears completely because the film becomes that frame.

29. Leslie Fiedler similarly argues in *Love and Death* that in the interval between *Tom Sawyer* and *Huck Finn,* Twain has matured artistically and "is only *playing* now

at producing an entertainment for children" (278). Fiedler details some of the ways in which *Huck Finn* deviates from the earlier book in apparently parallel scenes; see *Love and Death,* 278–85. Unlike *Tom Sawyer,* Twain's masterpiece is "not merely an adult but a subversive novel" (278).

30. Fishkin claims that Huck was modeled not only on Tom Blankenship, the poor white boy whose company Twain enjoyed in Hannibal, but also on an African American servant child whom Twain later met and celebrated in an 1874 *New York Times* sketch called "Sociable Jimmy." She traces parallels between the attributes and speech of Huck and Jimmy to suggest that Twain realized through his encounter with Jimmy "the possibilities of a vernacular narrator" (4).

31. Sherwood Cummings's *Mark Twain and Science: Adventures of a Mind* usefully explores the influence of Twain's philosophical and scientific reading on his creative work. As Cummings shows in his chapter on realism, Twain's familiarity with evolutionary thinkers such as Hippolyte Taine—famous, like Spencer, for applying the methodologies of physical science to social science—paved the way for Twain's begrudging acceptance of Darwinism. Taine's emphasis on the importance of environmental factors in tandem with Darwin's theory of natural selection led Twain, according to Cummings, first to a faith in the perfectibility of humanity, and then to a pessimistic determinism, as evidenced in later writings such as *What Is Man?* (1898). Although Twain at first resisted Darwinian biology—and the "newer" physical sciences such as archaeology, paleontology, and anthropology—because it seemed too deterministic, he eventually found social as well as biological Darwinism compelling to a significant degree, once remarking (apparently not in jest, and certainly in the spirit of the age) that "it is not immoral for one nation to seize another man's property or life if it is strong enough and wants to take it" (cited in Paine, *Mark Twain,* 1335).

32. See *A Case Book on Mark Twain's Wound,* ed. Lewis Leary.

33. Bernard DeVoto mocks this assumption: "Mark Twain was clearly designed to be an artist, in rebellion against the Philistinism of America, because he played pirate and absented himself from school" (*Mark Twain's America,* 230). Despite his lambasting of Brooks, DeVoto does some romanticizing of his own, describing *Tom Sawyer* as "the supreme American idyll," a "familiar landscape, so intimate to our experience," "immortal," and "eternally true about children" (304).

34. For an intriguing discussion of Brooks's ambivalence about the possibility of culture and cultural analysis, and his various classificatory schemes, see chapter 3 of Susan Hegeman's *Patterns for America,* esp. 78–80.

35. Bernard DeVoto dismisses Brooks's book as "lay-psychoanalysis" and "a species of dinner-table annotation" (228). Calling his own study, *Mark Twain's America,* "an essay in the correction of ideas" (viii), DeVoto notes with exasperation that "nothing can be done with such thinking. It represents not a superficial knowledge of America before the War but no knowledge whatever. A theory that is capable of calling the America of 1700–1860 homogeneous racially, intellectually, emotionally, philosophically, economically, or aesthetically, is powerless to describe America" (226).

36. Other critics have likewise characterized Twain as a split subject, at once the "Hartford literary gentleman" and the "sagebrush bohemian" (Kaplan, *Mr. Clemens and Mark Twain*, 18). This tradition of scholarship, in tandem with Twain's own fascination with doubling and twinning, has inspired a cottage industry in Twain studies.

37. Fiedler's understanding of the myth is distinctly Freudian; he sees it as a collective screen memory against the painful historical reality of racial dispossession and genocide. Even so, Fiedler questions what Emerson celebrates in "Self-Reliance"— boyish self-reliance, aboriginal masculinity—even if he thus invokes recapitulation (as mediated through psychoanalysis). Emerson's valorization of the infantile and the self enabled what seemed to him a bold refusal of normative masculinities but what looks now like misogyny, bigotry, and solipsism.

38. It is also important to note that Fiedler describes Bad Boy writing, and thus American classic writing, as part of a sentimental (romance) rather than a realist tradition. It's hard to know what Fiedler might expect a truly realist (or at least non-sentimental) literature to look like, aside from fewer figurations of love and death. He is clearly just as dismissive of realist literature as Aldrich and Howells are of sentimental writing.

39. He points to the cultural differentiation of male-male sex and a spiritualized male homoeroticism understood as the very antithesis of, even insulation against, the "sexual" (i.e., the feminine/heterosexual): "Mothers, indeed, rejoiced at 'harmless' romantic attachments between their sons, conceiving of them as protections against the lure of . . . undesirable lower-class girls" (*Love and Death*, 350). Fiedler acknowledges the ways in which such attachments "always threaten to develop into sexuality," and that "sexuality would turn the pure anti-female romance into the travesty of inversion" (182). While a phrase like "travesty of inversion" should certainly give us pause, Fiedler understands, even as he exhibits, homosexual panic.

40. Our most cherished texts, Fiedler proclaims, "celebrate, all of them, the mutual love of a white man and a colored. So buried at a level of acceptance which does not touch reason, so desperately repressed from overt recognition, so contrary to what is usually thought of as our ultimate level of taboo—the sense of that love can survive only in the obliquity of a symbol, persistent, obsessive, in short, an archetype: the boy's homoerotic crush, the love of the black fused at this level into a single thing" ("Come Back," 146).

3. Wolf-Boys, Street Rats, and the Vanishing Sioux

1. The senior Kipling also argues that prior to British intervention, the indigenous culture was despotic and violent. "No mention," he claims, is typically "made of the horrible pit from which the country was digged" (3). *Beast and Man in India* functions as an imperialist bestiary written for men of culture. Its author comments only briefly on the wolf-boy stories, ignoring the issue of authenticity; he simply invokes them as proof of the proximity of native people and native animals.

2. Fresh from medical school, Itard was only twenty-six when he began work

with Victor, but he was an expert on many medical topics, notably speech training. His innovative experiments with Victor inspired advances in behavior modification, sign language, and eventually the Montessori method.

3. Itard's faith in culture is shared by later French commentators, notably Lucien Malson in *Wolf Children and the Problem of Human Nature* (1964), in which Itard's reports are reprinted.

4. Of the published reports, only Sleeman's 1852 pamphlet precedes the Great Mutiny of 1857. After 1857 the Government of India was organized to replace the East India Company, and Sleeman's *Journey through the Kingdom of Oude in 1849–1850* was packaged by that government as an overview of "the real state of the country, condition, and feeling of the people of all classes" (v).

5. The first case, of a boy still living in Sultanpoor at the time of Sleeman's report, is taken from the rajah of Hasunpoor's report, and from Sleeman's correspondence with Captain Nicholetts, commander of the First Regiment of Oude Local Infantry at Sultanpoor. The other cases are reported as factual, but we don't know exactly how Sleeman learned of them. And yet several are quite detailed and elaborate, told as miniadventure tales. Oddly, these children either disappear or don't survive to adulthood. "It is remarkable," writes Sleeman, "that I can discover no well-established instance of a man who had been nurtured in a wolf's den having been found" (221). The seventh boy, the only one Sleeman actually interviews, is still living in Lucknow, now a grown man dubbed the "wild man of the woods." Sleeman finds him "very inoffensive," if also a bit dull and "impatient." Sleeman doubts that he ever actually cohabited with wolves.

6. Tylor points out that the motif surfaces in Indian mythology, mentioning the *Panchatantra* and the *Kathâ-sarit-sâgara*, or *Oceans of Rivers of Story*, a collection of Sanskrit stories from the twelfth century (29), but Tylor's Orientalism affirms Anglicist science. Like other architects of empire, he implies that the natives mistake mythology as history or science, noting the tendency of "ignorant and superstitious men" to apply "abstract belief in such stories" to particular people (30).

7. Ironically, the wolf-boy had already been an emblem for an uncultured life—but not necessarily to the discredit of native parents. Some historians have argued that Britain's early-nineteenth-century commitment to Indian uplift came in part as an attempt to redress the depredations of British merchants and administrators, which suggests that the wolf-boy motif also serves as an index to the inhumane or negligent parenting of the imperialists, or at least to their residual guilt. It's as if Sleeman and Tylor exaggerate the depravity of the wolf-boy to make such guilt ridiculous, just as modern accounts of street kids try to disclaim responsibility through images of a priori delinquency and violence

8. Tylor's anxiety about the easy confusion of fact and fiction isn't surprising, given the extent to which even the most authoritative feral tales borrow from mythology and popular entertainment. In 1800, the scientists working with the Wild Boy of Aveyron attended a popular melodrama in Paris about a fictitious *enfant sauvage* entitled *The Forest's Child* and named their own wild child Victor after the play's protagonist. Soon a new play supplanted the first, a vaudeville number inspired

by Victor's case called *The Savage of Aveyron* or *Don't Swear by Anything* (Rymer, *Genie*, 65–66). Some two hundred years later, doctors and scientists studying a severely neglected and abused California girl attended a special screening of Truffaut's *The Wild Child* in Los Angeles. They did not name the girl Victor but rather called her Genie; they in turn were known as the "Genie team," inspired by Truffaut's upbeat film, hoping to work miracles.

9. Indian himself, Ball aims to chronicle the lives of common men, beasts, and plants, deciding against a planned ethnology of Indian tribes. But as Ball's report reveals, geology functions much like geography in the colonialist scheme, as yet another way of mapping empire. "There is a great, an indescribable pleasure," writes Ball, "in being the first to take up the geological exploration of a hitherto quite unknown tract—in being the first to interpret the past history of a portion of the earth's crust which no geologist has ever seen before" (xi). Ball's attention to wolf-boys, like Sleeman's, is part of a cartography of empire in which the fledgling fields of anthropology and child study are inseparable. Whatever its narrative spin, the British feral tale seems to be the Robinsonade of the soldier-scholar, with the wolf-boys playing invisible Friday to the intrepid cartographer.

10. It was not, of course, the only such charitable institution. Other prominent organizations were the Boston's Children's Mission, the New England Home for Little Wanderers, the (Catholic) New York Foundling Hospital, and the New York Association for Improving the Condition of the Poor, which incorporated the New York Juvenile Asylum. Boston was the only city that rivaled New York in child-saving activities, and Peter C. Holloran's *Boston's Wayward Children* is an excellent analysis of its programs of social uplift and child transformation. New York's CAS, however, conducted philanthropic rescue on a grander scale and influenced the activities of most other groups, and the fearless Brace seems to have been the most outspoken child saver.

11. By 1840 five schools had been opened in London "exclusively for children raggedly clothed" (Cunningham, *Children of the Poor*, 103); the urban reformer Lord Ashley, Brace's English counterpart, devoted his life to working with the Ragged School Union, formed in 1844. Henry Mayhew, journalist and author of *London Labour and the London Poor: A Cyclopedia of the Conditions and Earnings of Those That Will Work, Those That Cannot Work, and Those That Will Not Work* (1851–1852), was a critic of the Ragged Schools and of evangelical reforms more generally, but he shared Ashley's concerns about child vagrancy in the metropolis. Mayhew describes in detail the everyday life of criminals and other "wandering tribes" on the city streets. Anticipating Brace, he divides people into "two distinct and broadly marked races—viz., the wanderers and the settlers—the vagabond and the citizen—the nomadic and the civilized tribes" (1:1).

12. For a thorough account of this historical process, see Leps, *Apprehending the Criminal*, esp. 18–31.

13. "John Hollingshead wrote of 'human child-rats,' and Blanchard Jerrold of the 'claws' of the 'wretched children' in the street," notes Hugh Cunningham. Poor children were seen as "alien beings, far removed not only from civilization, but, more

important, from any likeness to children as they existed in the middle-class world" (122).

14. Between 1853 and 1890, Brace and the CAS relocated around 90,000 children, most of them boys, from New York City to Christian homes in rural areas. Marilyn Irvin Holt offers an even more staggering body count: more than 200,000 infants, children, teenagers, and adults on the eastern seaboard were transported by several organizations, including the CAS. Most of these children were not literally orphans but were often described as such for effect. There were so many of them that CAS agents were hard-pressed to make follow-up evaluations. Despite the society's talk of placements "out West," over 40 percent of its charges were relocated only to rural New York, and nearly all the rest went to the Midwest (Langsam, *Children West*, 25). The placing-out scheme was based on the classic indenture system; the primary difference was that parents never relinquished legal guardianship, meaning that the CAS assumed no real legal responsibility for its charges or their placements. Placing out also bore strong resemblances to the British system of "transportation," and to the American practice of Indian removal or relocation. Both emphasized farming, vocational training, and land ownership as antidotes to the nomadic life. In 1894, to reinforce his general emphasis on the redemptive power of rural life, Brace founded the Brace Farm School in Valhalla, New York.

Placing out drew sharp criticism from various quarters, however, and by the early twentieth century, child savers were opting instead for settlement houses and other urban solutions. New child labor laws, in tandem with the professionalization of social work and sociology, also helped curb enthusiasm for placing out. Even so, the practice did not stop until 1929. Reformers sometimes shipped kids to the country for a day or so, in the hopes that brief exposure to the "great outdoors" might work wonders. "Country Weeks" and "Fresh Air" funds were financed by major newspapers; nature study was introduced into urban school curricula. Brace himself commissioned a series of before-and-after sketches of children benefiting from farm excursions.

15. Mr. Macy's real-life counterpart was apparently C. C. Tracy, a friend and CAS advocate.

16. Whereas Riis called immigrant street children "street rats," as if their depravity simply reflected their slum surroundings, for Goldberg the feral is an indictment of bad parenting and political apathy. Goldberg's subjects have been driven out of family dens and into the streets. How the other half lives, in other words, is only part of the story. The cover of *Raised by Wolves* features a silhouette of Victor of Aveyron, and throughout, Goldberg toys with classic feral types: the wild child, the wolf-boy, Tarzan, and Kaspar Hauser. He titles one section "The Same Ol' Story, Romulus and Remus." Most of the kids featured in the book give themselves folkloric nicknames, such as Vyper, Cookie, Blade, Tank, Animal, Casper, Rusty Boy, Tiger, Echo, Beaver, and Tweeky Dave. We watch as these kids shoot up, sketch out, hustle, and even die. We tour the squalid urban spaces they claim: condemned warehouses, tenements, alleys, and underpasses. We meet sugar daddies and social workers, cops and pimps. *Raised by Wolves* tells many stories, through letters, diary

entries, and drawings, as well as Goldberg's photos and interview transcripts. While Goldberg doesn't quite relinquish the classic role of scandalized ethnographer, his concern for these kids shines through. Above all, he questions the very nature of family, noting that kids "would rather live in filth and hunger with a group that will accept them than . . . with a family that will meet all their physical needs, yet inflict on them emotional pain and torment" (130).

17. We could assume that by the time *My Indian Boyhood* appeared, the street boy had become a less reprehensible creature, or a less sensationalistic one, as the more explicitly racist writing of Brace and other child savers was rejected in favor of more comparative and relativist perspectives on culture. We might also argue that Alger-style series fiction, which romanticized the street boy, helped shift the representational ethos, as did the more complex treatments of the urban poor in psychology and literary naturalism. While street rat thinking persisted, it also lost ground to more sympathetic, if still custodial, figurations of difference and disenfranchisement.

18. With the exception of Lewis Henry Morgan, anthropologists did not, to my knowledge, forge connections between the Indians of Asia and the "Indians" of North America. Morgan, the putative father of American anthropology and a committed monogenist, noted patterns of resemblance between Iroquois culture in North America and the Tamil people of Southern India and theorized an Asian origin for American Indians in both *The Indian Journals* (1859–1862) and *Systems of Consanguinity and Affinity of the Human Family* (1871) (see Bieder, *Science Encounters the Indian*, 221–29). As far as I can tell, however, Morgan's theories had little influence beyond academic circles.

19. These include *Red Hunters and the Animal People* (1904), *Old Indian Days* (1907), and *Wigwam Evenings: Sioux Folktales Retold* (1909). Eastman cowrote several of these with his wife, Elaine Goodale Eastman, an accomplished Indian activist and educator.

20. Cheyfitz suggests that by setting his jungle fantasy in colonial Africa, Burroughs could at once savor and deny America's own imperial ventures and a "foreign policy of forgetfulness" ("Tarzan of the Apes," 345).

21. Sheffield was chosen by MGM to play Tarzan's foundling son, Boy, in the 1940s Tarzan films. Two years after he was kicked out of that series, at age eighteen, Sheffield was cast as Bomba. The twelve Bomba features include *Bomba the Jungle Boy* (1949), *Bomba on Panther Island* (1949), *Bomba and the Hidden City* (1950), *Bomba and the Elephant Stampede* (1951), and, of course, *Bomba and the Jungle Girl* (1952). Footage from the documentary *Africa Speaks* was used in all twelve features.

22. In the next installment, Mr. Bartow sails to Africa to "paint the gorgeous scenery of that continent" and immediately gets captured by cannibals. Bomba and his sidekick Gibo charge to the rescue, their destination not Brazil but Africa—Tarzan country—where Bomba pits his rippling muscles against lions, leopards, crocodiles, and gorillas.

23. On an uncharted island, Bomba and his cohorts discover a cavern studded with precious stones inside a volcanic mountain: the "steaming grotto." Every five minutes or so, the mountain's "Caves of Steam" emit poisonous fumes, and our

explorers protect themselves with special leaves and nuts. "Crush your nuts in your pouches," Bomba instructs, "and hold them over your noses. It is only our hope" (160). Readers hoping for some meaningful closure will be disappointed; a few minor skirmishes with the natives plus a clever act of ventriloquism, and the series is over.

4. Father Flanagan's Boys Town

1. There have been two other films made about Boys Town besides the original and its 1941 sequel, *Miracle of the Heart: A Boys Town Story* (1986), a television movie starring Art Carney as Father Michael T. O'Halloran, and *The Road Home* (1996), set in the 1930s, in which two orphans travel cross-country to reach Boys Town.

2. The Ourslers interviewed Flanagan at length, speaking with him, in fact, just before he departed for Austria and Germany at the request of General MacArthur, to inspect postwar conditions for youth. Flanagan never returned; he suffered a sudden heart attack while in Berlin and died overnight. The book went to press shortly afterward and functions as much as eulogy as biography. It remains the only biography of Flanagan.

3. Such exposés, of course, register and codify as much as dictate public sentiment, but nonetheless, contemporary readers are more likely than their midcentury counterparts to question the church's particular investment in boyhood. So far Flanagan has escaped accusations of abuse, although one of his more illustrious descendants in the Catholic child-saving campaign, Father Bruce Ritter of Covenant House, has been at the center of a massive sex scandal.

4. One of the more important early studies of juvenile delinquency was conducted by Thomas Earl Sullenger, a sociology professor at the University of Omaha, and written up in 1930 as *Social Determinants in Juvenile Delinquency: A Community Challenge*. A "careful analysis" of 1,145 cases of juveniles appearing before the courts between 1922 and 1927, Sullenger's study echoes and supports Flanagan's emphasis on the social causes of delinquency, among them family dysfunction, lack of organized recreational opportunities, and widespread poverty. Sullenger quotes at length from the reports of Judge Lindsey (of personal touch advocacy), affirming Lindsey's admonition that "the fact that juvenile delinquency is a product of the community must be faced squarely" (69). I would be surprised if Sullenger and Father Flanagan didn't know each other.

5. Rooney and Tracy had previously worked together on *Captains Courageous* (1937). As Robert B. Ray reminds us, Rooney was the box office champion in 1939, 1940, and 1941, thanks largely to the Andy Hardy series.

6. In his television commentary, Gingrich puzzles over the absence of African American boys in the film, ignoring the fact that in the 1930s Hollywood rarely cast African American actors. He is silent about the blackface episode.

7. In their witty and engaging study, the Keysers identify six major subgenres of the priest film: the epic film, the crime movie, the clerical melodrama, the war film, the horror movie, and the romance.

8. *Boys Town* bears striking resemblances to another 1938 film, *Angels with Dirty Faces*, in which a priest must confront his boyhood pal, who has turned to a life of crime after a stint in reform school. The priest, Jerry (played by Pat O'Brien), has dedicated his life to saving at-risk kids from such a fate, while Rocky (James Cagney) is keeping a low profile while waiting to jump-start his career as a racketeer. *Angels with Dirty Faces* is one of the so-called Dead End Kids films, named after *Dead End: The Cradle of Crime* (1937).

9. See McAvoy, *History of the Catholic Church,* chap. 12.

10. For more detailed accounts of this Americanism, see Herberg and Dohen.

11. From 1940 to 1960, the Catholic population doubled, in keeping with the postwar baby boom.

12. I refer to *"I Think of My Homelessness": Stories from Boys Town* (1991), by Father Peter, and the more elaborate *Dreams Fulfilled: Success Stories from Boys Town* (1992), written by Terry Hyland and Kevin Warnecke and edited by Father Peter and Ron Herron. The books feature case histories of boys and girls both. In one, a boy heads for Boys Town and away from gang life after seeing the 1938 film on late-night television.

13. Father Peter also writes a regular advice column available on the Web site, called "Father's Letters." In one, he advises parents on how to explain the impeachment of President Clinton to their children: "The Republicans describe the President as being immoral in these matters. The Democrats point out that although he acted immorally, he is a political giant," he writes. "There is truth to both arguments. Let your children know the President is both a political giant and a moral midget" (http://www.ffbh.boystown.org/aboutus/letters/impeachment.htm). No wonder Gingrich likes Boys Town.

14. Boys Town is not technically an orphanage. Today, in fact, most of its residents have at least one living parent. According to Web site statistics, the number of orphans declined nationally from 1920 to 1960 (though no sources are given). In any case, most of the residents are victims of abuse or neglect; some have been abandoned by their parents. In that sense, they are homeless, if not exactly orphaned.

15. Over the years, Boys Town has been visited by many political and cultural celebrities, such as Franklin Roosevelt, John Philip Sousa, Bing Crosby, Bob Hope, George Burns, Gracie Allen, Bud Abbott and Lou Costello, Lou Gehrig, and Babe Ruth. More recent visitors include Newt himself, as well as Colin Powell, Nancy Reagan, and baseball commissioner Peter Ueberroth.

16. The screening process for prospective parent-teachers is extremely rigorous. Jendryka reports that only one of every eighteen couples who apply to become family-teachers at Boys Town is selected.

5. From Freud's Wolf Man to Teen Wolf

1. For Freud, the challenge for the feral subject is the transformation of pathology into speech. As adults, his patients are already speaking subjects, and although Freud had much to say about the function of language in relation to the

unconscious, he does not give much attention to the little Dicks of the world who have yet to enter the symbolic realm.

2. Given his interest in the nonhuman or presymbolic world, it shouldn't surprise us that in his famous essay on the mirror stage, Lacan cites animal evidence of the visual and spatial impetus to development (but not, significantly, of the ability to self-identify). Apparently the sexual development of the female pigeon depends upon a primitive gestalt or imago, as does the social life of the migratory locust (*Écrits*, 3). Shuli Barzilai devotes a fascinating chapter of *Lacan and the Matter of Origins* to Lacan's largely unacknowledged debts to the French psychologist Henry Wallon, whose research on "mirroring" and subjectivity among children and animals helped Lacan fashion his theory of specular identity. Wallon and Lacan after him proposed that children, unlike animals, can recognize (if also misconstrue) themselves in the mirror from an early age. See chapter 4, "On Chimpanzees and Children in the Looking Glass."

3. In *The Philosophical Imaginary*, Le Doeuff seeks to recover the "shameful face" of philosophical discourse—not simply its repertoire of images and metaphors but its very language of disavowal, which depends on, and draws from, that repertoire. By "imaginary" she means a discursive realm or register, not an archetypal or collective imaginary. Her use of the term is obviously rather different from Lacan's; she makes no distinction between the imaginary and the symbolic. She specifically warns against the idea of an imaginary located outside of culture: "When one realizes that imagery copes with problems posed by the theoretical enterprise itself, it is no longer thinkable to attribute it to some primitive soul which, endlessly reworking the same themes, produces analogies, arbitrary valorizations and seductive images whose sweet solicitations abstract knowledge must absolutely oppose" (5). The feral child and other folkloric tropes may constitute the "shameful face" of psychoanalysis, although Freud does not disavow oral narrative as resolutely as classic philosophers disavow the philosophical imaginary.

4. In "Feral Children and Autistic Children" (1959), Bettelheim argues that most so-called feral children are really autistic; he attributes their wild behavior to experiences of isolation as well as various kinds of abuse. He develops this theme in his controversial book *The Empty Fortress: Infantile Autism and the Birth of the Self* (1967), drawing from cases of feral children as well as Holocaust survival stories to support his theory of autism.

5. Freud never studied children actually living in isolation or raised by animals, but one of his most persistent themes is the proximity of the human to the animal. In "One of the Difficulties of Psychoanalysis" (1917), for instance, Freud declares that psychoanalysis represents perhaps the most damaging assault on human narcissism chiefly because it exposes man as a confused bundle of animal instincts. He points out that the child "can see no difference between his own nature and that of animals; he is not astonished at animals thinking and talking in fairy-tales; he will transfer to a dog or a horse an emotion of fear which refers to his human father, without thereby intending any derogation of his father" (186). Every child, then, might imagine himself raised and/or persecuted by animals. In the family romance,

Oedipal anxieties "naturally" find expression in animal associations, perhaps because animals surround us, perhaps because we easily revert to less distinctly human acts and identities.

6. Drawing out Foucault's biohistory of childhood (to which he planned to devote an entire volume in his planned six-volume series on sexuality), Ann Laura Stoler points out that in the nineteenth-century discourse on children's sexuality, children are at once normal and abnormal creatures, thanks to the logic of (perverse) specification. "Children," she writes, thus entered "on *both* sides of the equation, for theirs is both an endangered and dangerous sexuality. They must be protected against exposure to the dangerous sexuality of the racial and class Other, not because their sexuality is so different, but because it is 'savage,' unrestrained, and very much the same" (141). We can see this sort of logic at work in depictions of feral children, who are at once dangerous and endangered sexually as well as culturally.

7. Diagnostic case writing on childhood disorders is hardly restricted to this psychoanalytic approach—which (unlike Freudian ego psychology) concentrates on the pre-Oedipal relationship between mother and child—but many prominent child analysts have worked in this tradition.

8. Like other critics of Freud, Masson wants to recover the child abuse that Freud allegedly denied. Masson's first effort in this direction was *The Assault on Truth: Freud's Suppression of the Seduction Theory* (1984), but his latest attack takes the form of a meditation on Kaspar Hauser, entitled *Lost Prince: The Unsolved Mystery of Kaspar Hauser* (1996). This book features Masson's translation of Anselm Ritter von Feuerbach's 1832 account of Hauser and other source documents, along with a lengthy and polemical introduction.

9. Contemporary retellings of these and other cases use a rhetoric of heterosexuality to safeguard what is essentially a drama of highly unconventional human experience from accusations of perversion. Peter Lehman has explained the ways in which contemporary feral child films, notably Truffaut's *The Wild Child* and Herzog's *Kaspar Hauser,* obscure the very interesting source material on sexuality in these reports and presume either the asexuality or latent heterosexuality of feral boys.

10. In his discussion of the case, Christopher Herbert points out that if the feral boy lacks culture, then desire has no place to go, nothing to cathect. For Itard, as Herbert emphasizes, Victor's freedom from culture results (for Itard) in "a radical disablement of desire" (Herbert, *Culture and Anomie*, 49), his needs random, sudden, and explosive. Herbert doesn't address the heterosexual bias of Itard's reports but describes them more generally as "a parable of the sociocultural basis of desire" (48), one that debunks the fantasy that shedding social constraints will restore mankind to prelapsarian bliss. That parable also motivates psychoanalysis, although Freud's vision of culture seems far darker. Still, Freud's notion of the unconscious mind is a psychoanalytic formulation of what Herbert identifies (after Durkheim) as "anomie," or anarchic desire and restlessness.

11. Through his research and the creation of the Wissenschaftlich-Humanitäre Komite, Hirschfeld coordinated the first homosexual rights movement in 1897. Two

years later he launched a journal, *Jahrbuch für sexuelle Zwischenstufen,* which ran until 1923.

12. See Jonathan Ned Katz on the history of heterosexuality as a perversion, and the gradual normalization of opposite-sex relations outside of marriage.

13. For more information on Freud's clinical and theoretical sources on childhood sexuality (and child study more generally), see Stephen Roger Kern's dissertation "Freud and the Emergence of Child Psychology, 1880–1910." Kern provides a detailed history of work preceding Freud's, noting that the earliest was probably *The Physiology and Pathology of the Mind* (1867), by the English psychologist Henry Maudsley.

14. Freud admittedly isn't consistent in this view; he resorts to both teleology and tautology when he speaks of "inverted types" with "archaic constitutions" and presumably minoritizing "primitive psychical mechanisms" (12).

15. A psychiatry professor at the University of Vienna, Krafft-Ebing was Freud's distinguished colleague and advocate. The first edition of *Psychopathia Sexualis* appeared in 1886 and featured forty-five case histories; by 1903, the twelfth edition included 238 entries (Weeks, *Sexuality and Its Discontents,* 67). Krafft-Ebing encountered only a few of these people in his clinic; new entries came from other doctors or the perverts themselves. Unlike Freud, Krafft-Ebing is interested not in the border between nature and culture but in inheritance. Each case is prefaced with the psychiatric and medical history of the patient and his family, for example, "Case 145. *Homosexuality.* N., aged forty-one, unmarried. Father and mother near relatives, but both psychically normal. An uncle on the father's side was insane. N.'s brothers were hyper- and heterosexual" (158). Nearly everyone in his book is neurasthenic or just plain "nervous." Krafft-Ebing's histories are really impersonal case notes about organic disease; most run several paragraphs or less. No names are used, because these reports are not about individuals but about types. Individuals are simply manifestations or concrete examples of the disorder under review. Even so, such sexological profiles did make possible a proto-psychoanalytic orientation. Krafft-Ebing's guard sometimes drops, and he shares case details that seem tangential to the condition he's already diagnosed, the sort of cultural scripts in which Freud takes such pleasure and forges such meaning. Krafft-Ebing even calls attention to psychic experiences such as disassociation and dreaming.

16. Jeffrey Weeks accords *Psychopathia Sexualis* as much influence in sexology as the work of Darwin, writing that "it was the eruption into print of the speaking pervert, the individual marked, or marred, by his (or her) sexual impulses. The case studies were a model of what was to follow, the analyses were the rehearsal for a century of theorising" (67).

17. Sexology might even be considered a protoliterary enterprise, to the degree that it coincides with and enables both literary exposition and formalistic analysis, or "close reading" of the body-text. Pointing out that many prominent gay men of Victorian letters dabbled in sexology, Robert Sulcer proposes that the homosexual and the literary critic are intertwined in late-nineteenth-century culture. Sulcer suggests that as sexology deprived the ostensible pervert of agency by identifying him

as a passive sexual type, literary and rhetorical criticism offered him a compensatory power in the ability to discern and evaluate, to enjoy what Foucault calls the "formidable 'pleasures of analysis'" (71). Or at least the pervert *becomes* a sensitive, self-contained, but rather readerly text; as Foucault sees it in the first volume of *The History of Sexuality,* his sexuality is "written immodestly on his face and body because it was a secret that always gave itself away" (43).

18. Peter Stallybrass and Allon White make a compelling argument that in his major case studies, Freud rewrites the bourgeois body through the mediation of the slum, setting the body upright and distinguishing the lower regions from the higher faculties. "The vertical axis of the bourgeois body," they write, "is primarily emphasized in the *education* of the child: as s/he grows up/is cleaned up, the lower bodily stratum is regulated or denied, as far as possible" (145). The Rat Man and the Wolf Man just can't seem to renounce that lower stratum.

19. Saul Rosenzweig contends that Freud's determination to complete the narrative before sailing to America suggests a desire to remake himself from obscure neurotic into psychoanalytic powerhouse. Rosenzweig claims that Freud unconsciously reenacts the Oedipal myth of the hero through the Rat Man's narrative. "With that journey he would enter a new phase of his unconsciously determined life, and appear on the lecture platform in Worcester as if by the 'omnipotence' of his own thought and wishes he was fulfilling an 'incredible daydream'" (32–33).

20. Freud presented the case as the keynote address at the first psychoanalytic congress in April 1908. The analysis was then still in progress; it ended in September, when the patient seemed cured. The case is still used to train analysts.

21. Incidentally, Victor of Aveyron also bites; Itard provokes him, and the boy retaliates, and the bite fills Itard with glee: "It could only delight me, for the bite was a legitimate act of vengeance; it was an incontestable proof that the idea of justice and injustice, the permanent basis of the social order, was no longer foreign to my pupil's mind" (175). Victor's bite evinces maturity, not infantile sexuality.

22. At this point in Freud's narrative, we discover that the Rat Man's leading lady is unable to conceive, and that he wants desperately to have children. The patient allows himself to insult both his father and his lover and then punishes himself for doing so by imagining that the rat torture will be enacted on them both (despite the fact that his father is long dead). This self-reprimand or retroactive sanction is further fueled by two common infantile theories, namely, the belief that babies emerge from the anus and that men can thus give birth. Freud draws from his work on dreams to explain that "the notion of coming out of the rectum can be represented by the opposite notion of creeping into the rectum (as in the rat punishment), and *vice versa*" (57).

23. The rat punishment functions as a folkloric horror story and, in particular, as an Orientalist fantasy that begs for analysis as such (and not only because his beloved Czech nursemaid was written out of the Oedipus complex in favor of his mother). Freud reports that the Rat Man's fears of punishment "were entirely foreign and repugnant to him" (13).

24. In his lectures at Clark, Freud spoke about little Hans but not the Rat Man,

whose case he had just finished so feverishly. I suspect that he felt that the Rat Man's case was too sensationalistic for his American audience. He was probably right; Hall, for one, despite his general support of Freud, criticized Freud's remarks about the sexuality of little Hans and also "little Anna" (probably Jung's daughter).

25. A more sophisticated and persuasive form of the abuse hypothesis has been central to the feminist literature on the case of Dora (1900) especially, as evidenced by books such as *In Dora's Case: Freud, Hysteria, Feminism* (1983) and *Father Knows Best: The Use and Abuse of Power in Freud's Case of Dora* (1993).

26. Stallybrass and White historicize this rat currency as "a kind of debased coinage" of city, sewer, and slum. In Freud's hands, they argue, the rat is "a phobic mediator between high and low, a kind of debased coinage in the symbolic exchange underpinning the economy of the body" in the nineteenth-century discourse of sewer, slum, and city (146). Historically the rat has mediated between the public, noble city and the private, hermetically sealed underworld of the sewers; the rat embodied all that was not sanitary and hygienic. Stallybrass and White attempt to restore the "social terrain" that Freud represses in his narrative. See chapter 3 of *The Politics and Poetics of Transgression*, "The City: The Sewer, the Gaze, and the Contaminating Touch."

27. Shengold devotes two chapters in *Soul Murder* (1989) to the traumatic symptoms of "rat people," people abused during childhood, whose self-hatred manifests as cannibalistic impulses and sometimes even as conscious identification with rats. Thus what was for Freud the highly idiosyncratic history of one patient becomes for Shengold a constellation of reactive symptoms, a clinical archetype.

28. Third Reich ideologues held the Brothers Grimm in great esteem and interpreted Red Riding-Hood as representing the German people, victimized but finally rescued from the clutches of wolfish Jews. In American films of the 1940s, by contrast, the Nazis were portrayed as wolves and werewolves.

29. Like proponents of men's studies after him, Fromm decries the sexism and sex phobia at work in the Grimms' "Little Red Cap": "The male is portrayed as a ruthless and cunning animal . . . This view is not held by women who like men and enjoy sex. It is an expression of a deep antagonism against men and sex" (241).

30. In this line of interpretation, Freud's writerly strategies conceal/reveal his own sexual desires and the designs of psychoanalysis. For Stanley Fish, Freud's control over the Wolf Man's narrative is complete and tyrannical; "the Wolf Man got it right," explains Fish, when he declared "this man is a Jewish swindler, he wants to use me from behind and shit on my head" (Fish, "Witholding the Missing Portion," 526). Freud's account of the Wolf Man's childhood trauma, according to Fish, is the master's greatest moment of anal-sadistic triumph; Freud "withholds the missing portion" so that he can take a whopping dump on his patient. In his response to Fish's polemic, John Forrester points out that this line is a paraphrase of a quotation cited in Ernest Jones's biography of Freud, which itself was likely a misquote of the Wolf Man. In any case, the passage in Jones implies the opposite of what Fish assumes: the patient "initiated the first hour of treatment with the offer to have rectal intercourse with Freud and then to defecate on his head!" (Forrester, *Dispatches*

from the Freud Wars, 210). Fish implies that the Wolf Man originally knew that Freud intended to abuse him, but then was duped or shat upon. This case, notes Forrester, has long "served as a test case for the truth of psychoanalysis" (209).

In gay male studies, accounts of the case also emphasize Freud's rhetoric but range in their take on his "homosexual" politics. Whitney Davis offers a fairly sympathetic reading, but Leo Bersani condemns the case as "one of the most morbid genealogies of homosexual desire in psychoanalytic literature" (108). Lee Edelman's argument that Freud typically approaches the psyche "from behind" suggests perhaps that psychoanalysis is routinely *a tergo more ferarum*. Leo Bersani proposes, against the homopanic of "that decidedly nongay daddy," a more pleasurable primal scene; see *Homos*, 12.

31. Freud reminds us that vermin often represent babies. The column of feces, moreover, acts during the "cloacal epoch" as a foreshadowing or first version of the penis. "'Faeces,' 'child,' and 'penis' thus form a unity," concludes Freud, "an unconscious concept *(sit venia verbo)*—the concept, namely, of a little thing that can become separated from one's body" (243), which he later christens "the excrement baby."

32. Drawing from the Aaren-Thompson tale-type index, Alan Dundes notes in "Interpreting 'Little Red Riding Hood' Psychoanalytically" that the folktale is probably a cognate form of "The Wolf and the Seven Little Goats."

33. Freud's interest in ontogenetic-phylogenetic relation beyond recapitulation never waned. In a manuscript called *A Phylogenetic Fantasy*, written sometime during World War I but never published, Freud pursues his anthropological ideas about recapitulation and neurosis even further, after an exchange with Ferenczi about Lamarck. Freud hoped to demonstrate that both the transference and the narcissistic neuroses are ontogenetic reenactments of man's phylogenetic adaptations to his shifting historical environment. Freud's work was successful, in a disciplinary sense, even if his writings are not valued as science per se. Ontogenetic-phylogenetic correspondence—and speculation about that correspondence—still animates not only psychoanalysis but also the disciplines it nurtures, notably child psychology, progressive pedagogy, and folklore studies.

34. In this case study, Freud takes pains to distinguish the "widdler"-obsessed boy from the true penis-worshiping homosexual that he did not become ("Analysis of a Phobia," 146). Sounding strangely like Horatio Alger Jr., Freud assures his readers that Hans "was well formed physically, and was a cheerful, amiable, active-minded young fellow who might give pleasure to more people than his own father" (176). In a 1922 postscript to the case, Freud reports that the well-formed boy "was now a strapping lad of nineteen," who remembers nothing of his horse obsession or of Freud's analysis (182).

35. Macleod attributes this initial lack of enthusiasm to a distinctly American preoccupation with, and understanding of, adolescence, citing the influence of Hall's two-volume study *Adolescence* (1904). Scouting was officially restricted to boys age twelve through eighteen, and American leaders worried that Cubbing would bore potential Scouters (Macleod, *Building Character*, 296).

36. Incidentally, to illustrate the power of cultural context in an individual's

development of morality, Cushman turns to the example of Huck Finn, writing that Huck's "inability to see Jim in any frame other than as a piece of property, despite his friendship and affection for Jim, illustrates the profound power of a cultural frame of reference" (12).

37. Cushman's materialist history arrives at a conclusion familiar from other assessments of American mass culture: psychoanalysis and psychotherapy helped manufacture an "empty self," forever seeking new forms of stimulation and gratification. In his view, the self has displaced the citizen, even as the public sphere has virtually disappeared.

38. It's significant that Max is a boy. Max is Sendak's most famous character, and yet he emerged from Rosie. Rosie was a ten-year-old child who lived near Sendak in New York, and about whom Sendak wrote his first children's stories. Max is a lot like the spunky and imaginative Rosie in *The Sign on Rosie's Door* (1960), who choreographs many a wild rumpus in the neighborhood. Also derivative of Rosie are the little boys who show up in three of the four books that make up the Nutshell Library (published in 1962): *Pierre, One Was Johnny,* and *Chicken Soup with Rice.* The themes are familiar, too: adventure, rebellion, eating, and being eaten up. It's fair to assume that Rosie would make a less heroic wolf-child than Max and that the psychological realism and hypercanonicity of Sendak's book depend on this gender morph.

39. "What children's books tell us, finally," writes Fiedler in *Freaks,* "is that maturity involves the ability to believe the self normal, only the other a monster or a Freak" (31).

40. Music videos were only beginning to be popular in 1983, and *Thriller* set a formidable precedent for artistic vision and financial profit. Prior to its release, MTV didn't even pay record companies for the right to air videos because such airplay was deemed terrific promotion.

41. In *Between Men,* Eve Kosofsky Sedgwick appropriates the term "homosexual panic" from psychiatric and legal discourse, using it to suggest the ways in which "many twentieth-century western men experience their vulnerability to the social pressure of homophobic blackmail" (89). As Sedgwick demonstrates, homosexual panic is particularly resonant in gothic genres.

6. Reinventing the Boy Problem

1. Philip Wylie's *Generation of Vipers* (1942) seems to have inaugurated the critique of Momism, or overzealous mothering, linked to the alleged feminization of America's boys, followed by David M. Levy's *Maternal Overprotection* (1943) and Edward A. Strecker's *Their Mother's Sons: The Psychiatrist Examines an American Problem* (1946). More recent tirades along these lines are Wylie's follow-up book *Sons and Daughters of Mom* (1971) and Hans Sebald's *Momism: The Silent Disease of America* (1976). Sebald, a sociology professor, argues that "a boy is much more vulnerable to the effects of Momism than a girl" (14). For an extended critique, see *"Bad" Mothers,* ed. Molly Ladd-Taylor and Lauri Umansky.

2. For a treatment of Bly's misreading of this tale, see "Spreading Myths about

Iron John," chap. 4 in Jack Zipes's *Fairy Tale as Myth, Myth as Fairy Tale*. As Zipes demonstrates, Bly distorts *Der Eisenhans* to fashion his own myth of feminine meddling and masculine revenge.

3. If "self-esteem" is the buzzword for the girl crisis writers, then "emotional intelligence" is the emergent keyword for boy crisis writers; Will Glennon thus offers companion handbooks *Two Hundred Ways to Raise a Girl's Self-Esteem* (1999) and *Two Hundred Ways to Raise a Boy's Emotional Intelligence* (2000). The term "emotional intelligence" we owe to Daniel Goleman, whose 1995 book on the subject is smart and nuanced.

4. Gurian's confidence in brain science is uncomfortably reminiscent not only of phrenology but also of the nineteenth-century faith in encephalization as the interpretive key to human nature. For instance, my favorite recapitulationist, John Johnson Jr., insists in "The Savagery of Boyhood" (1887) that emotional precocity results from "unhealthy development of the brain," which like the rest of our organism "is subject to the all-embracing law of animal existence, which declares the development of the individual to be an epitome of the development of his race" (799).

5. Men were not the only ones to appropriate feral discourse to their own archetypal ends. Posed against *Iron John* and *Fire in the Belly* is Clarissa Pinkola Estés's 1992 best-seller *Women Who Run with the Wolves: Myths and Stories of the Wild Woman Archetype*. Inside every woman, asserts Estés, is a wild woman struggling for release, whose instinctive, creative energies have been repressed. A Jungian analyst and *cantadora,* Estés argues that women bear powerful resemblances to wolves; she began her study of the archetype, in fact, by studying wolf culture. Estés notes the ways in which folk narratives have been altered for specific audiences, but she also insists that beneath those changes lie the bare bones of female experience, emblematized by *La Loba,* the Wolf Woman. Estés's work is a compelling rejoinder to the contemporary mythopoetic men's movement, which has adapted classic folk mythology alongside Jungian pop psychology. Whereas Bly attacks women and gay men for the pain they inflict on heterosexual men, the mythology of Estés recuperates men as well as women, and homosexuality as well as heterosexuality.

6. Later Kimmel cites George Bancroft's description of Jackson as "the nursling of the wilds," "a pupil of the wilderness" (34).

7. In 1995, Gilligan, now affiliated with the Harvard Graduate School of Education, launched the Harvard Project on Women's Psychology, Boys' Development, and the Culture of Boyhood, a three-year study of the emotional life of preschool boys. Shortly thereafter she concluded that whereas girls experience psychosocial trauma as they begin adolescence, boys experience it much earlier. "Girls' psychological development in patriarchy," writes Gilligan, "involves a process of eclipse that is even more total for boys" (252). Gilligan attributes most boy problems to the patriarchal policing of masculinity, to the repression of boys' natural sensitivity and compassion. Boys are allegedly forced to separate from women but are not allowed to mourn that separation or even identify it as loss. She insists that we must find a way to allow boys to remain close to their mothers, and to refuse the straitjacket of masculinity.

Christina Hoff Sommers is sharply critical of Gilligan's conclusions (as well as her research methods) and argues that boys suffer less from patriarchal repression than from the widespread absence of fathers and male role models. In her chapter "Gilligan's Island," Sommers puts in "a good word for the capitalist patriarchy and martial values" (to cite a section title). Here again, at issue is the status and significance of feminism in our culture; Gilligan cries patriarchy, while Sommers rails against the "feminization" of public schools and (implicitly) of higher education.

8. For discussion of the "girl question," which predated the "boy problem," see Claudia Nelson and Lynne Vallone's introduction to *The Girl's Own*. Some critics have reversed the usual rhetorical order, notably Sally Mitchell, who discusses boyhood as a developmental phase for the (English) New Girl (137).

9. Foucault's perhaps too persuasive *Discipline and Punish* has reinforced the association of men with brute force and women with less tangible influence. Men punish, the story goes, whereas women offer a kinder, gentler form of control; boys are spanked (even if we call it discipline), while girls are taught the moral lessons they must come to symbolize. One challenge facing scholars of girl culture is to avoid the assumption that since girls were removed from the public sphere, their presence is best understood as an indirect moral influence. Lynne Vallone's account of girl culture in *Disciplines of Virtue* is instructive along these lines, demonstrating how Foucauldian analysis can resist its own rhetorical power. Vallone complicates the punishment-discipline narrative, suggesting that some "disciplinary" forms of eighteenth-century girl culture set the stage for subsequent body-centered institutions such as the Magdalen Hospital for penitent prostitutes.

10. Gibson also explains the physiological benefits of assorted sports, disparaging the "anemic boy prodigy" and the bookworm with "soft hands, tender feet, and tough rump from too much sitting" (*Boyology*, 18).

11. Biddulph is allegedly "Australia's best-known family therapist and parenting author" (according to the jacket blurb), and his book was published in Australia in 1997 and in America the following year.

Works Cited

Aarne, Antti. *The Types of the Folktale.* Trans. and expanded by Stith Thompson. 2d rev. ed. Helsinki: Academia Scientiarum Fennica, 1961.

Abbott, Franklin, ed. *Boyhood, Growing Up Male: A Multicultural Anthology.* Freedom, Calif.: Crossing Press, 1993.

Abbott, Mather Almon. *The Boy Today.* 3d ed. New York: Fleming H. Revell, 1930.

Alcott, Louisa May. *Little Men.* 1871. New York: Penguin, 1987.

Aldrich, Thomas Bailey. *The Story of a Bad Boy.* 1869. Hanover, N.H.: University Press of New England, 1990.

Alger, Horatio. *Ragged Dick, or Street Life in New York.* 1868. New York: Penguin, 1985.

Arac, Jonathan. *Huckleberry Finn as Idol and Target: The Functions of Criticism in Our Time.* Madison: University of Wisconsin Press, 1997.

Armstrong, Nancy. "The Rise of the Domestic Woman." In *The Ideology of Conduct: Essays on Literature and the History of Sexuality,* ed. Nancy Armstrong and Leonard Tennenhouse. New York: Methuen, 1987.

Backus, Margot Gayle. *The Gothic Family Romance: Heterosexuality, Child Sacrifice, and the Anglo-Irish Colonial Order.* Durham, N.C.: Duke University Press, 1999.

Ball, Valentine. *Tribal and Peasant Life in Nineteenth Century India.* Darya Ganj, New Delhi: Usha Publications, 1985. Originally published in 1880 as *Jungle Life in India, or The Journeys and Journals of an Indian Geologist.*

Barrie, J. M. *The Little White Bird.* London: Hodder and Stoughton, 1902.

Barzilai, Shuli. *Lacan and the Matter of Origins.* Stanford: Stanford University Press, 1999.

Beecher, Henry Ward. *Eyes and Ears.* Boston: Ticknor and Fields, 1862.

Bersani, Leo. *Homos.* Cambridge: Harvard University Press, 1995.

Bettelheim, Bruno. "Feral Children and Autistic Children." *American Journal of Sociology* 64, no. 5 (March 1959): 455–67.

———. *The Empty Fortress: Infantile Autism and the Birth of the Self.* 1967. New York: Free Press, 1972.

———. *The Uses of Enchantment: The Meaning and Importance of Fairy Tales.* New York: Alfred A. Knopf, 1976. New York: Random House, 1977.

Biddulph, Steve. *Raising Boys: Why Boys Are Different — and How to Help Them Become Happy and Well-Balanced Men.* Berkeley: CelestialArts, 1998.

Bieder, Robert E. *Science Encounters the Indian, 1820–1880: The Early Years of American Ethnology.* Norman: University of Oklahoma Press, 1986.

Bloomfield, Robert. *The Farmer's Boy: Collected Poems (1800–1822) of Robert Bloomfield.* Ed. Jonathan N. Lawson. Gainesville, Fla.: Scholars' Facsimiles and Reprints, 1971.

Bly, Robert. *Iron John: A Book about Men.* Reading, Mass.: Addison-Wesley, 1990.

Boone, Joseph Allen. "Male Independence and the American Quest Romance as Counter-traditional Genre: Hidden Sexual Politics in the Male World of *Moby Dick, Huckleberry Finn, Billy Budd,* and *The Sea Wolf.*" In *Tradition counter Tradition: Love and the Form of Fiction.* Chicago: University of Chicago Press, 1987.

Boyle, Patrick. *Scout's Honor: Sexual Abuse in America's Most Trusted Institution.* Rocklin, Calif.: Prima Publishing, 1994.

Boys Town. Dir. Norman Taurog. Perf. Spencer Tracy, Mickey Rooney, Henry Hull, Leslie Fenton, Addison Richards, Bobs Watson, Minor Watson, and Martin Spellman. MGM, 1938.

Boys Town: Memories and Dreams. Boys Town, Nebr.: Boys Town Press, 1995.

Brace, Charles Loring. *The Dangerous Classes of New York and Twenty Years' Work among Them.* 1872. 3d ed. New York: Hougton, Mifflin, 1880.

———. "Wolf-Reared Children." *St. Nicholas* 9, no. 7 (May 1882): 542–54.

Brace, Emma. *The Life of Charles Loring Brace, Chiefly Told in His Own Letters.* New York: Charles Scribner's Sons, 1894.

Brogan, Hugh. *Mowgli's Sons: Kipling and Baden-Powell's Scouts.* London: Jonathan Cape, 1987.

Brooks, Bruce. *Boys Will Be.* 1993. New York: Hyperion, 1995.

Brooks, Van Wyck. *The Ordeal of Mark Twain.* New York: E. P. Dutton, 1920.

———. *The Writer in America.* New York: Avon Books, 1953.

Brown, Bill. *The Material Unconscious: American Amusement, Stephen Crane, and the Economics of Play.* Cambridge: Harvard University Press, 1996.

Burkett, Elinor, and Frank Bruni. *A Gospel of Shame: Children, Sexual Abuse, and the Catholic Church.* New York: Viking, 1993.

Burns, Sarah. *Pastoral Inventions: Rural Life in Nineteenth-Century American Art and Culture.* Philadelphia: Temple University Press, 1989.

Burr, Hanford. *Studies in Adolescent Boyhood.* 5th ed. 1910. New York: Association Press, 1918.

Burroughs, Edgar Rice. *Tarzan of the Apes.* 1912. New York: Ballantine, 1963.

Butler, Judith. *The Psychic Life of Power: Theories in Subjection.* Stanford: Stanford University Press, 1997.

Candland, Douglas Keith. *Feral Children and Clever Animals: Reflections on Human Nature.* New York: Oxford University Press, 1993.

Carroll, Michael P. "The Folkloric Origins of Modern 'Animal-Parented' Stories." *Journal of Folklore Research* 21, no. 1 (January–April 1984): 63–85.

Carter, Angela. "The Company of Wolves." In *The Bloody Chamber and Other Stories.* New York: Penguin, 1979.

Cech, John. *Angels and Wild Things: The Archetypal Poetics of Maurice Sendak.* University Park: Pennsylvania State University Press, 1996.

Chamberlain, A. F. *The Child: A Study in the Evolution of Man.* London: Walter Scott, 1900.

Chesley, Albert M. *Social Activities for Men and Boys.* New York: YMCA Press, 1910.

Cheyfitz, Eric. "Tarzan of the Apes: U.S. Foreign Policy in the Twentieth Century." *American Literary History* 1, no. 2 (summer 1989): 339–60.

Chudacoff, Howard P. *The Age of the Bachelor: Creating an American Subculture.* Princeton: Princeton University Press, 1999.

Connell, R. W. *Masculinities*. Berkeley: University of California Press, 1995.

Craig, Eleanor. *One, Two, Three: The Story of Matt, a Feral Child*. New York: Signet-Penguin, 1978.

Crow, Martha Foote. *The American Country Girl*. New York: Frederick A. Stokes, 1915.

Crowley, John W. "*Little Women* and the Boy Book." *New England Quarterly* 58, no. 3 (September 1985): 384–99.

———. "Polymorphously Perverse? Childhood Sexuality in the American Boy Book." *American Literary Realism* 19, no. 1 (fall 1986): 2–15.

Cummings, Sherwood. *Mark Twain and Science: Adventures of a Mind*. Baton Rouge: Louisiana State University Press, 1988.

Cunningham, Hugh. *The Children of the Poor: Representations of Childhood since the Seventeenth Century*. Oxford: Basil Blackwell, 1991.

Cushman, Philip. *Constructing the Self, Constructing America: A Cultural History of Psychotherapy*. Reading, Mass.: Addison-Wesley, 1995.

Darling, Richard L. *The Rise of Children's Book Reviewing in America, 1865–1881*. New York: R. R. Bowker, 1968.

Darwin, Charles. *The Origin of the Species* and *The Descent of Man*. New York: Modern Library, 1955.

Davis, Whitney. *Drawing the Dream of the Wolves: Homosexuality, Interpretation, and Freud's "Wolf Man."* Bloomington: Indiana University Press, 1995.

Deloria, Philip J. *Playing Indian*. New Haven: Yale University Press, 1998.

Demos, John. "Oedipus and America: Historical Perspectives on the Reception of Psychoanalysis in the United States" (1978). In *Inventing the Psychological: Toward a Cultural History of Emotional Life in America,* ed. Joel Pfister and Nancy Schnog. New Haven: Yale University Press, 1997.

Derrick, Scott S. *Monumental Anxieties: Homoerotic Desire and Feminine Influence in Nineteenth-Century U.S. Literature*. New Brunswick: Rutgers University Press, 1997.

DeVoto, Bernard. *Mark Twain's America*. Boston: Little, Brown, 1932.

Dippie, Brian W. *The Vanishing American: White Attitudes and U.S. Indian Policy*. Lawrence: University of Kansas Press, 1982.

Dohen, Dorothy. *Nationalism and American Catholicism*. New York: Sheed and Ward, 1967.

Douthwaite, Julia V. *The Wild Girl, Natural Man, and the Monster: Dangerous Experiments in the Age of Enlightenment*. Chicago: University of Chicago Press, 2002.

Dundes, Alan. "The Psychoanalytic Study of Folklore." In *Parsing through Customs: Essays by a Freudian Folklorist*. Madison: University of Wisconsin Press, 1987.

———. "Interpreting 'Little Red Riding Hood' Psychoanalytically." In *Little Red Riding Hood: A Casebook,* ed. Alan Dundes. Madison: University of Wisconsin Press, 1989.

Eastman, Charles Alexander (Ohiyesa). *Indian Boyhood*. New York: Dover, 1971.

————. *From the Deep Woods to Civilization*. Lincoln: University of Nebraska Press, 1977.

————. *The Soul of an Indian: An Interpretation*. Lincoln: University of Nebraska Press, 1980.

Eckert, Allan W. *Incident at Hawk's Hill*. Boston: Little, Brown, 1971.

Edelman, Lee. "Seeing Things: Representation, the Scene of Surveillance, and the Spectacle of Gay Male Sex." In *Inside/Out: Lesbian Theories, Gay Theories*, ed. Diana Fuss. New York: Routledge, 1991.

Eells, Eleanor. *Eleanor Eells' History of Organized Camping: The First One Hundred Years*. Martinsville, Ind.: American Camping Association, 1986.

Ellis, Havelock. *Man and Woman: A Study of Human Secondary Sexuality Characteristics*. 4th ed. New York: Charles Scribner's Sons, 1904.

Emerson, Ralph Waldo. "Nature." In *Selected Writings of Ralph Waldo Emerson*, ed. William H. Gilman. New York: Penguin, 1965.

————. "Self-Reliance." In *Selected Writings of Ralph Waldo Emerson*, ed. William H. Gilman. New York: Penguin, 1965.

Estés, Clarissa Pinkola. *Women Who Run with the Wolves: Myths and the Stories of the Wild Woman Archetype*. New York: Ballantine, 1992.

Faludi, Susan. *Stiffed: The Betrayal of the American Man*. New York: William Morrow, 1999.

Farming for Boys: What They Have Done, and What Others May Do, in the Cultivation of Farm and Garden. Boston: D. Lothrop, 1868.

Fellows, Will. *Farm Boys: Lives of Gay Men from the Rural Midwest*. Madison: University of Wisconsin Press, 1996.

Fetterley, Judith. "The Sanctioned Rebel." *SNNTS* 3 (fall 1971): 293–304.

Fiedler, Leslie. *Love and Death in the American Novel*. New York: Dell, 1960.

————. "Come Back to the Raft Ag'in, Huck Honey!" In *An End to Innocence*. New York: Stein and Day, 1972.

————. *Freaks: Myths and Images of the Secret Self*. New York: Doubleday, 1978.

Fine, Gary Alan. *With the Boys: Little League Baseball and Preadolescent Culture*. Chicago: University of Chicago Press, 1987.

Fish, Stanley. "Withholding the Missing Portion: Psychoanalysis and Rhetoric." In *Doing What Comes Naturally: Change, Rhetoric, and the Practice of Theory in Literary and Legal Studies*. Durham, N.C.: Duke University Press, 1989.

Fisher, James Terence. *The Catholic Counterculture in America, 1933–1962*. Chapel Hill: University of North Carolina Press, 1989.

Fisher, Philip. *Hard Facts: Setting and Form in the American Novel*. New York: Oxford University Press, 1987.

Fishkin, Shelley Fisher. *Was Huck Black? Mark Twain and African-American Voices*. New York: Oxford University Press, 1993.

Fiske, George Walter. *Boy Life and Self-Government*. 1910. New York: Association Press, 1912.

Forbush, William Byron. *The Boy Problem: A Study in Social Pedagogy*. Boston: Pilgrim's Press, 1901.

————. *Guide Book to Childhood*. Philadelphia: George W. Jacobs, 1915.

Forrester, John. *Dispatches from the Freud Wars: Psychoanalysis and Its Passions.* Cambridge: Harvard University Press, 1997.

Foucault, Michel. *Discipline and Punish: The Birth of the Prison.* Trans. Alan Sheridan. 1975. New York: Vintage Books, 1979.

———. *The History of Sexuality: An Introduction, Volume I.* Trans. Robert Hurley. 1976. New York: Vintage, 1980.

Freud, Sigmund. *Totem and Taboo: Resemblances between the Psychic Lives of Savages and Neurotics.* Trans. A. A. Brill. New York: Vintage Books, 1946.

———. *Three Essays on the Theory of Sexuality.* Trans. and ed. James Strachey. New York: Basic Books, 1962.

———. "Analysis of a Phobia in a Five-Year-Old Boy" (1909). In *The Sexual Enlightenment of Children,* ed. Philip Rieff. New York: Collier-Macmillan, 1963.

———. "One of the Difficulties of Psychoanalysis" (1917). In *Character and Culture,* ed. Philip Rieff. New York: Collier-Macmillan, 1963.

———. *Three Case Histories: The "Wolf Man," the "Rat Man," and the Psychotic Doctor Schreber.* Ed. Philip Rieff. New York: Collier-Macmillan, 1963.

———. *The Interpretation of Dreams.* Ed. and trans. James Strachey. New York: Avon Books, 1965.

———. *A Phylogenetic Fantasy: Overview of the Transference of Neuroses.* Ed. Ilse Grubrich-Simitis. Trans. Axel Hoffer and Peter T. Hoffer. Cambridge: Belknap–Harvard University Press, 1987.

Freud, Sigmund, and Carl Jung. *The Freud/Jung Letters: The Correspondence between Sigmund Freud and C. G. Jung.* Ed. William McGuire. Trans. Ralph Manheim and R. F. C. Hull. Princeton: Princeton University Press, 1974.

Freud, Sigmund, and Sándor Ferenczi. *The Correspondence of Sigmund Freud and Sándor Ferenczi: Volume 1, 1908-1914.* Ed. Eva Brabant and Ernst Falzeder, with Patrizia Giampieri-Deutsch. Trans. Peter T. Hoffer. Introduction by André Haynal. Cambridge: Belknap–Harvard University Press, 1993.

Froebel, Friedrich Wilhelm August. *The Education of Man.* 1826. New York: D. Appleton, 1902.

Gandal, Keith. *The Virtues of the Vicious: Jacob Riis, Stephen Crane, and the Spectacle of the Slum.* New York: Oxford University Press, 1997.

Garbarino, James. *Lost Boys: Why Our Sons Turn Violent and How We Can Save Them.* New York: Free Press, 1999.

Gay, Peter. *Reading Freud: Explorations and Entertainments.* New Haven: Yale University Press, 1990.

Gesell, Arnold. *Wolf Child and Human Child: Being a Narrative Interpretation of the Life History of Kamala, the Wolf Girl.* New York: Harper and Bros., 1940.

Gibson, H. W. *Boyology or Boy Analysis.* 1916. New York: Association Press, 1922.

———. *Camping for Boys.* New York: Association Press, 1911.

———. *Camp Management: A Manual on Organized Camping.* New York: Greenberg, 1923.

Glazener, Nancy. *Reading for Realism: The History of a U.S. Literary Institution, 1850–1910.* Durham, N.C.: Duke University Press, 1997.

Goldberg, Jim. *Raised by Wolves.* New York: Scalo, 1995.

Goleman, Daniel. *Emotional Intelligence.* New York: Bantam, 1995.

Gould, Stephen Jay. *Ontogeny and Phylogeny.* Cambridge: Harvard University Press, 1977.

Gribben, Alan. "'I Did Wish Tom Sawyer Was There': Boy-Book Elements in *Tom Sawyer* and *Huckleberry Finn.*" In *One Hundred Years of Huckleberry Finn: The Boy, His Book, and American Culture,* ed. Robert Sattelmeyer and J. Donald Crowley. Columbia: University of Missouri Press, 1985.

Gurian, Michael. *The Wonder of Boys: What Parents, Mentors, and Educators Can Do to Shape Boys into Exceptional Men.* 1996. New York: Tarcher-Penguin Putnam, 1997.

———. *A Fine Young Man: What Parents, Mentors, and Educators Can Do to Shape Adolescent Boys into Exceptional Men.* New York: Tarcher-Penguin Putnam, 1998.

Hale, Nathan G., Jr. *Freud and the Americans: The Beginnings of Psychoanalysis in the United States, 1876–1917.* New York: Oxford University Press, 1995.

———. *The Rise and Crisis of Psychoanalysis in the United States: Freud and the Americans, 1917–1985.* New York: Oxford University Press, 1995.

Hall, Granville Stanley. "Boy Life in a Massachusetts Country Town Thirty Years Ago." *American Antiquarian Society* 7, no. 5 (October 1890): 107–28.

———. *Adolescence: Its Psychology and Its Relations to Physiology, Anthropology, Sociology, Sex, Crime, Religion, and Education.* 2 vols. 1904. New York: D. Appleton, 1992.

Hedrick, Tace. *Mestizo Modernism: Race, Nation, and Identity in Latin American Culture, 1900–1940.* Piscataway, N.J.: Rutgers University Press, 2003.

Hegeman, Susan. *Patterns for America: Modernism and the Concept of Culture.* Princeton: Princeton University Press, 1999.

Hendler, Glenn. "Tom Sawyer's Masculinity." *Arizona Quarterly* 49, no. 4 (winter 1993): 33–59.

Herberg, Will. *Protestant-Catholic-Jew.* 2d rev. ed. Garden City, N.Y.: Doubleday Anchor, 1960.

Herbert, Christopher. *Culture and Anomie: Ethnographic Imagination in the Nineteenth Century.* Chicago: University of Chicago Press, 1991.

Herman, Ellen. *The Romance of American Psychology: Political Culture in the Age of Experts.* Berkeley: University of California Press, 1995.

Hilkey, Judy. *Character Is Capital: Success Manuals and Manhood in Gilded Age America.* Chapel Hill: University of North Carolina Press, 1997.

Holland, Rupert S. *Historic Boyhoods.* Philadelphia: George W. Jacobs, 1909.

Holloran, Peter C. *Boston's Wayward Children: Social Services for Homeless Children, 1830–1930.* Cranbury, N.J.: Associated University Presses, 1989.

Holt, Marilyn Irvin. *The Orphan Trains: Placing Out in America.* Lincoln: University of Nebraska Press, 1992.

Hook. Dir. Steven Spielberg. Perf. Dustin Hoffman, Robin Williams, Julia Roberts, Bob Hoskins, Maggie Smith, Carolyn Goodall, Charlie Korsmo. Columbia-Tristar, 1991.

Howe, Lawrence. *Mark Twain and the Novel: The Double-Cross of Authority.* Cambridge: Cambridge University Press, 1998.

Howells, William Dean. Review of *The Story of a Bad Boy. Atlantic Monthly,* January 1870, 124–25.

———. Review of *The Adventures of Tom Sawyer. Atlantic Monthly,* May 1876, 621–22.

———. *A Boy's Town.* New York: Harper and Brothers, 1890.

———. *My Mark Twain: Reminiscences and Criticisms.* Baton Rouge: Louisiana State University Press, 1967.

Hunter, Jim. "Mark Twain and the Boy Book in Nineteenth-Century America." *College English* 24, no. 6 (March 1963): 430–38.

Hupp, Robert P. *The New Boys Town: The Story of Father Flanagan's Boys' Home and How Its Programs Were Reshaped to Meet the Complicated Needs of Today's Troubled Youth.* New York: Newcomen Society/Princeton University Press, 1985.

Hyland, Terry, and Kevin Warneke. *Dreams Fulfilled: Success Stories from Boys Town.* Ed. Father Val J. Peter and Ron Herron. Boys Town, Nebr.: Boys Town Press, 1992.

Itard, Jean-Marc-Gaspard. "Preface" and "Of the First Developments of the Young Savage of Aveyron." Trans. Edmund Fawcett, Peter Ayrton, and Joan White. 1801. In *Wolf Children and the Problem of Human Nature,* ed. Lucien Malson. New York: Monthly Review Press, 1972. Trans. of *Les enfants sauvages.* Paris: Union Générale d' Editions, 1964.

———. "Report on the Progress of Victor of Aveyron." Trans. Joan White. 1806. In *Wolf Children and the Problem of Human Nature,* ed. Lucien Malson. New York: Monthly Review Press, 1972. Trans. of *Les enfants sauvages.* Paris: Union Générale d' Editions, 1964.

Jackson, Michael. "Thriller." *Thriller.* Sony Music, 1983. Music video. Dir. John Landis. MTV.

Jacobson, Marcia. *Being a Boy Again: Autobiography and the American Boy Book.* Tuscaloosa: University of Alabama Press, 1994.

James, Hartwell. *The Boys of the Bible.* 1905. Philadelphia: Henry Altemus, 1916.

Jeal, Timothy. *The Boy-Man: The Life of Lord Baden-Powell.* New York: William Morrow, 1990.

Jendryka, Brian. "Flanagan's Island." *Policy Review,* summer 1994, 44–51.

Johnson, Clifton. *The Farmer's Boy.* New York: D. Appleton, 1894.

Johnson, John, Jr. "The Savagery of Boyhood." *Popular Science Monthly* 31 (1887): 796–800.

Jon Nones, Eric. *Caleb's Friend.* New York: Farrar, Straus and Giroux, 1993.

Jordan, Mary Kate. *Losing Uncle Tim.* Illustrated by Judith Friedman. Niles, Ill.: Albert Whitman, 1989.

The Jungle Book. Dir. Stephen Sommers. Perf. Jason Scott Lee, Cary Elwes, Lena Headey, Sam Neill, John Cleese, Jason Flemying. Disney, 1994.

Kantrowitz, Barbara, and Claudia Kalb. "Boys Will Be Boys." *Newsweek,* 11 May 1998, 55–60.

Kaplan, Justice. *Mr. Clemens and Mark Twain.* New York: Simon and Schuster, 1966.

Karlin, Daniel. Introduction to *The Jungle Books,* by Rudyard Kipling. New York: Penguin, 1987.

Karttunen, Frances. *Between Worlds: Interpreters, Guides, and Survivors.* New Brunswick: Rutgers University Press, 1994.

Katz, Illana. *Uncle Jimmy.* Northridge, Calif.: Real Life Storybooks, 1994.

Katz, Jonathan Ned. *The Invention of Heterosexuality.* New York: Dutton-Penguin, 1995.

Kellerman, Jonathan. *Savage Spawn: Reflections on Violent Children.* New York: Ballantine, 1999.

Kelley, R. Gordon. *Mother Was a Lady: Self and Society in Selected American Children's Periodicals, 1865–1890.* Westport, Conn.: Greenwood Press, 1974.

Kelsey, Darwin P. "Outdoor Museums and Historical Agriculture." In *Farming in the New Nation: Interpreting American Agriculture, 1790–1840,* ed. Darwin P. Kelsey. Washington, D.C.: Agricultural History Society, 1972. Special issue of *Agricultural History* (publication of symposium) 46, no. 1 (January 1972).

Kennedy, Dana. "Time to Face the Music." *Entertainment Weekly,* 17 December 1993, 30.

Kett, Joseph F. *Rites of Passage: Adolescence in America, 1790 to the Present.* New York: Basic Books, 1977.

Kern, Stephen Roger. *Freud and the Emergence of Child Psychology, 1880–1910.* Ph.D. diss., Columbia University, 1970. Ann Arbor: UMI, 1989.

Keyser, Les, and Barbara Keyser. *Hollywood and the Catholic Church: The Image of Roman Catholicism in American Movies.* Chicago: Loyola University Press, 1984.

Kiley, Dan. *The Peter Pan Syndrome: Men Who Have Never Grown Up.* New York: Dodd, Mead, 1983.

Kimmel, Michael. *Manhood in America: A Cultural History.* New York: Free Press, 1996.

Kindlon, Dan, and Michael Thompson, with Teresa Baker. *Raising Cain: Protecting the Emotional Life of Boys.* New York: Ballantine, 1999.

Kipling, John Lockwood. *Beast and Man in India: A Popular Sketch of Indian Animals in Their Relations with the People.* London: Macmillan, 1891.

Kipling, Rudyard. "In the Rukh" (appendix A). 1893. In *The Jungle Books,* ed. Daniel Karlin. New York: Penguin Books, 1987.

———. *The Jungle Books.* Ed. W. W. Robson. New York: Oxford University Press, 1992.

Klein, Melanie. "The Importance of Symbol-Formation in the Development of the Ego" ("Little Dick"). 1930. In *Melanie Klein: Love, Guilt, and Reparation and Other Works, 1921–1945.* Introduction by Hanna Segal. London: Vintage, 1998.

Kliebard, Herbert M. *Forging the American Curriculum: Essays in Curriculum History and Theory.* New York: Routledge, 1992.

Krafft-Ebing, Richard. *Psychopathia Sexualis.* Introduction by Terence Sellers. 1886. London: Velvet Publications, 1997.

Lacan, Jacques. *Écrits: A Selection.* Trans. Alan Sheridan. New York: W. W. Norton, 1977.

———. *The Seminar of Jacques Lacan, Book I: Freud's Papers on Technique, 1953–1954.* Ed. Jacques-Alain Miller. Trans. John Forrester. New York: W. W. Norton, 1991.

Ladd-Taylor, Molly, and Lauri Umansky. *"Bad" Mothers: The Politics of Blame in Twentieth-Century America.* New York: New York University Press, 1998.

Lane, Harlan. *The Wild Boy of Aveyron.* Cambridge: Harvard University Press, 1979.

Langsam, Miriam Z. *Children West: A History of the Placing-Out System of the New York Children's Aid Society, 1853–1890.* Madison: State Historical Society of Wisconsin, 1964.

Leary, Lewis, ed. *A Case Book on Mark Twain's Wound.* New York: E. P. Dutton, 1962.

Le Doeuff, Michèle. *The Philosophical Imaginary.* Trans. Colin Gordon. Stanford: Stanford University Press, 1989.

Lehman, Peter. "'I Will Suppress Nothing': Sexuality in Male Feral-Child Narratives." In *Running Scared: Masculinity and the Representation of the Male Body.* Philadelphia: Temple University Press, 1993.

Lenard, Mary. *Preaching Pity: Dickens, Gaskell, and Sentimentalism in Victorian Culture.* New York: Peter Lang, 1999.

Leps, Marie-Christine. *Apprehending the Criminal: The Production of Deviance in Nineteenth-Century Discourse.* Durham, N.C.: Duke University Press, 1992.

Lieberman, Archie. *Farm Boy.* New York: Abrams, 1974.

Lonnborg, Barbara A., ed. *Boys Town: A Photographic History.* Boys Town, Nebr.: Boys Town Press/Donning, 1992.

The Lost Boys. Dir. Joel Shumacher. Perf. Jason Patric, Dianne Wiest, Corey Haim, Barnard Hughes, Edward Hermann, Kiefer Sutherland, Jami Gertz, Corey Feldman. 1987.

Lowry, Richard S. *"Littery Man": Mark Twain and Modern Authorship.* New York: Oxford University Press, 1996.

———. "Domestic Interiors: Boyhood Nostalgia and Affective Labor in the Gilded Age." In *Inventing the Psychological: Toward a Cultural History of Emotional Life in America,* ed. Joel Pfister and Nancy Schnog. New Haven: Yale University Press, 1997.

Lutz, Tom. *American Nervousness, 1903: An Anecdotal History.* Ithaca: Cornell University Press, 1991.

MacDonald, Robert H. *Sons of the Empire: The Frontier and the Boy Scout Movement, 1890–1918.* Toronto: University of Toronto Press, 1993.

Macleod, David I. *Building Character in the American Boy: The Boy Scouts, YMCA, and Their Forerunners, 1870–1920.* Madison: University of Wisconsin Press, 1983.

Mailloux, Steven. *Rhetorical Power.* Ithaca: Cornell University Press, 1989.

Malcolm, Janet. *In the Freud Archives.* New York: Random House, 1983.

Malson, Lucien. *Wolf Children and the Problem of Human Nature.* Trans. Edmund Fawcett, Peter Ayrton, and Joan White. New York: Monthly Review Press, 1972. Trans. of *Les enfants sauvages.* Paris: Union Générale d'Editions, 1964.

Martin, Robert K. *Hero, Captain, Stranger: Male Friendship, Social Critique, and Literary Form in the Sea Novels of Herman Melville.* Chapel Hill: University of North Carolina Press, 1986.

Martin, T. T. *The 4-H Club Leader's Handbook: Principles and Procedures.* New York: Harper and Bros., 1956.

Masson, Jeffrey Moussaieff. *Lost Prince: The Unsolved Mystery of Kaspar Hauser.* New York: Free Press, 1996.

Mayhew, Henry. *London Labour and the London Poor.* 4 vols. London: Charles Griffin, 1865.

McAvoy, Thomas T. *A History of the Catholic Church in the United States.* Notre Dame, Ind.: University of Notre Dame Press, 1969.

Mechling, Jay. *On My Honor: Boys Scouts and the Making of American Youth.* Chicago: University of Chicago Press, 2001.

Melville, Herman. *Billy Budd, Sailor and Other Stories.* Ed. Harold Beaver. New York: Penguin, 1967.

Mennel, Robert M. *Thorns and Thistles: Juvenile Delinquents in the United States, 1825–1940.* Hanover, N.H.: University Press of New England, 1973.

Mercer, Kobena. "Monster Metaphors: Notes on Michael Jackson's *Thriller.*" Chap. 1 of *Welcome to the Jungle: New Positions in Black Cultural Studies.* New York: Routledge, 1994.

Merrill, Lilburn. *Winning the Boy.* New York: Fleming H. Revell, 1908.

Merrow, John. *Will Boys Be Boys? The Merrow Report.* Interview with Michael Gurian. National Public Radio. Originally broadcast from the UCLA Graduate School of Education and Information Studies. Audiocassette. 1998.

Middleton, Peter. "Are Men Rats? Freud's History of an Obsessional Neurosis." In *The Inward Gaze: Masculinity and Subjectivity in Modern Culture.* New York: Routledge, 1992.

Miller, Elise. "The Feminization of American Realist Theory." *American Literary Realism* 23, no. 1 (fall 1990): 20–41.

Mitchell, Sally. *The New Girl: Girls' Culture in England, 1880–1915.* New York: Columbia University Press, 1995.

Moore, Robert L., and Douglass Gillette. *King, Warrior, Magician, Lover: Rediscovering the Archetypes of the Mature Masculine.* San Francisco: HarperCollins, 1990.

Moore, Sheila, and Roon Frost. *The Little Boy Book: A Guide to the First Eight Years.* 1986. New York: Ballantine Books, 1987.

Munn, Charles Clark. *Boyhood Days on the Farm: A Story for Young and Old Boys.* Boston: Lothrop, Lee and Shepard, 1907.

My Best Friend Is a Vampire. Dir. Jimmy Huston. Perf. Robert Sean Leonard, Cheryl Pollack, René Auberjonois, Fannie Flagg. 1986.

Nelson, Claudia. *Boys Will Be Girls: The Feminine Ethic and British Children's Fiction, 1857–1917.* New Brunswick: Rutgers University Press, 1991.

Nelson, Claudia, and Lynne Vallone, eds. *The Girl's Own: Cultural Histories of the Anglo-American Girl, 1830–1915.* Athens: University of Georgia Press, 1994.

Newberger, Eli H. *The Men They Will Become: The Nature and Nurture of Male Character.* Reading, Mass.: Perseus Books, 1999.

Newton, Michael. *Savage Girls and Wild Boys: A History of Feral Children.* London: Faber and Faber, 2002.

Nikolova, Vassilka. "The Oedipus Myth: An Attempt at Interpretation of Its Symbolic Systems." In *Freud and Forbidden Knowledge*, ed. Peter L. Rudnytsky and Ellen Handler Spitz. New York: New York University Press, 1994.

O'Brien, David. *Public Catholicism*. New York: Macmillan, 1989.

Oursler, Fulton, and Will Oursler. *Father Flanagan of Boys Town*. Garden City, N.J.: Doubleday, 1949.

Paine, Albert Bigelow. *Mark Twain: A Biography*. 5 vols. New York: Harper and Row, 1912.

———. *The Boys' Life of Mark Twain: The Story of a Man Who Made the World Laugh and Love Him*. New York: Harper and Brothers, 1915.

Pauly, Thomas H. "*Ragged Dick* and *Little Women*: Idealized Homes and Unwanted Marriages." *Journal of Popular Culture* 9, no. 3 (winter 1975): 583–92.

Peck, George Wilbur. *How Private Geo. W. Peck Put Down the Rebellion*. Philadelphia: David McKay, 1908.

———. *Peck's Bad Boy and His Pa*. Introduction by E. F. Bleir. New York: Dover, 1958.

———. *Peck's Bad Boy with the Cowboys*. Philadelphia: David McKay, 1987.

Peter, Father Val J. "*I Think of My Homelessness*": *Stories from Boys Town*. Boys Town, Nebr.: Boys Town Press, 1991.

Pfister, Joel. "Glamorizing the Psychological: The Politics of the Performances of Modern Psychological Identities." In *Inventing the Psychological: Toward a Cultural History of Emotional Life in America*, ed. Joel Pfister and Nancy Schnog. New Haven: Yale University Press, 1997.

Platt, Anthony M. *The Child Savers: The Invention of Delinquency*. Chicago: University of Chicago Press, 1977.

Pollack, William. *Real Boys: Rescuing Our Sons from the Myths of Boyhood*. New York: Random House, 1998.

Pollak, Richard. *The Creation of Dr. B: A Biography of Bruno Bettelheim*. New York: Touchstone Books, 1998.

Prager, Arthur. *Rascals at Large, or The Clue in the Old Nostalgia*. New York: Doubleday, 1971.

Prawer, S. S. *Caligari's Children: The Film as Tale of Terror*. New York: Oxford University Press, 1980.

Propp, Vladimir. "Oedipus in Light of Folklore." 1944. In *Oedipus: A Casebook*, ed. Lowell Edmunds and Alan Dundes. Trans. Polly Coote. New York: Garland, 1984.

Quart, Leonard. "A Second Look." *Cineaste* 21, no. 3 (1995): 55–57.

Randall, Don. *Kipling's Imperial Boy: Adolescence and Cultural Hybridity*. New York: Palgrave, 2000.

Ray, Robert B. *The Avant-Garde Finds Andy Hardy*. Cambridge: Harvard University Press, 1995.

Reck, Franklin M. "*The American Boy* Magazine, 1899–1941." In *The American Boy Anthology*, ed. Franklin M. Reck. New York: Thomas Y. Crowell, 1951.

Riis, Jacob. *How the Other Half Lives*. New York: Hill and Wang, 1957.

Ritvo, Lucille B. *Darwin's Influence on Freud: A Tale of Two Sciences*. New Haven: Yale University Press, 1990.

Rockwood, Roy. *Bomba the Jungle Boy*. New York: Clover, 1926.

———. *Bomba the Jungle Boy among the Slaves*. New York: Clover, 1929.

———. *Bomba the Jungle Boy in the Swamp of Death*. New York: Clover, 1929.

———. *Bomba the Jungle Boy and the Lost Explorers*. New York: Grosset and Dunlap, 1930.

———. *Bomba the Jungle Boy in the Steaming Grotto*. New York: Cupples and Leon, 1938.

Robinson, Forrest C. *In Bad Faith: The Dynamics of Deception in Mark Twain's America*. 1986. Cambridge: Harvard University Press, 1992.

Rodgers, Daniel T. *The Work Ethic in Industrial America, 1850–1920*. Chicago: University of Chicago Press, 1974.

Rolt-Wheeler, Francis. *The Boy with the U.S. Mail*. Boston: Lothrop, Lee and Shepard, 1916.

Romero, Lora. *Home Fronts: Domesticity and Its Critics in the Antebellum United States*. Durham, N.C.: Duke University Press, 1997.

Roosevelt, Theodore. "The American Boy." In *The Strenuous Life: Essays and Addresses*. New York: Century, 1899.

Rosenthal, Michael. *The Character Factory: Baden-Powell and the Origins of the Boy Scout Movement*. New York: Pantheon, 1986.

Rosenzweig, Saul. *Freud, Jung, and Hall the King-Maker: The Historic Expedition to America (1909)*. Seattle: Hogrefe and Huber, 1992.

Rossiter, Margaret W. *The Emergence of Agricultural Science: Justus Liebig and the Americans*. New Haven: Yale University Press, 1975.

Rotundo, E. Anthony. *American Manhood: Transformations in Masculinity from the Revolution to the Modern Era*. New York: Basic Books, 1993.

Rural Manhood 1, no. 1 (January 1910)–11, no. 10 (December 1920).

Rymer, Russ. *Genie: A Scientific Tragedy*. New York: HarperCollins, 1993.

Sadoff, Dianne F. *Sciences of the Flesh: Representing Body and Subject in Psychoanalysis*. Stanford: Stanford University Press, 1998.

Salinger, J. D. *The Catcher in the Rye*. New York: Bantam Books, 1981.

Sanders, Barry. *A Is for Ox: The Collapse of Literacy and the Rise of Violence in an Electronic Age*. New York: Random House, 1994.

Schlebecker, John T. "Curatorial Agriculture." In *Farming in the New Nation: Interpreting American Agriculture, 1790–1840*, ed. Darwin P. Kelsey. Washington, D.C.: Agricultural History Society, 1972. Special issue of *Agricultural History* (publication of symposium), 46, no. 1 (January 1972): 95–103.

The Secret of the Wild Child. Prod. and dir. Linda Garmon. Narr. Stacy Keach. NOVA program no. 2112. WGBH Educational Programming, 18 October 1994.

Sedgwick, Eve Kosofsky. *Between Men: English Literature and Male Homosocial Desire*. New York: Columbia University Press, 1985.

———. *Epistemology of the Closet*. Berkeley: University of California Press, 1990.

———. "How to Bring Your Kids Up Gay: The War on Effeminate Boys." In *Tendencies*. Durham, N.C.: Duke University Press, 1993.

———. "Tales of the Avunculate: Queer Tutelage in *The Importance of Being Earnest*." In *Tendencies*. Durham, N.C.: Duke University Press, 1993.

Seltzer, Mark. *Bodies and Machines*. New York: Routledge, 1992.

Sendak, Maurice. *Where the Wild Things Are*. New York: Harper, 1963.

Sennott, Charles M. *Broken Covenant*. New York: Simon and Schuster, 1992.

Seton, Ernest Thompson. *Two Little Savages: Being the Adventures of Two Boys Who Lived as Indians and What They Learned*. New York: Grosset and Dunlap, 1903.

Shaddock, Jennifer. "*Where the Wild Things Are*: Sendak's Journey into the Heart of Darkness." *Children's Literature Association Quarterly* 22, no. 4 (winter 1997–1998): 155–59.

Shengold, Leonard. *Soul Murder: The Effects of Childhood Abuse and Deprivation*. New Haven: Yale University Press, 1989.

———. *Soul Murder Revisited: Thoughts about Therapy, Hate, Love, and Memory*. New Haven: Yale University Press, 1999.

Shideler, James H. "Agricultural History Studies: A Retrospective View." In *Outstanding in His Field: Perspectives on American Agriculture in Honor of Wayne D. Rasmussen*, ed. Frederick V. Carstensen, Morton Rothstein, and Joseph A. Swanson. The Henry A. Wallace Series on Agricultural History and Rural Studies. Ames: Iowa State University Press, 1993.

Singh, Rev. J. A. L., and Robert M. Zingg. *Wolf-Children and Feral Man*. New York: Harper and Brothers, 1939.

Skal, David J. *The Monster Show: A Cultural History of Horror*. New York: Penguin, 1993.

Sleeman, Sir Henry William. *Journey through the Kingdom of Oude in 1849–1850*. 2 vols. 1858. Lucknow: Helicon Publications, 1989.

Smith, Henry Nash, and William M. Gibson, eds. *Mark Twain–Howells Letters: The Correspondence of Samuel L. Clemens and William D. Howells, 1872–1910*. Cambridge: Harvard University Press, 1960.

Sommers, Christina Hoff. *The War against Boys: How Misguided Feminism Is Harming Our Young Men*. New York: Simon and Schuster, 2000.

Spencer, Herbert. "Progress: Its Law and Cause." In *Herbert Spencer on Social Evolution: Selected Writings*, ed. J. D. Y. Peel. 1857. Chicago: University of Chicago Press, 1972.

Stallybrass, Peter, and Allon White. *The Politics and Poetics of Transgression*. Ithaca: Cornell University Press, 1986.

Standing Bear, Luther. *My Indian Boyhood*. 1931. Bison Books, 1988.

Stephens, John, ed. *Ways of Being Male: Representing Masculinities in Children's Literature and Film*. New York: Routledge, 2002.

Stine, R. L. *Bad Moonlight*. New York: Archway, 1995.

———. *My Hairiest Adventure*. New York: Scholastic, 1995.

Stoler, Ann Laura. *Race and the Education of Desire: Foucault's "History of Sexuality" and the Colonial Order of Things.* Durham, N.C.: Duke University Press, 1995.

Stuart, Dorothy Margaret. *The Boy through the Ages.* New York: George H. Doran, 1926.

Sullenger, Thomas Earl. *Social Determinants in Juvenile Delinquency: A Community Challenge.* Omaha: Douglas Printing, 1930.

Sulloway, Frank J. *Freud, Biologist of the Mind: Beyond the Psychoanalytic Legend.* New York: Basic Books, 1979.

Sumner, William Graham. *What Social Classes Owe to Each Other.* New York: Harper and Brothers, 1883.

Tarkington, Booth. *Penrod and Sam.* New York: Grosset and Dunlap, 1916.

———. *Penrod.* Garden City, N.J.: Doubleday, Page, 1927.

Taylor, Bayard. *Boys of Other Countries: Stories for American Boys.* New York: G. P. Putnam's Sons, 1876.

Teen Wolf. Dir. Rod Daniel. Perf. Michael J. Fox, James Hampton, Susan Ursitti, Jerry Levine, Matt Adler, Lorie Griffin. 1985.

Thayer, V. T. *The Passing of Recitation.* New York: D. C. Heath, 1928.

Thompson, Michael, with Teresa Barker. *Speaking of Boys: Answers to the Most Asked Questions about Raising Sons.* New York: Ballantine, 2000.

Toth, Jennifer. *The Mole People: Life in the Tunnels beneath New York City.* Chicago: Chicago Review Press, 1995.

Trensky, Anne. "The Bad Boy in Nineteenth-Century American Fiction." *Georgia Review* 27, no. 4 (winter 1973): 503–17.

Twain, Mark. *The Adventures of Tom Sawyer.* New York: Signet, 1980.

———. *Adventures of Huckleberry Finn.* Ed. Walter Blair and Victor Fischer. Berkeley: University of California Press, 1985.

Tylor, Edward Burnet. "Wild Men and Beast-Children." *Anthropological Review,* 1, no. 1 (1863): 21–32.

———. *Primitive Culture: Researches into the Development of Mythology.* 2 vols. 1871. New York: Putnam, 1920.

Uncle Buck. Dir. John Hughes. Perf. John Candy, Jean Louisa Kelly, Gaby Hoffman, Macauley Culkin, Amy Madigan. Universal Studios, 1989.

Vallone, Lynne. *Disciplines of Virtue: Girls' Culture in the Eighteenth and Nineteenth Centuries.* New Haven: Yale University Press, 1995.

Veblen, Thorstein. *The Theory of the Leisure Class: An Economic Study of Institutions.* New York: Macmillan, 1899.

Vidal, Gore. "Goin' South." *GQ,* November 1992, 226–31.

Viswanathan, Gauri. *Masks of Conquest: Literary Study and British Rule in India.* New York: Columbia University Press, 1989.

Warner, Charles Dudley. *Being a Boy.* Boston: Houghton, Mifflin, 1897.

Weeks, Jeffrey. *Sexuality and Its Discontents: Meanings, Myths, and Modern Sexualities.* New York: Routledge, 1989.

Weiner, Bernard. *Boy into Man: A Father's Guide to Initiation of Teenage Sons.* San Franciso: Transformation Press, 1992.

Wessel, Thomas, and Marilyn Wessel. *4-H: An American Idea, 1900–1980.* Chevy Chase, Md.: National 4-H Council, 1982.

White, Hayden. *Tropics of Discourse: Essays in Cultural Criticism.* Baltimore: Johns Hopkins University Press, 1978.

White, William Allen. *The Court of Boyville.* New York: McClure, 1908.

Wiegman, Robyn. *American Anatomies: Theorizing Race and Gender.* Durham, N.C.: Duke University Press, 1995.

Wilder, Laura Ingalls. *Farmer Boy.* New York: Harper and Row, 1971.

Winter, Sarah. *Freud and the Institution of Psychoanalytic Knowledge.* Stanford: Stanford University Press, 1999.

The Wolves of Kromer. Dir. Will Gould. Narr. Boy George. Perf. Rita Davies, Matthew Dean, James Layton, Kevin Moore, David Prescott, Lee Williams. First Run Features, 1998.

Woodress, James. *Booth Tarkington: Gentleman from Indiana.* Philadelphia: J. B. Lippincott, 1954.

Wyllie, Irvin G. *The Self-Made Man in America.* New York: Free Press, 1954.

Zipes, Jack. *Fairy Tales and the Art of Subversion: The Classical Genre for Children and the Process of Civilization.* London: Heinemann, 1983.

———. *Fairy Tale as Myth, Myth as Fairy Tale.* Lexington: University of Kentucky Press, 1994.

Index

AAUW report on girls, 170
Abbott, Franklin, 183
Abbott, Jacob, 30
Abbott, Mather Almon, 73
"aboriginal Self." *See under* Emerson, Ralph Waldo
Abraham, Karl, 154
Account of Wolves Nurturing Children in Their Dens (Sleeman), 89–90, 92. *See also* wolf-boys
Adams, William T. (Oliver Optic), 200n5
ADD (attention deficit disorder), 170, 181
Adolescence (Hall), 59, 67, 69, 217n35
Adventures of Huck Finn, The (Disney), 203nn27–28
Adventures of Huckleberry Finn (Twain); 49–52, 54, 58–59; and the Bad Boy boom, 77–85; boy book frame of, 58, 80–81; hypercanonicity of, 19, 51–52, 66, 78–81; and the immaturity critique, 81–84; and juvenile delinquency, 79–80; as literary boy work, 52, 78–81; racial politics of, 78–81, 204n30; title character, 2, 60, 175, 177, 183, 185, 218n36
Adventures of Tom Sawyer, The (Twain), 52–53, 78, 203n25
Agricultural History Society, 38
agricultural museums, 34, 37–38, 197–98nn16–17
agricultural science, 27, 196n8
A Is for Ox (Sanders), 49–50, 84, 199nn1–3
Alcott, Louisa May, 28; *Little Men,* 52; *Little Women,* 200n7
Alcott, William, 26
Aldrich, Thomas Bailey, 28, 50–53, 55, 57, 61, 63, 78–79
Alger, Horatio, Jr., 32, 44, 52, 71, 200n5,

200n7, 217n34; *Frank's Campaign,* 198n24; *Ragged Dick,* 99–100
Allen, Tim, 163
American Antiquarian Society, 34
"American Boy, The" (Roosevelt), 53. *See also* Roosevelt, Theodore (Teddy)
American Boy magazine, 67, 202n21
American Country Girl, The (Crowe), 198n21
American Historical Association, 36
American Indian Stories (Zitkala Ša), 103
American International Pictures, 157
Americanization strategies, 41–42, 71
American Journal of Psychology, 36
American Magazine, The, 66
American Manhood (Rotundo), 179
American Psychiatric Association, 187
American Werewolf in London, 158
Anderson, Hans Christian, 154
Angels with Dirty Faces, 211n8
Anthropological Review, 87
anthropology, 51, 90–91, 189, 207n9, 209n18
Arac, Jonathan, 19, 52, 81
"Are Men Rats?" (Middleton), 145–46
Armstrong, Nancy, 30
Arnold, Matthew, 105
Arpád the chicken-boy (Ferenczi/Freud), 150–51
Atlantic Monthly magazine, 52
attention deficit disorder (ADD), 170, 181
avunculate: and African Americans, 196n6; and the Bad Boy genre, 53–54; boy workers as, 25–26, 30, 32, 35, 43, 46, 48–49, 53; and gay men, 25–26, 188, 199n26; Sedgwick on, 25–26, 188

Backus, Margot, 192n13
Bad Boy genre, 12, 14, 16, 22, 26, 28,

49–66, 98, 193n15; as avuncular,
53; and the Bomba books, 108;
compared to Brace's wolf-boy tale,
97–99; depiction of African
Americans, 55–56, 78–81; and Father
Flanagan's Boys Town, 125; major
authors and titles, 52, 200n5; and
Native Americans, 56–58, 60–61; and
Twain, 77–85
Baden-Powell, Lord Robert, 7, 42–43,
67, 87, 111, 179, 191–92n6
Bad Moonlight (Stine), 161
Baer, Karl Ernst von, 16
Baldwin, James Mark, 75
Ball, Valentine, 92, 95, 207n9
Barnum, P. T., 121
Barrie, J. M., 11, 162. *See also* Peter Pan
Barzilai, Shuli, 212n2
Beard, Daniel, 42
Beast and Man in India (Kipling), 87,
90, 205n1
Beecher, Rev. Henry Ward, 32; *Eyes and
Ears*, 62, 175; "Farm Creed," 40; on
"real" boys, 62, 175
Being a Boy (Warner), 16, 28, 37, 54,
58, 60–61, 73–74, 98
Being a Boy Again (Jacobson), 64,
193n15, 200n7, 201n9, 202n19
Bell, Sanford, 140
Bersani, Leo, 217n30
Bettelheim, Bruno, 8; *The Empty
Fortress*, 212n4; "Feral Children and
Autistic Children," 21, 212n4; feral
children as autistic, 20–21, 136, 152,
212n4; Pollak's biography of, 155;
The Uses of Enchantment, 147, 155.
See also fairy tales; feral tale;
psychoanalysis
Between Men (Sedgwick), 218n41
Biddulph, Steve, 220n11; on ADD as
Dad Deficit Disorder (DDD), 181
Big, 162
Billy Budd (Melville), 5, 111
Bloomfield, Robert, 31

Blumenbach, Joseph Friedrich, 4
Bly, Robert, 6, 169, 171–72, 176
Boas, Franz, 51
Bodies and Machines (Seltzer), 194n23,
196n3
Bomba the Jungle Boy series (Rockwood), 87, 106–9, 209–10nn21–23
boy books (non–Bad Boy), 72–74,
200n5; Abbott's Rollo books, 20,
200n5; Alcott titles, 28, 52; Alger
titles, 32, 44, 52, 71, 99, 200n5; Bomba
series, 105–9; Native American
memoirs as, 100–105; school story,
64; Wilder's *Farmer Boy*, 32
"Boy Code," 170, 182
boy culture: as democracy, 76–77,
121–22; and the new boyology, 170;
spatialization of, 72
Boyhood Days on the Farm (Munn), 37,
199n27
Boyhood: Growing Up Male (Abbott),
183
Boy into Man (Weiner), 176
Boyle, Patrick, 198–99n25
Boy Life and Self Government (Fiske),
75–77
"Boy Life in a Massachusetts Town
Thirty Years Ago" (Hall), 34–36, 41,
47, 197n14
Boy Life on the Prairie (Garland), 28
Boy Man, The (Jeal), 196n7
boyology: anxieties about feminism
and feminization, 2, 61–63, 169–70,
179–80, 197n11; avuncular tendencies of, 26, 30, 32, 35, 43, 46, 48–49,
53–54; biological faith of, 186–88;
as capitalist ideology, 98–99; and
citizenship, 41–42; contemporary
primers, 2–3; 167–88; "cultural
epochs" idea, 74–77; as curatorial,
19, 25, 34–38; early primers, 66–77;
early vs. contemporary, 167–69; as
entangled with the feral tale, 1, 6–12,
15–22, 168–71; first use of term, 25,

39; and homosexuality, 186–88; legitimacy of concerns, 170; as lingua franca of boy work, 2; and middle-class therapeutic culture, 2–3, 167–88; and "realism," 2, 31, 61–63, 65, 82, 202n15, 202n17; as "social pedagogy," 73–74; urbanization of, 34; and white privilege, 78–81, 184–86; women in, 61–63, 197n11. *See also* avunculate; boy culture; boy work; feral tale

Boyology or Boy Analysis (Gibson), 1, 19, 25, 66–67, 72, 176, 180–81

"boy power," 39–40

Boy Problem, The (Forbush), 1, 67, 74–75

boy-savage trope, 28, 52, 55–60, 64–65, 67, 79–81, 84, 194n21

Boy Scouts. See Scouting

Boys of Other Countries (Taylor), 73

Boys of the Bible (James), 72

boys' play. See war as child's play

Boys Town (Father Flanagan's), 111–33, 211nn14–16; admission of girls, 130; and the Catholic Church, 111, 114, 123–26; compared to Taurog's film, 126–33; and conservative family values, 127–28, 131–33; contemporary scene, 126–33, 211n16; early history, 117, 125–26, 129; funding structure, 114; Jekyndra on, 128, 131; as manifest destiny, 127; my tour of, 128–31; as nation-state, 118, 133; Newt Gingrich and, 20, 114, 127–28, 132–33; post-Flanagan administration, 125–26; and privatization, 133; progressive accomplishments of, 126; publicity for, 117–18, 130. See also *Boys Town* film (Taurog); Catholicism; Flanagan, Father Edward Joseph

Boy's Town, A (Howells), 28, 33, 56–57, 60–61, 64–66, 103

Boys Town film (Taurog), 20, 111–14, 116–23, 127–28, 133; and crime films, 119–20, 211n8; as melodrama, 118; and *Miracle of the Heart*, 210n1; and the nation-state, 118; Newt Gingrich and, 20, 114, 127–28; racial politics of, 119–20, 210n6; and *The Road Home*, 210n1; and sentimentality, 118

Boys Will Be (Brooks), 176–77

"Boys Will Be Boys" (Kantrowitz and Kalb), 167

Boy through the Ages, The (Stuart), 72–73

Boy Today, The (Abbott), 73

Boy with the U.S. Mail, The (Rolt-Wheeler), 73

boy work, 1–2, 7–8, 10–13, 15, 18–20, 26; as avuncular, 26, 30, 32, 35, 43, 46, 48, 49, 53; and the Catholic Church, 111; and the "contrasexed," 19, 42–48; as "farming," 1–2, 23–42; and the juvenile court system, 115–16; literature as, 13–15, 27, 52, 49–66, 78–81, 103. *See also* Bad Boy genre; boyology; Boys Town (Father Flanagan's); Eastman, Charles Alexander; Scouting; YMCA

Brace, Charles Loring, 34; and the child-saving movement, 93–99, 102, 105; *The Dangerous Classes of New York*, 94–97, 100, 102; founding of Children's Aid Society of New York, 94; and placing out, 94–95, 97, 99, 208n14; training of, 93–99; and the urban feral tale, 93–100; "Wolf-Reared Children," 95–99, 102, 105, 119. *See also* Children's Aid Society of New York; child-saving movement; feral tale; wolf-boys

Brogan, Hugh, 7

Brooks, Bruce, 176–77

Brooks, Van Wyck, 19, 50–51, 66, 78, 81–83, 173

Brothers Grimm, The, 89, 154, 169; *Der Eisenhans* ("Iron Hans"), 169, 219n2;

Nazi interpretations, 216n28; sexism of, 216n29. *See also* fairy tales; *Iron John*; Perrault, Charles; Zipes, Jack
Brown, Bill, 72, 192n14, 194n23, 201n8
Brunswick, Ruth Mae, 150
Buel, Jesse, 27
Building Character in the American Boy (Macleod), 1, 38, 42, 198n23
Buni, Frank, 199n25
Burkett, Elinor, 199n25
Burns, Sarah, 202n16
Burroughs, Edgar Rice, 8, 10; Tarzan (character), 5, 7, 10, 105–7, 209n20, 209n21
Bush, George H., 171
Bush, George W., 6
Bushnell, Horace, 26
Butler, Judith, 11–12

Cable, George W., 79
Caleb's Friend (Jon Nones), 163–65
Camping for Boys (Gibson), 45–47
Camp Management (Gibson), 42–43
camps and camping, 26, 40, 42–48, 105, 189–90, 198n23
"Camp That Failed, A" (Holliday), 44–45
Candland, Douglas, 191n4
Candy, John, 196n5
Carroll, Michael, 9–10
Carter, Angela, 150
Catcher in the Rye, The (Salinger), 135
Catholicism: as "Americanism," 124; and Boys Town, 111, 114, 123–26; compared to Scouting, 112; condemnation of homosexuality, 132; Dorothy Day and the Catholic Worker Movement, 124; in early twentieth-century America, 123–24; and Irish immigrants, 123–24; sexual scandals of, 111–12, 199n25
Caveman within Us, The (Fielding), 153
Caxton, William, 147
Cech, John, 156

Chamberlain, A. F., 54, 59, 75
character building, 25, 167. *See also* Scouting; Sons of Daniel Boone; YMCA
"character contagion," 39, 42–47
Character Is Capital (Hilkey), 70–71
Chelsey, Albert M., 69
Cheyfitz, Eric, 105, 209n20
Child, Lydia Maria, 28
Children of the Wolf (Yolen), 163
Children's Aid Society of New York, 93–96, 207n10, 208n14. *See also* Brace, Charles Loring; child-saving movement; wolf-boys
children's literature, 20, 160–61, 172; Alcott, 28, 56; Alger, 32, 44, 52, 71; Bomba the Jungle Boy, 106–9; *Boys Will Be* (Brooks), 176–77; *Caleb's Friend*, 163–64; classics influenced by Wild Peter case, 194–95nn24–25; Defoe, 194–95nn24–25; *Farming for Boys*, 25–34; as feral tale, 20, 89, 163–65; Fiedler on, 195n25; *Incident at Hawk's Hill*, 163–64; *Our Young Folks* magazine, 25, 28, 32, 52; and pop-psychoanalysis, 154–56; as racial elegy, 102; R. L. Stine, 160–61; *St. Nicholas* magazine, 28, 72, 93–99; *Where the Wild Things Are*, 6, 138, 155–56; and wolf-boy reports, 89; *Youth's Companion* magazine, 28. *See also* Bad Boy genre; boy books; *St. Nicholas* magazine; Twain, Mark
children's literature scholarship, 154–55
child-saving movement, 88, 94–99, 207n10; and Charles Loring Brace, 93–99, 102, 105
child sexuality, 46–48, 138–42, 213n6, 214n13
child study, 25–26, 34, 36, 178; and boyology, 68–69, 108; and the feral boy, 5; Freud's *Three Essays* as contribution to, 140–41; and G. Stanley Hall, 34–36, 69, 178,

197n15; and Midnapore wolf-girls case, 151; and psychoanalysis, 140, 151. *See also* Gesell, Arnold; Hall, Granville Stanley

china-painting Henry, 44–45

Chodorow, Nancy, 179

Chudacoff, Howard P., 179

Clark University, 36, 140, 142, 152, 178

Cleese, John, 162

Clemens, Samuel. *See* Twain, Mark

Clinton, Bill, 85, 211n13

Clinton, Hillary, 114

coitus a tergo more ferarum, 147–50

colonial India, 87

Colonial Williamsburg, 37

"Come Back to the Raft Ag'in, Huck Honey!" (Fiedler), 49–50, 205n40

"Company of Wolves, The" (Carter), 150

conduct manuals, 27

Conlon, E. P., 25, 39

Connell, R. W., 189

Cooper, James Fenimore: heady influence of, 37; *The Last of the Mohicans*, 15; Natty Bumppo and Tarzan, 105–6

Cope, Edward Drinker, 59

Coughlin, Father Charles, 123

Country Gentleman, 27

Court of Boyville, The (White), 28, 63

Covington, Dennis, 163

Craig, Eleanor, 192n13

Creation of Dr. B, The (Pollak), 155

crime films, 119–20, 211n8

Crocodile Dundee, 163

Crowe, Martha Foote, 198n21

Crowley, John, 54, 201–2n14

"'Cruiser' program," 46

Cubbing. *See under* Scouting

Culkin, Macauley, 196n5

Cultivator, The, 27

Culture and Anomie (Herbert), 74

Cummings, Sherwood, 204n31

Cunningham, Hugh, 207n13

curriculum theory, 74

Cushman, Philip, 142, 153–54, 218nn36–37; on the unconscious as "enchanted interior," 153

Dangerous Classes of New York, The (Brace), 94–97, 100, 102. *See also* Brace, Charles Loring; child-saving movement; wolf-boys

Daniel, Rod, 138, 158

Darwin, Charles: and Darwinism, 9, 94, 98, 122, 151

Davis, Whitney, 217n30

Day, Dorothy, 124

Defoe, Daniel, 194–95n24

Degeneracy (Talbot), 59

Deloria, Philip J., 101

Demos, John, 13, 153, 193n16

Dennis the Menace cartoon strip, 175–76

Derrick, Scott S., 193n17

DeVoto, Bernard, 81–83, 204n34; *Mark Twain's America*, 83, 204n33, 204n35; praise of *Tom Sawyer*, 204n33; *The Writer in America*, 83

Dewey, John, 69

Diagnostic and Statistical Manual, 187

Dippie, Brian, 101

Discipline and Punish (Foucault), 45, 220n5

Disciplines of Virtue (Vallone), 220n9

Disney. *See* Walt Disney film

Dodge, Mary Mapes, 102. See also *St. Nicholas* magazine

Douthwaite, Julia, 21

Doyle, Richard, 171–72

Dr. Dolittle, 163

Dundes, Alan, 154, 217n32

Earp, Edwin L., 39, 41

Eastman, Charles Alexander (Ohiyesa), 102–5; *From the Deep Woods to Civilization*, 104–5; *Indian Boyhood*, 102–5; as Native American activist,

102–5; and Scouting, 104–5; *The Soul of an Indian,* 103–4; volumes of folklore, 209n19; youth among Dakota Sioux, 102. *See also* Native Americans

Eastman, Elaine Goodale, 209n19

Eckert, Allan W., 163–64

Edelman, Lee, 217n30

Education of Man, The (Froebel), 72, 74, 202–3n24

Eggleston, Edward, 200n6

Ellis, Havelock, 140

Emerson, Ralph Waldo, 14–15, 43, 55, 70, 98, 105; on the "aboriginal Self," 12, 14–15, 101, 105; "Nature," 15, 194n19; "Self-Reliance," 14–15, 55, 193n18, 205n37

Empty Fortress, The (Bettelheim), 212n4

Encino Man, 163

Epistemology of the Closet (Sedgwick), 63, 202n18

Estés, Clarissa Pinkola, 219n5

evolutionary theory: and the Bad Boy genre, 51, 53, 63–64, 82, 87, 201n11; and *Boys Town,* 122; centrality to boyology and the feral tale, 15–18; and child saving, 94, 98; Darwin, 94, 98, 151; and *Farming for Boys,* 31, 36; Haeckel, 16, 200n4; Lamarck and Lamarckianism, 16–18, 122; in Latin American modernism, 118; and psychoanalysis, 18, 142, 217n33; and sexology, 139–40; Spencer, 16–17, 200n4

Eyes and Ears (Beecher), 62, 175

fairy tales, 3, 135–36, 142, 147, 149–50, 154–55, 162, 169, 182, 216n28, 218–19n2

Fairy Tales and the Art of Subversion (Zipes), 3, 147, 154–55

Faludi, Susan, 173–74, 189

Family Circle cartoon strip, 175

"family film," 163

Farm Boy, The (Lieberman), 47

Farm Boys (Fellows), 47

Farmer Boy (Wilder), 32

Farmer's Boy, The (Bloomfield), 31

Farmer's Boy, The (Johnson), 37

Farming for Boys (serial), 25–34, 52, 125; and avuncular boy work, 25–26; and Brace's wolf-boy tale, 97; compared to *Rural Manhood,* 40, 42; miniaturization in, 31–33; and self-reliance, 32–33

farming programs for boys: and agricultural science, 27–28; 4-H, 1, 24, 27; YMCA efforts, 24, 38–42

Farrell, Warren, 171

Fasteau, Marc Feigen, 171

father figures. *See* Bad Boy genre; Bomba the Jungle Boy series; boy work; Flanagan, Father Edward Joseph; paternalism; the personal/personnel touch; priests in crime films; Scouting; YMCA

Father Flanagan of Boys Town (Oursler), 112–13, 120, 122–24, 210n2

FDR (Franklin Delano Roosevelt), 123

Fellows, Will: *Farm Boys,* 47–48

"Feral Children and Autistic Children" (Bettelheim), 21, 212n4

Feral Children and Clever Animals (Candland), 191n4

feral tale: Americanization(s) of, 6–8, 18–22, 105–9, 151–63; Anglo-American lineage, 1; and autism, 21, 136, 152 (*see also* Bettelheim, Bruno); Bomba series, 106–9; Burroughs's Tarzan stories, 5, 7, 10, 105–7; as children's literature, 6, 137–38, 163–66; as "civilizing" discourse, 3; as colonialist narrative of British India, 5, 87–90, 92; compulsory heterosexuality in, 138, 157–62, 213n9; and English literature, 89; and "family film," 6, 157–63; Freud's variants, 5, 8–10, 136–37, 141–51,

212–13n5; Elián González case, 5–6; Kipling's Mowgli stories, 5, 7, 8, 10–11, 90, 92, 107, 136, 156, 162; and Linnaeus, 3; and men's studies, 174, 179, 219n5; and the Oedipus myth, 9–10; origins in mythology and science, 3–5, 191n3; pop-clinical variants, 192n13; and Sioux culture, 100–105; as urban American cautionary tale, 93–99, 207n11. *See also* Hauser, Kaspar; Victor of Aveyron

Ferenczi, Sándor, 142; case of Arpád the chicken-boy, 150–51

FFA (Future Farmers of America), 24, 27, 196n2

Fiedler, Leslie: on appeal of the feral, 5; on children as "freaks," 151, 218n39; "Come Back to the Raft Ag'in, Huck Honey!" 49–50, 205n40; *Freaks*, 84, 151, 195n25, 218n39; Freudian influences on, 205n37; homo-economics of, 64, 83–84, 205nn37–40; immaturity critique, 51, 54, 61, 64, 81–84, 173, 205n37; *Love and Death in the American Novel*, 50, 203–4n29, 205nn37–40; *Return of the Vanishing American*, 84; on Twain, 78–81, 81–84, 203–4n29

Fielding, William J., 153

Field of Dreams, 127

Fine, Gary Alan, 181

Fire in the Belly (Keen), 172

Fish, Stanley, 149, 216–17n30

Fisher, James Terence, 124

Fisher, Philip, 196–97n10

Fishkin, Shelley Fisher, 81, 177, 204n30

Fiske, George Walter, 75–77

Fiske, John, 54, 60, 193n18

Flanagan, Father Edward Joseph, 20, 111–33; beliefs of, 114–15; and Catholicism, 114, 120, 123–26; early life, 122–23; fame as boy worker, 111–12, 124–25; founding of

Boys Town, 117, 123, 125–26, 129; masculinity of, 113–14; Oursler biography of, 112–13, 120, 122–24; and the personal/personnel touch, 70, 114–17; as public figure, 124–25; Spencer Tracy as, 118, 121. *See also* Boys Town; *Boys Town* film (Taurog)

"Flanagan's Island" (Jekyndra), 128, 131

Flight of Pony Baker, The (Howells), 54, 201–2n14

"forbidden experiment," 88

Forbush, William Byron: *The Boy Problem*, 1, 67–69, 74, 181; *Guide Book to Childhood*, 69, 202n22

Ford, Harrison, 127

Forgotten Language, The (Fromm), 147, 216n29

Forrester, John, 216–17n30

Forrest Gump, 127

Foucault, Michel: biohistory of childhood, 213n6; *Discipline and Punish*, 45, 220n5; on the family cell, 13; *The History of Sexuality*, 194n22, 215n17

4-H programs, 1, 24, 27, 195–96n2

Fox, Michael J., 158

Frank's Campaign (Alger), 198n24

Frazer, Sir James, 3

Freaks (Fiedler), 84, 151, 195n25

Freud, Sigmund: Americanization(s) of, 151–65, 168; and Arpád the chicken-boy, 150–51; and Ferenczi, 150–51; on heterosexuality as precarious, 139, 165; *History of an Infantile Neurosis* (Wolf Man case), 8, 10, 12, 136–38, 146–51, 156, 216–17n30; and "hysterical" women, 142, 216n25; *The Interpretation of Dreams*, 140, 192n8; and Itard, 141–42; on Kipling's *Jungle Books*, 8; Lacan on, 135–36; Little Hans case, 147, 151, 217n34; *Notes upon a Case of Obsession Neurosis* (Rat Man case), 8, 10, 137–38, 143–49, 215nn19–20, 215nn22–23; "The Occurrence in

Dreams of Material from Fairy Tales," 149; "One of the Difficulties of Psychoanalysis," 212–13n5; *A Phylogenetic Fantasy*, 217n33; psychoanalytic feral tales of, 8–10, 20–21, 136–38, 141–51, 156; revisions of sexology, 136, 139–42; *Totem and Taboo*, 150; *Three Essays on the Theory of Sexuality*, 140–41; visit to Clark University, 36, 142, 145, 215–16n24

Froebel, Friedrich Willhelm, 72, 74, 202–3n24

Fromm, Erich, 147, 216n29

From the Deep Woods to Civilization (Eastman), 104–5

frontier hypothesis (Turner), 36–37

Frost, Roon, 175

Future Farmers of America (FFA), 24, 27, 196n2

Galton, Francis, 3

Gandal, Keith, 99

Garbarino, James, 167, 185–86

Gardiner, Muriel, 150

Garland, Hamlin, 28

Gay, Peter, 192n7

Gay Farm Boys Project, 47

gay farmers, 47–48

Gender Identity Disorder, 187–88

Genesee Farmer, 27

"Genie team," 4

Gerstein, Mordicai, 163–64

Gesell, Arnold: *Wolf Child and Human Child*, 152, 154; and the Yale Clinic of Child Behavior, 151

Gibson, Henry William: *Boyology or Boy Analysis*, 1, 19, 25, 66–70, 72, 176, 180–81; *Camping for Boys*, 45–47; *Camp Management*, 42–43; involvement with YMCA, 39, 66

Gillette, Douglass, 172

Gilligan, Carol, 178, 219–20n7

Gilman, Charlotte Perkins, 198n20

Gingrich, Newt, 20, 114, 127–28, 132–33, 210n6

girl culture, 180, 220n8

girls: and the Bad Boy genre, 59–61; and contemporary boyology, 170, 178; in farming narrative, 40–41, 198n21; in feral narrative, 137

Girls Own, The (Nelson and Vallone), 220n8

Glazener, Nancy, 202n15, 202n17

Glennon, Will, 219n3

Goldberg, Herb, 171

Goldberg, Jim, 99, 208–9n16

Goleman, Daniel, 219n3

González, Elián, 5, 6

Goodenough, Elizabeth, 128

Goosebumps (Stine), 161

Gore, Al, 85

Gould, Stephen Jay, 194n20

GQ magazine, 85

Grey, Zane, 101

Gribben, Alan, 78, 203n25

Griffin, Eleanore, 118

Guide Book to Childhood (Gibson), 69

Gulick, Luther, 202n22

Gunn, Frederick William, 45

Gurian, Michael: ethnographic language of, 181–82; trust in biology, 167–69, 177–78, 180–81, 186; *The Wonder of Boys*, 2, 72, 77, 167–70, 177–78, 180–83, 186

Haeckel, Ernst, 16, 200n4

Hale, Edward Everett, 200n6

Hale, Nathan, 153, 195n27

Hall, Granville Stanley, 75; *Adolescence*, 59, 67, 69, 217n35; agricultural interests of, 34–36; as anti-avuncular, 26, 35; "Boy Life in a Massachusetts Town Thirty Years Ago," 34–36, 41, 47, 197n14; on child play as recapitulation, 57; and child study, 34–36, 69, 178, 197n15; contributions to (child) psychology, 36; founding of

American Journal of Psychology and *Pedagogical Seminary*, 36; Freud's host at Clark, 142

Hamlet, 168

Harper's magazine, 52

Harty, Archbishop Jeremiah, 124–25

Hauser, Kaspar: and Billy Budd, 5; as cautionary figure, 5, 49, 137, 213n8; fame of, 4–5, 21; Herzog's film, 213n9; indifference to women, 139; as royal heir, 4

Hedrick, Tace, 118

Hegeman, Susan, 204n34

Hendler, Glenn, 199–200n4

Herbart, Johann Friedrich, 74

Herbert, Christopher, 74, 213n10

Herman, Ellen, 21, 153

Heroines of Fiction (Howells), 62

Herrick, Christine Terhume, 68

Herzog, Werner, 213n9

Hesse, Karen, 163–64

Hilkey, Judy, 70–71

Hine, Lewis, 99

Hirsch, E. D., 179

Hirschfield, Magnus, 139, 213–14n11

Historic Boyhoods (Holland), 72

History of an Infantile Neurosis. See under Freud, Sigmund

History of Sexuality, The (Foucault), 194n22, 215n17

Holland, Rupert S., 72

Holliday, W. B., 44–45

Holloran, Peter C., 207n10

Hollywood, 172

Holt, Marilyn Irvin, 208n14

Home Fronts (Romero), 15, 62, 196n9

Homestead Act, 27

homo-economics: and *A Boy's Town*, 63–66; and Bad Boy writing, 63–66, 205nn37–40; and the Bomba books, 107–8; in boyology, 10–12, 19, 43–46, 63–66, 172–73, 186–88; and Boys Town (Father Flanagan's), 132; and Catholicism, 111–13; and the cost of

heterosexuality, 11–12; in feral picture books, 164–65; in the feral tale, 138, 143, 147–48, 157–62, 164–65; and Freud's case histories, 143, 147–48; and homosexual panic, 26, 43–46, 158, 218n41; and horror film, 158; Kimmel on, 174; and the mythopoets, 172–73; and the Peter Pan Syndrome, 172–73; and Scouting, 10–11, 186–87; Sedgwick on, 25–26, 63, 133, 187–88, 218n41; and Spencer, 16–18; teen film, 158–62. *See also* Fiedler, Leslie; queer studies; Sedgwick, Eve Kosofsky

Homo ferus, 3, 4, 148

Hook (Spielberg), 6, 158, 162–63

Hoover, J. Edgar, 115

hothouse thesis, 13–14

Howe, Lawrence, 78

Howells, William Dean: *A Boy's Town*, 28, 33, 52, 56–57, 60–61, 103; on the Bad Boy books, 53; *The Flight of Pony Baker*, 54, 201–2, n14; *Heroines of Fiction*, 62; on Twain, 50, 78, 203n25

How Schools Shortchange Girls (AAUW), 170

How the Other Half Lives (Riis), 95, 208n16

"How to Bring Your Kids Up Gay" (Sedgwick), 187

Huck Finn (character), 2, 60, 175, 177, 183, 185, 218n36; as "black," 81, 204n30. *See also Adventures of Huckleberry Finn*

Hughes, Henry, 196n9

Hughes, John, 196n5

Hunter, Jim, 78

Hupp, Father Robert P., 125

Hurley, Timothy, 115

Huston, Jimmy, 160

Ibsen, Henrik, 144–45

immaturity critique: of Brooks and Fiedler, 51, 81–84; of Kiley, 172–73, 186

Incident at Hawk's Hill (Eckert), 163–64
Indian Boyhood (Eastman), 102–5
Indian Reorganization Act, 101
infancy theory of John Fiske, 54, 60–61
Interpretation of Dreams, The (Freud), 140
"In the Rukh" (Kipling), 92
"Iron Hans." *See under* Brothers Grimm, The
Iron John (Bly), 6, 169, 172, 176, 218–19n2
Israel, Henry, 195
Itard, Jean-Marc-Gaspard, 4, 88, 91, 135–36, 205–6n1, 213n10, 215n21; concern about Victor's sexuality, 138–40; and Freud, 141–42. *See also* Victor of Aveyron
I Was a Teenage Werewolf, 161

Jackson, Andrew, 174
Jackson, Michael, 138, 157–58, 162
Jacobson, Marcia, 66, 193n15, 200n7, 201n9, 202n19
James, Hartwell, 72
Jeal, Tim, 196n7
Jefferson, Thomas, 27, 33, 71, 101
Jeffords, Susan, 172
Jendryka, Brian, 128, 131
Johnson, Clifton, 37
Johnson, John, Jr., 219n4
Jones, Ernest, 154, 216n30
Jon Nones, Eric, 163–65
Jordan, Mary Kate, 199n26
Jumanji, 163
Jung, Carl, 142, 154
Jungle Book, The (Disney), 162
Jungle Books (Kipling), 5, 7–8, 10–11, 92, 136, 156. *See also* Kipling, Rudyard
jungle films, 106, 162–63, 209n21
Jungle Life in India (Ball), 92, 95, 207n9
Jungle 2 Jungle, 163
juvenile delinquency: and the Bad Boy genre, 51–53; and Boys Town,

113–15, 128, 210n4; and the courts, 114–16; and *Huck Finn,* 79–80; in nineteenth-century culture, 51, 79

Kalb, Claudia, 167
Kantrowitz, Barbara, 167
Karlin, Daniel, 92
Karttunen, Frances, 105
Katz, Illana, 199n26
Katz, Jonathan Ned, 214n12
Keen, Sam, 172
Kellerman, Jonathan, 184–86
Kern, Stephen Roger, 140, 214n13
Kett, Joseph, 93
Keyser, Les and Barbara, 119–20, 210n7
Kiley, Dan, 172–73, 186
Kimmel, Michael, 156, 171, 173–74, 179, 188–89, 219n6
Kindlon, Dan, 167
King, Warrior, Magician, Lover (Moore and Gillette), 172
Kipling, John Lockwood, 87, 90, 205n1
Kipling, Rudyard: and Baden-Powell, 7–8; influence on Scouting, 7–8; "In the Rukh," 92; *Jungle Books,* 5, 7–8, 10–11, 92, 136, 156; *Kim,* 5, 7; Mowgli (character), 5, 7–8, 10–11, 90, 92, 107, 136, 156, 162
Kipling's Imperial Boy (Randall), 191n1
Klein, Melanie, 135–37, 155
Krafft-Ebing, Richard von, 139–40; *Psychopathia Sexualis,* 141–42, 214nn15–16
Kristeva, Julia, 137
Kuznets, Lois, 128

Lacan, Jacques, 135–36, 212nn2–3
Ladd-Taylor, Molly, 218n1
laissez-faire capitalism, 98
Lamarck, Jean-Baptiste, 16, 17, 122
Lamarckian theory, 16–18
Landau, Elaine, 163
Landis, Jonathan, 158
Landon, Michael, 161

Lanzer, Ernst, 143
Last of the Mohicans, The (Cooper), 15
Leary, Lewis, 204n32
Le Doeuff, Michèle, 136, 212n3
Lee, Jason Scott, 162
Lefort, Rosine, 135–36
Lehman, Peter, 213n9
Lenard, Mary, 118
Leps, Christine, 207
LeVay, Simon, 186
Library of Contemporary American
Thought, 184
Lieberman, Archie, 47
Liebig, Justus, 196n8
Like Father, Like Son, 163
Lincoln, Abraham, 33
Lindsey, Benjamin Barr, 116
Linnaeus, Carolus (Carl von Linné),
3, 4
Lion King, The (Disney), 168
literature as boy work, 14–15, 52,
49–66, 78–81, 103. *See also* Bad Boy
genre; boyology; boy work; *Farming
for Boys* (serial)
literature as conservation, 101
Little Boy Book, The (Moore and Frost),
175–76
"Little Chanticleer." *See* Arpád the
chicken-boy
little Dick (Klein/Lacan), 135–36
Little Eyolf (Ibsen), 144–45
Little Hans (Freud), 147, 151, 217n34
Little League, 181
Little Men (Alcott), 52
Little White Bird, The (Barrie), 162
Little Women (Alcott), 200n7
London Labour and the London Poor
(Mayhew), 207n11
Longfellow, Henry Wadsworth, 28, 105
Losing Uncle Tim (Jordan), 199n26
Lost Boys (Garbarino), 167, 185–86
Lost Boys, The (Schumacher), 160
Lost Boy trope, 11, 37, 160, 168,
185–86

Lost Prince (Masson), 5, 137, 199n2,
213n8
Love and Death in the American Novel
(Fiedler), 50, 203–4n29
Lowell, James Russell, 28
Lowry, Richard S., 26, 192–93n14
Lutz, Tom, 59, 62
lycanthropy, 157–58

Macleod, David I., 1, 38, 42, 198n23,
217n35
Mailloux, Steven, 79–81
Malcolm, Janet, 137
Male Machine, The (Fasteau), 171
Malson, Lucien, 206n3
Manhood in America (Kimmel), 156,
171, 173–74, 179, 219n6
Manson, Marilyn, 185
Mark Twain and Science (Cummings),
204n31
Martin, Robert K., 83–84
Martin, T. T., 196n2
masculinity: American social history
of, 156, 171–75, 179, 185–90;
democratic potential of, 188–89; and
violence, 145–46. *See also* homo
economics; men's liberation
movement; men's studies; Scouting
Maslow, Abraham, 156
Masson, Jeffrey Moussaieff, 5, 137,
199n2, 213n8
Matsell, George, 93
Maudsley, Henry, 214n13
Mayhew, Henry, 207n11
Mayne, William, 163
Mazer, Harry, 163
McDonough School, 76–77
Mechling, Jay, 10–11, 181, 186–88
Mennel, Robert M., 115
men's liberation movement, 171–72
Men's Rights Association, 172
men's studies, 173–74, 179–80, 188–89
Men They Will Become, The
(Newberger), 77, 167

Mercer, Kobena, 158
Merrill, Lilburn, 70, 169
Merrow Report, The, 167, 178, 182
Mestizo Modernism (Hedrick), 118
Middleton, Peter, 145–46
Midnapore wolf-girls, 151–52
Miller, Elise, 62
miniaturization, 31–34
Miracle of the Heart, 210n1
Mirbeau, Octave, 145
Mitchell, Sally, 220n8
Mole People, The (Toth), 99
Moll, Albert, 140
"momism," 218n1
Montessori, Maria, 4
Monumental Anxieties (Derrick), 193n17
Moore, Robert L., 172
Moore, Sheila, 175
Morgan, Lewis Henry, 209n18
Mowgli. *See under* Kipling, Rudyard
Mowgli's Sons (Brogan), 7
Mrs. Frisby and the Rats of NIMH, 163
Munn, Charles Clark, 37, 199n27
Murphy, Eddie, 163
Music of the Dolphins, The (Hesse), 163–64
My Best Friend Is a Vampire (Huston), 160
My Boy and I (Herrick), 68
My Hairiest Adventure (Stine), 161
My Indian Boyhood (Standing Bear), 100–101
mythopoetic men's movement, 21–22, 168–69, 171; attitudes toward boyhood, 172; and the "deep masculine," 172. *See also* Bly, Robert

National Association for the Study of Childhood, 36
National Catholic Welfare Conference, 123
Native Americans: appropriation(s) of, 42, 56–58, 60–61, 67, 101, 103, 105; in Bad Boy writing, 56–58, 60–61;

and boyhood memoirs, 3, 100–105; Charles Alexander Eastman (Ohiyesa), 102–5; federal policies on, 100–101; folklore of, 92, 103–4; resemblances to street boys, 100; Luther Standing Bear, 100, 102; and trope of vanishing native, 88, 101–5; and U.S. nationalism, 101–2; white settlers as, 42; and Woodcraft Indians, 67, 105
Natty Bumppo, 106
"Nature" (Emerson), 15, 194n19
Nelson, Claudia, 220n8
Neverland, 11
Newberger, Eli, 71, 167
New Deal programs, 123, 128
New England Boyhood (Hale), 200n6
Newton, Michael, 139, 195n26
New York City as urban jungle, 95–99, 108
Nichols, Jack, 171
Nikolova, Vassilka, 192n11
Notes upon a Case of Obsession Neurosis (Rat Man case). *See under* Freud, Sigmund

O'Brien, David, 123–24
Oedipality: in boyology, 12–14, 53–54, 106, 119, 121; in the feral tale, 9–10, 136, 142; Kimmel on, 174; and mythopoetic writing, 169, 172; and psychoanalysis, 136, 142–44, 151; and Scouting, 152–53
"Oedipus in America" (Demos), 193n16
"Oedipus in Light of Folklore" (Propp), 9–10, 192n10–12
Oedipus myth, 9–10, 136, 192nn10–12
"Oedipus Myth" (Nikolova), 192n11
Oedipus Tyrannus (Sophocles), 10
Ohiyesa. *See* Eastman, Charles Alexander
Old Sturbridge Village, 38
One, Two, Three (Craig), 192n13

On My Honor (Mechling), 10–11, 181, 186–88
Ontogeny and Phylogeny (Gould), 194n20
Optic, Oliver, 200n5
Ordeal of Mark Twain, The (Brooks), 19, 50–51, 66, 81–83
Orenstein, Peggy, 180
Oursler, Fulton and Will, 112–13, 120, 122–24, 210n2
Our Young Folks magazine, 25, 28, 32, 52

Paine, Alfred Bigelow, 203n25
Pankejeff, Serge, 147, 150
parens patriae, 114
parenting manuals, 175–76
Parkman, Francis, 105
paternalism, 113–15
Patten, Gilbert, 200n5
Patterns for America (Hegeman), 204n34
Patterson, "Uncle" Robert, 43
Peck, George Wilbur: *How Private Geo. W. Peck Put Down the Rebellion*, 57; *Peck's Bad Boy with the Cowboys*, 61
Peck, Sylvia, 163–64
Pedagogical Seminary, 36
Penrod (Tarkington), 52, 55–56, 60
Penrod and Sam (Tarkington), 52, 58, 66
Perrault, Charles, 89, 154
personal/personnel touch, 70, 114–17
Peter, Father Valentine J., 112, 125–27, 133; books written by, 211n12; on Bill Clinton, 211n13
Peter Pan, 11, 158, 162, 168
Peter Pan Syndrome, The (Kiley), 172–73, 186
Pfister, Joel, 153
Phelps, Elizabeth Stuart, 28
Philosophical Imaginary, The (Le Doeuff), 136, 212n3
Pinocchio, 2, 168

Pipher, Mary, 170, 178, 180
placing out, 94–95, 97, 99. *See also* Brace, Charles Loring
Playing Indian (Deloria), 101
Pollack, William: on the "Boy Code," 170, 182; *Real Boys*, 77, 167, 170, 178, 181–83
Pollak, Richard, 155
Prawer, S. S., 157
Preaching Pity (Lenard), 118
priests in crime films, 119–20, 210n7
Primitive Culture (Tylor), 73, 91
Propp, Vladimir, 9–10, 192n10, 192n12
Psychic Life of Power, The (Butler), 11
psychoanalysis: Americanization(s) of, 151–63; and ego/humanist psychology, 156; and fairy tales, 154–55; and the feral tale, 5, 8–10, 136–37, 141–51; Ferenczi, 142, 150–51; Klein, 135–37, 155; Lacan, 135–36; reception in the United States, 13, 20–21, 137–38, 152–56; as "schoolboy psychology," 10, 12; and Scouting, 7–12, 20, 152; as textualization of oral narrative, 8. *See also* Bettelheim, Bruno; Freud, Sigmund
"psychoanalytic imaginary," 136
Psychopathia Sexualis (Krafft-Ebing), 141–42, 214nn15–16
Public Catholicism (O'Brien), 123–24

Quart, Leonard, 127–28
queer studies, 11–12, 25–26, 47–48, 63, 147–48, 205nn37–40

Ragged Dick (Alger), 99–100
Raised by Wolves (Goldberg), 99, 208–9n16
Raising Boys (Biddulph), 181
Raising Cain (Kindlon and Thompson), 167
Randall, Don, 191n1
Rank, Otto, 154

rat as signifier, 143–46, 163, 216n26
Rat Man case. *See under* Freud,
  Sigmund
"rat people," 147, 163, 216n27
Ray, Ola, 157
Ray, Robert B., 210n5
Reagan, Ronald, 171
Real Boys (Pollack), 77, 167, 170, 178,
  181–83
realism of boyology, 2, 19, 31, 61–63,
  65, 82, 202n15, 202n17
recapitulation theory, 15, 16, 194n20;
  in Bad Boy narrative, 53, 59, 57, 74,
  98, 201n11; in psychoanalysis, 18,
  217n33; and Sumner, 98; and
  Veblen, 98
Remus and Romulus legend, 136, 160,
  191n3
Return of the Vanishing American
  (Fiedler), 84
Reviving Ophelia (Pipher), 170, 178
Reynard the Fox (Caxton), 147
RFD magazine, 47
Rhetorical Power (Mailloux), 79–81
Riis, Jacob, 95, 208n16
Ritter, Father Bruce, 199n25, 210n3
Road Home, The, 201n1
Robinson, Forrest C., 78
Rockwood, Roy (Edward Stratemeyer),
  106
Rodman, Dennis, 182
Rogers, Carl, 156
Rollo books (Abbott), 30
Rolt-Wheeler, Francis, 73
Romero, Lora, 15, 62, 196n9
Rooney, Mickey, 117–18, 121, 210n5
Roosevelt, Franklin Delano (FDR), 123
Roosevelt, Theodore (Teddy), 32, 53,
  58, 198n22
Rosenthal, Michael, 201n12
Rosenzweig, Saul, 215n19
Rotundo, E. Anthony, 179
Rural Manhood (YMCA journal),
  24–26, 34, 37, 38–42, 198nn18–20,

198n22. *See also Farming for Boys*
  (serial); YMCA

Sadoff, Dianne, 148
Sanders, Barry, 49–50, 84, 199nn1–3
Savage Spawn (Kellerman), 184–86
Sawyer, Jack, 171
Schary, Dore, 118
"schoolboy psychology," 10, 12
Schoolcraft, Henry Rowe, 91–92
school story, 64
Schumacher, Joel, 160
Scouting, 1, 2, 24, 67, 71, 114; anal-
  erotics of, 11–12; appropriation(s)
  of Native Americans, 101, 105; as
  British-American amalgam, 105;
  Cubbing in the States, 7, 152,
  217n35; homophobia of, 112,
  186–89; Kipling's contributions to,
  7–8, 10, 87, 191–92n6; Mechling's
  ethnographic work on, 10–11, 181,
  186–88; and Native Americans, 105;
  and psychoanalysis, 7–12, 20, 152;
  Scouting for All (gay Scouts), 187;
  Seton's contributions to, 105; and
  sexual abuse, 43, 112, 198–99n25.
  See also Baden-Powell, Lord
  Robert
Scoutmaster(s), 14, 112, 152, 188
Seal Child (Peck), 163–64
"Second Look, A" (Quart), 127–28
Secret of the Wild Child, The (NOVA),
  20–21
Sedgwick, Eve Kosofsky: *Between Men*,
  218n41; *Epistemology of the Closet*,
  63, 202n18; "How to Bring Your
  Kids Up Gay," 187; "Tales of the
  Avunculate," 25–26, 133, 188
"Self-Reliance" (Emerson), 14–15, 55,
  193n18
Seltzer, Mark, 194n23, 196n3
Sendak, Maurice, 6, 138, 155–56,
  218n38
Sennott, Charles M., 199n25

Seton, Ernest Thompson, 42; appropriation(s) of Native Americans, 101, 105; contributions to Scouting, 105, 201n12; *Two Little Savages*, 58, 60, 105

sexology, 138–42, 214–15n17

sexual abuse, 43–45, 111–13, 198–99n25, 210n3. *See also* child sexuality; homo-economics

Sexual Life of the Child, The (Moll), 140

Shaddock, Jennifer, 155–56

Sheffield, Johnny, 106

Shengold, Leonard, 147, 216n27

Singh, Rev. J. A. L., 152

Sioux Indians, 100–105. *See also* Native Americans

"sissy boys," 187–88

Sleeman, Sir William Henry, 89–90, 92, 206nn4–5, 206n7

Social Activities for Men and Boys (Chesley), 69

social Darwinism, 98

Society of American Indians, 103

Sommers, Christina Hoff, 178–81, 220n7

Sons of Daniel Boone, 18, 67, 105

Sophocles, 10

Soul Murder (Shengold), 147, 216n27

Soul of an Indian (Eastman), 103–4

Speaking of Boys (Thompson), 156

Spencer, Herbert, 16–17, 51, 63, 70, 82, 98, 193n18, 200n4

Spielberg, Steven, 6, 158, 162

Stallybrass, Peter, 94, 146, 215n18, 216n26

Stand by Me (Reiner), 168

Standing Bear, Luther, 100, 102

Stephens, John, 189

Stevermer, Caroline, 163

Stiffed (Faludi), 173–74

Stine, R. L., 161

St. Nicholas magazine, 28, 72, 93–99; editorship of Dodge, 102

Stoler, Ann Laura, 213n6

Story of a Bad Boy, The (Aldrich), 28, 50–53, 55, 57, 61, 63, 78–79

Stowe, Harriet Beecher, 28, 61, 196n9

Stratemeyer, Edward, 106, 109, 200n5

"street Arabs," 94

"street rat," 34, 94, 97–100, 207n13

Stuart, Dorothy Margaret, 72–73

Stuart Little films, 163

success manuals, 70–71

Sulcer, Robert P., 214–15n17

Sullenger, Thomas Earl, 210n4

Sulloway, Frank, 140

Sumner, William Graham, 98

Tafel, Johann, 3

Talbot, E. S., 59

"Tales of the Avunculate" (Sedgwick), 25–26, 133, 188

Tarkington, Booth, 201n11; *Penrod*, 52, 55–56, 60; *Penrod and Sam*, 52, 58, 66; as "spokesman on boyhood," 66

Tarzan. *See under* Burroughs, Edgar Rice

Tatar, Maria, 155

Taurog, Norman, 20, 111, 116–18, 127

Taylor, Bayard, 28; *Boys of Other Countries*, 73

Teenage Boys! (Beausay), 167

teen monster movies, 157–62

Teen Wolf (Daniel), 138, 158–61

Teen Wolf Too, 161

Theory of the Leisure Class, The (Veblen), 98

Thomas, Jonathan Taylor, 129

Thompson, Michael: *Raising Cain*, 167; *Speaking of Boys*, 156

Thorndike, Edward L., 140

Three Essays on the Theory of Sexuality (Freud), 140–41, 143

Thriller (Jackson), 138, 157–58, 218n40

Tiernan-Lang, J. B., 127

Tom Sawyer (Twain), 52–53, 78, 203n25

Torture Garden, The (Mirbeau), 145

Totem and Taboo (Freud), 150

Toth, Jennifer, 99
Tracy, Spencer, 118, 121
Trensky, Anne, 78
Truffaut, François, 4, 88
Turner, Frederick Jackson, 36
Turner Network Television (TNT), 127
Twain, Mark (Samuel Clemens), 26, 66; *Adventures of Huckleberry Finn*, 19, 49–50, 52, 54, 66, 58–59, 78–81, 204n30; *The Adventures of Tom Sawyer*, 52–53, 78, 203n25; and the Bad Boy boom, 77–85; beliefs about science, 204n31; as boyish, 50; as divided personality, 81–83, 105, 205n36; and Howells, 50, 78; immaturity of, 81–84
Two Brothers statue, 117
Two Little Savages (Seton), 58, 60, 105
Tylor, Edward Burnett, 51; *Primitive Culture*, 73, 91; "Wild Men and Beast-Children," 87, 90–92, 138, 206–7nn6–8
Types of the Folktale (Aarne and Thompson), 9

Ulrichs, Karl, 139
Umansky, Lauri, 218n1
Uncle Benny, 25–34, 38–39, 45–46, 52, 58, 97, 196n6, 197n13
Uncle Buck (Hughes), 196n5
Uncle Jimmy (Katz), 199n26
uncles and aunts. *See* avunculate
Uses of Enchantment, The (Bettelheim), 147, 155

Vallone, Lynne, 220nn8–9
vampire films, 160
Vanishing American, The (Grey), 101
vanishing American trope, 67, 88, 101; and the Dakota Sioux, 101–5
Veblen, Thorstein, 98
Vice Versa, 163
Victor (Gerstein), 164

Victor of Aveyron, 4, 5, 21, 87–89, 135, 138–39, 141–42, 163–64, 213n10, 215n21; Gerstein's retellings, 164–64; sexual indifference to women, 138–39; and *The Wild Child*, 4, 88. *See also* Itard, Jean-Marc-Gaspard
Vidal, Gore, 85
Virey, J. J., 88
Viswanathan, Gauri, 89

Walk Like a Man, 163
Wallon, Henry, 212n2
Walt Disney film: *The Adventures of Huck Finn*, 203nn27–28; *The Jungle Book*, 162; *The Lion King*, 168
War against Boys, The (Sommers), 178–79
war as child's play, 57–59, 72, 80
Warner, Charles Dudley, 16, 28, 37, 54, 58, 60–61, 73–74, 98
Warner, Marina, 155
Was Huck Black? (Fishkin), 81, 204n30
Ways of Being Male (Stephens), 189
Weeks, Jeffrey, 214nn15–16
Wegner, Monsignor Nicholas H., 125
Weiner, Bernard, 176
werewolf movies, 157–61
What Social Classes Owe to Each Other (Sumner), 98
Where the Wild Things Are (Sendak), 6, 138, 155–56, 218n38
White, Allon, 94, 146, 215n18, 216n26
White, Hayden, 8, 18, 20, 137
White, William Allen, 28, 63
white primitive, 153
"Whitey Marsh." *See* Rooney, Mickey
Wiegman, Robyn, 83–84
Wild Boy (Gerstein), 164
Wild Boy of Aveyron. *See* Victor of Aveyron
Wild Child, The (Truffaut), 4, 207n8, 213n9
Wilde, Oscar, 26
Wilder, Laura Ingalls, 32

Wild Girl of Champagne, 21
"Wild Men and Beast-Children" (Tylor), 87, 90–92, 138
Wild Peter, 4, 142, 194n24
Will Boys Be Boys? (The Merrow Report), 167, 178, 182
Williams, Robin, 158
Winning the Boy (Merrill), 70, 169
Winter, Sarah, 10, 12
wolf-boys, 38, 49, 206nn3–8, 207n9; Brace's tale of Pickety, 95–99; in British India, 87–93; and English literature, 87; in fairy tales, 147, 149–50; Mowgli (character), 5, 7–8, 10–11, 90, 92, 107, 136, 156, 162; in psychoanalysis and child study, 8, 10, 12, 135–38, 141–42, 146–52, 156; and Scouting, 7–8, 10, 87; *Where the Wild Things Are*, 6, 138, 155–56. *See also* feral tale
Wolf Child and Human Child (Gesell), 152, 154
Wolf-Children and Feral Man (Singh and Zingg), 142, 152
Wolf Children and the Problem of Human Nature (Malson), 206n3
Wolf Cub's Handbook, The (Baden-Powell), 7
Wolfe, Thomas, 160
wolf-girls of Midnapore, 151–52
Wolf Man case. *See under* Freud, Sigmund

"Wolf-Reared Children" (Brace), 95–99, 102, 105, 119. *See also* Brace, Charles Loring
Wolves of Kromer, The (Gould), 162
Women Who Run with the Wolves (Estés), 219n5
Wonder of Boys, The (Gurian), 2, 72, 77, 167–70, 177–78, 180–83; ethnographic rhetoric in, 181–82; faith in biology, 167–69, 177–78, 180–81, 186
Woodcraft Indians, 67, 105, 201n12. *See also* Seton, Ernest Thompson
Wounded Knee, 102
Writer in America, The (Brooks), 83
Wyllie, Irving, 70

Yale Clinic of Child Behavior, 151
YMCA, 1, 18, 24–27, 34, 38–46, 66–67, 69, 71, 105, 114, 167, 195n2; sexual scandal in, 44–46
Yolen, Jane, 163
Youth's Companion magazine, 28, 202n21

Zingg, R. M., 142
Zipes, Jack: on Bly's misreadings, 218–19n2; *Fairy Tale as Myth, Myth as Fairy Tale*, 218–19n2; *Fairy Tales and the Art of Subversion*, 3, 147, 154–55
Zitkala-Ša, 103

Kenneth B. Kidd is assistant professor of English at the University of Florida and associate director of the Center for Children's Literature and Culture.